THE IMPACT OF UNION THE EU'S MARKET FREEDOMS

The book's aim is to consider the impact that the introduction and development of the status of Union citizenship has had on the interpretation of the EU's market freedoms. Starting by providing, in its introductory part (part one), a comprehensive and up-to-date analysis of the status of Union citizenship and its development from 1998 onwards, the book proceeds in part two to provide an in-depth examination of the relationship between this status and the Union's market freedoms. The central argument of the book is that, as a result of the move towards the creation of a meaningful status of Union citizenship, the market freedoms have been reconceptualised as fundamental Union citizenship rights and their interpretation has adapted accordingly.

Part three of the book analyses the result of this process of transforming the market freedoms into sources of fundamental Union citizenship rights and considers where it is likely to lead in the future. It demonstrates that, despite the fact that this development appears to be the next natural step in the process of constructing a meaningful notion of Union citizenship, it brings with it a number of issues that the EU will have to consider and carefully address. In particular, the method which the Court seems, up until now, to have employed to facilitate the metamorphosis of the market freedoms into citizenship rights, has led to criticisms on the grounds of legitimacy and coherence and will, undoubtedly, lead to further problems in the future. Hence part three of the book also identifies the difficulties that may emerge as a result of this process and suggests ways in which they may be overcome.

Volume 60 in the Series Modern Studies in European Law

Modern Studies in European Law
Recent titles in this series:

Nationalism and Private Law in Europe
Guido Comparato

EU Asylum Procedures and the Right to an Effective Remedy
Marcelle Reneman

The EU Accession to the ECHR
Edited by Vasiliki Kosta, Nikos Skoutaris and Vassilis P Tzevelekos

The European Court of Justice and External Relations: Constitutional Challenges
Edited by Marise Cremona and Anne Thies

A Critique of Codification
Leone Niglia

Protecting Vulnerable Groups: The European Human Rights Framework
Edited by Francesca Ippolito and Sara Iglesias Sanchez

EU International Relations Law Second Edition
Panos Koutrakos

Fundamental Rights in the EU: A Matter for Two Courts
Edited by Sonia Morano-Foadi and Lucy Vickers

What Form of Government for the European Union and the Eurozone?
Federico Fabbrini, Ernst Hirsch Ballin and Han Somsen

The UK and European Human Rights: A Strained Relationship?
Edited by Katja S Ziegler, Elizabeth Wicks and Loveday Hodson

The European Union in International Organisations and Global Governance: Recent Developments
Edited by Christine Kaddous

Nudge and the Law: What Can EU Law Learn From Behavioural Sciences?
Edited by Alberto Alemanno and Anne-Lise Sibony

Fundamental Rights in EU Internal Market Legislation
Vasiliki Kosta

Uniformity of Customs Administration in the European Union
Kathrin Limbach

**For the complete list of titles in this series, see
'Modern Studies in European Law' link at
www.hartpub.co.uk/books/series.asp**

The Impact of Union Citizenship on the EU's Market Freedoms

Alina Tryfonidou

·HART·
OXFORD · LONDON · NEW YORK · NEW DELHI · SYDNEY

HART PUBLISHING
Bloomsbury Publishing Plc
Kemp House, Chawley Park, Cumnor Hill, Oxford, OX2 9PH, UK

HART PUBLISHING, the Hart/Stag logo, BLOOMSBURY and the Diana logo are
trademarks of Bloomsbury Publishing Plc
First published in Great Britain 2016

First published in hardback, 2016
Paperback edition, 2018

Copyright © Alina Tryfonidou 2016

Alina Tryfonidou has asserted her right under the Copyright, Designs and Patents Act 1988 to be
identified as the Author of this work.

All rights reserved. No part of this publication may be reproduced or transmitted in any form or by
any means, electronic or mechanical, including photocopying, recording, or any information
storage or retrieval system, without prior permission in writing from the publishers.

While every care has been taken to ensure the accuracy of this work, no responsibility for loss or
damage occasioned to any person acting or refraining from action as a result of any statement in it
can be accepted by the authors, editors or publishers.

All UK Government legislation and other public sector information used in the work is Crown
Copyright ©. All House of Lords and House of Commons information used in the work is
Parliamentary Copyright ©. This information is reused under the terms of the Open Government
Licence v3.0 (http://www.nationalarchives.gov.uk/doc/open-government-licence/version/3) except
where otherwise stated.

All Eur-lex material used in the work is © European Union,
http://eur-lex.europa.eu/, 1998-2018.

A catalogue record for this book is available from the British Library.

Library of Congress Cataloging-in-Publication Data

Names: Tryfonidou, Alina, author.

Title: The impact of Union citizenship on the EU's market freedoms / Alina Tryfonidou.

Description: Portland, Oregon : Hart Publishing, 2016. | Series: Modern studies
in european law 60 | Includes bibliographical references and index.

Identifiers: LCCN 2015039917 | ISBN 9781849461672 (hardback : alk. paper)

Subjects: LCSH: Citizenship—European Union countries. | Free trade—European
Union countries. | Capitalism—European Union countries.

Classification: LCC KJE5124.T79 2016 | DDC 343.2408—dc23 LC record
available at http://lccn.loc.gov/2015039917

ISBN: PB: 978-1-50992-207-9
HB: 978-1-84946-167-2

Typeset by Compuscript Ltd, Shannon

To find out more about our authors and books visit www.hartpublishing.co.uk. Here you will find
extracts, author information, details of forthcoming events and the option to sign up for our
newsletters.

Acknowledgements

The process of writing this book has been enriched by the assistance and support of a number of persons and institutions.

I would like to thank the Universities of Leicester and Reading for generously granting me periods of sabbatical leave fittingly coinciding with the first and last stages of writing this book. Parts of this book have, also, been written during the time I spent as a Visiting Fellow at the Institute of Advanced Legal Studies (IALS) in London and I would like to thank the library staff at the Institute for their assistance in finding a wealth of resources.

I am very grateful to Tawhida Ahmed, Behnam Balalimood, Dimitry Kochenov, Christos Marneros, Clemens Rieder and Pedro Caro de Sousa for reading (the whole or parts of) the book manuscript and for offering incisive comments; needless to say, all errors remain mine.

I would also like to thank the staff at Hart Publishing for their patience in waiting for a delayed manuscript, as well as for always replying promptly and efficiently to all my queries.

Finally, I am extremely grateful to family and friends for offering their unfailing support throughout the period of researching and writing this book.

The book is dedicated to my family, who has always been there for me, for better or for worse.

Alina Tryfonidou
July 2015

Table of Contents

Acknowledgements v
List of Abbreviations xi
Table of Cases (numerical) xiii
Table of Secondary Legislation xxiii

Part I: Introductory Chapters

1. Introduction 3
   I. Setting the Background 3
   II. Aim of the Book 11
   III. Terminology 13
   IV. Structure of the Book 18
   V. A Taxonomy of Rights for the Market Freedoms 21

2. Taking Stock of Union Citizenship 23
   I. Introduction 23
   II. The Current Legal Regime 25
   III. The Infancy Phase (1993–97) 27
   IV. The Growth Phase (1998–2005) 29
      A. The Right to Non-Discrimination on
         Grounds of Nationality 30
      B. The Right to Free Movement 35
      C. The Right of Residence 36
      D. Comments 41
   V. Turbulent (Early) Adolescence (2006–09) 43
   VI. Coming of Age: Towards a Meaningful Status of
       Union Citizenship? (2010-Onwards) 48
   VII. Conclusion 57

Part II: The Impact of Union Citizenship on the EU's Market Freedoms

3. Union Citizenship and the Personal Market Freedoms 61
   I. Introduction 61
   II. The Personal Market Freedoms: A Sketch of the
       Current Legal Framework 62
   III. The Personal Market Freedoms as Sources of Instrumental
        Freedoms and Rights: The Pre-Maastricht Approach to
        their Interpretation 64
      A. Personal Market Freedoms: From Instrumental
         Freedoms to Instrumental Rights 66

	B.	The Pre-Maastricht Interpretation of the Personal Market Freedoms 73
IV.		The Court's Post-Maastricht Case-Law: (Re-)Reading the Personal Market Freedoms in the Light of Union Citizenship 79
	A.	The Court's Explicit Recognition of the Need to (Re-)Read the Personal Market Freedoms in the Light of Union Citizenship 80
	B.	Scope *Ratione Personae* 82
	C.	Scope *Ratione Materiae* 86
		i. The Addition of a Second Primary Right in the Material Scope of the More Stationary Personal Market Freedoms 88
		ii. Dispensing with the Requirement of Cross-Border Specificity 91
	D.	The Reconceptualisation of the Personal Market Freedoms as (Also) Sources of Fundamental Economic Rights for the Union Citizen 109
V.		Conclusion 116

4. Union Citizenship and the Free Movement of Goods 118
   I. Introduction 118
   II. The Traditional Interpretation of the Free Movement of Goods Provisions 119
       A. The Court's Traditional Approach to the Personal Scope of Article 34 TFEU 121
       B. The Court's Traditional Approach to 'Restrictions' Caught by Article 34 TFEU: *Dassonville*, *Cassis*, and *Keck*, and the Requirement of Cross-Border Specificity 124
   III. The Court's Stance on the Question of Whether the Free Movement of Goods Provisions are Sources of (Fundamental) Rights for Individuals 132
   IV. Some Signs in the Court's Case-Law that the Free Movement of Goods Provisions may now be the Source of Individual Rights for Persons 134
       A. The Rights of Consumers Under Article 34 TFEU 135
       B. The Right of Persons to *Move* to Another Member State for the Purpose of Selling Goods 140
       C. The Fundamental Right to Trade Goods in a Cross-Border Context Without Being Restricted by Unjustified National Regulation 143
   V. Conclusion 151

Part III: The Future

5. (Re-)Interpreting the Market Freedoms in the Light of
   Union Citizenship: Emerging Questions 155
   I. Introduction 155
   II. Can the Market Freedoms be (Re-)Interpreted in the
       Manner Documented in the Previous Two Chapters? 155
       A. Is the Expansion of the Scope of the Market Freedoms
          in the Manner Documented Warranted Under a Literal
          Interpretation of their Text? 158
       B. What are the Current Aims of the Market Freedoms? 162
   III. How should the Market Freedoms Now be Interpreted
        when Invoked by Union Citizens? 173
        A. A *De Minimis* Test? 177
        B. A Remoteness Test? 179
        C. The Purely Internal Rule 182
   IV. How should the Assessment as to Whether there is a
       Breach of the Market Freedoms Now be Made? 192
   V. Conclusion 194

6. (Re-)Interpreting the Market Freedoms in the Light of
   Union Citizenship: Persisting Conundrums 197
   I. Introduction 197
   II. The Persisting Distinction Between Union Citizens
       Who are Nationals of Member States and Union Citizens
       Who are Not 197
   III. Should there Still be a Number of Different Free
        Movement of Persons Provisions? 204
   IV. The Distinction Between Natural and Legal Persons
       Under the Market Freedoms 207
   V. Should the Personal Scope of the Personal Market
      Freedoms be Extended to Cover Third-Country Nationals? 212
   VI. (Fundamental) Human Rights vs (Fundamental)
       Economic Rights 219
   VII. Individual Rights vs Collective Rights 226
   VIII. Conclusion 230

Part IV: Conclusion

7. Conclusions 235

Bibliography 242
Index 257

List of Abbreviations

AG	Advocate General
AJCL	American Journal of Comparative Law
Art	Article
CFI	Court of First Instance
CJEL	Columbia Journal of European Law
CJEU	Court of Justice of the EU
CLJ	Cambridge Law Journal
CMLRev	Common Market Law Review
COM	Communication
CUP	Cambridge University Press
CYELS	Cambridge Yearbook of European Legal Studies
EBLRev	European Business Law Review
EC	European Community
ECJ	European Court of Justice
ECR	European Court Reports
ECSC	European Coal and Steel Community
ECHR	European Convention on Human Rights
ECtHR	European Court of Human Rights
Ed	Editor
Eds	Editors
EEC	European Economic Community
EGC	European General Court
EJML	European Journal of Migration and Law
ELJ	European Law Journal
ELRev	European Law Review
EPL	European Public Law
EU	European Union
EUCFR	EU Charter of Fundamental Rights
EUConst	European Constitutional Law Review
EUI	European University Institute
Euratom	European Atomic Energy Community
Fordham Int'l LJ	Fordham International Law Journal
GLJ	German Law Journal
IANL	Journal of Immigration, Asylum and Nationality Law
ICLQ	International and Comparative Law Quarterly
IJEL	Irish Journal of European Law
JCMS	Journal of Common Market Studies
JEPP	Journal of European Public Policy
KCLJ	Kings College Law Journal

LIEI	Legal Issues of Economic Integration/Legal Issues of European Integration
LQR	Law Quarterly Review
MEQR	Measure having equivalent effect to quantitative restrictions
MLR	Modern Law Review
MJ	Maastricht Journal of European and Comparative Law
OJ	Official Journal of the European Union
OUP	Oxford University Press
SEA	Single European Act
TEC	European Community Treaty
TEU	Treaty on European Union
TFEU	Treaty on the Functioning of the European Union
UEFA	Union of European Football Associations
UK	United Kingdom
YEL	Yearbook of European Law

Table of Cases (numerical)

ECJ CASES

Case 26/62 Van Gend en Loos [1963] ECR 13..66
Case 75/63 Hoekstra [1964] ECR 1771..75
Case 6/64 Costa v ENEL [1964] ECR 585..66
Case 7/68 Commission v Italy [1968] ECR 423 ....121, 178
Joined Cases 2 & 3/69 Diamantarbeiders [1969] ECR 211..124
Case 29/69 Stauder [1969] ECR 419..10, 66
Case 11/70 Internationale Handelsgesellschaft [1970] ECR 1125.......................................10
Case 2/73 Geddo [1973] ECR 865...120, 121, 124
Case 4/73 Nold [1974] ECR 491..10
Case 152/73 Sotgiu [1974] ECR 153..78, 199–200
Case 167/73 Commission v France [1974] ECR 359..16, 68
Case 2/74 Reyners [1974] ECR 631..68, 200
Case 8/74 Dassonville [1974] ECR 837...124–26, 143, 146
Case 12/74 Commission v Germany [1975] ECR 181 128
Case 33/74 Van Binsbergen [1974] ECR 1299 ....7, 68, 76, 77
Case 41/74 Van Duyn [1974] ECR 1337...47, 201
Case 32/75 Cristini [1975] ECR 1085..69
Case 36/75 Rutili [1975] ECR 1219..68
Case 48/75 Royer [1976] ECR 497..74, 83
Case 104/75 de Peijper [1976] ECR 613 125
Case 118/75 Watson and Belmann [1976] ECR 1185 70
Case 41/76 Donckerwolcke [1976] ECR 1921 215
Case 63/76 Inzirillo [1976] ECR 2057..69
Case 74/76 Iannelli [1977] ECR 557 ....122, 133
Case 15/78 Koestler [1978] ECR 1971 ....76–77, 79, 91, 139, 161
Case 120/78 Rewe-Zentral AG v Bundesmonopolverwaltung
  für Branntwein [1979] ECR 649 ....7, 120
Case 115/78 Knoors [1979] ECR 399...182
Case 170/78 Commission v UK [1983] ECR 2265 188
Case 175/78 Saunders [1979] ECR 1129...56, 75, 182
Case 15/79 Groenveld [1979] ECR 3409...120
Case 34/79 Henn and Darby [1979] ECR 3795..121, 124
Case 52/79 Debauve [1980] ECR 833 75
Case 149/79 Commission v Belgium [1980] ECR 3883...200
Case 788/79 Gilli and Andres [1980] ECR 2071..126
Case 155/80 Oebel [1981] ECR 1993..128
Case 279/80 Webb [1981] ECR 3305 17
Case 15/81 Gaston Schul [1982] ECR 1409..133
Case 53/81 Levin [1982] ECR 1035...83, 84

xiv *Table of Cases*

Case 65/81 Reina [1982] ECR 33 69
Case 75/81 Blesgen [1982] ECR 1211 ....127, 179
Joined Cases 115 & 116/81 Adoui and Cornuaille [1982] ECR 1665............................202
Case 249/81 Commission v Ireland [1982] ECR 4005..125, 128
Case 261/81 Rau [1982] ECR 3961 126
Case 266/81 SIOT [1983] ECR 731 121
Case 286/81 Criminal Proceedings against Oosthoek's
    Uitgeversmaatschappij BV [1982] ECR 4575 .... 16, 121, 123, 136, 140
Case 152/82 Forcheri [1983] ECR 2323 69
Joined Cases 177 & 178/82 Van de Haar [1984] ECR 1797 178
Joined Cases 286/82 & 26/83 Luisi and Carbone [1984] ECR 377 ....69, 70, 76, 84
Case 16/83 Prantl [1984] ECR 1299 127
Case 107/83 Klopp [1984] ECR 2971..76
Case 180/83 Moser [1984] ECR 2539 185
Case 240/83 ABDHU [1985] ECR 531..133
Case 238/83 Meade [1984] ECR 2631 ....67, 75, 213
Case 288/83 Commission v Ireland [1985] ECR 1761..124
Case 293/83 Gravier [1985] ECR 593 ....48, 70
Joined Cases 60 & 61/84 Cinetheque, [1985] ECR 2605...127, 128
Case 94/84 Deak [1985] ECR 1873 69
Case 103/84 Commission v Italy [1986] ECR 1759 178
Case 300/84 Van Roosmalen [1986] ECR 3097 83
Case 59/85 Reed [1985] ECR 1283..69
Case 66/85 Lawrie-Blum [1986] ECR 2121..75
Case 121/85 Conegate [1986] ECR 1007 202
Case 124/85 Commission v Greece [1986] ECR 3935 128
Case 139/85 Kempf [1986] ECR 1741...83, 229
Case 148/85 Forest [1986] ECR 3448..127
Case 221/85 Commission v Belgium [1987] ECR 719..79
Case 316/85 Lebon [1987] ECR 2811 ....80, 81
Case 352/85 Bond van Adverteerters [1988] ECR 2085 83
Case 407/85 3 Glocken [1988] ECR 4233 137
Case 197/86 Brown [1988] ECR 3205...81
Case 198/86 Conradi [1987] ECR 4469 79
Case 222/86 Heylens [1987] ECR 4097...194
Case 263/86 Humbel [1988] ECR 5365 84
Case 292/86 Gullung [1988] ECR 111 97
Case 20/87 Gauchard [1987] ECR 4879..127
Case 81/87 Daily Mail [1988] ECR 5500 76
Case 143/87 Stanton [1988] ECR 3877..67
Case 186/87 Cowan [1989] ECR 195 ....31, 67, 71, 72
Case 196/87 Steymann [1988] ECR 6159 ....75, 83
Case 215/87 Schumacher [1989] ECR 617 121
Case 298/87 Smanor [1988] ECR 4489...137
Case 328/87 Buet [1989] ECR 1235 ....136, 140
Case 344/87 Bettray [1989] ECR 1621 84
Joined Cases 389 & 390/87 Echternach and Moritz [1989] ECR 723 ....85, 199

Table of Cases xv

Joined Cases C-54 & 91/88 and 14/89 Niño [1990] ECR 3537 75
Case C-69/88 Krantz [1990] ECR I-583 179
Case 145/88 Torfaen [1989] ECR 765 ....127, 128
Case C-362/88 GB-INNO-BM [1990] ECR I-667 138
Case C-154/89 Commission v France [1991] ECR I-659 ....76, 160
Case C-205/89 Commission v Greece [1991] ECR I-1361 134
Case C-221/89 Factortame [1991] ECR I-3905 76
Case C-260/89 ERT [1991] ECR I-2925 ....10, 220
Case C-288/89 Gouda [1991] ECR I-4007 16
Case C-292/89 Antonissen [1991] ECR I-745 ....63, 83
Case C-308/89 Di Leo [1990] ECR I-4185 85
Case C-312/89 Conforama [1991] ECR I-997 127
Case 340/89 Vlassopoulou [1991] ECR 2357 194
Case C-2/90 Commission v Belgium [1992] ECR I-4431
Case C-62/90 Commission v Germany [1992] ECR I-2575 ....121, 137
Case C-76/90 Säger [1991] ECR I-4221 95
Case C-159/90 Grogan [1991] ECR I-4621 138
Case C-239/90 Boscher [1991] ECR I-2023 140
Case C-369/90 Micheletti [1992] ECR I-4239 ....54, 86
Case C-370/90 Singh [1992] ECR I-4265 ....67, 102, 104–05, 109, 201
Case C-106/91 Ramrath [1992] ECR I-3351 74
Case C-112/91 Werner [1993] ECR I-429 ....77, 88
Case C-126/91 Yves Rocher [1993] ECR I-2361 ....16, 137, 178
Case C-168/91 Konstantinidis [1993] ECR I-1191 ....71, 87, 178
Joined Cases C-267 & 268/91 Keck and Mithouard
  [1993] ECR I-6097 ....94, 129, 142
Case C-19/92 Kraus [1993] ECR I-1663 ....16, 36
Case C-91/92 Faccini Dori [1994] ECR I-3225 28
Case C-93/92 Baskiciogullari [1993] ECR I-5009 179
Case C-275/92 Schindler [1994] ECR I-1039 96
Case C-292/92 Hünermund [1993] ECR I-6787 ....16, 127–28, 129,
                                                                                   132, 149, 178
Case C-315/92 Clinique [1994] ECR I-317 137
Case C-379/92 Peralta [1994] ECR I-3453 ....179, 180
Case C-45/93 Commission v Spain [1994] ECR I-911 71
Joined Cases C-363 & 407-411/93 Lancry [1994] ECR I-3957 121
Case C-379/93 Schumacker [1995] ECR I-225 ....78, 86
Case C-384/93 Alpine Investments [1995] ECR I-1141 ....76, 94, 139, 187
Case C-412/93 Leclerc-Siplec [1995] ECR I-179 ....17, 129, 130, 145
Case C-415/93 Bosman [1995] ECR I-4921 ....6, 74, 96–98, 113, 184
Joined Cases C-418-421/93, 460-462/93, 464/93, 9-11/94,
  14-15/94, 23-24/94 and 332/94 Semeraro Casa Uno Srl
  [1996] ECR I-2975 127
Case C-470/93 Mars [1995] ECR I-1923 137
Case C-484/93 Svensson and Gustavsson [1995] ECR I-3955 ....217, 218
Joined Cases C-485 & 486/93 Simitzi v Kos [1995] ECR I-2655 121
Case C-7/94 Gaal [1996] ECR I-1031 85

xvi *Table of Cases*

Case C-55/94 Gebhard [1995] ECR I-4165 .... 7, 74, 75, 76, 96–97,
98, 101, 184
Case C-63/94 Belgapom [1995] ECR I-2467 .... 144, 185
Case C-193/94 Skanavi and Chryssanthakopoulos
[1996] ECR I-929 28
Case C-194/94 CIA [1996] ECR I-2201 134
Case C-214/94 Boukhalfa [1996] ECR I-2253 28
Case C-237/94 O'Flynn [1996] ECR I-2617 69
Case C-278/94 Commission v Belgium [1996] ECR I-4307 80
Joined Cases C-321-324/94 Pistre [1997] ECR I-2343 190
Joined Cases C-4 & 5/95 Stöber and Pereira [1997] ECR I-511 .... 25, 28
Case C-18/95 Terhoeve [1999] ECR I-345 .... 36, 78
Joined Cases C-65 & 111/95 Shingara and Radiom [1997] ECR I-3343 ..... 28, 201
Case C-70/95 Sodemare [1997] ECR I-3395 79
Case C-120/95 Decker [1998] ECR I-1831 .... 137, 140
Case C-265/95 Commission v France [1997] ECR I-6959 134
Case C-299/95 Kremzow [1997] ECR I-2629 185
Case C-368/95 Familiapress [1997] ECR I-3689 220
Case C-398/95 SETTG [1997] ECR I-3091 98
Joined Cases C-51/96 and C-191/97 Deliège [2000] ECR I-2549 95
Joined Cases 64 & 65/96 Ueckcr and Jacquct [1997] ECR I-3171 .... 29, 33
Case C-85/96 Martínez Sala [1998] ECR I-269 .... 30–32, 33–34,
37, 38, 53

Case C-108/96 Mac Quen [2001] ECR I-837 98
Case C-158/96 Kohll [1998] ECR I-1931 84
Case C-171/96 Pereira Roque [1998] ECR I-4607 202
Case C-184/96 Commission v France [1998] ECR I-6197 .... 191, 194
Case C-196/96 Lehtonen [2000] ECR I-2681 98
Case C-212/96 Centros [1999] ECR I-1459 84
Case C-266/96 Corsica Ferries [1998] ECR I-3949 179
Case C-274/96 Bickel and Franz [1998] ECR I-7637 .... 32–33, 34, 35, 37, 49
Case C-348/96 Calfa [1999] ECR I-11 .... 28, 86, 186, 201
Case C-350/96 Clean Car [1998] ECR I-2521 70
Case C-369/96 Arblade [1999] ECR I-8453 95
Case C-67/97 Bluhme [1998] ECR I-8033 180
Case C-230/97 Awoyemi [1998] ECR I-6781 213
Case 337/97 Meeusen [1999] ECR I-3289 75
Case C-378/97 Wijsenbeek [1999] ECR I-6207 .... 35, 37, 41
Case C-394/97 Heinonen [1999] ECR I-3231 134
Case C-6/98 PRO Sieben Media [1999] ECR I-7599 100
Case C-44/98 BASF [1998] ECR I-6269 180
Case C-58/98 Corsten [2000] ECR I-7919 94
Case C-108/98 RI.SAN [1999] ECR I-5219 185
Case C-190/98 Graf [2000] ECR I-493 .... 132, 144, 179
Case C-224/98 D'Hoop [2002] ECR I-6191 .... 34, 35, 36, 43, 86
Case C-228/98 Dounias [2000] ECR I-577 133
Case C-254/98 TK-Heimdienst [2000] ECR I-151 140

Table of Cases xvii

Case C-281/98 Angonese [2000] ECR I-4139..16
Case C-367/98 Commission v Portugal [2002] ECR I-4732 146
Case C-368/98 Vanbraekel [2001] ECR I-5473 ....84, 115
Case C-376/98 Germany v Parliament and Council [2000]
 ECR I-8419..9
Case C-379/98 PreussenElektra [2001] ECR I-2099 .... 16, 137, 191
Case C-405/98 Gourmet [2001] ECR I-1795 .... 17, 98, 99–100,
101, 113, 175
Case C-54/99 Association Eglise de Scientologie de Paris
 [2000] ECR I-1335...176
Case C-94/99 ARGE [2000] ECR I-11037 189
Case C-157/99 Geraets Smits and Peerbooms [2001]
 ECR I-5473..84, 86, 115
Case C-184/99 Grzelczyk [2001] ECR I-6193 ....30, 34, 37, 38, 40, 81,
82, 86, 192, 203, 229
Case C-205/99 Analir [2001] ECR I-1271 114
Case C-268/99 Jany [2001] ECR I-8615..75, 202
Case C-358/99 Müller Fauré [2003] ECR I-4509..84, 115
Case C-390/99 Canal Satélite [2002] ECR I-607 ....114, 134
Case C-413/99 Baumbast [2002] ECR I-7091 .... 30, 37, 38, 82, 85, 192
Case C-483/99 Commission v France [2002] ECR I-4781 ....114, 146
Case C-60/00 Carpenter [2002] ECR I-6279................................ 42, 48, 107–08, 115, 165
Case C-112/00 Schmidberger [2003] ECR I-5659 .... 134, 145, 221,
222, 223, 228
Case C-294/00 Gräbner [2002] ECR I-6515..98
Case C-355/00 Freskot [2003] ECR I-5263..187
Case C-56/01 Inizan [2003] ECR I-12403 ....84, 115
Case C-79/01 Payroll [2002] ECR I-8923 98
Case C-92/01 Stylianakis [2003] ECR I-1291..28
Case C-98/01 Commission v UK [2003] ECR I-4641 146
Case C-100/01 Oteiza Olazabal [2002] ECR I-10981 28
Case C-109/01 Akrich [2003] ECR I-9607 ....84, 102, 103
Case C-285/01 Burbaud [2003] ECR I-8219 95
Case C-322/01 DocMorris [2003] ECR I-14887 .... 123, 139, 144, 145
Case C-387/01 Weigel [2004] ECR I-4981..121
Case C-463/01 Commission v Germany [2004] ECR I-11705 ....178, 193
Joined Cases C-482/01 and C-493/01 Orfanopoulos and Oliveri
 [2004] ECR I-5257...82, 114, 211, 227
Case C-36/02 Omega [2004] ECR I-9609..222, 223
Case C-138/02 Collins [2004] ECR I-2703 ....42, 80, 81, 82
Case C-148/02 Garcia Avello [2003] ECR I-11613..........................33, 34, 35, 44, 53, 55, 86
Case C-200/02 Zhu and Chen [2004] ECR I-9925..30, 40, 41
Case C-224/02 Pusa [2004] ECR I-5763 ....35, 36, 43
Case C-293/02 Jersey Produce Marketing Organisation v States
 of Jersey and Jersey Potato Export Marketing
 Board [2005] ECR I-9543..122
Case C-309/02 Radlberger [2004] ECR I-11763 178

xviii *Table of Cases*

Case C-442/02 CaixaBank [2004] ECR I-8961 ....92, 132
Case C- 456/02 Trojani [2004] ECR I-7573 ....31, 38
Case C-20/03 Burmanjer [2005] ECR I-4133 ....140, 141, 178
Case C-72/03 Carbonati Apuani [2004] ECR I-8027 121
Case C-134/03 Viacom Outdoor [2005] ECR I-1167 178
Case C-152/03 Ritter-Coulais [2006] ECR I-1711 ....88–91, 111, 112,
159, 166, 171
Case C-209/03 Bidar [2005] ECR I-2119 .... 30, 37, 40, 44, 45, 81
Case C-215/03 Oulane [2005] ECR I-1215 ....61, 205
Case C-231/03 Coname [2005] ECR I-7287 190
Case C-293/03 My [2004] ECR I-12013 ....28, 53
Case C-320/03 Commission v Austria [2005] ECR I-9871 193
Case C-403/03 Schempp [2005] ECR I-6421 ....33, 35
Case C-446/03 Marks and Spencer [2005] ECR I-10837 ....17, 116
Case C-458/03 Parking Brixen [2005] ECR I-8585 ....17, 188–89
Case C-109/04 Kranemann [2005] ECR I-2421 36
Joined Cases C-158 & 159/04 Vassilopoulos [2006] ECR I-8135 ....92, 132, 168
Case C-168/04 Commission v Austria [2006] ECR I-9041 95
Case C-258/04 Ioannidis [2005] ECR I-8275 81
Joined Cases C-282 & 283/04 Commission v Netherlands
  [2006] ECR I-9141 ....146, 179
Case C-290/04 Scorpio [2006] ECR I-9461 ....213, 217
Case C-300/04 Eman and Sevinger [2006] ECR I-8055 32
Case C-372/04 Watts [2006] ECR I-4325 ....84, 115
Case C-386/04 Stauffer [2006] ECR I-8203 90
Case C-406/04 De Cuyper [2006] ECR I-6947 43
Case C-410/04 ANAV [2006] ECR I-3303 189
Case C-434/04 Ahokainen [2006] ECR I-9171 146
Case C-441/04 A-Punkt [2006] ECR I-2093 141
Case C-452/04 Fidium Finanz [2006] ECR I-9251 218
Case C-470/04 N [2006] ECR I-7409 ....88, 89–90, 159
Case C-520/04 Turpeinen [2006] ECR I-10685 43
Case C-1/05 Jia [2007] ECR I-1 103
Case C-65/05 Commission v Greece [2006] ECR I-10341 146
Case C-76/05 Schwarz [2007] ECR I-6849 ....28, 43
Case C-110/05 Commission v Italy (mopeds)
  [2009] ECR I-519 .... 131, 136, 144, 145, 146–47,
149–50, 170, 178
Case C-142/05 Mickelsson and Roos
  [2009] ECR I-4273 .... 136, 144, 146, 147,
149, 170, 178, 180
Case C-173/05 Commission v Italy [2007] ECR I-4917 121
Case C-192/05 Tas-Hagen and Tas [2006] ECR I-451 43
Case C-208/05 ITC [2007] ECR I-181 28
Case C-291/05 Eind [2007] ECR I-10719 ....105–06, 107
Case C-341/05 Laval [2007] ECR I-11767 ....222–23, 228
Case C-380/05 Europa 7 [2008] ECR I-349 ....17, 189

Table of Cases xix

Case C-392/05 Alevizos [2007] ECR I-3505 28
Case C-438/05 Viking [2007] ECR I-10779 .... 222–23, 228
Case C-464/05 Geurts [2007] ECR I-9325 .... 88, 90, 159
Joined Cases C-11 & 12/06 Morgan and Bucher [2007] ECR I-9161 43
Case C-182/06 Lakebrink [2007] ECR I-6705 78
Case C-212/06 Government of the French Community and Walloon
 Government v Flemish Government [2008] ECR I-1683 41
Case C-250/06 United Pan-Europe Communications [2007] ECR I-11135 114
Case C-256/06 Jäger [2008] ECR I-123 179
Case C-265/06 Commission v Portugal [2008] ECR I-2245 .... 136, 145
Case C-281/06 Jundt [2007] ECR I-12231 83
Case C-346/06, Rüffert [2008] ECR I-1989 223
Case C-347/06 ASM Brescia [2008] ECR I-5641 189
Case C-353/06 Grunkin and Paul [2008] ECR I-7639 43
Case C-445/06 Danske Slangterier [2009] ECR I-2119 133
Case C-499/06 Nerkowska [2008] ECR I-3993 43
Case C-524/06 Huber [2008] ECR I-9705 46
Case C-527/06 Renneberg [2008] ECR I-7735 .... 88, 159
Case C-33/07 Jipa [2008] ECR I-5157 43
Case C-158/07 Förster [2008] ECR I-8507 .... 44–45, 46, 49, 53, 198
Case C-164/07 Wood [2008] ECR I-4143 71
Case C-205/07 Gysbrechts [2008] ECR I-9947 .... 17, 120
Case C-221/07 Zablocka [2008] ECR I-9029 43
Case C-228/07 Petersen [2008] ECR I-6989 .... 57, 114
Case C-544/07 Rüffler [2009] ECR I-3389 .... 43, 91
Joined Cases C-22 & 23/08 Vatsouras and Koupatantze
 [2009] ECR I-4585 .... 47, 81
Case C-73/08 Bressol [2010] ECR I-2735 49
Case C-103/08 Gottwald [2009] ECR I-9117 .... 32, 44
Case C-123/08 Wolzenburg [2009] ECR I-9621 .... 44, 46, 198
Case C-127/08 Metock [2008] ECR I-6241 .... 48, 103
Case C-135/08 Rottmann [2010] ECR I-1449 .... 30, 48, 53–54, 55,
                                                                                                                  56, 57, 115, 183
Case C-211/08 Commission v Spain [2010] ECR I-5267 179
Case C-271/08 Commission v Germany [2010] ECR I-7091 .... 223, 224–25
Case C-310/08 Ibrahim [2010] ECR I-1965 .... 48, 85
Case C-371/08 Ziebell [2011] ECR I-12735 .... 162, 212
Case C-480/08 Teixeira [2010] ECR I-1107 .... 48, 85
Case C-515/08 Santos Palhota [2010] ECR I-9133 .... 96, 224
Case C-34/09 Ruiz Zambrano [2011] ECR I-1177 .... 48, 53, 55, 56,
                                                                                                                       57, 182, 183
Case C-56/09 Zanotti [2010] ECR I-4517 .... 28, 48
Case C-89/09 Commission v France [2010] ECR I-12941 57
Case C-108/09 Ker-Optika [2010] ECR I-12213 139
Case C-137/09 Josemans [2010] ECR I-13019 28
Case C-145/09 Tsakouridis [2010] ECR I-11979 .... 51, 52, 53, 115
Case C-162/09 Lassal [2010] ECR I-9217 50

xx *Table of Cases*

Case C-173/09 Elchinov [2010] ECR I-8889 ....84, 115
Case C-208/09 Sayn-Wittgenstein [2010] ECR I-13693 ....48, 50, 178
Case C-291/09 Guarnieri & Cie [2011] ECR I-2685 180
Case C-325/09 Dias [2011] ECR I-6387 50
Case C-348/09 PI ECLI:EU:C:2012:300..52, 53
Case C-391/09 Runevič-Vardyn [2011] ECR-3787 ....48, 50, 178
Case C-434/09 McCarthy [2011] ECR I-3375 ....55, 183
Case C-503/09 Stewart [2011] ECR I-6497 35
Joined Cases C-424 & 425/10 Ziolkowski [2011] ECR I-14035 50
Case C-434/10 Aladzhov [2011] ECR I-11569 ....37, 49
Joined Cases C-357-359/10 Duomo ECLI:EU:C:2012:283..189
Case C-364/10 Hungary v Slovak Republic ECLI:EU:C:2012:630 30
Case C-385/10 Elenca ECLI:EU:C:2012:634...143
Case C-430/10 Gaydarov [2011] ECR I-11637 ....49, 51
Case C-443/10 Bonnarde [2011] ECR I-9327 ....17, 148, 178
Case C-456/10 ANETT ECLI:EU:C:2012:241 ....135, 148
Case C-602/10 SC Volksbank România SA ECLI:EU:C:2012:443 179
Case C-40/11 Iida ECLI:EU:C:2012:691 186
Case C-75/11 Commission v Austria ECLI:EU:C:2012:605 ....44, 49
Joined Cases C-147 & 148/11 Czop ECLI:EU:C:2012:538..51, 85
Case C-171/11 Fra.bo ECLI:EU:C:2012:453...143
Case C-221/11 Demirkan ECLI:EU:C:2013:583...70
Case C-249/11 Byankov ECLI:EU:C:2012:608 49
Case C-256/11 Dereci [2011] ECR I-11315 ....53, 55, 183
Joined Cases C-356 & 357/11 O, S and L ECLI:EU:C:2012:776 55
Case C-379/11 Caves Krier ECLI:EU:C:2012:798 ....88, 91, 159
Joined Cases C-523 & 585/11 Prinz ECLI:EU:C:2013:524.................................49, 184, 204
Case C-639/11 Commission v Poland ECLI:EU:C:2014:173..148
Case C-61/12 Commission v Lithuania ECLI:EU:C:2014:172 148
Case C-86/12 Alokpa ECLI:EU:C:2013:645..41
Case C-87/12 Ymeraga ECLI:EU:C:2013:291 ....53, 55
Case C-139/12 Caixa d'Estalvis i Pensions de Barcelona
    ECLI:EU:C:2014:174..191
Case C-140/12 Brey ECLI:EU:C:2013:565 38
Joined Cases C-162 & 163/12 Airport Shuttle Express
    ECLI:EU:C:2014:74..191
Joined Cases C-204-208/12 Essent Belgium
    ECLI:EU:C:2014:2192 ....137, 148, 191
Case C-220/12 Thiele Meneses ECLI:EU:C:2013:683 49
Case C-303/12 Imfeld ECLI:EU:C:2013:822 ....91, 159
Case C-367/12 Sokoll-Seebacher ECLI:EU:C:2014:68 187
Case C-378/12 Onuekwere ECLI:EU:C:2014:13 51
Case C-400/12 MG ECLI:EU:C:2014:9 ....52, 53
Case C-423/12 Reyes ECLI:EU:C:2014:16 104
Case C-456/12 O and B ECLI:EU:C:2014:135 ....71, 101, 105, 106, 107
Case C-457/12 S and G ECLI:EU:C:2014:136 ....28, 71, 101, 107, 108, 165
Case C-474/12 Schiebel Aircraft ECLI:EU:C:2014:2139 70

Case C-481/12 Juvelta ECLI:EU:C:2014:11 137
Case C-483/12 Pelckmans ECLI:EU:C:2014:304..127
Case C-573/12 Ålands Vindkraft ECLI:EU:C:2014:2037 .... 134, 148, 191
Case C-87/13 X ECLI:EU:C:2014:2459... 88, 91, 159
Case C-133/13 Q ECLI:EU:C:2014:2460 122
Case C-202/13 McCarthy ECLI:EU:C:2014:2450...50
Case C-244/13 Ogieriakhi ECLI:EU:C:2014:2068..51
Case C-268/13 Petru ECLI:EU:C:2014:2271 ....84, 115
Case C-315/13 De Clercq ECLI:EU:C:2014:2408 ....69, 178
Case C-322/13 Rüffer ECLI:EU:C:2014:189 ....32, 49
Case C-333/13 Dano ECLI:EU:C:2014:2358 .... 39, 48, 115, 230
Case C-359/13 B Martens ECLI:EU:C:2015:118 ....49, 204
Case C-423/13 UAB Vilniaus Energija ECLI:EU:C:2014:2186 148
Case C-512/13 Sopora ECLI:EU:C:2015:108..16

CFI CASE

Case T-66/95 Hedwig Kuchlenz-Winter v Commission [1997] ECR II-637 38

ECtHR CASE

Chassagnou and others v France App nos 25088/94, 28331/95
  and 28443/95 (ECtHR, 24 April 1999) 225

Table of Secondary Legislation

REGULATIONS

Regulation 1612/68 on freedom of movement for workers
within the Community [1968] OJ L257/2 .... 8, 29, 64, 68, 69,
80, 85, 101, 106
Regulation 1408/71 on the application of social security
schemes to employed persons and their families moving
within the Community [1971] L149/2 31
Regulation 883/2004 on the coordination of social security
systems, as amended by Regulation 988/2009 [2004] OJ L166/1 .... 8, 64
Regulation 987/2009 laying down the procedure for implementing
Regulation 883/2004 on the coordination of social security
systems [2009] OJ L284/1 .... 8, 64
Regulation 492/2011 on freedom of movement for
workers within the Union [2011] OJ L141/1 .... 8, 29, 64, 69, 85, 213

DIRECTIVES

Directive 64/220 on the abolition of restrictions on movement
and residence within the Community for nationals of Member
States with regard to establishment and the provision of services
[1963–1964] Special Edition OJ 115 .... 68, 69
Directive 64/221 on the coordination of special measures
concerning the movement and residence of foreign nationals
which are justified on grounds of public policy, public security
or public health [1964] OJ L56/50 68
Directive 68/360 on the abolition of restrictions on movement
and residence within the Community for workers of Member
States and their families [1968] OJ L257/13 8
Directive 70/50 on the abolition of measures which have an
effect equivalent to quantitative restrictions on imports
and are not covered by other provisions adopted in
pursuance of the EEC Treaty [1970] OJ L13/29 .... 8, 124, 126
Directive 73/148 on the abolition of restrictions on movement
and residence within the Community for nationals of
Member States with regard to establishment and the provision
of services [1973] OJ L172/14 .... 8, 68, 69, 101, 104
Directive 88/361 for the implementation of Art 67 of the Treaty
[1988] OJ L178/5 8
Directive 90/364 on the right of residence [1990] OJ L180/26 .... 36, 82

Directive 90/365 on the right of residence for employees and
self-employed persons who have ceased their occupational
activity [1990] OJ L180/28 ....36, 82
Directive 93/96 on the right of residence for students
[1993] OJ L317/59 ....36, 82
Directive 2004/38 on the right of citizens of the Union and
their family members [2004] OJ L158/77.. 8, 27, 50, 51, 52,
56, 64, 101, 192,
202, 205, 229
Directive 2005/36 on the recognition of professional
qualifications [2005] OJ L255/22...64
Directive 2006/123 on services in the internal market
[2006] OJ L376/36 64
Directive 2011/24 on the application of patients' rights in
cross-border healthcare [2011] OJ L88/45 85
Directive 2014/54 on measures facilitating the exercise of
rights conferred on workers in the context of freedom
of movement for workers [2014] OJ L128/8 64

Part I

Introductory Chapters

1
Introduction

THIS BOOK IS a study of the impact that the status of Union citizenship has had on the market freedoms. In particular, the book seeks to consider what has been, and what may have been, the impact of this status on the interpretation of these provisions to date and to consider whether the way that these provisions are now interpreted (as a result of this) can be supported under a literal and/or teleological approach to their interpretation. Moreover, the book considers the broader implications of this: once it is accepted that the market freedoms should, indeed, be interpreted in the light of Union citizenship, what further issues have to be addressed?

I. SETTING THE BACKGROUND

Once upon a time, six European countries decided to pool their coal and steel resources in an attempt to build a European Coal and Steel Community (ECSC). Although it was clear that loftier aspirations for this project were entertained from the very beginning,[1] none of the drafters of the Treaty which gave birth to this Community could dare imagine that this new form of economic cooperation among a handful of western European nations would be the first, modest, seed, in what would become four decades later, the huge EU construct which would come as far as to have its own citizenry.

However, let us take things from the very beginning.

With the coming to an end of the Second Word War in the mid-1940s, Europe was faced with the challenge of having to be rebuilt from its ashes, the ensuing Cold War, re-establishing international relations but also, and perhaps more importantly, ensuring that the mistakes that were perpetrated in the past, would not be repeated in the future. This latter challenge was what led to the realisation that, in order to make a future conflict in the Continent 'not merely unthinkable, but materially impossible',[2] the areas of the economy essential for the building and running of military machines would have to be joined and put together under the

---

[1] This is made explicit in the text of the Schuman Declaration of 9 May 1950, which is the proposal that led to the establishment of the ECSC. The Declaration is available at europa.eu/abc/symbols/9-may/decl_en.htm.
[2] See ibid.

control and administration of a supranational authority. It was, hence, decided that the coal and steel resources of Germany and France should be pulled together, and if they wished, other western European countries would be welcome to participate in this Franco-German venture. Italy and the Benelux countries thereby decided to join, and this led to the signature of the ECSC Treaty in 1951, and its coming into force in the subsequent year.[3]

The main aim of the ECSC Treaty was to organise the free movement of coal and steel between the participating Member States and to ensure free access to the sources of production. The achievement of these aims would, mainly, be implemented and overseen by the High Authority, a supranational institution that was established for this purpose, and the latter would be assisted by a handful of other institutions that bore elements of both supranationalism and intergovernmentalism. As explained by Craig and de Búrca, the establishment of the ECSC 'was the first significant step towards European integration going beyond intergovernmentalism, and establishing a supranational authority whose independent institutions had the power to bind its constituent Member States'.[4]

Although this form of cooperation proved successful, it was clear that the ECSC was merely a first step in the process of European integration and, thus, it was the beginning rather than the culmination of this process. Accordingly, even before this Community was formed, plans for further integration had been made, namely the 1950 Pleven plan, which proposed the creation of a European Defence Community with a European army, and soon after, there were proposals for a European Political Community. Needless to say, both proposals were rejected as, at the time, it was obviously too much to ask of the Member States to cede their sovereignty in these sensitive fields to supranational institutions.[5]

Despite the fact that this was a major setback for the integration process, it clearly did not signal the end of it. Therefore, in 1955, the foreign ministers of the six ECSC Member States met in Messina in Sicily and agreed to move European integration further in the direction of economic integration—an area which was less contentious and sensitive from the point of view of Member State sovereignty. They, consequently, agreed to establish two additional Communities, the European Atomic Energy Community (Euratom) and the European Economic Community (EEC), the respective Treaties of which were signed in 1957 and came into force in 1958.

---

[3] Treaty Establishing the European Coal and Steel Community (ECSC Treaty) [1951], available at http://eur-lex.europa.eu/legal-content/EN/TXT/?uri=CELEX:11951K/TXT. The Treaty had, according to its Art 97, a limited life-span of 50 years and, therefore, it expired on 23 July 2002. Since then, the rules of, initially, the EU Treaty (Consolidated Version of The Treaty on European Union [2012] OJ C326/13) and, now, the Consolidated Version of The Treaty on the Functioning of the European Union (TFEU) [2012] OJ C326/47, have applied to coal and steel trade.
[4] P Craig and G de Búrca, *EU Law: Texts, Cases and Materials* (Oxford, Oxford University Press, 2011) 5.
[5] ibid, 8–9 for more on this.

As its name suggests, Euratom was established in order to coordinate the Member States' actions in the field of nuclear energy. The EEC, on the other hand, had a much broader remit. Its main objective was to establish an internal market[6] where goods, (economically active) Member State nationals, services and capital, would be free to move between Member States and, hence, any obstacle to their movement would be prohibited.[7] Building the internal market was, therefore, the EEC's core policy. Yet, even at this early stage, it was clear that the establishment of the internal market was 'viewed as an *instrument* to enhance social welfare through a variety of objectives (that have expanded over time) and *not* as an end in itself'.[8] In other words, despite the fact that the Communities would initially focus their efforts on the building of an internal market, this would not be their ultimate goal. Rather, as is clear from the Schuman Declaration, the pursuit of European (economic) integration was aiming at lasting peace in Europe and at safeguarding the well-being of Europeans.[9]

In order to achieve the economic aims of the Communities, it was considered necessary to include within the EEC Treaty a number of additional policies, such as a common agricultural policy, a social policy, and a common transport policy.[10] The Communities were given the power to intervene in these fields in varied ways, such as by adopting a common organisation of the market, by (merely) coordinating the actions of the Member States, by promulgating legislative measures to (partly or wholly) harmonise the relevant sectors, or by resorting to negative harmonisation.

This latter method—negative harmonisation—has been the main tool used by the EEC and, later, its successors (the EC and the EU), in the process of executing the internal market policy. The emphasis placed on the use of this method for the removal of obstacles to the free movement of products and factors of production has led to a mainly decentralised system of governance, whereby the power to make legislation for the purpose of regulating economic activity continues to rest with the Member States, whilst the EU institutions (in cooperation with the

---

[6] The initial objective of (what was) the EEC was to build a 'common' market. In the 1980s, however, the terms 'single' and 'internal' market were also introduced to signify this objective. The Treaty of Lisbon has replaced all references in the Treaties to the 'common market' or the 'single market' with the term 'internal market'. In this book the term 'internal market' will be used throughout, unless historical accuracy requires otherwise.

[7] The Single European Act amended (what was at the time) the EEC Treaty and introduced for the first time a definition for the term 'internal market'. This is now found in Art 26(2) TFEU which provides that the internal market 'is an area without internal frontiers in which the free movement of goods, persons, services and capital is ensured in accordance with the provisions of the Treaties'.

[8] E Szyszczak, 'Building a Socioeconomic Constitution: A Fantastic Object?' (2012) 35 *Fordham International Law Journal* 1364, 1370.

[9] Schuman Declaration (n 1). See J Snell, '"European Constitutional Settlement", an ever Closer Union, and the Treaty of Lisbon: Democracy or Relevance?' (2008) 33 *European Law Review* 619, 637–38; S O'Leary, 'Free Movement of Persons and Services' in P Craig and G de Búrca, *The Evolution of EU Law* 2nd edn (Oxford, Oxford University Press, 2011) 506; D Kochenov, 'The Citizenship Paradigm' (2012–13) 15 *Cambridge Yearbook of European Legal Studies* 196.

[10] Each Treaty revision added further policy areas to the EU's remit.

6   *Introduction*

national ones) police national measures to ensure that they do not create any obstacles to free movement.[11]

The main tools used for pursuing negative harmonisation in the area of the internal market have been—what I shall henceforth collectively call—'the market freedoms', which prohibit Member States from applying national measures that (unjustifiably) restrict the freedom of products, services, capital and economic actors to move between Member States. These provisions were, originally, found in the EEC Treaty, from 1993 until 2009 in the EC Treaty, and from 2009 onwards in the TFEU. As Kingreen has characteristically put it, the market freedoms 'are the public law "trampoline" that gives all participants in the EU economy the opportunity to leap over the normative "turnpikes" between the national markets'.[12]

There are a number of different 'market freedoms', each devoted to a different aspect of the 'production process'. Articles 34 and 35 TFEU prohibit the imposition of quantitative restrictions and measures having equivalent effect on, respectively, imports and exports of goods. Article 45 TFEU requires that the free movement of workers is secured within the Union, it prohibits any discriminatory (on the ground of nationality)—and as made clear by the Court[13]—non-discriminatory obstacles to the free movement of workers, and it provides a non-exhaustive list of rights to which migrant workers are entitled. Article 49 TFEU governs the right of establishment and prohibits any obstacles to the exercise of this freedom by (natural or legal) persons in the territory of another Member State. Like Article 45 TFEU, it makes explicit reference to 'rights' to which persons who fall within its scope are entitled. The freedom to provide services is protected by Article 56 TFEU, which prohibits any restrictions on the freedom to provide or receive (as clarified by the Court and the EU legislature) services from one Member State to another. Finally, Article 63 TFEU, governing the free movement of capital, is the only provision that has not remained the same since the birth of the EEC Treaty. This has always been considered as 'the Cinderella freedom',[14] since it started life as a mere obligation imposed on the Member States to progressively abolish restrictions on the movement of capital during the transitional period, 'only to the extent necessary to ensure the proper functioning of the common market'.[15] The Article currently provides that all restrictions on payments, and on the movement of capital, between Member States and between Member States and third countries, are prohibited.

---

[11] M Poiares Maduro, *We, The Court* (Oxford, Hart Publishing, 1998) 126–43. For more on this system of governance see C Barnard, *The Substantive Law of the EU: The Four Freedoms* (Oxford, Oxford University Press, 2013) 17–27.
[12] T Kingreen, 'Fundamental Freedoms' in A von Bogdandy and J Bast (eds), *Principles of European Constitutional Law* (Oxford, München, Hart Publishing, CH Beck, Nomos, 2011) 525.
[13] Case C-415/93 *Bosman* [1995] ECR I-4921.
[14] T Tridimas and P Nebbia, 'Introduction' in T Tridimas and P Nebbia (eds), *European Union Law for the Twenty-First Century* (Oxford, Hart Publishing, 2004) 3.
[15] Art 67 EEC.

Negative harmonisation on its own would, however, never suffice in building an internal market. This is due to the fact that in certain instances, national measures that do impede free movement are, nonetheless, necessary for protecting other (equally valued) non-economic interests, such as public health, consumer protection, and public security, and, as such, there is a good reason for these actions to continue or for the measures to stay in force and for the Member States to continue applying them even in situations involving a cross-border element.[16] The drafters of the EEC Treaty were well aware of this and the latter, from its inception, included an exhaustive list of derogations from the market freedoms. These have survived the subsequent amendments to this Treaty and are, now, found, in its current successor, the TFEU.[17] This has also been recognised by the Court of Justice in its case-law, where the so-called 'mandatory requirements' or 'objective justifications' have been developed,[18] which comprise, in essence, an additional non-exhaustive list of derogations.[19] However, recognising that if an internal market is to be built, it is not possible to allow the existence of such (justified) obstacles in the long run, the EEC was given competence to make legislation having as its aim to ensure that obstacles to free movement are removed whilst non-economic interests which are deemed worthy of protection are secured, albeit that they are secured by a harmonising piece of *EEC* (and later EC, and now, EU) legislation.[20]

The original internal market harmonising provision was—what is now—Article 115 TFEU, which requires unanimity in the Council and which gives competence to the Union to 'issue directives for the approximation of such laws, regulations or administrative provisions of the Member States as directly affect the establishment or functioning of the internal market'. Moreover, the more broadly-worded Article 352 TFEU (under the current numbering), has often been used (especially prior to the mid-1980s) as a legal basis for measures necessary for the establishment of the internal market. As will be seen below, with the coming into force of the Single

---

[16] P Craig, 'The Evolution of the Single Market' in C Barnard and J Scott (eds), *The Law of the Single European Market: Unpacking the Premises* (Oxford, Hart Publishing, 2002) 12.

[17] Art 36 TFEU (goods); Art 45(3) TFEU (workers); Art 52 TFEU (establishment); Art 62 TFEU, which makes Art 52 TFEU applicable in the context of services; Arts 65 and 66 TFEU (capital—though note that these grounds are not, in reality, 'non-economic').

[18] See, among others, Case 33/74 *Van Binsbergen* [1974] ECR 1299; Case 120/78 *Rewe-Zentral AG v Bundesmonopolverwaltung für Branntwein* ('*Cassis de Dijon*') [1979] ECR 649; Case C-55/94 *Gebhard* [1995] ECR I-4165.

[19] The focus of this book will be on the first stage of examining whether a measure is contrary to the market freedoms (ie on the question whether the measure amounts to a 'restriction' contrary to the relevant market freedom) and, hence, there will be little reference to the Treaty derogations and the mandatory requirements/objective justifications. For more on these see J Scott, 'Mandatory or Imperative Requires in the EU and the WTO' in C Barnard and J Scott (eds) *The Law of the Single Market: Unpacking the Premises* (Oxford, Hart Publishing, 2002); S O'Leary and JM Fernández-Martín, 'Judicially-Created Exceptions to the Free Provision of Services' in M Andenas and W-H Roth (eds), *Services and Free Movement in EU Law* (Oxford, Oxford University Press, 2002); C Barnard, 'Derogations, Justifications and the Four Freedoms: Is State Interest Really Protected?' in C Barnard and O Odudu (eds), *The Outer Limits of European Union Law* (Oxford, Hart Publishing, 2009).

[20] JHH Weiler, 'The Constitution of the Common Market Place: Text and Context in the Evolution of the Free Movement of Goods' in P Craig and G de Búrca (eds), *The Evolution of EU Law* (Oxford, Oxford University Press, 1999) 362.

8 *Introduction*

European Act in 1987, a new general legal basis for internal market measures was added (what is now Article 114 TFEU) which did away with the requirement of unanimity. Furthermore, the TFEU, like its predecessors, includes a number of more specific legal bases for making legislation for the purpose of furthering the internal market aims of the Treaty: Article 50 TFEU (freedom of establishment), Article 53 TFEU (recognition of diplomas) and Article 59 TFEU (services), are just a few examples.

Hence, it does not come as a surprise that the market freedoms were supplemented by secondary legislation early on, which sought to put flesh on their bare bones. The main pieces were Regulation 1612/68, which has now been replaced by Regulation 492/2011 which governs the position of migrant workers;[21] Directives 73/148[22] and 68/360[23] which covered the practical aspects of the free movement of workers and the self-employed, but which have been repealed and replaced by the main secondary legislation instrument that currently governs the position of (all) mobile Member State nationals (Directive 2004/38[24]); and a number of social security Regulations, which have been repealed and replaced over the years, the ones currently applicable being Regulations 883/2004 and 987/2009.[25] In addition, Directive 70/50 was adopted to clarify the meaning of the free movement of goods provisions,[26] whilst Directive 88/361 had been promulgated for the purpose of establishing the basic principles governing the free movement of capital.[27]

The requirement of unanimity in the original internal market legal bases, in combination with the so-called 'Luxembourg accords' in the mid-1960s,[28] meant that during the 1970s and 1980s the competence to make legislation in order to

---

[21] Reg 1612/68 on freedom of movement for workers within the Community [1968] OJ L257/2. Repealed and replaced by Reg 492/2011 on freedom of movement for workers within the Union [2011] OJ L141/1.

[22] Dir 73/148 on the abolition of restrictions on movement and residence within the Community for nationals of Member States with regard to establishment and the provision of services [1973] OJ L172/14. Repealed and replaced by Dir 2004/38 on the right of citizens of the Union and their family members [2004] OJ L158/77 (the Citizens' Rights Directive).

[23] Dir 68/360 on the abolition of restrictions on movement and residence within the Community for workers of Member States and their families [1968] OJ L257/13. Repealed and replaced by Dir 2004/38 (n 22).

[24] Dir 2004/38 (n 22).

[25] Reg 883/2004 on the coordination of social security systems, as amended by Reg 988/2009 [2004] OJ L166/1; Reg 987/2009 laying down the procedure for implementing Reg 883/2004 on the coordination of social security systems [2009] OJ L284/1.

[26] Dir 70/50 on the abolition of measures which have an effect equivalent to quantitative restrictions on imports and are not covered by other provisions adopted in pursuance of the EEC Treaty [1970] OJ L13/29.

[27] Dir 88/361 for the implementation of Art 67 of the Treaty [1988] OJ L178/5.

[28] The EEC Treaty provided that with the coming to an end of the transitional period (the transitional period came to an end at midnight on 31 December 1969), in most policy areas decisions would be taken by majority voting. However France objected to the entry into force of the Treaty provisions that would introduce majority voting and adopted the 'empty chair' policy and abstained from Council meetings until it was agreed in 1966 that even in cases where the Treaty provided for majority voting, discussion should continue until unanimity was reached in cases where important national interests were at stake; this agreement is what has been named the 'Luxembourg accords'—see P Craig and G de Búrca (n 4) 7–8.

facilitate the establishment of the internal market was only sporadically resorted to.[29] This placed the burden for the removal of barriers to free movement on the Court of Justice.[30] Accordingly, and as will be seen in more detail in subsequent chapters, the Court interpreted the market freedoms very broadly. Nonetheless, as already noted, negative harmonisation in itself could not suffice in establishing the internal market and in the early 1980s it was realised that the achievement of the central aim of the EEC Treaty, was lagging behind.

As a result of that, in the mid-1980s, the Commissioner for the internal market (Lord Cockfield) prepared a precise timetable—the 'White Paper'[31]—which set out a list of barriers to free movement which impeded the establishment of the internal market, and set the end of 1992 as the deadline for their removal. The deadline—which was not legally binding but 'was psychologically and politically significant'[32]—was endorsed by the Single European Act.[33] In order to facilitate the removal of these barriers, the Single European Act introduced a new legal basis for internal market measures—what is now Article 114 TFEU, which was mentioned earlier—which does not require unanimity and which allows the promulgation of not only directives but of any measures 'which have as their object the establishment and functioning of the internal market'.[34] Despite its wording which signified that this was a 'secondary' legal basis that would only come to be applicable if the other legal bases in the Treaty were not available,[35] this has steadily become the default legal basis for measures aiming to remove obstacles to inter-State movement and/or ensure the proper functioning of the internal market,[36] and this is now reflected in the wording of Articles 114 and 115 TFEU.[37]

---

[29] Weiler has made the very interesting argument that because the Member States found it increasingly difficult during the first two decades of the Community's existence to avoid Community obligations (due to the doctrines of direct effect and supremacy in combination with the preliminary rulings procedure)—which he called 'the closure of Exit'—the need for 'Voice' increased. This, according to him, is what lies beneath the increase in the intergovernmental elements in the decision-making process. See JHH Weiler, 'The Transformation of Europe' in JHH Weiler, *The Constitution of Europe* (Cambridge, Cambridge University Press, 2005) 30–31.

[30] As Kingreen has noted, the ECJ considered 'itself "an emergency power stand-by unit" of integration'—T Kingreen (n 12) 519; and see more generally pp 519–20.

[31] White Paper 'Completing the Internal Market' COM(85)310 final.

[32] C Barnard (n 11) 11.

[33] Art 8a of the EEC Treaty (as amended by the Single European Act) provided that 'The Community shall adopt measures with the aim of progressively establishing the internal market over a period expiring on 31 December 1992, in accordance with the provisions of this Article … and without prejudice to the other provisions of this Treaty'.

[34] It should be noted that qualified majority voting was not for the first time introduced by Art 114 TFEU. Rather, the latter provision 'revived' qualified majority voting since, lest for the Luxembourg Accords, the EEC would have moved away from unanimity and towards majority voting in most areas with the coming to an end of the transitional period.

[35] 'By way of derogation from Art 100 [now Art 115 TFEU] and save where otherwise provided in this Treaty'.

[36] Case C-376/98 *Germany v Parliament and Council (Tobacco Advertising I)* [2000] ECR I-8419.

[37] Art 114 TFEU now simply provides 'Save where otherwise provided in the Treaties' and does not make reference to Art 115 TFEU; Art 115 TFEU now starts by noting: 'Without prejudice to Article 114 TFEU'. Moreover, whereas in the pre-Lisbon setting what is now Art 115 TFEU preceded the equivalent

10 *Introduction*

Despite the fact that the Single European Act was the most significant revision of the EEC Treaty since its inception and that it was particularly important for the internal market policy since it revived the momentum for economic integration, it has not been without its critics.[38] One of the major criticisms levelled towards it was that it was too narrowly-focused on the economic aspects of European integration, at the expense of achieving further progress in the political field.[39]

As an answer to that came the Maastricht Treaty, which was signed in 1992 and came into force in 1993.[40] Maastricht is a milestone for a number of reasons: it signalled the beginning of full economic and monetary union; it brought considerable institutional change by establishing the 'three-pillar' structure of what, since then, has become known as the EU; and it amended the name of the EEC, by scrapping the reference to economic, thus emphasising that this form of European integration would now be about more than just establishing an internal market. This latter aspect of Maastricht was further reflected in a number of more specific changes to the Treaties, such as the expanded competence in the fields of education and culture, the reference in the Treaties, for the first time, to fundamental (human) rights which was, in essence, a consolidation of the ECJ case-law on the matter,[41] and, most importantly for our purposes, the introduction of a new Part Two into—what was then—the EC Treaty, which established a completely new status for Member State nationals: that of Union citizenship.

Hence, Maastricht has been very important in that it made it clear that the (newly-established) EU would no longer focus on achieving the economic aspirations of (what became) the EC, but would, also, set to contribute to the achievement of a number of non-economic objectives. Following Maastricht, '[t]he single market and economic convergence are no longer the predominant objectives of the EC Treaty but merely the first among equals in a whole series of other objectives'.[42] This became even more obvious with subsequent Treaty revisions and is, now, reflected in, inter alia, the text of Article 3 TEU, which provides only in its third paragraph that the 'Union shall establish an internal market', and this comes after the statement in the second paragraph that '[t]he Union shall offer its citizens an area of freedom, security and justice', whilst the word 'aim' is used only in the first paragraph, where it is stated that '[t]he Union's aim is to promote peace, its values and the well-being of its peoples'.

---

to what is now Art 114 TFEU, now the situation is the reverse. For a treatise on EU positive harmonisation see I Maletic, *The Law and Policy of Harmonisation in Europe's Internal Market* (Cheltenham, Edward Elgar, 2013).

[38] See, most prominently, P Pescatore, 'Some Critical Remarks on the Single European Act' (1987) 24 *Common Market Law Review* 9.
[39] W Maas, *Creating European Citizens* (Lanham MD, Rowman & Littlefield Publishers, 2007) 40.
[40] Treaty on European Union [1992] OJ C 191/1.
[41] See eg Case 29/69 *Stauder* [1969] ECR 419; Case 11/70 *Internationale Handelsgesellschaft* [1970] ECR 1125; Case 4/73 *Nold* [1974] ECR 491; Case C-260/89 *ERT* [1991] ECR I-2925.
[42] D Chalmers, 'The Single Market: From Prima Donna to Journeyman' in J Shaw and G More (eds), *New Legal Dynamics of European Union* (Oxford, Clarendon Press, 1995) 68.

The subsequent years saw further Treaty revisions (Amsterdam in 1997 and Nice in 2001), a failed Constitutional Treaty (2004), and the culmination of the reform process with the coming into force of the Lisbon Treaty in 2009, which, inter alia, abolished the three-pillar structure, amended the EU and EC Treaties, and renamed the latter 'TFEU'.[43] From these it is worth highlighting the introduction of the notion of 'an area of Freedom, Security and Justice' by the Treaty of Amsterdam in 1999—the 'central monument' of Amsterdam, as observed by Chalmers, Davies and Monti[44]—which has since been strengthened and, with the coming into force of the Treaty of Lisbon, saw the injection of further supranational elements; and the creation of a bill of rights for the EU, the EU Charter of Fundamental Rights ('the Charter' or 'EUCFR'),[45] which became legally binding in 2009, after surviving in a state of legal limbo since its drafting and proclamation by the EU institutions in 2000.

The last few pages have taken us on a swift journey through time, which sought to describe how the EU has developed from a narrowly-focused Community concerned with the administration of coal and steel in Western Europe, to an elaborate, (almost) pan-European,[46] political organisation with a highly complex legal system and its own citizenry. The aim has not been to provide a comprehensive analysis of the history of the EU but, rather, to sketch the main historical highlights and to place the market freedoms in a historical context, that will facilitate the reader in following the main analysis in the remainder of this book. Accordingly, I hope to be forgiven for, what may appear to some, a rather haste and selective exposition of the EU's history.[47]

In the next chapter we are going to see in more detail how the status of EU citizenship has been developed since its introduction in 1993. Before moving there, however, it will first be explained what the main aim of this book is and how this aim shall be achieved.

II. AIM OF THE BOOK

This book seeks to address the relationship between the status of Union citizenship and the market freedoms and, in particular, to examine the impact that Union citizenship has had, and should have, on the development of the market freedoms. It has a threefold objective: firstly, to consider how the introduction

---

[43] For a full analysis of the Lisbon Treaty and the changes made by it see M Dougan, 'The Treaty of Lisbon 2007: Winning Minds, Not Hearts' (2008) 45 *Common Market Law Review* 617; P Craig, 'The Treaty of Lisbon: Process, Architecture and Substance' (2008) 33 *European Law Review* 137.

[44] D Chalmers, G Davies and G Monti, *European Union Law: Cases and Materials* (Cambridge, Cambridge University Press, 2014) 29.

[45] Charter of Fundamental Rights of the European Union [2007] OJ C303/17.

[46] The EU currently has 28 Member States.

[47] For more detailed explorations of the EU's history see, inter alia, L Middelaar, *The Passage to Europe: How a Continent Became a Union* (Yale, Yale University Press, 2013); D Dinan, *Europe Recast: A History of European Union* (Basingstoke, Palgrave Macmillan, 2014).

and development of the status of Union citizenship has affected, and may have affected, the interpretation of the market freedoms; secondly, to assess whether the way that these provisions are now interpreted (as a result of this) is legally warranted, taking into account both their text and their current aims; and, thirdly, to identify any conundrums or problems that have emerged or are likely to emerge as a result of the re-interpretation of the market freedoms in the light of Union citizenship, and to offer some thoughts as to how, if at all, these can best be (re)solved.

The decision to write this book was made shortly after the publication of my previous monograph,[48] which examined the issue of reverse discrimination in purely internal situations and sought to establish whether permitting this form of differential treatment is still acceptable in today's EU. My research for that project revealed that the interpretation of the market freedoms—and, mainly, those concerned with the free movement of persons—had changed in recent years and especially after the introduction of the status of Union citizenship. In fact, in some cases, the Court had even acknowledged the need to re-read these provisions in a manner that takes into account that their beneficiaries are now, also, Union citizens. Accordingly, that project had demonstrated that different clusters of cases that did not make sense when a purely internal market-based rationale was employed could, nonetheless, be explained under a citizenship-based rationale. Although the focus of that project precluded a detailed examination of this issue, it became clear that the question of the impact of Union citizenship on the interpretation of the market freedoms was becoming increasingly important and deserved its own long project; this is what led to the proposal for this book.

It is true that in the literature that has been published in the last couple of decades, it has been widely recognised that Union citizenship has had a significant impact on the development of EU free movement law. However, this has not been expressly acknowledged by the Court, bar from a few instances in its personal market freedoms case-law, which will be seen in subsequent parts of the book. Moreover, the topic is relatively unexplored in literature as, although there have been a number of articles and books which explore certain aspects of this question,[49] there has not been a systematic study which illustrates the overall

---

[48] A Tryfonidou, *Reverse Discrimination in EC Law* (The Hague, Kluwer, 2009).
[49] See, most prominently, E Spaventa, 'From *Gebhard* to *Carpenter*: Towards a (Non)-Economic European Constitution' (2004) 41 *Common Market Law Review* 743; E Spaventa, *Free Movement of Persons in the European Union: Barriers to Movement in their Constitutional Context* (The Hague, Kluwer, 2007); S O'Leary, 'Developing an Ever Closer Union between the Peoples of Europe? A Reappraisal of the Case Law of the Court of Justice on the Free Movement of Persons and EU Citizenship' (2008) 27 *Yearbook of European Law* 167; E Spaventa, 'Seeing the Wood Despite the Trees? On the Scope of Union Citizenship and its Constitutional Effects' (2008) 45 *Common Market Law Review* 13; N Nic Shuibhne, 'The Outer Limits of EU Citizenship: Displacing Economic Free Movement Rights?' in C Barnard and O Odudu (n 19); A Tryfonidou, 'Family Reunification Rights of (Migrant) Union Citizens: Towards a Liberal Approach' (2009) 15 *European Law Journal* 634; A Tryfonidou, 'In Search of the Aim of the Free Movement of Persons Provisions: Has the Court of Justice Missed the Point?' (2009) 46 *Common Market Law Review* 1591; A Tryfonidou, 'Further Steps on the Road to Convergence among the Market Freedoms' (2010) 35 *European Law Review* 36; F de Cecco, 'Fundamental Freedoms, Fundamental Rights and the Scope of Free Movement Law' (2014) 15 *German Law Journal* 383.

impact of citizenship on the interpretation of *all* the market freedoms (and not just the personal market freedoms) *and* the (possible) implications of this.[50] This book will, therefore, aim to do just this.

As a broader, secondary, aim, the book will also seek to deepen the understanding of the nature and mechanisms of the market freedoms, as these have now been re-defined in the post-citizenship era. The developments in this area of EU law are inexorably linked to more general issues of EU law. In particular, the book will seek to illustrate and analyse the interminable tensions between the EU and the Member States when determining the power-sharing arrangements between them, how these tensions have been resolved so far, and how they could best be resolved.

III. TERMINOLOGY

Before proceeding to the main chapters, key concepts used in this book have to be defined. It should be noted that some of these terms have also been used by the ECJ, its Advocates General, or by other commentators, however, the usage here may in some respects differ.

The term 'market freedoms' refers to Articles 34, 35, 45, 49, 56 and 63 TFEU. The market freedoms which govern the rights of economically-active persons—Articles 45, 49 and 56 TFEU—will be collectively referred to as the 'personal market freedoms', whereas the phrase 'the free movement of goods provisions'—for the reasons explained in chapter four—will be used, mainly, to refer to Article 34 TFEU. As regards the personal market freedoms and Article 21 TFEU, these will be referred to collectively as 'the free movement of persons provisions'. The provisions situated in Part Two of the TFEU and, in particular, Articles 20 and 21, are collectively called the 'citizenship provisions'.

In some instances, there will be a need to distinguish between the freedom of movement for workers provisions and the establishment provisions, on the one hand, and the provisions governing the freedom to provide services, on the other. For this purpose, the term 'more stationary personal market freedoms' will be used to refer to the former, given that these provisions aim to ensure that an economic activity is *permanently* pursued in the territory of another Member State/ in a cross-border context and the cross-border element emerges from a *single* act, traditionally comprised of a change in the location of the economic activity and/ or the economic base of the economic actor, whereas the freedom to provide services provisions aim to protect the *continuous* provision of services *across borders* during a *specific* period of time, without there being a change in the economic base

---

[50] Moreover, and more broadly, as Nic Shuibhne has pointed out, 'the extent to which the legal meaningfulness of EU citizenship infuses the Treaty more generally has never been clearly determined'—N Nic Shuibhne, 'EU Citizenship after Lisbon' in D Ashiagbor, N Countouris and I Lianos (eds), *The European Union after the Treaty of Lisbon* (Cambridge, Cambridge University Press, 2012) 137.

of the economic actor (eg the service-provider maintains his business in the home State whilst he provides services to persons in other Member States or temporarily travels to other Member States for this purpose). Accordingly, whilst the 'more stationary personal market freedoms' have traditionally aimed to enable Member State nationals to change their economic base through a single instance of exercise of free movement, the whole point of granting the freedom to provide services has always been to ensure that economic actors can maintain their economic base in their home State whilst they can temporarily provide services to persons established in other Member States.

In this book, the phrase 'fundamental right' is taken to mean any right that is respected for its own sake and not in order to contribute to the achievement of another aim.[51] However, what is the difference between fundamental rights and instrumental rights/freedoms, which is a distinction central to the analysis in this book? In order to answer this question, I shall use the words of De Cecco who, relying on the writings of Joseph Raz, explained this distinction very clearly:

> a right is fundamental if the right-holder's interest is considered to be 'of ultimate value', that is, an interest that 'does not derive from some other interest of the right-holder or of other persons.' Furthermore, the values protected by fundamental rights are those that 'need not be explained or be justified by (their contribution to) other values.' If this is the case, when determining whether a certain right is a fundamental right, it is necessary to separate out those interests that are protected for their intrinsic value from those interests that are protected for their instrumental role.[52]

Consequently, in this book when it is said that the rights granted by the market freedoms are *fundamental* rights, this means that they are protected for their own sake, whereas when it is stated that these provisions are the sources of, merely, instrumental rights/freedoms, this means that the rights/freedoms stemming from them are protected because of their contribution to the internal market aims of the Treaty and not for their own sake. Moreover, and related to the previous point, although the terms 'freedom' and 'right' can, clearly, be treated as synonymous,[53] for the purposes of this book, a threefold distinction will be drawn when categorising the various entitlements stemming from the market freedoms: a) instrumental

---

[51] For an explanation of the consequences of the categorisation of a right as a fundamental one see C Hilson, 'What's in a Right? The Relationship between Community, Fundamental and Citizenship Rights in EU Law' (2004) 29 *European Law Review* 636, 646–49.

[52] F de Cecco (n 49) 385. A different definition of fundamental rights, though one which does not contradict the one provided by de Cecco and which can, in fact, be viewed as complementary, was provided by de Boer—NJ de Boer, 'Fundamental Rights and the EU Internal Market: Just how Fundamental are the EU Treaty Freedoms? A Normative Enquiry Based on John Rawls Political Philosophy' (2013) 9 *Utrecht Law Review* 148, 151.

[53] eg Hansen has noted that '[w]here a state's sovereignty is restricted towards a person, that person is said to enjoy a freedom, eg a freedom of speech, etc. The freedom in this respect could also be described as a right of that individual, eg a right of free speech. This parlance of what is usually national constitutional law can equally well describe the position of an individual of the European Union'— JL Hansen, 'Full Circle: Is there a Difference between the Freedom of Establishment and the Freedom to Provide Services?' in M Andenas and W-H Roth (n 19)200.

freedoms, when these are granted to third-country nationals (eg when they seek to move goods or capital between Member States) or *inanimate objects* (eg the freedom of movement of goods, capital and services; and the freedom of establishment/to provide or receive services/to sell or purchase goods/to move capital of corporate entities), in order to ensure that the economic aims of the Treaty are going to be achieved; b) instrumental rights, when these are granted to Member State nationals simply for the purpose of furthering the EU's economic aims; and c) fundamental (economic) rights, when these are granted to *Union citizens* and must be protected and respected *for their own sake*. The Court and EU law scholars have never adopted the above categorisation and, in particular, the distinction between *rights* (for Union citizens) and *freedoms* (for third-country nationals and inanimate objects), in the market freedoms context; rather, they use the terms interchangeably. Moreover, the fact that the market freedoms are directly effective irrespective of who seeks to invoke them and, thus, they are considered sources of enforceable *rights* for everyone and everything that falls within their personal scope, in fact contradicts this scheme of classification. Nonetheless, since—as will be seen in chapters five and six—the book argues that the market freedoms must be interpreted differently when they are relied on by Union citizens (in which case they must be read together with the citizenship provisions) than when they are invoked by legal persons or third-country nationals, using a different term to describe the entitlements that are derived from these provisions in each of the above scenarios is more apt and more conducive to legal certainty.

Another important notion which will play a cardinal role in the analysis in this book, is 'cross-border specificity'.[54] Cross-border specificity exists in a particular factual scenario, if the exercise of the rights stemming from the market freedoms (which are, by nature, cross-border), leads to a certain disadvantage. In other words, there is cross-border specificity in a situation if it involves a person or economic activity that is treated worse *as a result of the fact that* a right or freedom stemming from the market freedoms has been exercised. The less favourable treatment can be suffered when the person moves to another Member State (eg if the latter does not permit him or her to be accompanied there by close family members who, therefore, have to stay in the State of origin) or when (s)he is refused benefits or more beneficial treatment by his/her State of origin, to which (s)he was entitled prior to the exercise of the rights stemming from the market freedoms (eg (s)he loses entitlement to certain tax advantages). Moreover, when it comes to economic activities, cross-border specificity usually exists if cross-border economic activities are treated worse than economic activities that are pursued within the territory of a single Member State (eg if the provision of cross-border services or sale of goods is subject to more burdensome requirements than the provision of services or sale of goods within one and the same Member State). Accordingly, there is cross-border specificity when the contested national measure

---

[54] This term has been used by a number of scholars, most prominently E Spaventa, *Free Movement of Persons in the European Union* (n 49).

specifically (and only) negatively affects persons who have exercised the freedoms/ rights stemming from the market freedoms or economic transactions which are cross-border, whilst it does not have such a negative impact on persons in a similar position who have not exercised those freedoms/rights. The existence of cross-border specificity demonstrates that the contested national measure is biased against situations that involve the exercise of the rights or freedoms stemming from the market freedoms and, hence, instead of being a measure or action that seeks to ensure that the said matter or economic activity is (neutrally) regulated, it has the effect of *specifically* discouraging the taking-up and pursuit of cross-border economic activities. Needless to say, measures of the host State which (directly or indirectly) discriminate against nationals of other Member States who have made use of the freedoms or rights stemming from the market freedoms do, clearly, have cross-border specificity.

The requirement of cross-border specificity seems to be the basis of the discrimination-based approach, traditionally employed for delimiting the scope of application of the market freedoms.[55] In this context, of course, discrimination has been read very broadly,[56] as encompassing both direct and indirect discrimination on the grounds of nationality or origin (ie discrimination against the nationals of other Member States or goods/services/capital originating in other Member States)[57] *and* discrimination on the ground of free movement (ie discrimination against persons who have exercised their rights stemming from the market freedoms or against goods, services or capital that have moved or are to move between Member States).[58] Very recently, the Court has held that a discriminatory measure that leads to nationals of some Members States being favoured over nationals of other Member States is also prohibited by Article 45 TFEU,[59] and there is no reason why the prohibition of nationality discrimination stemming from the other market freedoms and, even, from Article 18 TFEU, should not be read in the same manner. Moreover, even measures which are more subtle and do not make any reference to nationality/origin or to the exercise of free movement, but are by nature such as they will (perhaps merely potentially) result in less favourable treatment for cross-border situations than for purely internal ones, appear to be having cross-border specificity. Hence, if a national measure has the effect of preventing an economic actor from elaborating a pan-European advertising strategy or from continuing to pursue such a strategy,[60] or if it is such as to

---

[55] As Davies has noted, 'any measure acting specifically upon cross-border movement is discriminatory in at least some sense'—G Davies, *Nationality Discrimination in the European Internal Market* (The Hague, Kluwer, 2003) 53, fn 3.

[56] N Nic Shuibhne, *The Coherence of EU Free Movement Law: Constitutional Responsibility and the Court of Justice* (Oxford, Oxford University Press, 2013) 198–99.

[57] See eg Case 167/73 *Commission v France* [1974] ECR 359; Case C-281/98 *Angonese* [2000] ECR I-4139; Case C-379/98 *PreussenElektra* [2001] ECR I-2099.

[58] See eg Case C-288/89 *Gouda* [1991] ECR I-4007; Case C-19/92 *Kraus* [1993] ECR I-1663.

[59] Case C-512/13 *Sopora* ECLI:EU:C:2015:108, para 25.

[60] See paragraphs 16–18 of the Opinion of AG Tesauro in Case C-292/92 *Hünermund* [1993] ECR I-6787. See eg Case 286/81 *Criminal Proceedings against Oosthoek's Uitgeversmaatschappij BV* [1982] ECR 4575, para 15; Case C-126/91 *Yves Rocher* [1993] ECR I-2361, para 10.

make access to the market for out-of-State goods, persons, or services more difficult (or even impossible) than access to the market for domestic ones, this being, usually, the case when the contested measure or rule seeks to maintain the status quo in the national market,[61] it, clearly, has cross-border specificity.[62] Similarly, national measures which do not require national authorities to take into account the 'history' of the product or person, or their background (eg whether they had to comply with certain requirements in their home State and, if so, whether those requirements safeguard the same interests that are protected under the legislation of the host State), may appear, on their face, to treat domestic and imported goods or services in the same manner or nationals and non-nationals equally, but in reality, they are treating two different situations in the same manner and they are, thus, discriminatory.[63]

As noted earlier, an approach which reads the market freedoms as requiring cross-border specificity in order to apply is, in essence, a discrimination-based approach. An alternative—broader—approach supported by certain commentators[64] and Advocates General,[65] the 'access to market' approach or test, will not be referred to much in this book, although 'access to market' language has been widely used in the Court's case-law, especially in recent years. This is for two reasons. Firstly, because it is an approach which has never been clearly defined and, thus, instead of providing some form of clarity, it introduces further confusion and gives rise to new questions.[66] For instance, the test is broad enough to cover both discriminatory and genuinely non-discriminatory measures (and most commentators treat it as such) but there is nothing to indicate that it cannot be read as encompassing merely discriminatory measures—hence, adopting this test (without providing further clarification) does not say anything about the exact types of measures that it brings within the scope of the market freedoms. Secondly, and more importantly, with its emphasis on access to *market*, the test appears to be too limited an approach to be adopted for the purposes of this book, since it is incapable of justifying the inclusion within the scope of the market freedoms of some of the measures that have been recently caught by them and which do not

---

[61] See eg Case C-405/98 *Gourmet* [2001] ECR I-1795; Case C-458/03 *Parking Brixen* [2005] ECR I-8585; Case C-380/05 *Europa 7* [2008] ECR I-349. For comments see G Davies (n 55) 69–70.
[62] See paragraphs 37–40 of the Opinion of AG Poiares Maduro in Case C-446/03 *Marks and Spencer* [2005] ECR I-10837, for examples of situations and measures which have cross-border specificity.
[63] See eg Case 279/80 *Webb* [1981] ECR 3305; Case C-443/10 *Bonnarde* [2011] ECR I-9327.
[64] See, most prominently, S Weatherill, 'After *Keck*: Some Thoughts on how to Clarify the Clarification' (1996) 33 *Common Market Law Review* 885; C Barnard, 'Fitting the Remaining Pieces into the Goods and Persons Jigsaw?' (2001) 26 *European Law Review* 35.
[65] See eg the Opinion of AG Jacobs in Case C-412/93 *Leclerc-Siplec* [1995] ECR I-179; the Opinion of AG Trstenjak in Case C-205/07 *Gysbrechts* [2008] ECR I-9947.
[66] See C Barnard and S Deakin, 'Market Access and Regulatory Competition' in C Barnard and J Scott (n 16) 204–13; C Barnard, 'Restricting Restrictions: Lessons for the EU from the US' (2009) 68 *Cambridge Law Journal* 575, 593–98; J Snell, 'The Notion of Market Access: A Concept or a Slogan?' (2010) 47 *Common Market Law Review* 437; G Davies, 'Understanding Market Access: Exploring the Economic Rationality of Different Conceptions of Free Movement Law' (2010) 11 *German Law Journal* 671; N Nic Shuibhne (n 56) 236–42.

18 *Introduction*

impede access to the *market* of another Member State but, more broadly, access to another Member State.[67]

Finally, it should be noted that the new Treaty of Lisbon numbering is used throughout, except where historical accuracy requires otherwise, in which case the old numbering is maintained, and the new numbering follows in brackets. The same is the case with terminology. Accordingly, it is the term 'EU' that will, generally, be used instead of 'EEC' or 'EC'. Similarly, as already noted, 'internal market'—as opposed to 'common' or 'single' market—will be used throughout the book, unless historical accuracy requires otherwise. As regards the EU courts, the (post-Lisbon) term 'CJEU' will be used to refer to the composite Court of Justice of the European Union, which includes the European Court of Justice ('ECJ', 'the Court of Justice' or 'the Court'), the European General Court (EGC) and the Civil Service Tribunal. As will be seen, given that the market freedoms and the citizenship provisions have been interpreted mostly—if not wholly—by the ECJ, it is the latter's case-law that will mainly be analysed in this book and, therefore, reference will, mostly, be made to the ECJ rather than to the other (lower) EU courts or to the term 'CJEU'.

IV. STRUCTURE OF THE BOOK

Traditional legal method has been used in conducting the research for this book. Building on analysis of (mostly) ECJ case-law, EU secondary legislation, documents of the EU institutions, and prior scholarly discourse, this monograph is the first study which sets to comprehensively analyse the impact that the development of the status of Union citizenship has had, may have had, and should have, on the interpretation of the market freedoms *and* to consider the overall implications of this for the development of EU law in this area.

The book is comprised of this introductory chapter, five main chapters, plus chapter seven, which concludes.

Chapter two will trace the development of the status of Union citizenship from its introduction to the present day, through the Court's case-law. The chapter will not seek to provide a detailed, critical, analysis of the Court's citizenship case-law, nor will it aim to explore the deeper, philosophical, questions that are often considered when the real value of this new status is assessed (for instance, whether the EU is a citizenship-capable polity and, if so, what type of citizenship it can aspire to develop). Rather, the aim will be to provide a clear explanation of the rights that (economically inactive) Union citizens now derive from EU law and, in particular, from the citizenship provisions of the Treaty.

Chapter three will focus on considering the impact that Union citizenship seems to have had to date on the interpretation of the personal market freedoms.

---

[67] Nic Shuibhne suggests that access should be conceived 'as a principle concerned with *access to the exercise of free movement rights*' as opposed to simply market access—N Nic Shuibhne (n 56) 210 and 241.

The chapter will begin by explaining that, originally, the latter provisions were viewed as sources of merely instrumental freedoms and, later, rights granted to Member State nationals, their main aim being to ensure that the latter would be encouraged to contribute to the achievement of the internal market aim of the Treaty. The lion's share of the analysis, however, will be taken by explaining how the scope of application of these provisions seems to have been affected by the fact that their beneficiaries are, since 1993, also Union citizens. Apart from referring to the (few) cases where the Court explicitly recognised the need to (re-)read the personal market freedoms in the light of Union citizenship, the chapter will focus on exploring how the personal and material scope of application of these provisions has changed in recent years. It will be concluded that given that the rights derived from the personal market freedoms are, now, in some cases granted to economic actors in situations where there does not appear to be a sufficient connection with the aim of building an internal market, they seem to have been transformed into *fundamental* economic rights which are granted to Member State nationals *simply* because they are Union citizens and not, merely, in order to ensure that they contribute to the EU's economic aims.

Chapter four will explore the impact that the status of Union citizenship *may* have had on the free movement of goods provisions. It will be seen that unlike the personal market freedoms, the Court in none of its judgments in this context did it point to a connection between the status of Union citizenship and the free movement of goods provisions. Nonetheless, there have been some changes in the interpretation of these provisions in recent years, which cannot be justified if they are read in the light of a purely internal market-based rationale. Accordingly, these may be taken as signs that the Court may now be re-considering the interpretation of the free movement of goods provisions and that it may be in a trajectory leading to a re-conceptualisation of these provisions as sources of fundamental rights for individuals. There is nothing, nonetheless, in the Court's case-law that illustrates that the rationale behind this move is the determination to read the free movement of goods provisions in the light of Union citizenship: the Court has neither admitted that these new rights are, indeed, fundamental, nor has it confined their availability to Union citizens, which would constitute an indication that this move has been effected as a result of the introduction of Union citizenship. Accordingly, it will be concluded that it is not yet possible to say with certainty whether the introduction and development of the status of Union citizenship has had any impact on the interpretation of the free movement of goods provisions.

The subsequent chapters are concerned with the implications of the process of re-interpreting the market freedoms in the light of Union citizenship.

Chapter five will focus on the question of whether the way the Court has interpreted these provisions after Maastricht—and which, it is argued in this book, is not justified by a purely internal market-based rationale—is legally warranted, when this is judged taking into account the text of these provisions and (what can be considered to be) their *current* aims. It will be concluded that the broader interpretation of the market freedoms in recent years, which cannot be justified by a purely internal market-based rationale can, indeed, be justified under a citizenship-based rationale. However—and this is a significant point—the market freedoms can only be read as sources of fundamental rights for Union citizens when they are read together with the citizenship provisions and, naturally, when they are invoked by Union citizens. From this it also follows that when the market freedoms are relied on by persons (whether legal or natural) that are *not* Union citizens, the Court should revert to its original (narrower) interpretation of them, under which the rights and freedoms stemming from them are purely instrumental to the economic aims of the Treaty. The chapter also proposes ways of avoiding an overly broad interpretation of the market freedoms, suggesting that the Court should ensure that the current filtering mechanisms employed in the context of the market freedoms are appropriately utilised for this purpose.

Chapter six will go further by identifying the conundrums and problems that have emerged or will emerge as a result of the re-interpretation of the market freedoms in the manner analysed in chapters three and four. Some of the main issues that will be considered are whether it is appropriate to exclude third-country nationals from entitlement to the fundamental rights stemming from the market freedoms; whether the market freedoms can be read as sources of different entitlements depending on who (if it is an EU citizen) or what (if it is a legal person) relies on them; whether fundamental economic rights now prevail over fundamental human rights and vice-versa; and, finally, whether these rights are/should be privileged over collective interests. The chapter will also seek to consider how these problems and conundrums can best be (re-)solved.

A few words should now be said about the scope of the study.

The book focuses on three of the market freedoms—the free movement of goods, persons and services—and not on the fourth, the free movement of capital. This is for the simple, practical, reason that the latter is the least developed freedom and there have not been any real signs in the Court's case-law that Union citizenship has had any impact on its interpretation. Nonetheless, reference to this freedom and to the Court's jurisprudence will be made, where appropriate.

Moreover, although, as will be seen, most of the market freedoms have both a personal and an economic aspect, the focus here will be on the personal aspect of these provisions.[68] Accordingly, the emphasis throughout the book will be on

---

[68] As explained by Nic Shuibhne, 'maybe divisions *within* the freedoms are becoming more critical than any divisions *across* them' (N Nic Shuibhne (n 49) 174) and, hence, instead of adopting the traditional fourfold division of the market freedoms into the provisions governing goods, persons, services, and capital, it would now make more sense to divide them into, on the one hand, the freedoms or the aspects of the freedoms which are merely used as tools for the construction and smooth functioning of the internal market (eg cases concerning the free movement of services as such, cases involving the free movement of companies, cases involving the free movement of capital and goods as such) and, on the other, the freedoms or the aspects of the freedoms which have now been reconceptualised as sources of constitutional fundamental rights for the Union citizen (eg cases involving the rights derived from the market freedoms by the service-provider or service-recipient who are natural persons, by the retailer, by the employed or self-employed worker).

the rights that *natural persons* and, in particular, Union citizens, derive from the market freedoms, whereas reference to the entitlements of legal persons will only be made in passing, when this is judged necessary for the purposes of the analysis or for reasons of completeness.

It should be noted that although the aim is to ensure balance of coverage across the market freedoms that form the subject-matter of this study, this will sometimes vary, due to the different issues that have emerged in the context of the various freedoms and which are relevant to this context.

It will be noticed that the book will neither seek to provide an exhaustive coverage of the Court's case-law interpreting the market freedoms, nor will it aim to find a coherent thread which unites the case-law and which demonstrates that in *all* its case-law, the Court appears to be taking into account that the beneficiaries of these provisions are, now, also Union citizens. Rather, the focus will be on ECJ case-law that cannot be justified under a purely market-based rationale and which can support the argument that the interpretation of the market freedoms has been affected by the introduction of Union citizenship.

The law is stated as at the end of May 2015.

V. A TAXONOMY OF RIGHTS FOR THE MARKET FREEDOMS

Taking into account the fact that the main argument of this book is that the market freedoms should (when read together with the citizenship provisions) be reconceptualised as sources of fundamental, economic, rights for the Union citizen, it is important to provide a taxonomy of rights which can be used when determining which rights are now stemming from these provisions.

At the core of this taxonomy lies the basic distinction between primary and secondary rights. As explained by Goudappel, '[p]rimary rights are the rights which are laid down in the Treaty texts'; on the other hand, secondary rights are derived from primary rights, 'like the right to bring your family members when you move to another Member State … Such rights are not laid down in the Treaty texts but follow from the rights laid down in there'.[69]

What is important in relation to primary rights is that whenever a person falls within the personal scope of the relevant market freedom, (s)he is entitled to those rights; they are 'master' rights and, thus, whenever *one* of these rights is breached (ie there is a *direct* restriction on their exercise), this automatically means that there is a violation of the relevant provision. Primary rights should not be confused with fundamental rights since, although primary rights are not dependent on any other rights granted by a Treaty provision for their existence, they may, however, be instrumental in the sense that they are granted to individuals in order to ensure the attainment of a particular objective, and, hence, they may not be

---

[69] F Goudappel, *The Effects of EU Citizenship: Economic, Social and Political Rights in a Time of Constitutional Change* (The Hague, TMC Asser Press, 2010) 55.

respected and protected merely for their own sake. Hence, as will be seen in chapter three, although the right to free movement (for the purpose of taking-up an economic activity) has always been considered a primary right stemming from the personal market freedoms, *traditionally* it could not be characterised as a fundamental right, since it was not respected for its own sake but as part of the process of building an internal market. On the other hand, a clear connection between a (claimed) secondary right and a primary right on the facts of the case must be proved, in order for the former to arise in the first place: a (secondary) right can only be considered as derived from the personal market freedoms if, *on the particular facts of the case*, its violation will lead to a violation of the primary right that has been (or was intended to be) exercised on the facts of the case. Obviously, the nature of secondary rights, which makes their existence and enjoyment dependent on another right, disqualifies them from being considered *fundamental* rights.

Although it is relatively simple to identify the primary rights granted by a Treaty provision, the same is not true for secondary rights: establishing which are the secondary rights bestowed by the personal market freedoms is a life-long task for the Court of Justice, which is fact-specific and, thus, cannot be done in a factually abstract setting but, rather, only on a case-by-case basis.

A violation of a primary right amounts to a direct restriction on that right, whilst a violation of a secondary right amounts to an indirect restriction on the relevant primary right.[70] Whenever there is a direct or indirect restriction on one of the primary rights stemming from the market freedoms, there is a prima facie breach of that provision, and the ECJ or the national court hearing the case will have to consider whether the measure which gives rise to the restriction is, nonetheless, justified.

---

[70] This is the approach followed in this book. It should be noted, however, that different approaches to what amounts to a direct or indirect restriction caught by the market freedoms are followed by different commentators and there is no consensus regarding the exact meaning of these terms. See eg the discussion in G Davies (n 55) 100–01.

2
Taking Stock of Union Citizenship

I. INTRODUCTION

IN THE PREVIOUS chapter, the background to this study was set, illustrating how the process of European integration developed from a narrowly focused Coal and Steel Community, to a Union with a much broader remit. In particular, it was seen that in the early 1990s, the Maastricht Treaty[1] established the status of Union citizenship, a move which—as will be seen in the next chapter—was not entirely unexpected, given the central role the individual had come to play in the EU construct.

Union citizenship celebrated its 21st birthday in 2014. Therefore, chronologically speaking, one could say that it has 'come of age'. This immediately leads to the question of whether Union citizenship has also come of age, if this is examined from the angle of the substance that has been given to this status.[2] Put differently, does this mean that Member State nationals today occupy a different—better—position under EU law than they did before they became Union citizens? Or is the status merely a consolidation of the pre-Maastricht *acquis*?

As will be seen, despite some retrograde steps taken in some of the Court's recent case-law, the overall conclusion that can be derived from the analysis in this chapter, is that Union citizenship has, indeed, granted to Member State nationals rights which are over and beyond those to which they were entitled under EEC law before the introduction and judicial development of this status. Accordingly, Union citizenship has come—or perhaps, more accurately, is very close to coming—of age.

As a background to what is going to follow in the subsequent chapters of the book, this chapter will seek to provide an explanation of the status of Union citizenship, viewed through the lens of the ECJ's jurisprudence. Much has been written about the introduction of this status, the history that preceded it, and its

---

[1] Consolidated Version of The Treaty on European Union [2012] OJ C326/13.
[2] For commentators supporting the view that EU citizenship has 'come of age' see, inter alia, D Kostakopoulou, 'Ideas, Norms and European Citizenship: Explaining Institutional Change' (2005) 68 *Modern Law Review* 233, 267; H de Waele, 'EU Citizenship: Revisiting its Meaning, Place and Potential' (2010) 12 *European Journal of Migration and Law* 319, 334.

significance.[3] The purpose of this chapter is, therefore, clearly not to offer another such account. Its aim is rather more humble, and it is to consider what has been achieved, in practice, through the Court's judgments, in the decades that followed the introduction of this status. As such, when it comes to the debate whether Union citizenship is, now, indeed, a 'real' citizenship status, the chapter will not take sides, though it will be concluded that EU citizenship has moved away from its initial 'incipient form' and market citizenship roots, and towards a status detached from economic and cross-border considerations.

The chapter will be heavily reliant on the Court's citizenship jurisprudence and, hence, it is imperative to provide a clear analysis of the relevant case-law and a categorisation of it which will enable meaningful conclusions to be drawn. Accordingly, a chronologically-based scheme of classification has been devised, which divides the Court's citizenship jurisprudence into four different phases: infancy, growth, adolescence, and coming of age.

Bearing in mind the large number of citizenship cases, it is clear that it is impossible to analyse in this chapter every single judgment where the Court has interpreted the citizenship provisions of the Treaty and/or the relevant secondary legislation in situations which involved *economically inactive* Union citizens.[4] However, an effort has been made to include as many citizenship cases as possible, even in a footnote. Readers who are already well-acquainted with the ECJ's citizenship jurisprudence, may wish to skip this chapter.

---

[3] See eg C Closa, 'The Concept of Citizenship in the Treaty on European Union' (1992) 29 *Common Market Law Review* 1137; HU Jessurun d'Oliveira, 'European Citizenship: Its Meaning, Its Potential' in Dehousse (ed), *Europe after Maastricht: An Ever Closer Union* (Munich, Beck, 1994); D O'Keeffe, 'Union Citizenship' in D O'Keeffe and P Twomey (eds), *Legal Issues of the Maastricht Treaty* (London, Chancery Law Publishing, 1994); S O'Leary, *The Evolving Concept of Community Citizenship: From the Free Movement of Persons to Union Citizenship* (The Hague, Kluwer, 1996); N Reich, 'Union Citizenship—Metaphor or Source of Rights?' (2001) 7 *European Law Journal* 4; RCA White, 'Citizenship of the Union, Governance, and Equality' (2006) 29 *Fordham International Law Journal* 790; W Maas, *Creating European Citizens* (Lanham MD, Rowman & Littlefield Publishers, 2007) Chs 2 and 3; FG Jacobs, 'Citizenship of the European Union—a Legal Analysis' (2007) 13 *European Law Journal* 591; D Kostakopoulou, 'European Union Citizenship: Writing the Future' (2007) 13 *European Law Journal* 623; D Kochenov, '*Ius tractum* of Many Faces: European Citizenship and the Difficult Relationship between Status and Rights' (2009) 15 *Columbia Journal of European Law* 169; S Currie, 'The Transformation of Union Citizenship' in M Dougan and S Currie (eds), *50 Years of the European Treaties: Looking Back and Thinking Forward* (Oxford, Hart Publishing, 2009); F Wollenschläger, 'A New Fundamental Freedom beyond Market Integration: Union Citizenship and its Dynamics for Shifting the Economic Paradigm of European Integration' (2011) 17 *European Law Journal* 1; J Shaw, 'Citizenship: Contrasting Dynamics at the Interface of Integration and Constitutionalism' in P Craig and G de Búrca (eds), *The Evolution of EU Law* (Oxford, Oxford University Press, 2011); S Kadelbach, 'Union Citizenship' in A von Bogdandy and J Bast (eds), *Principles of European Constitutional Law* (Oxford, München, Hart Publishing, CH Beck, Nomos, 2011); D Kochenov, 'The Essence of EU Citizenship Emerging from the Last Ten Years of Academic Debate: Beyond the Cherry Blossoms and the Moon?' (2013) 62 *International and Comparative Law Quarterly* 97.

[4] Since the position of economically active Union citizens who fall within the scope of the market freedoms will be analysed in the next two chapters, the analysis in this chapter shall be confined to examining the position of *economically inactive* Union citizens and shall, therefore, exclude case-law involving *economically active* Union citizens, unless such case-law has established principles which are equally applicable to economically inactive Union citizens.

II. THE CURRENT LEGAL REGIME

The Treaty of Maastricht came into force on 1 November 1993 and has been one of the landmark steps in the history of European integration for a plethora of reasons: the initiation of economic and monetary Union, the birth of the EU, and the creation of the pillar-structure, to name but a few.[5] The developments brought by Maastricht formed part of a coherent whole that signified a change in direction for the European integration project, which would now include further areas of integration and cooperation, some of which would not even be distinctly connected with the economic objectives that had traditionally formed the backbone of the EU. However, for the purposes of this book, the most important development brought about by this Treaty was the establishment of the status of Union citizenship and the addition of a new Part Two in (what was then) the EC Treaty:[6] a step of 'major significance in the construction of Europe'.[7]

Following the Treaty restructuring brought about by the Treaty of Lisbon,[8] which took effect in December 2009, the main[9] provisions on Citizenship are found in Part Two of the TFEU Treaty, which has been renamed 'Non-discrimination and Citizenship of the Union', in this way codifying 'an established conceptual link between citizenship and the principle of equality'.[10] This Part now begins with

---

[5] For more on the Treaty of Maastricht, see D O'Keeffe and P Twomey (n 3); D Chalmers, G Davies and G Monti, *European Union Law: Cases and Materials* 3rd edn (Cambridge, Cambridge University Press, 2014) 23–29; P Craig and G de Búrca, *EU Law: Text, Cases and Materials* (Oxford, Oxford University Press, 2011) 13–17.

[6] The provisions on this new status were to be found in the EC Treaty (now replaced by the TFEU) and, thus, were included within the first (Community) pillar. According to Neuwahl, 'the fact that European citizenship is placed inside that context can be taken as a clear sign that citizens' rights and concerns are to be taken seriously indeed'—see N Neuwahl, 'The Place of the Citizen in the European Construction' in P Lynch, N Neuwahl and W Rees (eds), *Reforming the European Union: From Maastricht to Amsterdam* (Harlow, Longman, 2000) 187. Moreover, it should be noted that Part Two was inserted in the EC Treaty immediately before the provisions on the customs union and the internal market, this probably signifying the importance intended to be attached to this status. According to Oliver et al, the fact that the 'fathers of the' EEC Treaty 'chose to set out the provisions relating to the customs union immediately after the eight introductory articles' showed that the customs union (and the common market) 'was the cornerstone of the venture which was the European Economic Community in 1958' (P Oliver, S Enchelmaier, M Jarvis, A Johnston, S Norberg, C Stothers and S Weatherill, *Oliver on Free Movement of Goods in the European Union* (Oxford, Hart Publishing, 2010) 1). Accordingly, one can say that the position of the provisions on Union citizenship signifies that it is this status that is, now, the 'cornerstone' of the EU venture.

[7] Opinion of Advocate General La Pergola in Joined Cases C-4 & 5/95 *Stöber and Pereira* [1997] ECR I-511, para 50.

[8] Treaty of Lisbon [2007] OJ C306/1.

[9] It should be noted that although it is only Part Two of the FEU Treaty that is considered the 'Citizenship part' of the Treaty, virtually all parts of the constituent Treaties of the EU are peppered with references to the rights that Union citizens derive from EU law.

[10] Consolidated Version of the Treaty on the Functioning of the European Union [2012] C326/47. N Nic Shuibhne, *The Coherence of EU Free Movement Law: Constitutional Responsibility and the Court of Justice* (Oxford, Oxford University Press, 2013) 144. For an analysis of the changes made by the Treaty of Lisbon to the citizenship provisions in the Treaties, see A Schrauwen, 'European Union Citizenship in the Treaty of Lisbon: Any Change at All?' (2008) 15 *Maastricht Journal of European and*

the two non-discrimination provisions (Articles 18 and 19 TFEU),[11] which were previously situated in a separate Part, and proceeds with the 'core' citizenship provision—Article 20(1) TFEU—which states: 'Citizenship of the Union is hereby established. Every person holding the nationality of a Member State shall be a citizen of the Union. Citizenship of the Union shall be additional to and not replace national citizenship'.[12] This maintains the essence of what used to be Article 8 EC—the original provision introducing Union citizenship—apart from the fact that the third sentence was only added (using somewhat different terminology)[13] in 1999, when the Treaty of Amsterdam came into force.[14] The second paragraph of Article 20 TFEU lists a number of rights that are granted to Union citizens, making it clear, nonetheless, that these are merely *some* of the rights which Union citizens enjoy and that the other provisions of the Treaties which are not on the Part Two list should, where appropriate, be read as rights bestowed on Union citizens.[15]

The subsequent provisions in Part Two TFEU make more specific reference to each of the citizenship rights appearing on the Article 20(2) TFEU list: the right to move and reside freely within the territory of the Member States (Article 21 TFEU); passive and active voting rights in municipal and European Parliament elections (Article 22 TFEU); diplomatic and consular protection in third countries (Article 23 TFEU); and rights to petition the European Parliament and the Ombudsman and to write to any of the EU institutions, bodies, offices or agencies in one of the 24 official languages of the EU and receive an answer in the same language, as well as the newly-introduced right of initiative (Article 24 TFEU). It should be underlined that one of the changes made by the Treaty of Lisbon is that *all* rights explicitly enumerated in this Part (and not, as in the EC Treaty, only the right to move and reside freely) 'shall be exercised in accordance with the conditions and limitations defined by the Treaties and by the measures adopted

---

Comparative Law 55; H de Waele (n 2); N Nic Shuibhne, 'EU Citizenship after Lisbon' in D Ashiagbor, N Countouris and I Lianos (eds), *The European Union after the Treaty of Lisbon* (Cambridge, Cambridge University Press, 2012) 138–42.

[11] Respectively, the traditional right to non-discrimination on the grounds of nationality (Art 12 EC) and the power granted to EU institutions to make legislation to combat discrimination on the grounds of sex, racial or ethnic origin, religion or belief, disability, age or sexual orientation (Art 13 EC). These provisions were previously situated in Part One of the EC Treaty, under the title 'Principles'.

[12] A similar statement is made in Art 9 TEU.

[13] 'Citizenship of the Union shall complement and not replace national citizenship'. For comments on this see H de Waele (n 2) 322–23; N Nic Shuibhne, 'EU Citizenship after Lisbon' (n 10) 139.

[14] Treaty of Amsterdam amending the Treaty on European Union, the Treaties establishing the European Communities and certain related acts [1997] C340/1. Amsterdam was considered a disappointment when judged from the perspective of the Union citizen. According to N Neuwahl (n 6) 197, '[a]fter Amsterdam the individual is not much more a fully fledged citizen than before, and not much less a subject'.

[15] 'Citizens of the Union shall enjoy the rights and be subject to the duties provided for in the Treaties. They shall have, inter alia:' and then the list follows. For a similar view see HU Jessurun d'Oliveira (n 3) 133–35; S O'Leary (n 3) 105.

thereunder'.[16] The practical effect of this, however, remains unclear, since, as will be noticed from the analysis in the remainder of this chapter, the Court's citizenship case-law has only been concerned with the elucidation of the meaning of Articles 20 and 21 TFEU, and not with the other citizenship provisions.[17] Citizenship rights are also mentioned in the EU Treaty (Articles 9–11 and 35 TEU) and in 'Title V' EUCFR,[18] which replicate the citizenship rights provided in the TFEU. Since the coming into force of the Lisbon Treaty in 2009, the Charter is legally binding.[19] Apart from the symbolic significance that the inclusion of a Citizenship Title in the Charter has had, which illustrates that Union citizenship rights are *fundamental* rights in the true meaning of the word, what, exactly, is added in practice by this move is as yet unclear.

The Treaty provisions governing Union citizenship are supplemented by Directive 2004/38,[20] which further defines the right of (economically active and inactive) Union citizens and their family members to move and reside freely in the territory of another Member State, and which has consolidated, updated, and replaced most of the legislation which previously governed the rights of movement and residence of Member State nationals under EU law. As will be seen, some of the citizenship judgments of the Court—especially those delivered in the last five years—are concerned with the interpretation of this Directive.

We will now proceed to examine the various phases of the Court's citizenship jurisprudence.

III. THE INFANCY PHASE (1993–97)

The period immediately following the coming into force of the Maastricht Treaty is, what I call, the 'Infancy phase' of Union citizenship. This period is characterised by diffidence on the part of the Court, by a hesitation to explore the real potential of this new status.[21] It was during this phase that the Court was, for the first time, confronted with questions concerning the interpretation of the citizenship provisions. Nonetheless, since in the case-law that emerged during this period it was possible to employ one of the market freedoms in order to find a violation of EU law, the Court refrained from delving into the mysteries of Union citizenship

---

[16] Last paragraph of Art 20(2) TFEU.

[17] For an analysis of the citizenship provisions governing political participation see S O'Leary (n 3) Chs 6 and 7; J Shaw, *The Transformation of Citizenship in the European Union: Electoral Rights and the Restructuring of Political Space* (Cambridge, Cambridge University Press, 2007); F Fabbrini, 'The Political Side of EU Citizenship in the Context of EU Federalism' in D Kochenov (ed), *Citizenship and Federalism in Europe* (Cambridge, Cambridge University Press 2016, forthcoming).

[18] Charter of Fundamental Rights of the European Union [2007] OJ C303/17.

[19] Art 6(1) TEU.

[20] Dir 2004/38 on the right of citizens of the Union and their family members to move and reside freely within the territory of the Member States [2004] OJ L158/77 (the Citizens' Rights Directive).

[21] Kostakopoulou has characterised this period as one of 'judicial minimalism'—see D Kostakopoulou (n 2).

and, noting that the citizenship provisions have a residual status, it left it for future case-law to draw the parameters of this new status.[22]

The first case where a question on, inter alia, the interpretation of one of the citizenship provisions was referred to the ECJ was that of *Skanavi and Chryssanthakopoulos*.[23] The issue was whether Articles 6, 8a and 52 EC (Articles 18, 21, and 49 TFEU) precluded the German authorities from requiring a driving licence issued by another Member State to be exchanged for a German driving licence within one year of the holder taking up normal residence in Germany. Following the Advocate General (Léger), the Court chose to decide the case on the basis of Article 52 EC (ie the freedom of establishment), saying that Article 8a EC finds 'specific expression' in Article 52 EC: 'Since the facts with which the main proceedings are concerned fall within the scope of the latter provision, it is not necessary to rule on the interpretation of Article 8a'.[24] The same approach was subsequently confirmed in numerous occasions in this and the phases that followed, and is still, at times, employed.[25]

The Court's reluctance to engage with the citizenship provisions of the Treaty and to initiate the process of transforming them into meaningful rights for Union citizens, came as a stark contrast to the much more progressive Opinions of its Advocates General during this phase.[26] For instance, in his Opinion in *Boukhalfa*, Advocate General Léger noted, referring to Union citizenship, that

> The concept embraces aspects which have already largely been established in the development of Community law and in this respect it represents a consolidation of existing Community law. However, it is for the Court to ensure that its full scope is attained. If all the conclusions inherent in that concept are drawn, every citizen of the Union must, whatever his nationality, enjoy exactly the same rights and be subject to the same obligations.[27]

During this phase the Court was also for the first time confronted with the question of whether reverse discrimination (ie the less favourable treatment suffered by persons that are in a purely internal situation in their Member State of nationality

---

[22] H Toner, 'Judicial Interpretation of European Union Citizenship—Transformation or Consolidation?' (2000) 7 *Maastricht Journal of European and Comparative Law* 158, 172–73.
[23] Case C-193/94 *Skanavi and Chryssanthakopoulos* [1996] ECR I-929.
[24] ibid, para 22.
[25] See, inter alia, Case C-348/96 *Calfa* [1999] ECR I-11, para 30; Case C-100/01 *Oteiza Olazabal* [2002] ECR I-10981, para 26; Case C-92/01 *Stylianakis* [2003] ECR I-1291, paras 18–20; Case C-293/03 *My* [2004] ECR I-12013, para 50; Case C-208/05 *ITC* [2007] ECR I-181, paras 64–65; Case C-76/05 *Schwarz* [2007] ECR I-6849, para 34; Case C-392/05 *Alevizos* [2007] ECR I-3505, para 80; Case C-137/09 *Josemans* [2010] ECR I-13019, para 53; Case C-56/09 *Zanotti* [2010] ECR I-4517, para 24; Case C-457/12 *S and G* ECLI:EU:C:2014:136, para 45. It should be noted, however, that following the first years after the introduction of Union citizenship, the Court's 'practice has since become more variable'—S O'Leary, 'Free Movement of Persons and Services' in P Craig and G de Búrca (n 3) 528.
[26] H Toner (n 22) 174–75.
[27] Opinion of the AG in Case C-214/94 *Boukhalfa* [1996] ECR I-2253, para 63. See also the Opinion of AG Lenz in Case C-91/92 *Faccini Dori* [1994] ECR I-3225, para 53; the Opinion of AG La Pergola *Stöber and Pereira* (n 7), para 50; and the Opinion of AG Colomer in Joined Cases C-65 & 111/95 *Shingara and Radiom* [1997] ECR I-3343, para 34.

and to whom EU law does not apply) is compatible with Union citizenship.[28] This question emerged in *Uecker and Jacquet*,[29] where two German nationals who were employed in that State and had never exercised their free movement rights, argued that they were 'workers' (within the meaning of the Treaty) and sought to rely on Regulation 1612/68,[30] so that their (third-country national) wives could derive certain rights from EU law. The Court held that the situation was a purely internal one and hence the 1968 Regulation was inapplicable. It also made it clear that reverse discrimination was not contrary to EU law, even now that Member State nationals were Union citizens:

> citizenship of the Union … is not intended to extend the scope ratione materiae of the Treaty also to internal situations which have no link with Community law. … Any discrimination which nationals of a Member State may suffer under the law of that State falls within the scope of that law and must therefore be dealt with within the framework of the internal legal system of that State.[31]

As will be seen subsequently, this appears to be the position of the Court to the present day, despite the fact that—as argued elsewhere—reverse discrimination appears to be an incongruity in an EU which aspires to develop a meaningful status of Union citizenship which requires that Union citizens are treated equally.[32]

Therefore, as a general conclusion to this section it can be said that in the first years following Maastricht, the Court appeared to have constantly avoided putting flesh on the bare bones of Union citizenship, which led to the criticism that this new status was an empty promise and a mere 'pie in the sky'.[33]

IV. THE GROWTH PHASE (1998–2005)

After its initial reticence, the Court, in the subsequent phase, appeared overly eager to clarify the meaning of the citizenship provisions of the Treaty and to develop this new status. The main question that floated around during the 'Growth phase' was whether Union citizenship was capable of affording rights to Member State nationals in situations which, if they arose before its introduction, would fall outside the scope of EU law. In other words, was Union citizenship capable of being a meaningful status detached from economic considerations, which had extended the veil of EU law protection to Member State nationals who did not contribute to the economic aims of the EU in any way, or was it merely a consolidation of

---

[28] For a detailed analysis of reverse discrimination and the doctrine of purely internal situations, see A Tryfonidou, *Reverse Discrimination in EC Law* (The Hague, Kluwer, 2009).
[29] Joined Cases 64 & 65/96 *Uecker and Jacquet* [1997] ECR I-3171.
[30] Reg 1612/68 on freedom of movement for workers within the Community [1968] OJ L257/2 (repealed and replaced by Reg 492/2011 on freedom of movement for workers within the Unions [2011] OJ L141/1).
[31] *Uecker and Jacquet* (n 29), para 23.
[32] A Tryfonidou (n 28) Ch 4.
[33] HU Jessurun d'Oliveira, 'Union Citizenship: Pie in the Sky?' in A Rosas and E Antola (eds), *A Citizens' Europe? In Search of a New Order* (London, Sage Publications, 1995).

the previous *acquis* which required an economic element—albeit not necessarily a direct one—before an individual could benefit from the provisions of EU law?[34] Through its rulings during this phase, the Court made it clear that it is the former.

During this phase, the Court made for the first time the important pronouncement that 'Citizenship of the Union is destined to be the fundamental status of nationals of the Member States',[35] this being the first express indication that—in the eyes of the Court—Member State nationals would now be, above all, Union citizens and any other status they might have (eg worker or service-provider) should come second and—as will be seen in subsequent chapters—should be 'coloured' by the fact that they are Union citizens.[36]

This period saw the delivery of landmark judgments such as *Martínez Sala*,[37] *Grzelczyk*,[38] *Baumbast*,[39] and *Bidar*,[40] and the emphasis of the Court was placed on elucidating the core citizenship rights: a) the right to non-discrimination on grounds of nationality; b) the right to free movement; and c) the right of residence in the territory of another Member State.[41] Accordingly, in the remainder of this section we shall see how the Court developed each of these rights during this phase.

A. The Right to Non-Discrimination on Grounds of Nationality

As explained by White when commenting on the importance attained by the principle of non-discrimination in EU law,

> In the early days of the Community, the prohibition of discrimination belonged to the market integration model, and was targeted at removing obstacles to economic activity. That approach had to develop organically as social integration became a stronger feature

---

[34] For an early view that the provisions on citizenship were merely a consolidation of 'existing Treaty law as regards economic actors, and secondary legislation as regards non-economic actors' see D O'Keeffe, (n 3) 94.

[35] Case C-184/99 *Grzelczyk* [2001] ECR I-6193, para 31. The Court may have been inspired by the statement of Advocate General La Pergola in paragraph 18 of his Opinion in Case C-85/96 *Martínez Sala* [1998] ECR I-269: 'Let us say that it [ie Union citizenship] is the fundamental legal status guaranteed to the citizen of every Member State by the legal order of the Community and now of the Union'.

[36] It should be noted that the Court may be considering that its view of Union citizenship as the fundamental status of nationals of the Member States is becoming more concrete as in some of its most recent cases it replaced the word 'destined' in the above statement, with the word 'intended'. See eg Case C-135/08 *Rottmann* [2010] ECR I-1449, para 43; Case C-364/10 *Hungary v Slovak Republic* ECLI:EU:C:2012:630, para 40.

[37] *Martínez Sala* (n 35).

[38] *Grzelczyk* (n 35).

[39] Case C-413/99 *Baumbast* [2002] ECR I-7091.

[40] Case C-209/03 *Bidar* [2005] ECR I-2119.

[41] Some other (secondary) rights were explored during this period such as rights to family reunification of economically inactive Union citizens and, in particular, the right of minor children to be accompanied in the territory of the host State by their primary carer—see eg *Baumbast* (n 39) and Case C-200/02 *Zhu and Chen* [2004] ECR I-9925. For reasons of space, the development of these—secondary—rights will not be discussed here.

of the ever-closer union of peoples envisaged by the EC Treaty. Now that the prohibition of discrimination has become attached to citizenship of the Union, its constitutional status has been confirmed.[42]

As will be seen in this section, this has clearly been reflected in the Court's citizenship case-law, especially during this phase.

Martínez Sala[43] is famous for being the very first citizenship judgment, in the sense that it is in this ruling that the Court for the first time employed (only) a citizenship provision—as opposed to one of the market freedoms—for bringing the situation within the scope of EU law and for finding a violation. In that case the question was whether a Spanish national who was lawfully resident in Germany since the late 1960s and who was in and out of work but at the relevant time was economically inactive and reliant on social assistance, could claim a child-raising allowance and require that its grant be subject to exactly the same conditions as those imposed on German nationals. The Court held that a Union citizen who is lawfully resident in the territory of another Member State has the right, by virtue of Article 8 EC (Article 20 TFEU), to rely on the prohibition of discrimination on the ground of nationality under Article 6 EC (Article 18 TFEU), in all situations that fall within the material scope of EU law.[44] Since, it was said, the claimed child-raising allowance had previously been held to fall within the scope of Regulations 1612/68 and 1408/71,[45] this sufficed for bringing it within the material scope of EU law and, thus, the claimant should be entitled to it under the same conditions as those imposed on German nationals. Due to the fact that Germany directly discriminated against nationals of other Member States by imposing different (more burdensome) conditions for the grant of the allowance than those imposed on its own nationals, the Court found that Article 6 EC (read together with Article 8 EC) was breached.[46]

The case confirmed the reasoning that was followed by the Court in its 'incipient citizenship' case-law developed in the context of the personal market freedoms (discussed in the next chapter),[47] in that it signified that in order for the principle of non-discrimination on the grounds of nationality to apply, it was no longer necessary to establish a link between the contested differential treatment and an impediment to the exercise of free movement between Member States: the German refusal to extend to Ms Martínez Sala the child-raising allowance under the same conditions as was granted to German nationals, would not appear to be capable of causing her to leave Germany; or, if it is asked whether she would in

---

[42] RCA White (n 3) 806–07.
[43] *Martínez Sala* (n 35). Annotated by C Tomuschat in (2000) 37 *Common Market Law Review* 449.
[44] *Martínez Sala* (n 35), paras 61–62.
[45] Respectively, Reg 1612/68 (n 30) and Reg 1408/71 on the application of social security schemes to employed persons and their families moving within the Community [1971] OJ L149/2.
[46] For a similar approach followed in another case in this phase, see Case C-456/02 *Trojani* [2004] ECR I-7573.
[47] See, most prominently, Case 186/87 *Cowan* [1989] ECR 195.

the first place be deterred from moving to Germany if she knew that she would be refused the benefit under the circumstances, again the answer would be in the negative. In any event, at the time that she had moved to Germany from Spain, Martínez Sala was not exercising EU free movement rights since Spain was not an EU Member State. Hence, this case demonstrated that in a Citizens' Europe, the principle of equality is important as such, and not merely as an instrument for the achievement of the EU's aims.[48] The Court endorsed this reasoning, by explicitly detaching the material from the personal scope of EU law. Hence, on the facts, a Union citizen who was lawfully resident in the territory of another Member State and, by virtue of that, fell within the personal scope of EU law via (what is now) Article 20 TFEU could rely on the prohibition of discrimination on the ground of nationality to claim a social assistance benefit that was traditionally granted only to 'workers'.[49]

Most importantly, however, with this case, the Court extended the 'incipient citizenship' reasoning to a situation which did not involve an economic element of any type. Martínez Sala was not a direct economic actor given that she was out of work, nor was she a passive economic actor as she was not economically self-sufficient. Accordingly, the Court in this ruling made it clear that Union citizens could now derive rights from EU law (or, at least, the right to non-discrimination on the ground of nationality), in situations which did not involve any contribution to the economic aims of the Treaty.

Half a year later, the same reasoning was followed in *Bickel and Franz*.[50] Here, again, the prohibition of discrimination on the ground of nationality was employed not in order to protect the exercise of free movement rights but, rather, to ensure that the Union citizens who had moved were not discriminated against on the ground of their nationality in the host State.[51] However, in this case we can detect traces of the Court's initial uneasiness with deciding a case solely on the basis of one of the citizenship provisions: although the case could easily and, perhaps, more aptly, be decided by simply applying Article 21 TFEU in combination with Article 18 TFEU, as was done in subsequent phases in the Court's jurisprudence in the cases of *Gottwald* and *Rüffer*,[52] the Court appears to have

---

[48] S Fries and J Shaw, 'Citizenship of the Union: First Steps in the European Court of Justice' (1998) 4 *European Public Law* 533, 536. This was made even clearer in the subsequent Case C-300/04 *Eman and Sevinger* [2006] ECR I-8055.

[49] For criticisms of this see C Tomuschat (n 43) 452; G Davies, *Nationality Discrimination in the European Internal Market* (The Hague, Kluwer, 2003) 192–93; S O'Leary, 'Developing an Ever Closer Union between the Peoples of Europe? A Reappraisal of the Case Law of the Court of Justice on the Free Movement of Persons and EU Citizenship' (2008) 27 *Yearbook of European Law* 167, 180.

[50] Case C-274/96 *Bickel and Franz* [1998] ECR I-7637.

[51] In fact, as explained by Kochenov, in this case the Court went further than simply requiring the host State to extend the rights afforded to (all) its nationals to nationals of other Member States: it required the host State to put mobile Union citizens who hold the nationality of another Member State on an equal footing with ethnic minorities (German-speaking *residents* of the said region) enjoying *extra* rights under regional law. See D Kochenov, 'Regional Citizenships and EU law: The Case of the Åland Islands and New Caledonia' (2010) 35 *European Law Review* 307, 310–11.

[52] Case C-103/08 *Gottwald* [2009] ECR I-9117 and Case C-322/13 *Rüffer* ECLI:EU:C:2014:189.

had its reservations, and whilst it did dip a toe in the (citizenship) water by using Article 8a EC (Article 21 TFEU) to bring the two applicants within the personal scope of EU law, it simultaneously used Article 59 EC (56 TFEU) for the same purpose.

During this phase two more judgments focused exclusively on the right to non-discrimination on the ground of nationality—*Garcia Avello*[53] and *Schempp*.[54] These cases affirmed what was clearly established in *Martínez Sala* and *Bickel and Franz*: the detachment of the citizenship provisions from an economic element and the importance attained by the principle of equality in EU law, which is no longer merely an instrument for achieving the EU's (free movement and/or economic) aims.[55] The main contribution of these rulings was, however, that they expanded the notion of a 'cross-border element', in a way which stretched the scope of EU law to encompass situations which would, traditionally, be considered purely internal to a Member State, in this way going against the Court's previous pronouncement in *Uecker and Jacquet*,[56] that the status of Union citizenship would not expand the material scope of EU law to cover situations which would traditionally be considered purely internal to a Member State. *Garcia Avello* expanded the scope of application of Article 20 TFEU, whereas *Schempp* did the same with respect to Article 21 TFEU.

Garcia Avello involved two children of dual Spanish and Belgian nationality who *were born and were always resident in Belgium*, ie they had never moved between Member States. Their parents wanted to register their surname in Belgium in accordance with Spanish practice. However, the Belgian authorities followed Belgian practice instead, and registered the children under their father's surname. When the children (through their father) applied for the surname to be changed, they met with the refusal of the Belgian authorities, which noted that the Belgian practice should be followed. The question was whether this amounted to a violation of EU law. The Court held that since the children were nationals of one Member State (Spain) lawfully resident in the territory of another (Belgium), they fell within the scope of EU law by virtue of Article 17 EC (Article 20 TFEU), and they were entitled to invoke Article 12 EC (Article 18 TFEU) in order to require the Belgian authorities not to discriminate against them on the basis of their nationality—the *Martínez Sala* reasoning. As the Court explained, '[a]lthough, as Community law stands at present, the rules governing a person's surname are matters coming within the competence of the Member States, the latter must none the less, when exercising that competence, comply with Community law'.[57] On the

---

[53] Case C-148/02 *Garcia Avello* [2003] ECR I-11613.
[54] Case C-403/03 *Schempp* [2005] ECR I-6421.
[55] For an elaborate analysis of this argument, see A Tryfonidou, 'The Notions of "Restriction" and "Discrimination" in the Context of the Free Movement of Persons Provisions: From a Relationship of Interdependence to One of (Almost Complete) Independence' (2014) 33 *Yearbook of European Law* 385.
[56] *Uecker and Jacquet* (n 29).
[57] *Garcia Avello* (n 53), para 25.

facts it was found that the situation of persons who bore only Belgian nationality was different from that of persons bearing dual Belgian-Spanish nationality since 'Belgian nationals who have divergent surnames by reason of the different laws to which they are attached by nationality may plead difficulties specific to their situation which distinguish them from persons holding only Belgian nationality'.[58] Accordingly, the Belgian authorities' decision to treat the two situations equally, amounted to discrimination on the ground of nationality which, the Court found, was not justified.

The result in *Garcia Avello* does not appear to differ in any important respect from *Martínez Sala*. What is important, nonetheless, is that this case made clear what was (only) implicit in *Martínez Sala*: that in order for a situation to fall within the scope of Article 20 TFEU, it is necessary to establish neither an impediment to inter-State movement as a result of the contested discrimination (a substantive requirement), nor to point to the exercise of inter-State movement on the facts of the case (a jurisdictional requirement); a point that was made even clearer in the 'Coming of Age phase' that will be analysed below.

In addition, although in *Martínez Sala* the Court expressly sought to establish whether the *claimed benefit* fell within the material scope of EU law, in *Garcia Avello* the Court appears to have followed a much broader approach,[59] considering that:

> The situations falling within the scope *ratione materiae* of Community law include those involving the exercise of the fundamental freedoms guaranteed by the Treaty, in particular those involving the freedom to move and reside within the territory of the Member States, as conferred by Article 18 EC.[60]

In other words, whenever a Union citizen exercises a right deriving from the market freedoms or Article 21 TFEU, her situation falls within the personal *and* material scope of EU law and it is no longer necessary to establish, in addition, that the right that is claimed (eg to change her surname, to a social assistance benefit, and so on) also falls within the material scope of EU law. This is an immensely important statement because it means that no areas of Member State competence can now remain insulated from the effects of EU law,[61] as any Union citizen who has exercised one of the rights stemming from the market freedoms or Article 21 TFEU can now rely on EU law in order to challenge the choices of a Member State in *any* area. We shall return to this point in the next chapter.

---

[58] ibid, para 37.
[59] Already apparent in, inter alia, the cases of *Bickel and Franz* (n 50), *Grzelczyk* (n 35) and Case C-224/98 *D'Hoop* [2002] ECR I-6191.
[60] *Garcia Avello* (n 53), para 24.
[61] HD Jarass, 'A Unified Approach to the Fundamental Freedoms' in M Andenas and W-H Roth (eds), *Services and Free Movement in EU Law* (Oxford, Oxford University Press, 2002) 143; A Tryfonidou, 'The Federal Implications of the Transformation of the Market Freedoms into Sources of Fundamental Rights for the Union Citizen' in D Kochenov (n 17).

Schempp[62]—unlike *Garcia Avello*—did involve the exercise of free movement rights, albeit not by the Union citizen who sought to rely on EU law on the facts. At issue was the compatibility with EU law of the German authorities' refusal to allow Mr Schempp—a German national who had never exercised any free movement rights—to deduct from his taxable income the maintenance payments he made to his former wife who was a German national but who was, at the relevant time, resident in Austria; such payments would have been deductible had his former wife still been resident in Germany. The Court found that the situation fell within the scope of EU law by virtue of Article 18 EC (Article 21 TFEU) and thus Mr Schempp could rely on this provision, either alone, or together with Article 12 EC (Article 18 TFEU), in order to claim that the contested refusal of the German authorities was contrary to EU law.[63] Accordingly, even the exercise of free movement rights by another person (which, quite arbitrarily, depends on whether that person holds the nationality of a Member State and, thus, can exercise such rights) may now be capable of bringing the situation of a Union citizen within the scope of EU law, if this exercise is capable of affecting the latter's situation in some way by subjecting him to treatment less favourable than that to which he would have been subjected if no such movement had been exercised.

B. The Right to Free Movement

The other main citizenship right that was elucidated in this phase was the right to free movement. This right (together with the right of residence, which will be analysed below) stems from Article 21 TFEU.

We have already mentioned *Bickel and Franz*,[64] where the Court employed the equivalent to what is now the above provision (together with the freedom to provide services) in order to bring within the scope of EU law two Union citizens who were discriminated against on the ground of nationality in the host State where they moved temporarily.

In the *Wijsenbeek* judgment,[65] which was delivered the subsequent year, the Court held that obstacles to free movement between Member States are contrary to Article 18 EC (Article 21 TFEU), and this is so even if they are non-discriminatory on the ground of nationality.[66] The judgment also demonstrated that this provision can be relied on by a Union citizen against his or her own Member State, if the latter impedes his/her movement to another Member State or his/her return to its territory.[67] In the same case, however, the Court also recognised that, as long as

---

[62] *Schempp* (n 54).
[63] In the end, however, the Court found that there was no violation of either of these provisions.
[64] *Bickel and Franz* (n 50).
[65] Case C-378/97 *Wijsenbeek* [1999] ECR I-6207.
[66] See, also, *D'Hoop* (n 59); Case C-224/02 *Pusa* [2004] ECR I-5763; *Schempp* (n 54); Case C-503/09 *Stewart* [2011] ECR I-6497, paras 83–86.
[67] *Wijsenbeek* (n 65), para 22.

common provisions on controls at the external EU borders have not been adopted, Member States can require Union citizens to establish their nationality by showing their passport, even when entering their territory through an *internal* EU frontier.

During this phase, the Court also made it clear that a form of discrimination that had already been held to be contrary to the personal market freedoms[68]—discrimination against free movers—is also caught by Article 18 EC (Article 21 TFEU), given that it is capable of impeding the exercise of the right to free movement. As the Court noted in the two cases that established this during this phase—*D'Hoop* in 2002 and *Pusa* in 2004:

> In that a citizen of the Union must be granted in all Member States, the same treatment in law as that accorded to the nationals of those Member States who find themselves in the same situation, it would be incompatible with the right to freedom of movement were a citizen, in the Member State of which he is a national, to receive treatment less favourable than he would enjoy if he had not availed himself of the opportunities offered by the Treaty in relation to freedom of movement.[69]

C. The Right of Residence

We should now move on to consider the third citizenship right elucidated through the Court's case-law during this phase—the right of residence in the territory of another Member State—which is also the most politically sensitive of the three, given that if its exercise goes unchecked, it may create opportunities for benefit tourism.[70] This is because the EU does not have its own welfare system and thus welfare systems remain national and, hence, each Member State makes different provision for social assistance.[71] This, in combination with the fact that from the 1990s onwards, economically inactive Member State nationals are free—by virtue of EU law—to move between Member States, creates the danger of benefit tourism, since they may choose to move to Member States that offer more generous social assistance benefits. As a response to this latter danger, when the EU legislature first extended the right of residence to economically inactive Union citizens with the promulgation of the three 1990 Residence Directives,[72] it made it subject to the—so-called—economic self-sufficiency requirements, which are now found in Article 7 of Regulation 2004/38: (economically inactive) Union citizens must 'have sufficient resources for themselves and their family members not to become

---

[68] See eg Case C-19/92 *Kraus* [1993] ECR I-1663; Case C-18/95 *Terhoeve* [1999] ECR I-345; Case C-109/04 *Kranemann* [2005] ECR I-2421.

[69] *D'Hoop* (n 59), para 30; *Pusa* (n 66), para 18.

[70] F Wollenschläger (n 3) 15.

[71] G Davies, *European Union Internal Market Law* (London, Routledge, 2003) 211.

[72] Dir 90/364 on the right of residence [1990] OJ L180/26; Dir 90/365 on the right of residence for employees and self-employed persons who have ceased their occupational activity [1990] OJ L180/28; Dir 93/96 on the right of residence for students [1993] OJ L317/59. For an analysis of the Directives as well as an explanation of the debate that preceded their adoption, see S O'Leary (n 3) 109–26.

a burden on the social assistance system of the host Member State during their period of residence and have comprehensive sickness insurance cover in the host Member State'.

The right of residence for economically inactive Union citizens is, since 1993, found in primary legislation and, in particular, in (what is now) Article 21 TFEU, which provides that

> [e]very citizen of the Union shall have the right to move and reside freely within the territory of the Member States, *subject to the limitations and conditions laid down in the Treaties and by the measures adopted to give them effect*.[73]

The subjection of this right to limitations and conditions has led some commentators to characterise it as 'half-hearted'.[74] Obviously, the limitations and conditions mentioned in this provision include the public policy, public security and public health exceptions on which Member States may rely in order to limit the exercise of the right to free movement and residence,[75] but—as demonstrated in the Court's case-law—they also include the self-sufficiency requirements which are (now) laid down in Article 7 of the 2004 Directive, quoted in the immediately preceding paragraph.[76]

In *Martínez Sala* the Court did not have to consider whether the (economically inactive) Union citizen that was involved on the facts of the case, had a right to reside in Germany *by virtue of EU law* (ie under, what is now, Article 21 TFEU), and whether, as a result of claiming the child-raising allowance, she no longer satisfied the conditions to which the exercise of this right was subject.[77] Rather, it was clear that the applicant in that case derived her right of residence in Germany from national law.[78] Nor did this issue emerge in the citizenship cases that followed soon after—*Bickel and Franz*[79] and *Wijsenbeek*[80]—which involved Union citizens that were merely visiting the host State, as opposed to wishing to establish their residence there. Rather, the question of whether the *EU right to reside* in the territory of another Member State can be exercised by (economically inactive) Union citizens even when the self-sufficiency conditions are not (or no longer) satisfied, emerged only in the new millennium, and the first cases where the scope of this right was examined were *Grzelczyk*,[81] *Baumbast*,[82] and *Bidar*.[83]

---

[73] Emphasis added. This was, from 1993 until 1999, Art 8a EC, and from 1999 until 2009, Art 18 EC.
[74] G Davies (n 49) 188.
[75] Case C-434/10 *Aladzhov* [2011] ECR I-11659, para 29.
[76] S O'Leary (n 3) 129; S Fries and J Shaw (n 48) 545.
[77] S O'Leary, 'Putting Flesh on the Bones of European Union Citizenship' (1999) 24 *European Law Review* 68, 77.
[78] *Martínez Sala* (n 35), para 60. See A Schrauwen, 'Sink or Swim Together? Developments in European Citizenship' (1999–2000) 23 *Fordham International Law Journal* 778, 785.
[79] *Bickel and Franz* (n 50).
[80] *Wijsenbeek* (n 65).
[81] *Grzelczyk* (n 35).
[82] *Baumbast* (n 39).
[83] *Bidar* (n 40).

Initially, it was thought that the financial self-sufficiency requirements were prior conditions that had to be satisfied before any right of residence could arise for economically inactive Union citizens.[84] Yet, in *Baumbast*,[85] the ECJ made it clear that the right to move and reside freely in the territory of another Member State, laid down in Article 21 TFEU, is a directly effective, *fundamental*, right and thus is automatically enjoyed by all Union citizens and can be relied on before national courts, either against the host State or against the State of origin/nationality. In other words, a fundamental right to free movement and residence *exists* for all Union citizens and is derived directly from the Treaty. However, as became clear in case-law that came after *Baumbast*, although the existence of this right cannot be questioned under any circumstances, given that it is a fundamental right bestowed on all Union citizens simply because they hold EU citizenship, its exercise *can* be circumscribed in case the Union citizen does not satisfy the financial self-sufficiency requirements laid down in secondary legislation.[86]

More specifically, as explained by the Court in *Grzelczyk* in 2001,[87] in case the Union citizen becomes an *unreasonable* burden on the social assistance system of the host State, the latter has the right to limit the exercise of this right in its territory. Yet, as made clear in the same case, an individual does not become an *unreasonable* burden on the social assistance system of the host State as soon as he seeks to rely on it, and thus that State cannot *automatically* limit the exercise of the right of residence in its territory in that case. Rather, it may do so only if this is proportionate,[88] that is, if the burden imposed on the social assistance system of the host State is not so insignificant that it would be disproportionate to deprive the Union citizen of his right of residence in that State.[89] Obviously, in order to make a proper assessment which accords with the above guidance, the court or national authority hearing the case must focus on the specific circumstances of the Union citizen involved and, thus, an individual case-by-case approach must be

---

[84] See eg the submissions of the German Government in *Martínez Sala* (n 35); and the judgment of (what was at the time) the Court of First Instance in Case T-66/95 *Hedwig Kuchlenz-Winter v Commission* [1997] ECR II-637, paras 47–48. See also S O'Leary (n 3) 125; A Schrauwen (n 78) 785.

[85] *Baumbast* (n 39).

[86] For commentators who draw this distinction between the 'existence' and the 'exercise' of the right to free movement and residence see, inter alia, Y Borgmann-Prebil, 'The Rule of Reason in European Citizenship' (2008) 14 *European Law Journal* 328, 341–42; J Shaw, 'A View of the Citizenship Classics: *Martínez Sala* and Subsequent Cases on Citizenship of the Union' in M Poiares Maduro and L Azoulai (eds), *The Past and Future of EU Law: The Classics of EU Law Revisited on the 50th Anniversary of the Rome Treaty* (Oxford, Hart Publishing, 2010) 358 and 361. This was also one of the arguments of the Commission in *Martínez Sala* (n 35), whilst this point was also made by AG La Pergola in paragraph 18 of his Opinion in the same case.

[87] *Grzelczyk* (n 35).

[88] This was expressly noted by the ECJ in, inter alia, *Grzelczyk* (n 35), paras 42–43, and was later confirmed in *Trojani* (n 46), para 45, and was consolidated in Recital 16 and Art 14 of the Citizens' Rights Directive (n 20). It has also been confirmed more recently in Case C-140/12 *Brey* ECLI:EU:C:2013:565, where the Court provided more detailed guidance to the national court.

[89] See eg the facts in *Baumbast* (n 39). For more on this see C Timmermans, '*Martínez* Sala and *Baumbast* revisited' in M Poiares Maduro and L Azoulai (n 86) 348–50.

followed. If it is found that the Union citizen can continue to exercise his/her right of residence in the host State this means—rather circularly—that (s)he is lawfully resident there under Article 21 TFEU and, hence, (s)he has the right to be treated equally with the nationals of the host State as regards a host of issues, including having recourse to the social assistance system of that State.[90]

Accordingly, through its case-law during this phase, the Court made it clear that the economic self-sufficiency requirements are no longer pre-conditions that must be satisfied in order for an economically inactive Union citizen to 'earn' the right to reside in the territory of another Member State (as seemed to be the case under the 1990 Directives regime), but are mere limitations attached to the exercise of the (fundamental) right to reside in the territory of another Member State, which is given automatically to *all* Union citizens.[91] This has made it clear that *all* Union citizens are now entitled to a fundamental right of residence in another Member State *by virtue of the fact that they are Union citizens* and not because they are economically active or economically self-sufficient. Moreover, the above rulings imposed a requirement on the court assessing the national rules/practices for their compliance with Article 21 TFEU—this, usually, being a national court—to consider whether the application of the national rules *to the particular circumstances of the case and to that particular individual*, is proportionate. This case-law, therefore, illustrates that Union citizenship not only 'impacts on the Member States' regulatory autonomy, but also on the Member States' regulatory practices, ie on the way the rules are applied to the particular circumstances of the case'.[92] A one-size-fits-all approach is, clearly, inappropriate when it comes to determining whether a constitutional, fundamental, right of a Union citizen is breached.

---

[90] For an explanation see P Minderhoud, 'Directive 2004/38 and Access to Social Assistance Benefits' in E Guild, C Gortázar Rotaeche and D Kostakopoulou (eds), *The Reconceptualization of European Union Citizenship* (Leiden, Boston, Brill Nijhoff, 2014).

[91] However in a very recent judgment, the Grand Chamber may have taken a retrograde step by using wording which illustrates that it is of the view that economic self-sufficiency is a *prior condition* that must be satisfied in order for a Union citizen to *acquire* the right of residence in the territory of another Member State: 'A Member State must therefore have the possibility, pursuant to Article 7 of Directive 2004/38, of refusing to grant social benefits to economically inactive Union citizens who exercise their right to freedom of movement solely in order to obtain another Member State's social assistance although *they do not have sufficient resources to claim a right of residence*'—Case C-333/13 *Dano* ECLI:EU:C:2014:2358, para 78 (emphasis added). Whether this will be the new, more restrictive, 'line' followed by the Court perhaps as a result of the economic crisis that has plagued the EU since the late 2000s and the—resultant—increased danger of benefit tourism, remains to be seen. For a view that the judgment is open to two different interpretations, see H Verschueren, 'Preventing "Benefit Tourism" in the EU: A Narrow or Broad Interpretation of the Possibilities Offered by the ECJ in *Dano*?' (2015) 52 *Common Market Law Review* 363. For a more pessimistic view see D Thym, 'When Union Citizens Turn into Illegal Migrants: The Dano Case' (2015) 40 *European Law Review* 249, who pointed out that the judgment 'presents a noteworthy shift towards doctrinal conservativism' (p 250) and has led to the reactivation of market citizenship (p 261). See also S Peers, 'Benefits for EU Citizens: A U-Turn by the Court of Justice?' (2015) 74 *Cambridge Law Journal* 195.

[92] E Spaventa, *Free Movement of Persons in the European Union: Barriers to Movement in their Constitutional Context* (The Hague, Kluwer, 2007) 155.

40 *Taking Stock of Union Citizenship*

Finally, in *Bidar*[93] the Court shed further light on the substance of the right of residence, by establishing that the longer a Union citizen resides in the territory of the host State, the greater the range of benefits (s)he receives on equal terms with nationals,[94] and the more difficult it becomes to argue that (s)he poses an unreasonable burden on the social assistance system of the host State.[95] On the facts of the case, it was held that a French teenager who had lawfully resided in the UK for three years whilst being in secondary education and who subsequently sought to obtain a maintenance grant for his university studies, was entitled to do so and did not, as a result, impose an unreasonable burden on the host State since he had established a sufficient link with its society.[96] The Court noted that the UK could reserve the claimed maintenance grant to students who demonstrated a certain degree of integration into its society, however, when determining whether such a degree of integration was attained, it should take into account all relevant factors establishing this and should not adopt criteria which might exclude Union citizens that were, indeed, sufficiently integrated into its society (as was the situation on the facts of the case).

Before proceeding to provide some concluding remarks for this phase, I should like to mention one more case—*Zhu and Chen*[97]—which confirmed *Grzelczyk* and *Bidar* (as regards the right of residence and the self-sufficiency conditions), but which I would like to highlight as another case in this phase which extended the meaning of the notion of a 'cross-border element', but this time in relation to the right of residence.

The case involved a baby—Catherine—who was born to Chinese parents in Northern Ireland (ie in the UK), but who possessed Irish nationality as a result of the fact that she was born in the island of Ireland (even though this was outside the political boundaries of the Republic of Ireland).[98] The baby (with her mother) moved to Wales (from Northern Ireland) where they sought to rely on EU law in order to obtain a long-term residence permit. One of the important questions that emerged on the facts was whether the case involved a sufficient cross-border

---

[93] *Bidar* (n 40).

[94] For an analysis see RCA White (n 3) 806–10.

[95] The gradual construction of a deeper link with the society of the host State is also reflected in a number of instances in the 2004 Citizens' Rights Directive (n 20) eg where provision is made for the right of permanent residence (Art 16), as well as the fact that the Directive provides that the longer individuals reside in the host State, the harder it is for that State to deport them (see Art 28, paragraphs (2) and (3) of the Directive).

[96] As explained by O'Leary, '[t]he objective behind the requirement of a real or genuine link is to ensure that the obligation of financial solidarity towards EU citizens is not, from the Member State's point of view, stretched beyond acceptable limits'—see S O'Leary (n 49) 182. For a commentator criticising the Court's approach towards solidarity in its citizenship case-law, see M Ross, 'The Struggle for EU Citizenship: Why Solidarity Matters' in A Arnull, C Barnard, M Dougan and E Spaventa (eds), *A Constitutional Order of States? Essays in EU Law in Honour of Alan Dashwood* (Oxford, Hart Publishing, 2011).

[97] *Zhu and Chen* (n 41).

[98] For an explanation of the factual background to this case, see A Tryfonidou, '*Kunqian Catherine Zhu and Man Lavette Chen v. Secretary of State for the Home Department*: Further Cracks in the "Great Wall" of the European Union?' (2005) 11 *European Public Law* 527.

element. As can be seen, the child (and her mother) had not moved between Member States but, rather, between two regions of one and the same Member State (from Northern Ireland to Wales). As has been repeatedly confirmed, Article 21 TFEU does not govern free movement within one and the same Member State.[99]

Although on the facts there was no (physical) cross-border movement, the Court found that the situation was not purely internal to a Member State, because baby Catherine held the nationality of one Member State (Ireland) whilst seeking to reside in the territory of another (UK). Hence, although there was no exercise of cross-border movement, one of the primary rights provided in Article 18 EC (Article 21 TFEU)—the right to reside in the territory of a Member State other than that of someone's nationality—was exercised and, hence, the situation was not a purely internal one. Accordingly, one could say that in *Zhu and Chen* it was established that in order for Article 21 TFEU to apply, there is a need to *either* exercise the (primary) right to free movement between Member States *or* to exercise the (other) primary right bestowed by that provision (ie the right to reside in the territory of a Member State other than that of that person's nationality). This does not appear to be inappropriately extending the scope of application of the above provision given that what appears to be the aim of this provision (ie to ensure that Union citizens can freely exercise their fundamental EU right to move and/*or* to reside in the territory of Member States other than that of their nationality) is achieved when EU rights are granted in such situations. The same approach was again taken by the Court more recently in *Alokpa*.[100]

D. Comments

At this point, we should pause to examine what is the importance of this phase and how it has contributed to the development of the status of Union citizenship. Three points will be highlighted.

Firstly, it was during this phase that it was made clear that the notion of Union citizenship is, indeed, detached from any economic considerations and that economically inactive Union citizens who are also *not* economically self-sufficient (and, thus, incapable of—even indirectly—contributing to the aim of establishing an EU internal market) may derive (fundamental) rights from EU law, purely and simply by virtue of their status as Union citizens. It was, therefore, during this phase that the Court for the first time 'established that the Treaty provisions on citizenship create certain autonomous rights, independent of other Treaty provisions governing movement and residence'.[101] Hence during this 'Growth phase'

---

[99] This was explicitly confirmed in the subsequent phase in Case C-212/06 *Government of the French Community and Walloon Government v Flemish Government* (*Flemish Care insurance scheme* case) [2008] ECR I-1683.
[100] Case C-86/12 *Alokpa* ECLI:EU:C:2013:645.
[101] P Craig and G de Búrca (n 5) 819. See also para 84 of the Opinion of AG Cosmas in *Wijsenbeek* (n 65).

the Court provided us with the first signs that 'market citizenship' is not the only form of European citizenship that we can aspire to and that, as pronounced by the Court, '[c]itizenship of the Union is destined to be the fundamental status of nationals of the Member States'.[102]

Secondly, during this phase, we had the placing of the first building blocks of a vertical relationship between the EU and the Union citizen. More specifically, it was made clear that the importance of the status of Union citizenship is not merely reduced to a requirement that the Union citizen should not be discriminated against in the host State and should thus be able to rely on EU law in order to require the host State to give him/her the status of a 'privileged alien'. Rather, it was made clear that Union citizens derive a number of rights directly from EU law (rights of free movement and residence; certain political rights), which Member States (including the Member State of nationality of the individual) have to respect and protect.[103] To use O'Leary's terminology, it seems, therefore, that we are moving away from a 'minimalist approach' to the concept of Union citizenship which 'limit[s] the extension of the benefits of each Member State's citizenship, to the citizens of the other Member states on a reciprocal basis', and towards a 'maximalist approach' which 'extends beyond the principle of equal treatment'.[104] And not only that but, in addition, the relationship between a Union citizen and his own Member State may now be affected.[105]

Thirdly, during this phase, the first signs of the truly transformative nature of the status of Union citizenship became visible and the Court appeared to have recognised, for the first time, the broader implications that the introduction of this status could have on the overall development of the EU polity and, more specifically, on the interpretation of the (personal) market freedoms. In particular, it was during this period that the Court, in some of its case-law, expressly noted that the personal market freedoms should be re-read in the light of Union citizenship[106]—a point to which we shall return in the next chapter.

Perhaps more significant, nonetheless, are the more implicit signs that can be deduced from some of the Court's rulings in this period, to the effect that (mobile) Union citizens must be brought within the scope of EU law (and thus enjoy the protection of EU law) in all instances, irrespective of whether the contested measure can specifically impede the exercise of cross-border economic activities. The typical example of this is *Carpenter*,[107] where the Court accepted that the situation fell within the scope of EU law via Article 49 EC (Article 56 TFEU) and, as a result, the Carpenters could rely on their right to family life in order to stop the UK authorities from deporting Mrs Carpenter, even though it was not clear how

---

[102] For a similar view see D Kostakopoulou (n 2).
[103] For a similar view see C Timmermans (n 89) 347.
[104] S O'Leary (n 2) 22. For a different view see S Kadelbach (n 3) 453.
[105] G Davies (n 49) 187.
[106] Case C-138/02 *Collins* [2004] ECR I-2703.
[107] Case C-60/00 *Carpenter* [2002] ECR I-6279.

this was in any way connected with the ability of Mr Carpenter to provide services across borders. As Jo Shaw has very rightly observed:

> the powerful notion of citizenship is regularly used in a symbolic manner by the Court of Justice, sometimes in conjunction with human rights arguments, in order to justify some of its most daring judgments on free movement and single market questions since the end of the 1990s onwards.[108]

As will be seen in the subsequent section, this tendency became even more pronounced in the next phase of the ECJ's jurisprudence.

V. TURBULENT (EARLY) ADOLESCENCE (2006–09)

In 2006—13 years after its introduction—the status of Union citizenship entered its period of 'adolescence'. The main characteristic of this phase is confusion, the cause of which are the mixed signals given by the Court in its judgments. In general, this is a period which is relatively uneventful, since in its case-law the Court mainly confirmed the principles established during the previous phase, without adding anything novel. However, at the same time, the Court also took some backward steps, indicating a desire to impose some limits on the principles established during the previous phase.

In this phase, the Court confirmed that Article 21 TFEU requires the abolition of any (unjustified) restrictions on the free movement of Union citizens,[109] whether these restrictions are imposed by the State of origin[110] or the host State.[111] The Court also confirmed that, as established in *D'Hoop*[112] and *Pusa*[113] during the previous phase, discrimination against free movers is contrary to Article 21 TFEU, unless justified. Accordingly, in *De Cuyper*,[114] it was found that the requirement to reside in Belgium in order to receive an unemployment allowance in that Member State amounted to a restriction on the free movement of a Belgian national to France (where he had established residence), albeit one that was justified by the need to monitor compliance with the statutory conditions laid down for retention of entitlement to that allowance; and in *Turpeinen*,[115] a case very similar to *Pusa*, it was held that Finnish legislation which treated, for tax purposes, Finnish nationals who were not resident in Finland worse than Finnish nationals who were resident in that Member State, amounted to a violation of (what is now) Article 21 TFEU.

---

[108] J Shaw (n 3) 582.
[109] Case C-353/06 *Grunkin and Paul* [2008] ECR I-7639.
[110] Case C-520/04 *Turpeinen* [2006] ECR I-10685; Case C-192/05 *Tas-Hagen and Tas* [2006] ECR I-451; Case C-406/04 *De Cuyper* [2006] ECR I-6947; *Schwarz* (n 25); Joined Cases C-11 & 12/06 *Morgan and Bucher* [2007] ECR I-9161; Case C-499/06 *Nerkowska* [2008] ECR I-3993; Case C-221/07 *Zablocka* [2008] ECR I-9029; Case C-33/07 *Jipa* [2008] ECR I-5157.
[111] Case C-544/07 *Rüffler* [2009] ECR I-3389.
[112] *D'Hoop* (n 59).
[113] *Pusa* (n 66).
[114] *De Cuyper* (n 110).
[115] *Turpeinen* (n 110).

44 *Taking Stock of Union Citizenship*

This phase also saw the delivery of a judgment in a case (*Grunkin-Paul*)[116] with facts quite similar to those in *Garcia Avello*,[117] but with the difference that the facts in this case did involve the exercise of free movement and, thus, the Court included the situation within the scope of Article 18 EC (Article 21 TFEU) (as opposed to Article 20 TFEU, as in *Garcia Avello*).

In its case-law examining the parameters of the prohibition of nationality discrimination, the Court seems to have more readily accepted the justifications put forward by the Member States. This can be seen, for instance, in *Gottwald*,[118] where the Court found that an Austrian rule which restricted the issue of an annual toll disc free of charge to those disabled persons who were resident or ordinarily resident in Austria, although (indirectly) discriminatory on the grounds of nationality, it was, nonetheless, justified by the need to promote the mobility and social integration of disabled persons and the wish to ensure that there is a connection between the society of the Member State concerned and the recipient of the benefit in question.[119] Those who consider that the fundamental rights afforded by the EU to its citizens should, in all instances, prevail over the (economic) interests of the Member States, may consider this a backward step, taking the case-law in the opposite direction from that leading to a meaningful status of Union citizenship.

However, an even clearer backward step[120] during this phase is the Court's judgment in *Förster*.[121] At issue in the case was a Dutch law which required five years uninterrupted residence before an economically inactive *national of another Member State* could receive a maintenance grant during university studies; this condition was not applicable to Dutch nationals. The Court held that Article 12 EC (Article 18 TFEU) did not preclude a Member State from applying (only) to nationals of other Member States a requirement of five years' prior residence before they could receive a maintenance grant, and this was so even if that State

---

[116] *Grunkin-Paul* (n 109).
[117] *Garcia Avello* (n 53).
[118] *Gottwald* (n 52).
[119] See, also, Case C-123/08 *Wolzenburg* [2009] ECR I-9621 (annotated by C Janssens in (2010) 47 *Common Market Law Review* 831). It should be noted that in *Gottwald*, Austria accepted that a connection between the society of the Member State concerned and the recipient of the benefit in question was established by mere residence or ordinary residence in its territory, without—as in *Bidar*—requiring a minimum period of residence. Probably, this was because of the less (financially) burdensome nature of the claimed benefit in this situation. As AG Kokott in paragraph 76 of her Opinion in Case C-75/11 *Commission v Austria* ECLI:EU:C:2012:605, explained, '[t]he degree of integration required cannot ... be determined uniformly for all benefits, and a distinction must be made by reference to the scale of the benefits.'
[120] As explained by de Waele, 'faint indications of judicial retreat may be observed in recent ECJ jurisprudence'—see H de Waele (n 2) 320 and 326–27.
[121] Case C-158/07 *Förster* [2008] ECR I-8507. For excellent analyses, see S O'Leary, 'Equal Treatment of and EU Citizens: A New Chapter on Cross-Border Educational Mobility and Access to Student Financial Assistance' (2009) 34 *European Law Review* 612; O Golynker, 'Annotation of *Förster*' (2009) 46 *Common Market Law Review* 2021; AP van der Mei, 'Union Citizenship and the Legality of Durational Residence Requirements for Entitlement to Student Financial Aid' (2009) 15 *Maastricht Journal of European and Comparative Law* 477.

did not take into account any other factors which might demonstrate that a certain degree of integration into the society of the host State was attained.

This decision is clearly a backward step.

Firstly, it is a step backwards from *Bidar*.[122] In the latter case, the Court had accepted that it is lawful for a Member State to limit the award of a maintenance grant only to students who are integrated into its society, provided that the law makes provision for the individual circumstances of the applicant to be taken into account and grants the assistance whenever it is proved that (s)he is integrated in the host society. In *Förster*, nonetheless, the Court—unlike its Advocate General[123]—appeared willing to accept that in case a Union citizen has not resided in the host State for the specific period of time laid down in its legislation, the latter is entitled to refuse the benefit, irrespective of whether (s)he is (as evidenced by a number of different factors) integrated into its society.[124] More specifically, the Court noted that the finding that the five years residence requirement is permissible 'is without prejudice to the option for Member States to award maintenance grants to students from other Member States who do not fulfil the five year residence requirement *should they so wish*',[125] thus leaving it to the discretion of the Member States to determine whether they will take into account other criteria when determining the degree of integration of a national of another Member State into their territory.

Secondly, as explained by Chalmers, Davies and Monti:

> The unusual aspect of *Förster* is that the Court does not see the Dutch rule as violating the principle of non-discrimination. Its conclusion is that Article 18 TFEU is not violated because the rule is justified. While it is clear that Dutch citizens are treated differently from those of other Member States, this is not discrimination because it corresponds to a genuine difference between them. ... What *Förster* embodies is the idea that there remains a special bond between a citizen and their home state, not just in the realm of security and high politics, but also in the socio-economic arena. In this respect, nationals and foreigners *are* different and thus may be treated differently without this being discrimination. For a foreigner, it takes time or work to integrate, but for a national, it does not.[126]

In other words, the Court still appears to be considering that the nationals of a Member State have a special bond with it, which does not need to be positively proved (irrespective of their *actual* link with it), whereas nationals of other

---

[122] *Bidar* (n 40).
[123] AG Opinion in *Förster* (n 121), para 33.
[124] For a criticism see AP van der Mei (n 121) 487.
[125] *Förster* (n 121), para 59.
[126] D Chalmers, G Davies and G Monti, *European Union Law: Cases and Materials* 2nd edn (Cambridge, Cambridge University Press, 2010) 459. Commenting on this point, O'Leary noted that this actually amounted to direct discrimination on the grounds of nationality and, thus, 'any examination of objective justification, beyond the express derogations provided by the EC Treaty, with reference to genuine links and degrees of integration and the principle of proportionality seems beside the point'—S O'Leary (n 121) 621.

Member States always need to prove such a link.[127] This, however, is an approach which is steeped in discrimination and is, thus, incongruous with a meaningful status of Union citizenship which seeks to ensure that all Union citizens are treated equally irrespective of their nationality. Why should a Union citizen who happens to possess the nationality of a Member State (because, for instance, his father possesses that nationality) but who has never set foot in that State, be considered to have a link with it (without this being challenged or double-checked), whereas a Union citizen who happens not to possess that nationality should have to *prove* a sufficient link with the society of that State, even though (s)he may have spent virtually all his or her life in that State? In a Citizens' Europe, drawing distinctions based wholly on the nationality of a person does not appear acceptable and, thus, there can no longer be a presumption that nationals and non-nationals are differently situated for all purposes. The presumption should, now, be that all Union citizens—irrespective of nationality—are similarly situated.

Conversely, the judgment in *Huber*,[128] delivered in the same period, can be considered a step forward in the protection of EU citizens' rights and a step in the opposite direction from *Förster* and the inherently discriminatory approach taken there. In *Huber*, at issue was the compatibility with EU law of German legislation which provided that the German Government would keep a central database with information about all (non-German) EU citizens resident in its territory, whilst such a register would not be kept for German citizens. One of the arguments of the German Government was that the database was necessary for enabling it to fight crime. The Court, nonetheless, found that the system unjustifiably violated the prohibition of discrimination on the ground of nationality under Article 12 EC (Article 18 TFEU), since there was no reason why the aim of combating crime required different treatment for non-Germans: 'the fight against crime ... necessarily involves the prosecution of crimes and offences committed, irrespective of the nationality of their perpetrators'.[129]

During this phase—as in the 'Infancy phase'—the Court was, once again, confronted with the question of whether reverse discrimination was in line with the developments that had taken place in the context of Union citizenship. This question emerged in the *Flemish Care insurance scheme* case,[130] and was considered extensively by Advocate General Sharpston in her Opinion in that case.[131] The Court (rightly) confirmed that the purely internal rule is—and should remain—applicable when determining whether a situation falls within the scope of the market freedoms. However, and despite the urgings of its Advocate General, the

---

[127] The same criticism can also be levelled at the Court's subsequent judgment in *Wolzenburg* (n 119), especially para 68.
[128] Case C-524/06 *Huber* [2008] ECR I-9705.
[129] ibid, para 78.
[130] *Flemish Care insurance scheme* case (n 99).
[131] For comments on the case see TAJA Vandamme, 'Annotation of *Government of the French Community and Walloon Government v Flemish Government*' (2009) 46 *Common Market Law Review* 287.

Court avoided responding to the all-important question of whether reverse discrimination is, still, permissible under EU law.

Finally, a word should be said about this phase and the Court's tendency to (re-)interpret the personal market freedoms in the light of Union citizenship. As explained, during the previous phase of 'Growth', the Court for the first time, both explicitly and implicitly, appreciated the extent to which the introduction of the status of Union citizenship could and should affect the interpretation of the personal market freedoms. Moreover, as O'Leary has rightly argued, there has been a cross-pollination of principles in the opposite direction, ie principles developed in the context of the market freedoms have been employed in the interpretation of the citizenship provisions.[132] During this phase, the Court continued to follow this approach of infusing the interpretation of the market freedoms with a citizenship rhetoric.[133]

Before proceeding to the final phase of the ECJ's case-law on citizenship, I would like to make some general comments regarding this phase of the Court's citizenship jurisprudence.

Between 2006 and 2009, the Court tried and tested some of the principles established in the previous phase and, as we saw, whilst it did confirm the main ones, it also took some backward steps and provided some limiting clarifications.

More specifically, in contrast to the previous phase, which saw the delivery of a number of progressive—some might say revolutionary—judgments, during this phase the Court's approach appeared to be somewhat more moderate. For instance, the Court confirmed that there are certain rights/benefits that Member States can reserve for persons who have a special bond with them (mainly burdensome social assistance benefits). That special bond is presumed to *automatically* exist between a Member State and its own nationals, whereas nationals of other Member States have to positively prove that they have established it with the host State. In addition, the Court appeared determined to give the Member States more leeway when deciding what criteria they will apply in deciding whether a national of another Member State has established such a bond, even if this means that in certain cases where such a bond has been developed, the national authorities refuse to recognise its existence. This appears to be in line with older case-law dating back to the 1970s, where the Court held that with regards to certain issues—most prominently—deportation, a Member State is allowed to treat its own nationals differently (ie more favourably) than nationals of other Member States, without this being contrary to EU law.[134] One, however, would no doubt wonder whether

---

[132] S O'Leary (n 49). For a similar view see S Schmidt, 'Who Cares about Nationality? The Path-Dependent Case Law of the ECJ from Goods to Citizens' (2012) 19 *Journal of European Public Policy* 8, 20; A Iliopoulou Penot, 'The Transnational Character of Union Citizenship' in M Dougan, N Nic Shuibhne and E Spaventa (eds), *Empowerment and Disempowerment of the European Citizen* (Oxford, Hart Publishing, 2012) 16.

[133] See eg Joined Cases C-22 & 23/08 *Vatsouras and Koupatantze* [2009] ECR I-4585, para 37.

[134] See eg Case 41/74 *Van Duyn* [1974] ECR 1337, paras 20–23.

48 *Taking Stock of Union Citizenship*

this is still acceptable in the light of Union citizenship and the importance that this status has attained—a point to which I shall return in chapter six.

In this phase the Court also confirmed its classic approach to the issue of reverse discrimination, which is that it is not contrary to EU law and is a matter to be settled—if at all—by the Member States.

One final, related, point is that during this phase, we also saw the continuation of the tendency—also seen in the previous phase—of interpreting the personal market freedoms in a manner which is not justified under a purely internal market-based rationale, this giving rise to results that are favourable for the Union citizen. It was seen before that the case of *Carpenter*[135]—delivered in the 'Growth phase'—is the paradigmatic case, which illustrates this approach. In this subsequent phase, the highlight of this approach is the *Metock* judgment[136] (to be seen in more detail in the next chapter), where it was made even clearer that the grant of family reunification rights does not need to be *specifically* connected with the exercise of the rights stemming from the free movement of persons provisions, ie such (secondary) rights can, now, be also granted in situations where there is no cross-border specificity.

VI. COMING OF AGE: TOWARDS A MEANINGFUL STATUS OF UNION CITIZENSHIP? (2010-ONWARDS)

2010 initiated a new, more dynamic, phase in the development of the status of Union citizenship. In contrast to the (partly) disheartening case-law of the latter half of the previous decade, this new phase has seen the delivery of citizenship-friendly rulings such as *Rottmann*[137] and *Ruiz Zambrano*[138] (in the context of citizenship) and *Ibrahim*[139] and *Texeira*[140] (in the context of the personal market freedoms—to be seen in the next chapter).[141]

The Court in this phase confirmed some of the cardinal principles it had established in previous phases. Hence, it confirmed that discrimination against free movers is contrary to Article 21 TFEU, since it directly impedes the exercise of the right to free movement stemming from that provision;[142] it confirmed the *Gravier* principle (established in the 1980s, ie before the introduction of Union citizenship),[143] according to which access to education must be free from

---

[135] *Carpenter* (n 107).
[136] Case C-127/08 *Metock* [2008] ECR I-6241.
[137] *Rottmann* (n 36).
[138] Case C-34/09 *Ruiz Zambrano* [2011] ECR I-1177.
[139] Case C-310/08 *Ibrahim* [2010] ECR I-1965.
[140] Case C-480/08 *Teixeira* [2010] ECR I-1107.
[141] Note, however, that some backward steps are not absent from this phase—see, in particular, *Dano* (see the comments in n 91 above) and the Court's rulings on the derogations from the free movement of persons provisions, analysed later in the main text.
[142] *Zanotti* (n 25); Case C-208/09 *Sayn-Wittgenstein* [2010] ECR I-13693; Case C-391/09 *Runevič-Vardyn* [2011] ECR-3787.
[143] Case 293/83 *Gravier* [1985] ECR 593. For an analysis of this principle see S O'Leary (n 3) 160–66.

(direct or indirect) discrimination on the ground of nationality;[144] it made it clear that Article 21 TFEU catches within its scope not only restrictions on the free movement of Union citizens into the territory of the host Member State but also any restrictions on their movement outside their State of nationality;[145] and it confirmed *Bickel and Franz* in a case which involved civil proceedings between two non-Italians (a German national and a Czech national) taking place in the same province (in Bolzano), albeit that in this judgment the Court did not have recourse to Article 56 TFEU (in addition to Article 21 TFEU) in order to bring the situation within the personal scope of EU law, but solely employed for this purpose Article 21 TFEU and found—again—a breach of Article 18 TFEU.[146]

Moreover, the Court in this phase took the opportunity to 'set right' some of the problematic aspects of its jurisprudence from the previous phase. For instance, in *Commission v Austria*,[147] the Court appeared determined to clarify that the requirement of a link with the society of the host State should be interpreted in the pre-*Förster* manner.

In particular, the Court pointed out, firstly, that

> the proof required to demonstrate the genuine link must not be too exclusive in nature or unduly favour an element which is not necessarily representative of the real and effective degree of connection between the claimant to reduced transport fares and the Member State where the claimant pursues his studies, to the exclusion of all other representative elements.[148]

Secondly, the Court stated that

> the genuine link required between the student claiming a benefit and the host Member State need not be fixed in a uniform manner for all benefits, but should be established according to the constitutive elements of the benefit in question, including its nature and purpose or purposes. The objective of the benefit must be analysed according to its results and not according to its formal structure.[149]

---

[144] Case C-73/08 *Bressol* [2010] ECR I-2735.
[145] Case C-430/10 *Gaydarov* [2011] ECR I-11637; *Aladzhov* (n 75); Case C-249/11 *Byankov* ECLI:EU:C:2012:608.
[146] *Rüffer* (n 52).
[147] *Commission v Austria* (n 119), para 56.
[148] ibid, para 62.
[149] ibid, para 63. See also, more recently, Joined Cases C-523 & 585/11 *Prinz* ECLI:EU:C:2013:524 (for comments see PJ Neuvonen, 'In Search of (Even) More Substance for the "Real Link" Test: Comment on *Prinz and Seeberger*' (2014) 39 *European Law Review* 125); Case C-220/12 *Thiele Meneses* ECLI:EU:C:2013:683; Case C-359/13 *B Martens* ECLI:EU:C:2015:118. See paragraph 85 of the AG's Opinion in *Prinz* for the distinction between these cases and *Förster* (n 121). Strumia and Brown have argued that these cases may not have overruled *Förster* but may in fact be demonstrating that stricter requirements are imposed on Member States by EU law, when their measures impede the *exit* of Union citizens from their territory than when they impede the right of entry of Union citizens to their territory. See F Strumia and C Brown, 'The Asymmetry in the Right to Free Movement of European Union Citizens: The Case of Students' available at eulawanalysis.blogspot.be/2015/07/the-asymmetry-in-right-to-free-movement.html.

50 *Taking Stock of Union Citizenship*

During this phase, there were also two cases (*Sayn-Wittgenstein*[150] and *Runevič-Vardyn*[151]) which concerned a Member State's refusal to register the surname of its own nationals according to the practice of another Member State and the compatibility of this refusal with EU law. Although the Court in both cases found that the contested refusal amounted to an obstacle to free movement, in the end it found that the measure was justified, paying particular attention to Article 4(2) TEU, which provides, inter alia, that the EU is to respect the national identities of its Member States. This may be an indication that post-Lisbon, the Court is particularly sensitive when it comes to certain matters which are considered as constitutive of the identity of the Member States, and for this reason is willing to apply a very 'light touch' approach when assessing the justifications put forward by Member States when seeking to defend their choices in relation to such matters.[152]

One of the novelties of this phase is that the Court took the opportunity to interpret a number of provisions of the 2004 Citizens' Rights Directive, with special emphasis being placed on a) the interpretation of the right of permanent residence provided by Article 16 and b) the public policy/public security exceptions, as elucidated in Articles 27 and 28 of the Directive.[153]

Starting with the right of permanent residence which, according to Article 16 of Directive 2004/38, is acquired by Union citizens and their family members who have legally resided in the host State for a period of five years, in *Lassal*,[154] the Court held that continuous periods of five years' residence completed *before* the date of transposition of the 2004 Directive (ie 30 April 2006), must be taken into account when determining whether the five-year lawful residence requirement for establishing this right is satisfied. The Court, moreover, held that absences from the host Member State of less than two consecutive years occurring after the continuous residence of five years but before 30 April 2006, are not such as to affect the link of integration of the citizen of the Union concerned. This was qualified subsequently, however, when the Court in *Dias*[155] held that periods of residence completed before the date of transposition of the 2004 Directive on the basis solely of a residence permit validly issued under EU secondary legislation that was applicable at the time, but *without the conditions governing entitlement to any right of residence having been met*, cannot be regarded as having been completed legally for the purposes of the acquisition of a right of permanent residence.

Similarly, in *Ziolkowski*,[156] it was ruled that a Union citizen who has been resident for more than five years in the territory of the host Member State on the sole basis of the national law of that Member State, cannot be regarded as having acquired

---

[150] *Sayn-Wittgenstein* (n 142).
[151] *Runevič-Vardyn* (n 142).
[152] For more on this see A Iliopoulou Penot (n 132) 23–26.
[153] For a recent case where the Court interpreted Art 35 of Dir 2004/38, see Case C-202/13 *McCarthy* ECLI:EU:C:2014:2450. Due to lack of space and the lack of novelty in the Court's pronouncement in that case, it will not be discussed further in this chapter.
[154] Case C-162/09 *Lassal* [2010] ECR I-9217.
[155] Case C-325/09 *Dias* [2011] ECR I-6387.
[156] Joined Cases C-424 & 425/10 *Ziolkowski* [2011] ECR I-14035.

the right of permanent residence if, during that period of residence, he did not satisfy the conditions laid down in Article 7(1) of the Directive.[157] More recently, in *Onuekwere*,[158] the Court held that continuity of residence for the purposes of the right of permanent residence is interrupted by periods of imprisonment in the host Member State. Similarly, periods of imprisonment cannot be taken into account when calculating the five-year period of residence required for establishing this right. *Ogieriakhi*,[159] on the other hand, concerned the acquisition of the right of permanent residence by the third-country national family member of a Union citizen who had exercised free movement rights and the Court held that the right is acquired even though during the period which is taken into consideration for the purpose of satisfying the five-year residence requirement, the spouses had decided to separate and were already residing with other partners.

Moving, now, to the Treaty derogations from the right to free movement, and, in particular, the principles established with respect to the public policy and public security derogations, in *Gaydarov*,[160] the Court made clear that these principles are the same as those established in case-law before Directive 2004/38 came into force. During this phase, the Court was also asked to clarify the meaning of principles which were only introduced by the Directive. In particular, the Court was asked to elucidate the meaning of Article 28 of the 2004 Directive, which provides enhanced protection from expulsion for Union citizens who are long-term residents in the host State. Article 28(3) of the Directive, in particular, provides that Union citizens who have resided in the host Member State for the previous 10 years, can only be expelled on 'imperative grounds of public security'.

Tsakouridis[161] concerned the question of the extent to which absences from the host Member State interrupt the above-mentioned 10-year period of residence and, thus, remove the enhanced protection available under Article 28(3). The Court noted that 'an overall assessment must be made of the persons' situation on each occasion at the precise time when the question of expulsion arises'[162] and that, in particular, '[i]t must be ascertained whether those absences involve the transfer to another State of the centre of the personal, family or occupational interests of the person concerned'.[163] The Court also, and more specifically, stated that the fight against trafficking in narcotics as part of an organised international network is capable of being covered by the concept of imperative grounds of public security and is definitely covered by the concept of serious grounds of public policy.

---

[157] See Joined Cases C-147 & 148/11 *Czop* ECLI:EU:C:2012:538, for the position of nationals of Member States that acceded to the EU after the Union citizen had moved to another Member State.
[158] Case C-378/12 *Onuekwere* ECLI:EU:C:2014:13.
[159] Case C-244/13 *Ogieriakhi* ECLI:EU:C:2014:2068.
[160] *Gaydarov* (n 145).
[161] Case C-145/09 *Tsakouridis* [2010] ECR I-11979.
[162] ibid, para 32.
[163] ibid, para 33.

The Court took things even further in the *PI* case.[164] The case concerned an Italian national who had been resident in Germany for more than 10 years and was, thus, entitled to the increased protection afforded by Article 28(3)(a) of Directive 2004/38, namely, he could only be expelled if Germany could prove that there were imperative grounds of public security. The reason for the deportation order issued against him was that he was sentenced in Germany to a term of imprisonment of seven years and six months for the sexual assault, sexual coercion, and rape of his former partner's minor daughter. The question was whether these acts could be brought within the notion of 'imperative grounds of public security'. The Court replied in the affirmative, pointing out that a number of Treaty provisions express the serious nature of criminal offences involving the sexual abuse and sexual exploitation of children, and, accordingly, 'it is open to the Member States to regard' such offences 'as constituting a particularly serious threat to one of the fundamental interests of society, which might pose a direct threat to the calm and physical security of the population' and thus be covered by the concept of 'imperative grounds of public security'.[165]

Tsakouridis and *PI* have been criticised by Kostakopoulou and Ferreira,[166] who have observed that these judgments have made it easier for Member States to prove that a certain kind of conduct satisfies the requirements of Article 28(3) and, hence, it is now easier for the host State to deport from its territory long-term residents and, even, Union citizens who have spent their whole life in the territory of that State. This is 'deeply problematic from an EU law standpoint' as it, inter alia, 'undermines the rationale of the Citizenship Directive and its objectives of promoting security of residence for long-term resident EU citizens and enhancing their citizenship status'.[167]

The effect of imprisonment on the enhanced protection provided by Article 28(3)(a) was considered in the *MG* case.[168] It was held that a period of imprisonment is, in principle, capable both of interrupting the continuity of the period of residence for the purposes of that provision and of affecting the decision regarding the grant of the enhanced protection provided for thereunder, even where the person concerned resided in the host Member State for the 10 years prior to imprisonment. Furthermore, such a period of imprisonment may be taken into consideration, as part of the overall assessment required for determining whether the integrating links previously forged with the host Member State

---

[164] Case C-348/09 *PI* ECLI:EU:C:2012:300. For comments, see D Kochenov and B Pirker, 'Deporting the Citizens within the Euroepan Union: A Counter-Intuitive Trend in Case C-348/09, P.I. V Oberbürgermeisterin der Stadt Remscheid' (2012-2013) 19 CJEL 369.

[165] ibid, para 28.

[166] D Kostakopoulou and N Ferreira, 'Testing Liberal Norms: The Public Policy and Public Security Derogations and the Cracks in European Union Citizenship' (2013–14) 20 *Columbia Journal of European Law* 167. See, also, D Kostakopoulou, 'When EU Citizens become Foreigners' (2014) 20 *European Law Journal* 447, 457–60.

[167] D Kostakopoulou and N Ferreira (n 166) 175.

[168] Case C-400/12 *MG* ECLI:EU:C:2014:9.

have been broken, and thus for determining whether the enhanced protection provided for in that provision will be granted.

The above three judgments (*Tsakouridis, PI* and *MG*) demonstrate a reticence on the part of the Court to require the host State to treat long-term residents who bear the nationality of another Member State in the same way as nationals of the host State, in this way preventing the development of 'denizenship' which would require all long-term residents in a Member State—irrespective of nationality—to be treated in the same way, including when it comes to deportation and expulsion. Accordingly, in this phase, the Court appears to have (partly) stood by its approach we saw during the previous phase in the case of *Förster*, where it was demonstrated that the bond of nationality continues to remain stronger than that of (long-term) residence, in this way permitting the host State to continue treating nationals of other Member States as 'foreigners', despite the fact that they may have developed a very strong bond with their society by having spent virtually their whole life in the host State.

We should now proceed to the last, important, group of ECJ judgments which can fairly be described as the 'jewel in the crown' of this phase: judgments through which, according to Kochenov, 'the Court seems to be hinting at the beginning of a new era of EU law where the text of Part II Treaty on the Functioning of the EU (TFEU) is finally taken seriously'.[169] This is the group comprised of two main cases—*Rottmann* and *Ruiz Zambrano*—and the cases that followed (*McCarthy, Dereci, Ymeraga, O, S & L*), which made it clear that, contrary to what was said in the *My* case back in 2004,[170] Article 20 TFEU *can* be applied independently of the other provisions in Part Two of the TFEU; and, in order for this provision to apply, there is no need to point either to an obstacle to free movement (ie a substantive element) or (even) to the *exercise* of inter-State movement, provided that there is either some other kind of a cross-border element (which is what has been established in cases like *Martínez Sala*[171] and *Garcia Avello*)[172] or, as established in this line of case-law, that the contested measure is capable of depriving Union citizens of the genuine enjoyment of the substance of their Union citizenship rights. With these judgments, therefore, the Court expanded the material scope of EU law, not only beyond *economic* activities but, also, beyond *cross-border* activities.

Rottmann[173] involved the all-important question of the effect of the status of Union citizenship on the actions of the Member States with regards to the grant

---

[169] D Kochenov, 'The Right to Have What Rights? EU Citizenship in Need of Clarification' (2013) 19 *European Law Journal* 502, 503.
[170] *My* (n 25), para 32.
[171] *Martínez Sala* (n 35).
[172] *Garcia Avello* (n 53).
[173] *Rottmann* (n 36). For comments see, inter alia, T Konstadinides, 'La fraternité europeene? The Extent of National Competence to Condition the Acquisition and Loss of Nationality from the Perspective of EU Citizenship' (2010) 35 *European Law Review* 401; D Kochenov, 'Annotation of *Rottmann*' (2010) 47 *Common Market Law Review* 1831; A Tryfonidou, 'The Impact of EU Law on Nationality Laws and Migration Control in the EU's Member States' (2011) 25 *Immigration, Asylum and Nationality Law* 358, 358–66.

or withdrawal of their nationality. Dr Rottmann was an Austrian doctor who transferred his residence to Germany in 1995, after criminal proceedings had been instigated against him by the Austrian authorities, on account of suspected serious fraud in the exercise of his profession. In 1998 he applied for German nationality, which he obtained in 1999 and, as a result of this, he lost his Austrian nationality. During the naturalisation procedure he failed to mention to the German authorities that criminal proceedings were pending against him in Austria. When the German authorities were informed of this, they decided to withdraw the naturalisation with retroactive effect; this would render Dr Rottmann stateless. The question that emerged was whether this would amount to a violation of EU law since the fact that Dr Rottmann would no longer possess any Member State nationality, meant that he would no longer be a Union citizen and, thus, that he would lose all rights deriving from that status.

In its judgment, the Court firstly dealt with the question of whether the situation fell within the scope of EU law. Although it was argued that the matter was a purely internal one, the Court found that the situation fell within the scope of EU law since

> the situation of a citizen of the Union who, like the applicant in the main proceedings, is faced with a decision withdrawing his naturalisation, adopted by the authorities of one Member State, and placing him, after he has lost the nationality of another Member State that he originally possessed, in a position capable of causing him to lose the status conferred by Article 17 EC and the rights attaching thereto falls, by reason of its nature and its consequences, within the ambit of European Union law.[174]

The Court, then, noted that when exercising their powers in the sphere of nationality, Member States must have due regard to EU law[175] and, by that, in effect, the Court meant that the exercise of Member States' powers in this area are 'amenable to judicial review carried out in the light of European Union law'.[176] This requires the Member States to prove that the decision withdrawing naturalisation corresponds to a reason relating to the public interest and that it is proportionate.[177]

Rottmann illustrates two things. Firstly, it is made clear (confirming previous case-law)[178] that Member State decisions in the field of nationality have to be compliant with EU law. Hence, although it is acknowledged that such decisions do continue to fall within the competence of the Member States, when these decisions concern the withdrawal of Member State nationality and, with it, of the status of Union citizenship and the rights that are attached to it, they have to be justified under EU law. Secondly, and most importantly, the case made it clear that when it is Article 20 TFEU that is employed in order to bring a situation within the scope of EU law, there is no need to point to a cross-border element in certain cases. From the judgment in *Rottmann*, we can deduce that a cross-border element is not

---

[174] *Rottmann* (n 36), para 42.
[175] ibid, para 45.
[176] ibid, para 48.
[177] ibid, paras 51 and 55.
[178] Case C-369/90 *Micheletti* [1992] ECR I-4239, para 10.

necessary in situations where the contested Member State action leads to the loss of Union citizenship and, as a result of this, to the complete loss of rights bestowed via that status on Member State nationals.

It was not made clear, however, whether the complete lack of a cross-border element is only acceptable for bringing a situation within the scope of EU law via Article 20 TFEU in only this limited instance, or whether the same rationale can be applied in other situations with similarly important consequences for Union citizens. This was clarified subsequently in the *Ruiz Zambrano* case,[179] which involved two Belgian children who sought to invoke EU law in order to claim that their third-country national parents should be allowed to continue residing with them in Belgium. On the facts, it was clear that no inter-State movement had been exercised, nor were there any *concrete* plans for its future exercise. Moreover, there was no other kind of cross-border element, such as the possession of the nationality of a Member State other than that where the children were residing, which could have brought the case within the scope of EU law as per *Garcia Avello*.[180] The Court, nonetheless, held that a 'refusal to grant a right of residence to a third country national with dependent minor children in the Member State where those children are nationals and reside, and also a refusal to grant such a person a work permit' has 'the effect of depriving citizens of the Union of the genuine enjoyment of the substance of the rights conferred by virtue of their status as citizens of the Union'.[181] This was because

> such a refusal would lead to a situation where those children, citizens of the Union, would have to leave the territory of the Union in order to accompany their parents. Similarly, if a work permit were not granted to such a person, he would risk not having sufficient resources to provide for himself and his family, which would also result in the children, citizens of the Union, having to leave the territory of the Union. In those circumstances, those citizens of the Union would, as a result, be unable to exercise the substance of the rights conferred on them by virtue of their status as citizens of the Union.[182]

The Court in *Ruiz Zambrano* appears, therefore, to have wished to make it clear that it is not only in the (very exceptional) case where a Union citizen is completely stripped of his EU rights as per *Rottmann*, that Article 20 TFEU applies in the absence of a cross-border element. Rather, in this case, the Court seized the opportunity to formulate a new principle, according to which Article 20 TFEU catches any national measure that deprives the Union citizen 'of the genuine enjoyment of the substance of the rights conferred by virtue of her status as a Union citizen'.

In the subsequent cases of *McCarthy*,[183] *Dereci*,[184] *O, S and L*,[185] and *Ymeraga*,[186] the Court confirmed that the new *Ruiz Zambrano*-type of restriction can now

---

[179] *Ruiz Zambrano* (n 138).
[180] *Garcia Avello* (n 53).
[181] *Ruiz Zambrano* (n 138), paras 42–43.
[182] ibid, para 44.
[183] Case C-434/09 *McCarthy* [2011] ECR I-3375.
[184] Case C-256/11 *Dereci* [2011] ECR I-11315.
[185] Joined Cases C-356 & 357/11 *O, S and L* ECLI:EU:C:2012:776.
[186] Case C-87/12 *Ymeraga* ECLI:EU:C:2013:291.

amount to a violation of Article 20 TFEU, but it also took the opportunity to place some (extensive) limits on its ambit; lack of space, however, precludes an analysis of this here.[187]

A few concluding remarks for this most recent phase of Union citizenship case-law are now in order.

The majority of the Court's jurisprudence from 2010 onwards were a) cases where an interpretation of Directive 2004/38 was required and, most importantly, b) cases where the Court was given the opportunity to establish that Union citizens now derive rights from EU law—rights which were traditionally only bestowed on *moving* Union citizens—in situations that lack a cross-border element of any kind.

The Court made it clear through *Rottmann* and *Ruiz Zambrano*, that Member State nationals can benefit from their status as Union citizens even in the complete absence of a cross-border element—this, after all, is not entirely unprecedented, given that certain EU law provisions do not require the existence of such an element in order to apply.[188] This is, clearly, a further step towards establishing a meaningful notion of Union citizenship: if the existence or even genuine enjoyment of Union citizenship rights is threatened by Member State measures, this should undoubtedly suffice for activating EU law, even in the absence of a cross-border element.[189] Member State nationals no longer become Union citizens only once they exercise their (by nature) cross-border rights stemming from the market freedoms and Article 21 TFEU, but they *are* Union citizens in all circumstances,

---

[187] For an analysis of the *Ruiz-Zambrano*-line of case-law see, inter alia, A Wiesbrock, 'Disentangling the "Union Citizenship Puzzle"? The McCarthy Case' (2011) 36 *European Law Review* 861; P Van Elsuwege and D Kochenov, 'On the Limits of Judicial Intervention: EU Citizenship and Family Reunification Rights' (2011) 13 *European Journal of Migration and Law* 443; R Morris, 'European Citizenship and the Right to Move Freely: Internal Situations, Reverse Discrimination and Fundamental Rights' (2011) 18 *Maastricht Journal of European and Comparative Law* 179; D Kochenov, 'A Real European Citizenship: A New Jurisdiction Test: A Novel Chapter in the Development of the Union in Europe' (2011) 18 *Columbia Journal of European Law* 55; A Tryfonidou, 'Redefining the Outer Boundaries of EU Law: The *Zambrano, McCarthy* and *Dereci* Trilogy' (2012) 18 *European Public Law* 493; S Mantu, 'European Union Citizenship Anno 2011: Zambrano, McCarthy and Dereci' (2012) 26 *Immigration, Asylum and Nationality Law* 40; S Peers and C Berneri, 'Iida and O and S: Further Developments in the Immigration Status of Static EU Citizens' (2013) 27 *Journal of Immigration, Asylum and Nationality Law* 162; S Reynolds, 'Exploring the "Intrinsic Connection" between Free Movement and the Genuine Enjoyment Test: Reflections on EU Citizenship after *Iida*' (2013) 38 *European Law Review* 376; M van den Brink, 'The Origins and the Potential Federalising Effects of the Substance of Rights Test' in D Kochenov (n 17).

[188] See eg Art 157 TFEU and the non-discrimination regime. Spaventa, writing in 2008, pointed out that 'If Union citizens fall within the personal scope of the Treaty by virtue of Article 17 EC [now Article 20 TFEU], and since that Article does not mention migration, then *any* citizen, and not only the migrant, now falls within the personal scope of the Treaty and is therefore able to rely on it whenever the situation falls within its material scope'—E Spaventa, 'Seeing the Wood Despite the Trees? On the Scope of Union Citizenship and its Constitutional effects' (2008) 45 *Common Market Law Review* 13, 22.

[189] This appears to echo the views of Advocate General Warner in his Opinion in Case 175/78 *Saunders* [1979] ECR 1129, 1142, where he noted that the true question 'is not whether the case has any connexion with another Member State, but whether and, if so, to what extent Community law confers rights on a person in Miss Saunders's position'.

and should, thus, be entitled to enjoy and exercise the rights attached to this status in all instances, and not solely in those where there is already an exercise of those rights.[190] The focus, thus, now seems to be no longer on the concept of movement and/or the achievement of the EU's aims, but has shifted to the individual.[191] As observed by Lenaerts, '*Ruiz Zambrano* has emancipated EU citizenship from the constraints inherent in its free movement origins'.[192]

Of course, this does not mean the purely internal rule has been abolished and that static Union citizens can now rely on EU law in all instances; after all, most of the rights derived from the personal market freedoms and the citizenship provisions are of a cross-border nature and, hence, will not be available in situations where a Union citizen seeks to claim them in a single-State scenario. It means, however, that all Union citizens—and not, merely, the slim majority who move—are now considered beneficiaries of EU law and, thus, the actions of the Member States that affect (or may potentially affect) the rights that (all) Union citizens derive from EU law, can be subjected to EU scrutiny.

Accordingly, whilst the 'Growth phase' of Union citizenship had as one of its main highlights the detachment of Union citizenship from any requirement of a contribution to the economic aims of the EU, in this most recent phase, the Court took the further—and highly important—step of establishing that the status of Union citizenship is detached also from the idea of free movement.

Moreover, the rulings delivered during this phase further enhance the vertical relationship between the Union and its citizens and the autonomy of the rights that Union citizens *directly* derive from EU law. The latter was, in particular, confirmed 'by the Court in *Rottmann*, when it stated that Member States cannot interfere in the bond between the citizen and the Union by unjustifiably depriving him of State nationality'.[193]

Consequently, we can now claim that we are very close to attaining a meaningful notion of Union citizenship which has added value and which is not merely a consolidation of the pre-1993 *acquis* and, hence, we can now speak of a Union citizenship which is coming of age.

VII. CONCLUSION

This introductory chapter sought to provide an up-to-date account of the development of the status of Union citizenship via the ECJ's case-law.

---

[190] Editorial Comment: 'Two-speed European Citizenship? Can the Lisbon Treaty Help Close the Gap?' (2008) 45 *Common Market Law Review* 1, 3.

[191] Opinion of AG Ruiz-Jarabo Colomer in Case C-228/07 *Petersen* [2008] ECR I-6989, para 28.

[192] K Lenaerts, '"Civis europeus sum": From the Cross-Border Link to the Status of Citizen of the Union' (2011) 3 *Online Journal on Free Movement of Workers within the European Union* 6, 7, available at ec.europa.eu/social/BlobServlet?docId=7281&langId=en.

[193] Opinion of AG Cruz Villalón in Case C-89/09 *Commission v France* [2010] ECR I-12941, para 136.

Judging from the quantity of cases that have been decided in this area in the last 20 years and, especially, from the 2000s onwards, it is obvious that there has clearly been a move towards establishing that Union citizenship was not an empty promise—as many argued when it was first established—but could attain real substance. The majority of the Court's rulings have ensured that Union citizenship does, indeed, grant to Member State nationals something above and beyond what was offered to them under the original Treaties, when they were merely viewed as factors of production that were to be 'used' instrumentally in the process of building an internal market. Thanks to this status, and to its development by the ECJ, Member State nationals now appear to enjoy a number of *fundamental* (citizenship) rights to which they were *not* entitled prior to its introduction; and to have a direct relationship with the EU which does not need to be 'mediated' by the Member States.

We have, in particular, seen that through a number of incremental steps, the Court has made it clear that Union citizens can, now, enjoy certain fundamental rights under EU law irrespective of whether they contribute, in any way, to the economic aims of the EU. And, equally importantly, they can derive rights from the citizenship provisions of the Treaty (and, in particular, Article 20 TFEU) even when they have not moved between Member States and their situation does not present any other kind of cross-border element.

Moreover, as we briefly saw (since this will be analysed in detail in the chapters that follow), Union citizenship also appears to have played an important role as a transformative element of the EU polity, having a spill-over effect in other areas of EU integration. In particular, the Court has explicitly recognised in some of its market freedoms case-law the need to (re-)interpret those provisions in a way which takes into account the introduction of this status, whilst in others, the impact that the introduction of this status has had on the interpretation of these provisions is obvious.

Having seen the main phases in the development of the status of Union citizenship and having sketched the main principles which have been developed to govern this status, we shall now proceed to chapters three and four, which will consider what the impact of this status has been on the interpretation of the market freedoms.

Part II

The Impact of Union Citizenship on the EU's Market Freedoms

3

Union Citizenship and the Personal Market Freedoms

I. INTRODUCTION

THIS CHAPTER AND the next will seek to consider what has been and what *may* have been, to date, the impact of Union citizenship on the interpretation of the market freedoms. As one commentator has rightly observed, in light of the importance attained by the status of Union citizenship and the resultant transformation of the EU in the last few decades, '[i]t would be rather surprising if, in this setting, the fundamental freedoms carved out an isolated existence as the kernel of the European economic constitution, remaining untouched'.[1]

The current chapter focuses on the relationship between Union citizenship and the *personal* market freedoms (Articles 45, 49 and 56 TFEU[2]). It will, in particular, seek to examine how the metamorphosis of the Member State national, from the initial persona of the economic agent to today's Union citizen, has influenced the Court's interpretation of these provisions. The main conclusion will be that, as part of the overall 'transformation of European integration from an economic to a political phenomenon based on individual rights'[3] and, most importantly, as a result of the introduction of the status of Union citizenship, the scope of the personal market freedoms seems to have adapted in order to reflect the fact that (some) of their beneficiaries are, now, Union citizens.[4] This becomes obvious from some of the Court's post-Maastricht rulings, which demonstrate that these provisions have been transformed from sources of merely instrumental freedoms

---

[1] C Krenn, 'A Missing Piece in the Horizontal Effect "Jigsaw": Horizontal Direct Effect and the Free Movement of Goods' (2012) 49 *Common Market Law Review* 177, 184–85.
[2] Consolidated Version of the Treaty on the Functioning of the European Union [2012] C326/47.
[3] W Maas, *Creating European Citizens* (Lanham MD, Rowman & Littlefield Publishers, 2007) 116.
[4] AG Léger in paragraph 50 of his Opinion in Case C-215/03 *Oulane* [2005] ECR I-1215, pointed out that 'although the protection given by the status of citizen of the Union does not have to be systematically called on as such, the development of Community law on the freedom of movement of persons, in the broad sense, which that entails cannot be disregarded. That is why Union citizenship, which "is destined to be the fundamental status of nationals of the Member States", is a factor which must be actively taken into account for interpreting all the Community rules on the freedom of movement of persons'.

and rights for legal and natural persons to, *also,* sources of fundamental economic rights for the Union citizen.

The backbone of this chapter will be the distinction between (what I call) the Court's instrumental and fundamental rights-based approaches to the personal market freedoms. Under the former, the Court views the market freedoms as merely sources of instrumental freedoms and rights which are given to persons for the purpose of enabling and encouraging them to contribute to the economic aims of the Treaty. Conversely, under the fundamental rights-based approach, these provisions are read as sources of fundamental rights that are granted to Union citizens for their own sake (simply because they are Union citizens and, as such, should have the right to take-up and/or pursue an economic activity in another Member State/in a cross-border context).

The main analysis in the chapter will begin by sketching the legal framework that governs the rights of economically active Union citizens within the EU (II). This will be followed by a section (III) that will document the process through which the personal market freedoms were—already before Maastricht—transformed into sources of *rights* for Member State nationals, albeit instrumental ones; and shall seek to explain how these provisions were interpreted before the status of Union citizenship was introduced, when they appeared to be viewed solely as the tools for the construction of an internal market. Section IV will, then, proceed to examine the overall impact that the introduction of Union citizenship seems to have had on the interpretation of the personal market freedoms. The section will begin by presenting the (handful of) instances where the Court has (explicitly) stressed the need to re-interpret the personal market freedoms in the light of Union citizenship and will then proceed to consider how the personal scope of these provisions was developed in the period after Maastricht. The greatest part of the section will, however, be devoted to an analysis of post-Maastricht case-law, which cannot be explained under a purely internal market rationale. It will be argued that the most plausible rationale that can justify the Court's approach in that case-law is the need to take into account the fact that (some of) the beneficiaries of the personal market freedoms are Union citizens who should (now) enjoy certain economic rights for their own sake and not, merely, for the purpose of contributing to the economic aims of the Treaty. Section VI will conclude.

II. THE PERSONAL MARKET FREEDOMS: A SKETCH OF THE CURRENT LEGAL FRAMEWORK

As seen in chapter one, since the birth of the EEC, there have been a number of Treaty provisions which govern the position of Member State nationals who wish to move between Member States for an economic purpose. These provisions are, now, Articles 45, 49 and 56 TFEU, and are all found in Title IV of Part Three of the TFEU.

Article 45 TFEU concerns 'workers'.[5] It begins by stating that '[f]reedom of movement for workers shall be secured within the Union',[6] and then proceeds to specify that such freedom shall entail the abolition of nationality discrimination as regards employment, remuneration, and other conditions of work and employment. The Article then provides a (non-exhaustive[7]) list of the rights that this freedom entails (eg the right to accept offers of employment actually made, the right to move freely within the territory of Member States for this purpose), and explains that the rights provided for in this Article are subject to limitations justified on grounds of public policy, public security, or public health. Article 45 TFEU concludes with stating that this provision shall not apply to employment in the public service (the 'public service exception').

Establishment is governed by Article 49 TFEU.[8] The provision begins with a prohibition of 'restrictions on the freedom of establishment of nationals of a Member State in the territory of another Member State', and moves on to explain that this prohibition 'shall also apply to restrictions on the setting-up of agencies, branches or subsidiaries by nationals of any Member State established in the territory of any Member State'. Article 49 TFEU then provides that this freedom

> shall include the right to take up and pursue activities as self-employed persons and to set up and manage undertakings, in particular companies or firms within the meaning of the second paragraph of Article 54, under the conditions laid down for its own nationals by the law of the country where such establishment is effected, subject to the provisions of the Chapter relating to capital.

Like in the context of Article 45 TFEU, the entitlements deriving from this provision are also subject to limitations justified on grounds of public policy, public security, or public health (Article 52 TFEU); and the Chapter does not apply to activities which are connected with the exercise of official authority (the 'official authority exception') (Article 51 TFEU).

It should be noted that unlike Article 45 TFEU, which only grants to *natural* persons the 'freedom of movement for workers', Article 54 TFEU makes it clear that the freedom of establishment is granted to both natural *and* legal persons.

Article 56 TFEU is the main provision concerning the freedom to provide services:[9]

> Within the framework of the provisions set out below, restrictions on freedom to provide services within the Union shall be prohibited in respect of nationals of Member States

---

[5] 'Workers' are, more broadly, covered in Chapter 1 of Title IV of Part Three TFEU.
[6] Interestingly, the draft Constitutional Treaty of 2004 would amend the first sentence of this provision by replacing the word 'freedom' with the word 'right' and would, thus, read: 'Workers shall have the right to move freely within the Union'. However, the Treaty of Lisbon did not take over this change but maintained the original wording.
[7] G Davies, *European Union Internal Market Law* (London, Routledge, 2003) 42. The Court has acknowledged the fact that the list of rights provided explicitly in the text of Art 45 TFEU is not exhaustive—Case C-292/89 *Antonissen* [1991] ECR I-745, para 13.
[8] Establishment is, more broadly, covered in Chapter 2 of Title IV of Part Three of the TFEU.
[9] The free movement of services is, more broadly, covered in Chapter 3 of Title IV of Part Three of the TFEU.

who are established in a Member State other than that of the person for whom the services are intended.

Article 57 TFEU then explains that '[s]ervices shall be considered to be "services" within the meaning of the Treaties where they are normally provided for remuneration, in so far as they are not governed by the provisions relating to' the other market freedoms. Like the other provisions seen above, this freedom is also subject to the public policy, public security, and public health derogations, as well as the official authority exception. Moreover, like the freedom of establishment, the freedom to provide services is granted to both natural *and legal* persons.

As noted in chapter one, the personal market freedoms are complemented by a number of pieces of secondary legislation, which together make a rather convoluted whole. For the purposes of this chapter, the most important piece is the Citizens' Rights Directive (Directive 2004/38)[10]—which we examined in the previous chapter—and which applies to all Union citizens (both economically active and inactive) who move to or reside in a Member State other than that of which they are a national, and to their family members who accompany or join them.[11] Needless to say, it does not apply to legal persons and the only non-EU nationals that derive rights from it are the family members of migrant Union citizens. Other important pieces of secondary legislation are Regulation 492/2011 on the free movement of workers,[12] which has recently repealed and replaced Regulation 1612/68;[13] Directive 2014/54 on measures facilitating the exercise of rights conferred on workers in the context of freedom of movement for workers;[14] Directive 2005/36, which governs the recognition of professional qualifications;[15] the Services Directive (Directive 2006/123), which—despite its name—applies to both services and establishment;[16] and the social security Regulations (Regulations 883/2004 and 987/2009).[17]

III. THE PERSONAL MARKET FREEDOMS AS SOURCES OF INSTRUMENTAL FREEDOMS AND RIGHTS: THE PRE-MAASTRICHT APPROACH TO THEIR INTERPRETATION

The aim of this section is to illustrate how the personal market freedoms were interpreted *before* the status of Union citizenship was introduced in 1993. The

---

[10] Dir 2004/38 on the right of citizens of the Union and their family members to move and reside freely within the territory of the Member States [2004] OJ L158/77.
[11] ibid, Art 3(1).
[12] Reg 492/2011 on freedom of movement for workers within the Union [2011] OJ L141/1.
[13] Reg 1612/68 on freedom of movement for workers within the Community [1968] OJ L257/2.
[14] Dir 2014/54 on measures facilitating the exercise of rights conferred on workers in the context of freedom of movement for workers [2014] OJ L128/8.
[15] Dir 2005/36 on the recognition of professional qualifications [2005] OJ L255/22.
[16] Dir 2006/123 on services in the internal market [2006] OJ L376/36.
[17] Reg 883/2004 on the coordination of social security systems, as amended by Reg 988/2009 [2004] OJ L166/1; Reg 987/2009 laying down the procedure for implementing Reg 883/2004 on the coordination of social security systems [2009] OJ L284/1.

analysis will be divided into two subsections: the first subsection will seek to document the *process* through which these provisions were transformed from, initially, instrumental *freedoms* which merely sought to *allow* natural and legal persons to take-up a cross-border economic activity into, also, sources of instrumental *rights* for natural persons; the second subsection will purport to explain how the personal market freedoms were interpreted before Maastricht, when an instrumental approach to their interpretation was adopted.

Before proceeding to the main analysis, one caveat should be inserted. This is that it is not the argument of this book that the personal market freedoms have become sources of rights only once and because the status of Union citizenship was introduced. Rather, the constitutionalisation of these provisions had been (implicitly) required by the Treaties and the broader (non-economic) aims, which had been set for European integration from the very beginning. Hence, although 'there was no *market* requirement for individual rights',[18] the incremental process of re-reading these provisions as sources of (instrumental, at first) rights, goes back as far as the 1960s and can be seen as one of the tools used for furthering the main aim of the EU, which has always been to achieve peace in Europe and a better life for all[19]—the ultimate goal of the EU which, according to Baquero Cruz, was hidden 'by the subsequent pragmatic stress on economic goals'.[20]

Having inserted the above caveat, it should, nonetheless, be noted that the introduction of Union citizenship has been immensely important in the process of constitutionalising the personal market freedoms and without it the (further) transformation of these provisions into sources of *fundamental* rights,[21] would probably not have taken place.[22] As will be seen in subsequent parts of this chapter, it is only after the introduction of this status that the Court took the further step of expanding the scope of application of the personal market freedoms to cover situations and measures which would not be covered had a purely internal market-based rationale still been applicable.

---

[18] W Maas (n 3) 6 (emphasis added).

[19] D Kochenov, 'The Citizenship Paradigm' (2012–13) 15 *Cambridge Yearbook of European Legal Studies* 196. For a similar view, see S O'Leary, 'Free Movement of Persons and Services' in P Craig and G de Búrca, *The Evolution of EU Law* 2nd edn (Oxford, Oxford University Press, 2011) 506. This is now reflected in Art 3(1) TEU.

[20] J Baquero Cruz, *Between Competition and Free Movement: The Economic Constitutional Law of the European Community* (Oxford, Hart Publishing, 2002) 44.

[21] Note, however, that other commentators—possibly relying on the wording used by the Court in its judgments—are of the view that the Court had interpreted the rights deriving from the personal market freedoms as fundamental rights even before the status of Union citizenship was introduced. See eg E Spaventa, *Free Movement of Persons in the European Union: Barriers to Movement in their Constitutional Context* (The Hague, Kluwer, 2007); W Maas (n 3) 21.

[22] P Oliver and W-H Roth, 'The Internal Market and the Four Freedoms' (2004) 41 *Common Market Law Review* 407, 439. According to Maas, 'Free movement rights for workers were first justified in terms of enabling the free movement of labor, and then as a measure to complete the single market. But they were extended and expanded even after the worker movement sufficient to support the common market had been achieved. This broadening of individual rights coincided with the introduction of European Union (EU) citizenship, which took over two decades to reach fruition'—W Maas (n 3) 29.

A. Personal Market Freedoms: From Instrumental Freedoms to Instrumental Rights

Through a series of landmark judgments in the second and third decades of the Community's existence, the Court of Justice put in place the foundations for a European (economic) constitution,[23] and signified that the Community was not intended to be merely an international organisation of the traditional kind, but was rather destined to have its own idiosyncratic character,[24] which would take the form of—as Alan Dashwood put it—a constitutional order of states.[25] This 'sui generis' nature of the EEC would mainly be reflected in the role that the individual would come to play in its development. In particular, by establishing the principles of direct effect[26] and supremacy,[27] and by ruling that fundamental (human) rights form part of the general principles of EEC law,[28] the ECJ 'had extracted and developed the constitutional seeds contained in the Treaty',[29] and placed the individual at the core of the process of EEC law-building and enforcement.[30] As Preuss has noted, 'to live under a constitution means the individual is not to be merely the object of domination but is to be recognized as a person vested with rights'.[31]

One important question that emerged in the very early years of the Community's existence was what the position of individuals was in its internal market policy. As already seen in chapter one, the EU started life as a rather modestly aimed Coal and Steel Community comprised of six western European States. Aiming at pulling together the coal and steel resources of the participating States and establishing a common market for these products, this Community appeared to have little place for individuals other than those who took part in the production

---

[23] For a discussion of the constitutionalisation of EU law see, inter alia, E Stein, 'Lawyers, Judges and the Making of a Transnational Constitution' (1981) 75 *American Journal of International Law* 1; GF Mancini, 'The Making of a Constitution for Europe' (1989) 26 *Common Market Law Review* 595; K Lenaerts, 'Constitutionalism and the Many Faces of Federalism' (1990) 38 *American Journal of Comparative Law* 205; J Temple Lang, 'The Development of European Community Constitutional Law' (1991) 25 *International Lawyer* 455; JHH Weiler, 'The Reformation of European Constitutionalism' (1997) 35 *Journal of Common Market Studies* 97; N Reich, 'A European Constitution for Citizens: Reflections on the Rethinking of Union and Community Law' (1997) 3 *European Law Journal* 131; P Craig, 'Constitutions, Constitutionalism, and the European Union' (2001) 7 *European Law Journal* 130.

[24] P Athanassiou and S Laulhé Shaelou, 'EU Accession from Within?—An Introduction' (2014) 33 *Yearbook of European Law* 335, 363–65.

[25] A Dashwood, 'The Limits of European Community Powers' (1996) 21 *European Law Review* 113, 114.

[26] Case 26/62 *Van Gend en Loos* [1963] ECR 13.

[27] Case 6/64 *Costa v ENEL* [1964] ECR 585.

[28] Case 29/69 *Stauder* [1969] ECR 419; Case 11/70 *Internationale Handelsgesellschaft* [1970] ECR 1125.

[29] J Baquero Cruz (n 20) 46.

[30] P Craig and G de Búrca, *EU Law: Text, Cases and Materials* (Oxford, Oxford University Press, 2011) 63. See, generally, JHH Weiler, 'The Transformation of Europe' (1991) 100 *Yale Law Journal* 2403; B de Witte, 'Direct Effect, Supremacy and the Nature of the Legal Order' in P Craig and G de Búrca (eds), *The Evolution of EU law* (Oxford, Oxford University Press, 1999).

[31] U Preuss, 'Constitutionalism—Meaning, Endangerment, Sustainability' in S Saberwal and H Sievers (eds), *Rules, Laws, Constitutions* (London, Sage Publications, 1998) 173–74.

and marketing process of coal and steel.[32] Moreover, as we saw in the same chapter, in the latter half of the 1950s, the same European States that formed the European Coal and Steel Community (ECSC), proceeded to sign the EEC Treaty, which had as its central aim to establish a 'common market'. The Treaty drafters recognised the important role that Member State nationals would come to play in the establishment and functioning of this market and, hence, made provision for them to be free to take-up an economic activity in the territory of another Member State or to initiate an economic activity that would be pursued in a cross-border context. For this purpose, the personal market freedoms were introduced into the EEC Treaty.

In the very early days of European integration, the personal market freedoms were simply viewed as 'instructions' given to the Member States as to what they should allow legal and natural persons to do in furtherance of the economic objectives of the—at the time—EEC; or, more precisely, as the binding provisions of a Treaty which limited the ability of Member States to act in ways that could impede the *freedom* of economic actors and corporations to initiate an economic activity that was going to be pursued in the territory of another Member State or in a cross-border context.[33] Accordingly, initially, it was not clear if Member State nationals (and corporations) could rely on these provisions and enforce them before their national courts. It was only certain that these provisions were enforceable by the EEC or the Member States themselves.[34]

Things began to change in the late 1960s, when a process of 'humanising' the market freedoms was initiated and successfully pursued, to the extent that certain commentators,[35] and, even, Commission officials,[36] started speaking about the emergence of 'European citizenship' or 'an incipient form of European citizenship', and the term 'Community citizen' made its first tentative appearance.[37]

---

[32] E Olsen, 'Work, Production, Free Movement and Then What? Conceptions of Citizenship in European Integration, 1951–1971', EUI Working Paper 2006/08, Department of Political and Social Sciences, San Domenico di Fiesole: European University Institute, available at cadmus.eui.eu/handle/1814/6405, pp 5–6. For some commentary on the provisions governing 'workers' in the ECSC Treaty, see W Maas (n 3) 12–17; M Condinanzi, A Lang and B Nascimbene, *Citizenship of the Union and Freedom of Movement of Persons* (The Hague, Martinus Nijhoff, 2008) 65–66.

[33] W Maas (n 3) 26.

[34] V Skouris, 'Fundamental Rights and Fundamental Freedoms: The Challenge of Striking a Delicate Balance' (2006) *European Business Law Review* 225, 227.

[35] See eg R Plender, 'An Incipient Form of European Citizenship' in FG Jacobs (ed), *European Law and the Individual* (Amsterdam, North Holland, 1976); A Durand, 'European Citizenship' (1979) 4 *European Law Review* 3; A Evans, 'European Citizenship' (1982) 45 *Maastricht Journal of European and Comparative Law* 497; A Evans, 'European Citizenship: A Novel Concept in EEC Law' (1984) 32 *American Journal of Comparative Law* 679. For a description of the (very) early stages of this process see W Maas (n 3) 17–22.

[36] See eg Commission Vice-President Sandri in 'Free Movement of Workers in the European Communities', Bull EC 11-1968, 5-vbb9. See also, the Tindemans Report (Report by Mr Leo Tindemans, Prime Minister of Belgium, to the European Council. Bulletin of the European Communities, Supplement 1/76).

[37] See eg Case 143/87 *Stanton* [1988] ECR 3877, para 13; Case C-370/90 *Singh* [1992] ECR I-4265, para 16. See also, the Opinion of AG Mancini in Case 238/83 *Meade* [1984] ECR 2631 and the Opinion of AG Lenz in Case 186/87 *Cowan* [1989] ECR 195. Moreover, this term was used in the 13th General Report on the Activities of the European Communities (1979), point 123.

68 *Citizenship and Persons Market Freedoms*

The process mainly consisted of the Court's rulings establishing the direct effect of the personal market freedoms,[38] which signified that these provisions were not simply sources of economic freedoms but they were also sources of *enforceable rights* for economic actors (whether these were legal or natural persons); and of a recognition in the Court's case-law as well as in secondary legislation in the area, that natural persons are human beings and that this needs to be taken into account when their situation—as factors of production—is governed by EU law.

The first important instrument that reflected the EEC's realisation that migrant economic actors are, also, human beings and must be treated as such, was Directive 64/221, which complemented all the personal market freedoms and which limited the restrictions Member States could impose on the exercise of the rights and freedoms derived from them.[39] As noted in *Rutili*,[40] some provisions of this Directive were specific expressions of the general principles enshrined in the European Convention on Human Rights (ECHR) and, hence, this is a first illustration of the ECJ's recognition that migrant economic actors—as human beings—are holders of human rights which must be protected and respected in situations that fall within the scope of EU law.

The most important instrument for our purposes, however, is Regulation 1612/68[41]—now repealed and replaced by Regulation 492/2011[42]—which governed the position of 'workers' and which had as its main aim to prohibit nationality discrimination with regards to access and pursuit of employment in the host State. It will be seen below that it is in the context of interpreting the provisions of this Regulation that the Court delivered some of its early 'proto-citizenship'[43] case-law.

As regards the self-employed, the main instrument was, initially, Directive 64/220[44] which was relatively soon repealed and replaced by Directive 73/148.[45] What is important for our purposes is that both the 1964 Directive and its successor made it clear that, although the text of Article 59 EEC (Article 56 TFEU) only made reference to service-providers, service-recipients—ie Member State

---

[38] Case 2/74 *Reyners* [1974] ECR 631 (establishment); Case 33/74 *Van Binsbergen* [1974] ECR 1299 (services); Case 167/73 *Commission v France* [1974] ECR 359 (workers).
[39] Dir 64/221 on the coordination of special measures concerning the movement and residence of foreign nationals which are justified on grounds of public policy, public security or public health [1964] OJ L56/50 (now repealed).
[40] Case 36/75 *Rutili* [1975] ECR 1219, para 32.
[41] Reg 1612/68 (n 13).
[42] Reg 492/2011(n 12).
[43] This term is borrowed from Jo Shaw—see J Shaw, 'Citizenship: Contrasting Dynamics at the Interface of Integration and Constitutionalism' in P Craig and G de Búrca (n 19) 584.
[44] Dir 64/220 on the abolition of restrictions on movement and residence within the Community for nationals of Member States with regard to establishment and the provision of services [1963-1964] Special Edition OJ 115.
[45] Dir 73/148 on the abolition of restrictions on movement and residence within the Community for nationals of Member States with regard to establishment and the provision of services [1973] OJ L172/14.

nationals who were not, strictly speaking, economic actors—were also covered by that provision and were, thus, equally entitled to rely on it.[46] Moreover, as made clear through the Court's case-law in the last few decades, Article 56 TFEU does not include within its scope merely the receipt of cross-border services *in a purely commercial context* (eg when both the provider and the recipient are parties to the transaction in their capacity as (respectively) active and passive, *economic actors*),[47] but it can, also, be relied on by individuals who wish to receive cross-border services in a more personal capacity as, simply, consumers (eg individuals who wish to move to another Member State to receive medical or tourist services or individuals who wish to receive online services (eg foreign language lessons) over the Internet).[48]

Apart from the above legislative measures, the ECJ has played an important role in the process of 'humanising' the personal market freedoms, and in their transformation into (also) sources of (secondary) personal rights for natural persons.[49]

This process initially involved an extension of the scope of application of the personal market freedoms (and of the accompanying secondary legislation) to cover migrant economic actors in situations where it did not appear that there was a *direct* impediment to the exercise of the primary (economic) right to take-up an economic activity pursued in the territory of another Member State or in a cross-border context.[50] More specifically, in a well-known body of case-law,[51] where the Court interpreted Article 7(2) of Regulation 1612/68,[52] which provided that migrant workers shall enjoy in the host State the same social and tax advantages as national workers, the Court noted that the contested refusal of such advantages in situations involving migrant workers and/or their family members would (directly) impede the smooth integration of the migrant worker (and his family) in the host State, to which they had moved permanently, which, in its turn, would, (indirectly) impede the worker's movement to that State for

---

[46] Art 1(1)(b) of Dir 64/220 (n 44); Art 1(b) of Dir 73/148 (n 45).
[47] See eg the facts in Case C-315/13 *De Clercq* ECLI:EU:C:2014:2408.
[48] See eg Joined Cases 286/82 & 26/83 *Luisi and Carbone* [1984] ECR 377.
[49] F Wollenschläger, 'A New Fundamental Freedom beyond Market Integration: Union Citizenship and its Dynamics for Shifting the Economic Paradigm of European Integration' (2011) 17 *European Law Journal* 1, 4–14. As Mancini submitted in the early 1990s, 'if it can be said to be a good thing that our Europe is not merely a Europe of commercial interests, it is the judges who must take much of the credit'—see GF Mancini, 'The Free Movement of Workers in the Case-Law of the Court of Justice' in D Curtin and D O'Keeffe (eds), *Constitutional Adjudication in EC and National Law. Essays in Honour of Justice T F O'Higgins* (Dublin, Butterworths, 1992) 67.
[50] For an analysis of this case-law see, inter alia, R Plender (n 35); D O'Keeffe, 'Equal Rights for Migrants: The Concept of Social Advantages in Article 7(2), Regulation 1612/68' (1985) 5 *Yearbook of European Law* 93; J Steiner, 'The Right to Welfare: Equality and Equity under Community law' (1985) 10 *European Law Review* 21, 35–39.
[51] There is a long list of such cases. See, inter alia, Case 32/75 *Cristini* [1975] ECR 1085; Case 63/76 *Inzirillo* [1976] ECR 2057; Case 65/81 *Reina* [1982] ECR 33; Case 152/82 *Forcheri* [1983] ECR 2323; Case 94/84 *Deak* [1985] ECR 1873; Case 59/85 *Reed* [1985] ECR 1283; Case C-237/94 *O'Flynn* [1996] ECR I-2617.
[52] Reg 1612/68 (n 13). This has now been replaced by Art 7(2) of Reg 492/2011 (n 12), which adopts exactly the same wording as its predecessor.

the purpose of taking-up an economic activity there. As explained by Craig and de Búrca, the ECJ

> was not willing to tolerate an EU in which migrant workers were treated as second-class citizens in the Member States where they worked. This would not only act as a disincentive to free movement, but was also fundamentally at odds with the very *raison d'être* of the EU.[53]

Hence, Member State nationals who moved to another Member State for an economic purpose should be able to rely on EU law to require the host Member State to extend to them benefits and entitlements, the availability of which was originally confined to its own nationals. The right to claim such benefits on an equal footing with the nationals of the host State was obviously a secondary right, which sought to ensure that the exercise of the primary (economic) right to move to another Member State for an economic purpose would not be impeded. Accordingly, in the 1970s, the Court began extending the material scope of the personal market freedoms, recognising the fact that migrant economic actors should also be viewed and treated as human beings and should, thus, be given certain personal (non-economic) secondary rights under EEC law.

In the 1980s and 1990s, on the other hand, it was the personal scope of these provisions that was broadened. As a result of that, it was no longer solely direct/active economic actors (ie workers (employed or self-employed) and service-providers) that were covered, but the rights derived from EEC law were extended to indirect economic actors (ie students studying in another Member State).[54] In addition, it was made clear that the free movement of workers provisions could be enforced not only by the persons who derived rights from them (ie workers) but also by persons who stood to benefit from the exercise of the rights stemming from them, ie employers.[55] Furthermore, during the same period the Court endorsed what was already provided in secondary legislation: that service-recipients (another category of passive economic actors) derive rights from the freedom to provide services and, in particular, the right to move to another Member State for the purpose of receiving a service or simply to receive a service across borders.[56]

The Court had also taken the further step of including such passive economic actors within the scope of EU law, even in situations where there was no link between what was claimed and the right that was exercised on the facts; and where the Member State national who had moved was present in the host State only temporarily and, hence, the contested national measure could not be considered capable of impeding his or her smooth integration into the society of the host State.

---

[53] P Craig and G de Búrca (n 30) 749.
[54] See Case 293/83 *Gravier* [1985] ECR 593.
[55] Case C-350/96 *Clean Car* [1998] ECR I-2521, paras 16–25, confirmed recently in Case C-474/12 *Schiebel Aircraft* ECLI:EU:C:2014:2139, paras 25–26.
[56] *Luisi and Carbone* (n 48). For an analysis, see paras 47–51 of the AG Opinion in Case C-221/11 *Demirkan* ECLI:EU:C:2013:583. For an (early) analysis of this step, see M Van der Woude and P Mead, 'Free Movement of the Tourist in Community Law' (1988) 25 *Common Market Law Review* 117. For a call for caution see AG Trabucchi in Case 118/75 *Watson and Belmann* [1976] ECR 1185, 1204.

The classic example of this is *Cowan*,[57] which involved a British tourist in France who was claiming compensation as a victim of a violent crime in that Member State, on the basis that such compensation was made available to French nationals who were also the victims of a violent crime, the perpetrator of which remained unidentified. It is obvious that nobody would seriously consider that someone would be deterred from going on a holiday to another Member State just because he is told that *in case* he is the victim of a violent crime there, he will be unable to claim compensation *in case* the perpetrator remains unidentified; this appears 'too remote'. Furthermore, Mr Cowan had moved to France only for a few days as a tourist, so it was not possible to argue that the discrimination complained of could impede his smooth integration into the society of that State which, in its turn, would be capable of impeding the exercise of his right to move to that Member State for an economic purpose (ie to receive tourist services). Accordingly, the contested measure in *Cowan* was not capable of restricting the (primary) right that had been exercised on the facts of the case: the right to move to another Member State for the purpose of receiving a service.

This, after all, appears to be the reason why the Court did not find a violation of the freedom to provide services provisions (which were the medium through which Mr Cowan was brought within the personal scope of EU law), but rather, ruled that it was Article 7 EEC (Article 18 TFEU) that was breached.[58] Because Mr Cowan had moved (temporarily) to another Member State as a service-recipient, the Court found that he was entitled to rely on a provision of the Treaty in order to stop the host Member State from discriminating against him on the ground of his nationality.[59]

It is not surprising, therefore, that *Cowan* has been viewed as the main (pre-Maastricht) judgment with a citizenship 'flavour', given that in this case the principle of non-discrimination (on the ground of nationality) was upgraded to a principle that had to be respected in its own right, and was not used instrumentally, in order to ensure that the achievement of the EEC's economic aims would not be impeded.[60]

Yet, it should be highlighted that in *Cowan*, as noted above, the Court did not find that there was a violation of the freedom to provide services provisions; in

---

[57] *Cowan* (n 37). See, also, Case C-45/93 *Commission v Spain (museum admission)* [1994] ECR I-911; Case C-164/07 *Wood* [2008] ECR I-4143. For comments see E Spaventa, 'Seeing the Wood despite the Trees? On the Scope of Union Citizenship and its Constitutional Effects' (2008) 45 *Common Market Law Review* 13, 33–34.

[58] S Weatherill, 'Annotation of *Cowan*' (1989) 26 *Common Market Law Review* 563, 565–68.

[59] It seems that AG Jacobs in paragraph 46 of his Opinion in Case C-168/91 *Konstantinidis* [1993] ECR I-1191, was largely inspired by the *Cowan* judgment, when he employed a similar mode of reasoning and transplanted it into a situation involving the violation of fundamental human rights in the host State. For a recent suggestion which appears to be quite similar (albeit with a somewhat different legal base), see paragraph 62 of the (joined) Opinion of AG Sharpston in Case C-456/12 *O and B* and in Case C-457/12 *S and G* ECLI:EU:C:2013:837.

[60] For more on this see A Tryfonidou, 'The Notions of "Restriction" and "Discrimination" in the Context of the Free Movement of Persons Provisions: From a Relationship of Interdependence to One of (Almost Complete) Independence' (2014) 33 *Yearbook of European Law* 385, 402–09.

other words, the Court's approach in this case demonstrates that a breach of Article 59 EEC (Article 56 TFEU) would only be found if the (discriminatory) refusal of the contested entitlement was shown to be capable of impeding the exercise of the right to move to another Member State for the purpose of receiving services. Accordingly, although *Cowan* is, clearly, a 'proto-citizenship' case for the reasons explained above, in it the Court had (rightly) not gone as far as to expand the material scope of the personal market freedoms to matters which are entirely unrelated to the exercise of free movement for an economic purpose. Hence, the case also confirmed the traditional reading of the personal market freedoms, according to which only rights which are necessary for enabling a Member State national to move for the purpose of taking-up an economic activity in another Member State or start pursuing (actively or passively) an economic activity in a cross-border context, can be derived from these provisions.

Accordingly, in the years that followed the establishment of the EEC there had not, merely, been a gradual erosion of the link between economic activity and the rights stemming from the Treaty, this culminating in the institutionalisation of the status of Union citizenship in 1993. There had also been a parallel—related—shift in perception away from viewing economically active Member State nationals as merely factors of production to also seeing them as individuals—as human beings—with personal rights which could be enforced against the host State and, on some occasions, even against their own Member State. Reflecting this, the personal market freedoms were progressively transformed from, merely, sources of the freedom, for natural and legal persons, to take-up an economic activity that was going to be pursued in another Member State or across borders into, also, sources of (primary, economic, and secondary, personal, non-economic) *rights* for natural persons.

However, when the Court recognised 'the humanity' of migrant economic actors and, as a result of that, granted them personal rights which seemed appropriate for enabling or encouraging them to exercise the primary economic rights stemming from these provisions, it did so only in order to ensure that the achievement of the internal market objectives of the Treaty would not be put in jeopardy; not out of any interest in granting genuine, fundamental, rights to them which would be protected and respected for their own sake. Accordingly, although—through the above developments—the personal market freedoms were reconceptualised as (also) sources of personal, non-economic, rights for Member State nationals, these rights were merely secondary, instrumental, rights, which were only granted in order to ensure that the primary rights stemming from these provisions would be freely exercised.[61] Moreover, the traditional interpretation of these

---

[61] As O'Leary has pointed out, '[t]his type of judicial creativity certainly points to the development of the social aspects of free movement, but in the last analysis, the cases generally demonstrate some sort of economic link (no matter how insignificant) and may be limited as future precedents on this basis'—S O'Leary, *The Evolving Concept of Community Citizenship: From the Free Movement of Persons to Union Citizenship* (The Hague, Kluwer, 1996) 70.

provisions—which will be described in the next subsection—demonstrated that the primary economic rights stemming from them (the right to take-up an economic activity in the territory of another Member State and the right to start pursuing an economic activity in a cross-border context) were purely instrumental to the aim of building an internal market and, hence, were not fundamental rights.

Therefore, the Court and the EEC legislature had developed a rudimentary form of European citizenship,[62] but one that was still attached to the economic aims of the Treaty and, as such, was merely a 'market citizenship'.[63] Under such a form of citizenship, Member State nationals were '"reached by" Community norms and legislation' only when '"acting as participants in or as beneficiaries of the common market"';[64] and the (primary and secondary) rights that they derived from EU law were instrumental to the achievement of the EU's economic aims and, hence, could not be characterised as fundamental rights.

The establishment of this rudimentary form of European citizenship is what had originally created the splintering in the material scope of the personal market freedoms that we are going to see in more detail in chapter six: natural persons would, now, derive from these provisions instrumental economic and non-economic *rights* as 'citizens' participating in the newly-created market, whilst legal persons continued to be merely afforded instrumental economic *freedoms*.

B. The Pre-Maastricht Interpretation of the Personal Market Freedoms

This subsection shall demonstrate how the personal market freedoms were interpreted prior to the introduction of the status of Union citizenship. Given that the book aims to examine how the interpretation of these provisions has been affected by the introduction of this status, what interests us the most, here, is the Court's fundamental rights-based approach towards these provisions which, it is argued,

---

[62] For a similar argument, see D O'Keeffe, 'Trends in the Free Movement of Persons within the European Communities' in J O'Reilly (ed), *Human Rights and Constitutional law: Essays in Honour of Brian Walsh* (Dublin, The Round Hall Press, 1992) 267–74; S O'Leary, ibid, 81.

[63] See M Everson, 'The Legacy of the Market Citizen' in J Shaw and G More (eds), *New Legal Dynamics of European Union* (Oxford, Clarendon Press, 1995). Niamh Nic Shuibhne and Charlotte O'Brien consider that market citizenship is still the only form that EU citizenship has taken (see N Nic Shuibhne, 'The Resilience of Market Citizenship' (2010) 47 *Common Market Law Review* 1597 and C O'Brien, 'I Trade, Therefore I am: Legal Personhood in the European Union' (2013) 50 *Common Market Law Review* 1643), whilst Kochenov and Plender are of the view that this was the case until recently, but as a result of a number of developments in the Court's jurisprudence in recent years it can now be said that the first steps for building a meaningful status of Union citizenship detached from any economic and free movement considerations, have now been taken (see D Kochenov and R Plender, 'EU Citizenship: From an Incipient Form to an Incipient Substance? The Discovery of the Treaty Text' (2012) 37 *European Law Review* 369). For a commentator who considers that the EU is, still, essentially an economic organisation and that 'the "internal market" rules on free movement are above all *market making*', see V Hatzopoulos, 'Turkish Service Recipients under the EU-Turkey Association Agreement: Demirkan' (2014) 51 *Common Market Law Review* 647, 658.

[64] M Everson (n 63) 73.

has only been adopted following the establishment of this status. Nonetheless, a meaningful understanding of the latter approach cannot be attained without a prior description of the pre-Maastricht, instrumental, approach of the Court, which will enable us to draw a comparison between the two. For this reason—and due to the fact that space precludes a more detailed analysis—this subsection will merely seek to provide a *basic* explanation of the Court's instrumental approach to the interpretation of these provisions.

It would, perhaps, be useful at this point to explain the relationship between the instrumental and fundamental rights-based readings of the personal market freedoms. There is clearly some overlap as regards the cases that fall under these two approaches, since a situation which falls within the scope of these provisions when an instrumental reading is employed would, in all instances, also fall within their scope under a fundamental rights-based reading. In fact, most of the case-law appears to be in line with both of these readings and, for this reason, it is not analysed in this book. Accordingly, in order to highlight the differences between these two readings, cases that can be explained under *only one* of them, shall be used as examples. Hence, in this section, which aims to describe the instrumental reading of the personal market freedoms, the cases that will be mentioned will be cases where the Court excluded from the scope of application of these provisions a situation which, with hindsight (taking into account the Court's post-Maastricht case-law), would be included under a fundamental rights-based reading. In the next section, on the other hand, the focus will be on case-law which involved situations which would not be included within the scope of these provisions if a purely instrumental reading was adopted.

The analysis will revolve around the two basic elements that together constitute the positive scope of the personal market freedoms: their personal scope (*ratione personae*) and their material scope (*ratione materiae*).

In order to answer the question of *who* derives freedoms and rights from the personal market freedoms (ie what is their scope *ratione personae*), one needs to look at the relevant Treaty provision(s) *and* the Court's case-law where different aspects of the meaning of the terms that make up the personal scope of each provision have been clarified in a piecemeal fashion. Their personal scope is, exactly, what differentiates the various personal market freedoms from each other and what determines which one is applicable to any particular factual scenario, given that the Court appears to have increasingly adopted a common approach as regards the other main element that makes up their positive scope (ie the material scope).[65] The material scope of a provision, on the other hand, refers to *what* is

---

[65] Case 48/75 *Royer* [1976] ECR 497, para 12; Case C-106/91 *Ramrath* [1992] ECR I-3351; Case C-55/94 *Gebhard* [1995] ECR I-4165; Opinion of AG Lenz in Case C-415/93 *Bosman* [1995] ECR I-4921, para 165. For comments see M Condinanzi et al (n 32) 22 and 131; P Caro de Sousa, 'Quest for the Holy Grail—Is a Unified Approach to the Market Freedoms and European Citizenship Justified?' (2014) 20 *European Law Journal* 499, 504–05. For a criticism of the fact that the same approach is followed in the context of the free movement of workers and establishment, on the one hand, and the free movement of services, on the other, see L Daniele, 'Non-Discriminatory Restrictions to the Free Movement of Persons' (1997) 22 *European Law Review* 191.

covered by that provision; on what kinds of activities or situations that provision can have an impact. Moreover, when a provision is a source of rights, it also refers to the list of rights that derive from it.

The basic principles governing the personal scope of the personal market freedoms were mainly laid down by the Court in its judgments that were delivered prior to the coming into force of the Treaty of Maastricht. Accordingly, in the next few paragraphs, I will briefly describe these basic principles. It should be noted that these principles are still applicable given that—as will be explained in the next section—the Court's post-Maastricht approach to the delimitation of the personal scope of these provisions is a linear continuation of its pre-Maastricht approach.

The Court had early on claimed a hermeneutic monopoly over the term 'worker',[66] holding that this is someone who is a Member State national[67] and who 'for a certain period of time' 'performs services for and under the direction of another person in return for which he receives remuneration'.[68] In the late 1970s, it was also established that the requisite cross-border element must be present in order for the situation to come within the scope of (what is now) Article 45 TFEU,[69] though this is an issue that mainly concerns the material scope of the relevant provision; the same cross-border requirement applies for (what are now) Articles 49[70] and 56[71] TFEU.

What distinguishes a worker from a service-provider or a person who falls within the personal scope of Article 49 TFEU is, exactly, the fact that the former is an *employed* person (ie there must be a relationship of subordination),[72] whereas the latter two are self-employed. Articles 45 and 49 TFEU govern, respectively, the rights of the employed (and, indirectly, of their employers, who, as noted earlier, can invoke Article 45 TFEU) and of the self-employed who have taken up and pursued an economic activity in the territory of another Member State or in a cross-border context on a *permanent* basis. Conversely, Article 56 TFEU aims to, inter alia, protect the rights of the self-employed who provide services across borders or in the territory of another Member State on a temporary basis; and, as we saw, the rights of those who move to receive services or who receive services across borders.[73]

The definition of establishment has given rise to less case-law than the free movement of workers.[74] In *Factortame*, the Court defined establishment as 'the actual pursuit of an economic activity through a fixed establishment in another

---

[66] Case 75/63 *Hoekstra* [1964] ECR 1771.
[67] *Meade* (n 37).
[68] Case 66/85 *Lawrie-Blum* [1986] ECR 2121, para 17. For the Court's broad approach to the meaning of remuneration, see Case 196/87 *Steymann* [1988] ECR 6159.
[69] Case 175/78 *Saunders* [1979] ECR 1129.
[70] Joined Cases C-54 & 91/88 and 14/89 *Niño* [1990] ECR 3537.
[71] Case 52/79 *Debauve* [1980] ECR 833.
[72] Case 337/97 *Meeusen* [1999] ECR 1-3289;Case C-268/99 *Jany* [2001] ECR I-8615.
[73] *Gebhard* (n 65), especially paras 25–27.
[74] RCA White, *Workers, Establishment, and Services in the European Union* (Oxford, Oxford University Press, 2004) 36.

Member State for an indefinite period';[75] and Advocate General Darmon in his Opinion in the *Daily Mail* case stressed that 'establishment means integration into a national economy'.[76] Article 49 TFEU governs the freedom of establishment of both natural and legal persons, and covers both primary establishment, where all links are severed with the home State and there is only one establishment in the EU,[77] and secondary establishment, where legal or natural persons maintain their establishment in their home State and, thus, pursue a self-employed economic activity on a permanent basis in both their home and host States.[78]

As regards services, although the wording of Article 56 TFEU (like the wording of its predecessors) focuses on the freedom of the self-employed to move to a Member State other than that of their establishment for the purpose of providing their services there temporarily,[79] it has been made clear through the Court's case-law that this provision covers a number of different situations.[80] Hence, it applies, also, where a person moves to another Member State in order to receive services;[81] where the recipient and the provider reside in the same Member State but have both moved to another Member State (temporarily) where the service is provided;[82] as well as to situations where neither the provider nor the recipient of the service moves, but the service itself is provided across borders.[83] Article 57 TFEU provides that a service is a 'service' for the purposes of Article 56 TFEU, if it is provided for remuneration and is not covered by the other provisions of the Treaty governing free movement.

Moving on to the material scope of the personal market freedoms, when viewed purely instrumentally, these provisions appear to be, mainly, considered as sources of the freedom (legal persons) or primary right (natural persons) to move for the purpose of taking-up an economic activity that is going to be pursued permanently in the territory of another Member State or in a cross-border context (workers and establishment); and the freedom or primary right to either move temporarily to another Member State to provide or receive services or to start providing or receiving services temporarily across borders, where the emphasis is placed on the free movement of services as such (services).[84]

The nature of the freedom to provide services is such that it seeks to ensure that whilst the economic base of the economic actor remains the same (eg (s)he maintains his/her establishment in the home State), either the location of the economic

---

[75] Case C-221/89 *Factortame* [1991] ECR I-3905.
[76] Section 3 of the Opinion of AG Darmon in Case 81/87 *Daily Mail* [1988] ECR 5500.
[77] See eg *Gebhard* (n 65).
[78] See eg Case 107/83 *Klopp* [1984] ECR 2971.
[79] See eg *Van Binsbergen* (n 38).
[80] J Snell, *Goods and Services in EU Law: A Study of the Relationship between the Freedoms* (Oxford, Oxford University Press, 2002) 16–17.
[81] *Luisi and Carbone* (n 48).
[82] Case C-154/89 *Commission v France (Tourist Guides)* [1991] ECR I-659.
[83] Case 15/78 *Koestler* [1978] ECR 1971; Case C-384/93 *Alpine Investments* [1995] ECR I-1141.
[84] This view was clearly held by early commentators—see eg A Evans, 'European Citizenship: A Novel Concept in EEC Law (n 35) 690.

activity changes *temporarily* (eg when the service-provider moves to another Member State to provide a service) or the mode of pursuit of the economic activity changes (from the service being provided in a purely domestic context to being provided across borders). Hence, what these provisions seek to ensure is that economic actors can maintain their economic base in their home State whilst services can be provided across borders.

This is reflected in the Court's traditional approach to the material scope of the services provisions and is obvious from *Koestler*,[85] where a German national who had originally been receiving banking services from a French bank whilst residing in France (a purely internal situation for the purposes of these provisions), subsequently moved back to Germany from where he continued to receive the said services. What brought the situation within the scope of Article 59 EEC (Article 56 TFEU) was the fact that from the moment that Mr Koestler had moved back to his State of origin, the said services had begun to be provided across borders. In other words, there was no change in the location of the economic activity (the bank maintained the base of its economic activity in France and continued providing the service *from* its premises in France) but there was, rather, a change in the mode of its pursuit (from initially a purely internal context to a cross-border one), and this sufficed for bringing the situation within the scope of that provision.[86]

The material scope of the more stationary market freedoms (ie workers and establishment) has, nonetheless, traditionally been delimited differently. The aim of these provisions has, traditionally, been considered to be to enable Member State nationals to take up economic activities *in another Member State*, which would then be *permanently* pursued there or in a cross-border context. Hence, unlike the freedom to provide services provisions, these market freedoms have traditionally required a transfer of the economic base of the economic actor and, with it, a change in the location of the economic activity.

This was made clear in *Werner*.[87] In that case, the applicant was a German national who had studied in Germany and had always pursued a self-employed activity in that Member State. At one point, however, he decided to move to the Netherlands where he set up his residence, whilst continuing to work permanently in a self-employed capacity in Germany; in other words, he was a 'reverse frontier worker'.[88] The case arose when he sought to challenge the German taxation regime

---

[85] *Koestler* (n 83).

[86] Moreover, in *Van Binsbergen* (n 38), a Dutch lawyer who had moved his residence *and establishment* to Belgium (ie unlike in *Koestler*, there was a change in the economic base of the economic actor), relied on the freedom to provide services provisions in order to require his State of nationality to allow him to continue to provide his services to persons in the Netherlands whilst maintaining his (new) economic and residence base in Belgium. The Dutch law that was challenged was a requirement that lawyers must be *habitually resident* in the Netherlands in order to provide their services and it was considered that this was capable of impeding the right of Member State nationals to provide services in the territory of another Member State.

[87] Case C-112/91 *Werner* [1993] ECR I-429.

[88] The term is taken from C O'Brien, 'Annotation of *Hartmann, Geven* and *Hendrix*' (2008) 45 Common Market Law Review 499.

which treated him worse than he would have been treated had he maintained his residence in Germany; and, for this purpose, he relied on Article 52 EEC (Article 49 TFEU).

The Court stressed that the only factor that took Mr Werner's situation out of a purely national context was that he lived in a Member State other than that in which he practised his profession and this did not suffice for bringing the situation within the scope of Article 52 EEC (Article 49 TFEU), in the absence of a change in the location of the economic activity. Despite the fact that Mr Werner was self-employed on a permanent basis in his State of nationality whilst he resided in the territory of another Member State and, thus, the economic activity had begun to be pursued in a cross-border context from the moment that he moved to another Member State *to take up residence*, the situation was excluded from the scope of that provision, because there was no prior exercise of the right to move to another Member State *for the purpose of taking up* an economic activity there.

Frontier workers, on the other hand—ie Member State nationals who have taken up an *economic activity in another Member State* whilst they have *maintained their residence* in their State of nationality—have, always, been included within the scope of the more stationary personal market freedoms, since their situation does involve the *initiation of an economic activity in another Member State* and, thus, there is a change in the location of the economic activity and the economic base of the economic actor.[89] Their only difference from classic workers is that they have maintained their residence in their State of origin and thus they pursue an economic activity in a cross-border context, but that—in itself—does not preclude the application of the above provisions.

The Court's pre-Maastricht jurisprudence, therefore, demonstrated that in order for the more stationary personal market freedoms to apply, there was, traditionally, a need in all instances for a change in the location of an economic activity and the economic base of the economic actor. Hence, the only primary right that was traditionally considered to be stemming from these provisions was the economic right to move to another Member State for the purpose of taking up an economic activity there that would be pursued permanently there or in a cross-border context.

The case-law prior to Maastricht also demonstrates that, traditionally, there was a requirement of cross-border specificity, in order for a situation to be included within the material scope of personal market freedoms. Accordingly, if national measures limited the freedom of economic actors or agents to take-up and/or pursue an economic activity in the territory of another Member State/in a cross-border context, in the same manner that this was limited in a purely internal context, this did not, traditionally, suffice for a finding that there was a restriction caught by these provisions. This is obvious from cases where the Court held that genuinely non-discriminatory measures (even those which limited in some way

---

[89] Case 152/73 *Sotgiu* [1974] ECR 153; Case C-379/93 *Schumacker* [1995] ECR I-225; Case C-18/95 *Terhoeve* [1999] ECR I-345; Case C-182/06 *Lakebrink* [2007] ECR I-6705.

the economic freedom of economic actors and agents) escaped the ambit of the personal market freedoms and did not have to be justified.[90] It will be explained in more detail in the next section (and in subsequent chapters), why the requirement of cross-border specificity is reflective of an instrumental reading of the personal market freedoms and, therefore, in order to avoid repetition, this will not be analysed here.

Accordingly, as a general conclusion, it can be noted that by 1993, the personal market freedoms had been transformed from, originally, merely sources of freedoms for legal and natural persons to, also, sources of *rights* for the latter. Nonetheless, the way that these provisions were interpreted before Maastricht shows that only primary (economic) and secondary (non-economic) rights, the exercise of which would contribute to the aim of building an internal market were originally derived from these provisions. Hence, it seems that these rights were not fundamental rights but were merely instrumental rights, granted to Member State nationals in order to ensure that the economic objectives of the EEC would be attained.

IV. THE COURT'S POST-MAASTRICHT CASE-LAW:
(RE-)READING THE PERSONAL MARKET FREEDOMS
IN THE LIGHT OF UNION CITIZENSHIP

We turn, now, to the most significant part of this chapter: the section that will set to explore what has been the impact of Union citizenship on the interpretation of the personal market freedoms.

Although, as was noted in the previous section, since the 1960s, the interpretation of the personal market freedoms had begun to reflect their gradual reconceptualisation as (also) sources of (instrumental) *rights* for Member State nationals, in this section, it will be argued that their further transformation into

---

[90] See eg *Koestler* (n 83); Case 221/85 *Commission v Belgium* [1987] ECR 719; Case 198/86 *Conradi* [1987] ECR 4469. This requirement seems to have been imposed even in some of the Court's post-Maastricht case-law—see eg Case C-70/95 *Sodemare* [1997] ECR I-3395, para 33. The imposition of a cross-border specificity requirement in this (post-Maastricht) case may be attributable to the fact that the contested legislation appeared in all instances merely capable of limiting the *freedoms* that legal persons derive from Art 49 TFEU (and could under no circumstances limit the *rights* of Union citizens). Moreover, the Court may have wished (like it does in the area of direct taxation) to maintain a requirement of cross-border specificity in this context (the system of social welfare of a Member State), given the sensitivity of this area from the point of view of the Member States. Other areas where there is, still, a requirement of cross-border specificity in order for a restriction to be found are the areas of direct taxation and social security—for comments (and for the rationale behind this) see E Spaventa (n 21) 71–73; A Tryfonidou, 'The Federal Implications of the Transformation of the Market Freedoms into Sources of Rights for the Union Citizen' in D Kochenov (ed), *Citizenship and Federalism in Europe* (Cambridge, Cambridge University Press, 2016, forthcoming). It should be noted that some commentators are of a different view, considering that throughout the 1980s the personal market freedoms were being applied to non-discriminatory measures under the cover of a discrimination test—see, for instance, the analysis in P Caro de Sousa, *The European Fundamental Freedoms: A Contextual Approach* (Oxford, Oxford University Press, 2015).

sources of *fundamental* rights only emerged once the status of Union citizenship was introduced and developed. In other words, it is only post-Maastricht and following the introduction of this status, that the Court extended the material scope of these provisions, firstly, by covering situations which would have been excluded under a purely instrumental reading of them and, secondly, by providing for rights which would not be read as stemming from these provisions under such a reading.

A central question, therefore, is what are the exact rights that Union citizens can now (ie post-Maastricht) derive from these provisions. Apart from this question, which will be dealt with in subsections C and D, the latter subsections will also explain why the most plausible normative explanation for the Court's post-Maastricht case-law, where it has departed from its traditional, instrumental, approach to the interpretation of the personal market freedoms, is that it has been determined to re-read these provisions in the light of Union citizenship. Subsection A will present the (handful of) instances where the Court *explicitly* recognised the need to re-interpret the personal market freedoms and the rights stemming from them in the light of Union citizenship; whilst subsection B will explain that the introduction of Union citizenship has not effected any significant change in the delimitation of the personal scope of these provisions, given that this had, already, been generously delimited in the Court's pre-Maastricht jurisprudence.

A. The Court's Explicit Recognition of the Need to (Re-)Read the Personal Market Freedoms in the Light of Union Citizenship

It seems to have been inevitable that the establishment of Union citizenship would sooner or later have an impact on the interpretation of the personal market freedoms and would require a reassessment of certain aspects of the Court's case-law in this area. Therefore, it was no surprise that the Court in 2004, in the case of *Collins*,[91] expressly noted that when interpreting these provisions, the status of the applicant as a Union citizen should be taken into account, thereby (explicitly) mainstreaming the demands of EU citizenship in the interpretation of these provisions.

The case concerned a dual Irish-US citizen who applied for UK Jobseeker's Allowance whilst looking for a job in the UK. In its judgment, the Court recalled that in *Lebon* and *Commission v Belgium*,[92] it was held that jobseekers are only entitled to rely on the principle of non-discrimination on the grounds of nationality as regards *access* to employment in the host State and not, also, as regards social and tax advantages within the meaning of Article 7(2) of Regulation 1612/68.[93]

---

[91] Case C-138/02 *Collins* [2004] ECR I-2703.
[92] Case 316/85 *Lebon* [1987] ECR 2811; Case C-278/94 *Commission v Belgium (tideover benefits)* [1996] ECR I-4307.
[93] *Collins* (n 91), para 58.

On this basis, Collins—not being a fully-fledged 'worker'—would not be entitled to the Jobseeker's Allowance.

However, the Court continued its analysis and went on to explain that the above rulings should be reconsidered in the light of Union citizenship and, in particular, in the light of *Grzelczyk*[94] and the principles established therein. In particular, the Court noted:

> In view of the establishment of citizenship of the Union and the interpretation in the case-law of the right to equal treatment enjoyed by citizens of the Union, it is no longer possible to exclude from the scope of 48(2) of the Treaty ... a benefit of a financial nature intended to facilitate access to employment in the labour market of a Member State.[95]

The Court, then, continued to explain that '[t]he interpretation of the scope of the principle of equal treatment in relation to access to employment must reflect this development, as compared with the interpretation followed in *Lebon* and *Commission v Belgium*'.[96] As a result, the Court held that a person such as Collins—a 'citizen-worker'[97]—could rely on Article 6 EC (Article 18 TFEU), to require the UK to refrain from using an (indirectly) discriminatory requirement such as habitual residence, for the purpose of determining whether it should grant the allowance applied for, unless, of course, this could be justified by a non-economic ground, such as the need to restrict the availability of the allowance only to persons who have a real link with its employment market. Very similar reasoning—including the need to take into account the establishment of Union citizenship—was applied the subsequent year in the case of *Ioannidis*[98] and, more recently, in *Vatsouras and Koupatantze*.[99]

The Court also used the introduction of Union citizenship as a justification for its decision to increase the areas of national competence that can come under EU scrutiny; this was done, mainly, through the Court's citizenship jurisprudence but it can, obviously, also affect the areas which can be subjected to scrutiny under the personal market freedoms. An example of this can be seen in *Grzelczyk*[100] (and confirmed in *Bidar*),[101] where the Court noted that, although it had previously—in the *Brown* case[102]—held that assistance given to (economically inactive) students for maintenance and training fell outside the scope of EU law:

> However, since *Brown*, the Treaty on European Union has introduced citizenship of the European Union into the EC Treaty and added to Title VIII of part Three a new chapter 3 devoted to education and vocational training. There is nothing in the amended text of

---

[94] Case C-184/99 *Grzelczyk* [2001] ECR I-6193.
[95] *Collins* (n 91), para 63.
[96] ibid, para 64.
[97] The term is taken from N Nic Shuibhne, *The Coherence of EU Free Movement Law: Constitutional Responsibility and the Court of Justice* (Oxford, Oxford University Press, 2013) 75–76.
[98] Case C-258/04 *Ioannidis* [2005] ECR I-8275, para 22.
[99] Joined Cases C-22 & 23/08 *Vatsouras and Koupatantze* [2009] ECR I-4585, para 37.
[100] *Grzelczyk* (n 94).
[101] Case C-209/03 *Bidar* [2005] ECR I-2119, para 39.
[102] Case 197/86 *Brown* [1988] ECR 3205.

the Treaty to suggest that students who are citizens of the Union, when they move to another Member State to study there, lose the rights which the Treaty confers on citizens of the Union.[103]

In addition, the effect that the introduction of Union citizenship should have on the interpretation of the derogations from the personal market freedoms, was acknowledged by the Court in *Orfanopoulos and Oliveri*,[104] which was delivered one month after the ruling in *Collins*. There, the Court pointed out that 'a particularly restrictive interpretation of the derogations from [the freedom of movement for workers] is required by virtue of a person's status as a citizen of the Union'.[105] Based on that, the Court held that national legislation that required the *automatic* expulsion of nationals of other Member States who had received certain sentences for specific offences, could not be justified on the grounds of public policy; their individual situation should be examined by the national authorities before a decision regarding their expulsion could be made.

Reflecting on the Court's approach in the above cases, Judge Timmermans (writing extra-judicially) noted a 'kind of spill-over effect' in the case-law, 'the newly created Union citizen rights appearing able to permeate the interpretation of the scope of the other, economic rights of free movement under the EC Treaty'.[106]

B. Scope *Ratione Personae*

As we saw in the previous chapter, even before the introduction of Union citizenship in 1993, the personal scope of free movement law had been broadened, via the 1990 Residence Directives,[107] to encompass economically inactive Member State nationals who were financially self-sufficient. The creation of Union citizenship was not entirely unimportant, however. In particular, the introduction of this new status was significant in that *primary law* now brought within the personal scope of EU law persons that were not contributing to the economic aims of the Treaty in any way.[108] As the Court noted in *Baumbast*,

> the Treaty does not require that citizens of the Union pursue a professional or trade activity, whether as an employed or self-employed person, in order to enjoy the rights provided in Part Two of the EC Treaty on citizenship of the Union.[109]

---

[103] *Grzelczyk* (n 94), para 35.
[104] Joined Cases C-482/01 and C-493/01 *Orfanopoulos and Oliveri* [2004] ECR I-5257.
[105] ibid, para 65.
[106] C Timmermans, '*Martínez Sala* and *Baumbast* revisited' in M Poiares Maduro and L Azoulai (eds), *The Past and Future of EU Law: The Classics of EU Law Revisited on the 50th Anniversary of the Rome Treaty* (Oxford, Hart Publishing, 2010) 353.
[107] Dir 90/364 on the right of residence [1990] OJ L180/26; Dir 90/365 on the right of residence for employees and self-employed persons who have ceased their occupational activity [1990] OJ L180/28; Dir 93/96 on the right of residence for students [1993] OJ L317/59 ('1990 Residence Directives').
[108] N Nic Shuibhne (n 97) 145.
[109] Case C-413/99 *Baumbast* [2002] ECR I-7091, para 83.

Accordingly, since Maastricht, the personal scope of free movement law is based on (what is seemingly) a clear-cut distinction: the personal market freedoms cover economically active Union citizens who have exercised or wish to exercise the rights stemming from these provisions, whereas the economically inactive can derive rights from the citizenship provisions of the Treaty.

The introduction of Union citizenship and its development via the Court's jurisprudence does not appear to have effected any major change in the delimitation of the scope *ratione personae* of the personal market freedoms. Rather, as noted in the previous section, the Court's post-Maastricht approach to this matter appears to be a linear continuation of what its position was before 1993. In particular, in its post-Maastricht jurisprudence, the Court built on what was already a very broadly-framed personal scope for these provisions and further diluted the notion of an economic activity and the need to participate *actively* in an economic activity of some sort, in order for someone to come within the personal scope of these provisions.[110]

Hence, in the early 1980s, the Court held that part-time workers can be 'workers' within the meaning of Article 45 TFEU,[111] and this is so even if they earn less than the necessary minimum and have to supplement their income by having recourse to private funds[112] or social assistance from public benefits.[113] The Court had also recognised that jobseekers have a quasi-worker status and so can come within the personal scope of Article 45 TFEU;[114] this was necessary in order to ensure the *effet utile* of this right.[115] Moreover, the requirement of remuneration—which is applicable in all the personal market freedoms in order to establish that an activity is 'economic'—was read very broadly to include anything which is money's worth, including food and lodging.[116] In addition, although 'the activity must not be provided for nothing', there is no need for the economic actor 'to be seeking to make a profit'.[117]

In the context of the freedom to provide services provisions, the Court held that the remuneration does not need to come from the person who has actually received the service, but it suffices if it comes from somewhere else.[118] Nevertheless, the requirement of remuneration (of some kind) needs always to be satisfied and, hence, services of a non-economic nature, such as those provided by the

---

[110] For an early discussion of this, see P Leleux, 'Recent Decisions of the Court of Justice in the Field of Free Movement of Persons and Free Supply of Services' in FG Jacobs (ed), *European Law and the Individual* (Amsterdam, North-Holland, 1976) 81–82.
[111] Case 53/81 *Levin* [1982] ECR 1035.
[112] ibid.
[113] Case 139/85 *Kempf* [1986] ECR 1741.
[114] *Antonissen* (n 7).
[115] *Royer* (n 65).
[116] *Steymann* (n 68).
[117] Case C-281/06 *Jundt* [2007] ECR I-12231, para 32.
[118] Case 300/84 *Van Roosmalen* [1986] ECR 3097; Case 352/85 *Bond van Adverteerters* [1988] ECR 2085.

State free of charge in fulfilment of its duties towards its own population, have traditionally been excluded from the ambit of the personal market freedoms.[119] Furthermore, as seen in the previous section, the Court in the 1980s confirmed that—as was already clear in secondary legislation—service-recipients directly derive from the freedom to provide services provisions the right to receive services across borders.[120] This created the potential for a very broad personal scope of these provisions—and, through them, of EEC (and then EC, and now EU) law— and this is especially so now during the Internet era, as virtually everyone appears to be a recipient of cross-border services.

As regards the nature of the activity pursued, the Court had adopted an equally broad approach in the context of all the personal market freedoms, whereby it simply required that the activity must be 'effective and genuine', 'to the exclusion of activities on such a small scale as to be regarded as purely marginal and ancillary'.[121] Moreover, the reason why the economic actor is engaged in the economic activity had relatively early on been considered immaterial,[122] and, as made clear post-Maastricht, even if (s)he has exercised the rights stemming from the personal market freedoms merely in order to bring his or her situation within the scope of EU law and to benefit from the more beneficial treatment offered by it (than by national law), this does not constitute an abuse of Treaty rights.[123]

This expansionary trend in the delimitation of the personal scope of the personal market freedoms, continued unabated post-Maastricht. An obvious example of this is the ECJ's cross-border healthcare case-law,[124] where the Court noted that Union citizens who move to another Member State to receive healthcare services, fall within the scope of Article 56 TFEU, and this is so despite the fact that they seek reimbursement for their costs (ie for the remuneration they provided to the healthcare provider in the host State) from their Member State of origin. This appears to contradict the Court's case-law on education, where it was held that the provision of State-funded education is not an economic activity and, hence, is not covered by Article 56 TFEU.[125] In its case-law, the Court held that the requirement of prior authorisation for reimbursement by the home State in respect of healthcare services received in other Member States (always) constitutes a barrier

---

[119] Case 263/86 *Humbel* [1988] ECR 5365.
[120] *Luisi and Carbone* (n 48).
[121] *Levin* (n 111).
[122] ibid. See, however, Case 344/87 *Bettray* [1989] ECR 1621.
[123] Case C-212/96 *Centros* [1999] ECR I-1459; Case C-109/01 *Akrich* [2003] ECR I-9607.
[124] See, inter alia, Case C-158/96 *Kohll* [1998] ECR I-1931; Case C-368/98 *Vanbraekel* [2001] ECR I-5473; Case C-157/99 *Geraets Smits and Peerbooms* [2001] ECR I-5473; Case C-358/99 *Müller Fauré* [2003] ECR I-4509; Case C-56/01 *Inizan* [2003] ECR I-12403; Case C-372/04 *Watts* [2006] ECR I-4325; Case C-173/09 *Elchinov* [2010] ECR I-8889; Case C-268/13 *Petru* ECLI:EU:C:2014:2271.
[125] *Humbel* (n 119). For a criticism of the Court's failure to reconcile these two lines of case-law, see A Kaczorowska, 'A Review of the Creation by the European Court of Justice of the Right to Effective and Speedy Medical Treatment and its Outcomes' (2006) 12 *European Law Journal* 345, 351–53; E Spaventa (n 21) 54–58. See, also, the Opinion of AG Ruiz-Jarabo Colomer in *Geraets Smits and Peerbooms* (n 124).

to the receipt of such services, and is, thus, contrary to Article 56 TFEU, unless justified.[126]

Other post-Maastricht examples of overstretching the personal scope of the personal market freedoms and/or of the accompanying secondary legislation, are the 'sister' cases of *Ibrahim*[127] and *Teixeira*,[128] where the Court—building on the already very generous regime developed for the children of migrant (or former migrant) workers[129]—held that the children of *former* migrant workers can continue residing in the host State by virtue of Article 12 of Regulation 1612/68[130] (which is now Article 10 of Regulation 492/2011[131]) as can their primary carer, *and* this right continues to exist even though the children and the primary carer are not financially self-sufficient and need to have recourse to the social assistance system of the host State. Because—as the Court noted—these were cases which involved the children of *former* migrant *workers* who, thus, fell within the scope of the freedom of movement of workers provisions, the self-sufficiency conditions applicable to economically inactive persons could not be applied, in this way drawing an illogical distinction between Union citizens who can point to a (very) remote economic element, as in *Ibrahim* and *Teixeira*, and those Union citizens who cannot and who, therefore, need to satisfy the above conditions.[132] The injustice of the situation has been further enhanced as a result of the Court's pronouncement in the subsequent case of *Czop*,[133] that Article 12 of Regulation 1612/68 was not applicable to the children of self-employed persons, and thus the rights stemming from that provision could not be extended to children whose parents were economically active but *happened* to be self-employed.

Accordingly, although the distinction between Union citizens who are involved in an economic activity and those who are not still exists in theory, in practice, the lines have been blurred to the extent that it is very difficult to find any coherence in

---

[126] For literature on the Court's healthcare case-law see, inter alia, AP Van der Mei, 'Cross-border Access to Health Care within the European Union: Some Reflections on *Geraets Smits and Peerbooms* and *Vanbraekel*' (2002) 9 *Maastricht Journal of European and Comparative Law* 189; C Newdick, 'Citizenship, Free Movement and Health Care: Cementing Individual Rights by Corroding Social Solidarity' (2006) 43 *Common Market Law Review* 1645; C Rieder, 'The EC Commission's New Adopted Baby: Health Care' (2007–08) 14 *Columbia Journal of European Law* 145; G Di Federico, 'Access to Healthcare in the Post-Lisbon Era and the Genuine Enjoyment of EU Citizens' Rights' in L Serena Rossi and F Casolari (eds), *The EU after Lisbon: Amending or Coping with the Existing Treaties?* (Heidelberg, Springer, 2014). The main principles established through the case-law have now been consolidated and supplemented by Dir 2011/24 on the application of patients' rights in cross-border healthcare [2011] OJ L88/45.
[127] Case C-310/08 *Ibrahim* [2010] ECR I-1065.
[128] Case C-480/08 *Teixeira* [2010] ECR I-1107.
[129] See eg Case C-308/89 *Di Leo* [1990] ECR I-4185; Case C-7/94 *Gaal* [1996] ECR I-1031; Joined Cases 389 & 390/87 *Echternach and Moritz* [1989] ECR 723; *Baumbast* (n 109).
[130] Reg 1612/68 (n 13).
[131] Reg 492/2011 (n 12).
[132] For comments on these cases, see P Starup and M Elsmore, 'Taking a Logical or Giant Step Forward? Comment on *Ibrahim* and *Teixeira*' (2010) 35 *European Law Review* 571.
[133] Joined Cases C-147 & 148/11 *Czop* ECLI:EU:C:2012:538, paras 30–33.

the way that it is determined whether a Union citizen falls within the scope of the personal market freedoms or whether his/her situation should be judged for its compliance with the citizenship provisions of the Treaty. Therefore, it is not surprising that it has been suggested that the way forward may simply be to abolish the personal market freedoms and consolidate all the rights that natural persons derive from EU law in the Citizenship Part of the TFEU—a point to which we shall return in chapter six.

C. Scope *Ratione Materiae*

In recent years and, in particular, following the coming into force of the Treaty of Maastricht, the scope *rationae materiae* of the personal market freedoms has been broadened.[134] This has been done in two ways.

Firstly, the Court in its citizenship case-law has extended the ambit of, inter alia, the personal market freedoms, in a principled manner, by noting that the situations that fall within their material scope 'include those involving the exercise of the fundamental freedoms guaranteed by the Treaty'.[135] As a result of the above pronouncement, a situation falls within the material scope of these provisions and has to be judged for its compatibility with EU law, *whenever* it involves a Union citizen who has exercised the primary rights stemming from these provisions. It is, therefore, no longer necessary to prove that the claimed right or entitlement or, more broadly, the policy area that is affected by the contested measure, *also* falls within the material scope of EU law. Accordingly, any Union citizen who has exercised the rights stemming from the personal market freedoms can, now, challenge the measures and regulatory choices of the Member States if they have a (negative) impact on the exercise of those rights. Moreover and more broadly, as already made clear prior to Maastricht, this is so even in areas that escape the ambit of EU legislative competence (eg nationality laws, direct taxation, criminal law, provision of healthcare, and so on).[136] In other words, although the EU can still *not* legislate in these areas, it can, nonetheless, subject the measures of the Member States in

---

[134] Caro de Sousa has pointed out that the expansion of the material scope of the personal market freedoms as a result of the introduction of Union citizenship 'is in certain cases easily justified independently of particular normative considerations. ... From a systematic perspective, if the autonomous function of European Citizenship is to protect those who are not encompassed by the economic fundamental freedoms, it would not make sense to protect non-workers more than workers, which is what would have happened had the material scope of the relevant market freedoms not been extended.'— P Caro de Sousa (n 90) 77–78.

[135] *Grzelczyk* (n 94), para 33; C-224/98 *D'Hoop* [2002] ECR I-6191, para 29; Case C-148/02 *Garcia Avello* [2003] ECR I-11613, para 24. In this sentence it is clear that the Court used the term 'fundamental freedoms' when referring to what in this book are referred to as the market freedoms.

[136] See, inter alia, Case C-369/90 *Micheletti* [1992] ECR I-4239; *Schumacker* (n 89); Case C-348/96 *Calfa* [1999] ECR I-11; *Geraets Smits and Peerbooms* (n 124).

these fields to EU scrutiny.[137] Therefore, although even before the introduction of Union citizenship it could be said that '[t]here simply is no nucleus of sovereignty that the Member States can invoke, as such, against the Community',[138] this is even more so now, following the above pronouncement, given that the rights that Union citizens derive from EU law touch, virtually, all areas of human life and, with it, all areas of national legislative competence.[139]

This broadening of the material scope of the personal market freedoms appears to reflect the view expressed by Advocate General Jacobs in the early 1990s, in his Opinion in the *Konstantinidis* case, when he noted that

> a Community national who goes to another Member State as a worker or self-employed person under Articles 48 [45 TFEU], 52 [49 TFEU] or 59 [56 TFEU] of the Treaty is entitled not just to pursue his trade or profession and to enjoy the same living and working conditions as nationals of the host State; he is in addition entitled to assume that, wherever he goes to earn his living in the European Community, he will be treated in accordance with a common code of fundamental values, in particular those laid down in the European Convention on Human Rights. In other words, he is entitled to say 'civis europeus sum' and to invoke that status in order to oppose any violation of his fundamental rights.[140]

Yet, it should be noted that whilst the Advocate General was merely concerned with the protection of the fundamental human rights of economic actors in the host State, the Court's pronouncement in its recent case-law to the effect that the material scope of the market freedoms includes all situations where a Union citizen has exercised the rights stemming from these provisions is broader, in that in such situations *any* national measure and not merely, as per the Advocate General's suggestion, national measures that breach the fundamental human rights of a mobile Union citizen, should be assessed for its compatibility with EU law.

The second way in which the material scope of the personal market freedoms has been expanded after Maastricht is based on two parameters: a) the addition of a second, primary, right which is now considered to be stemming from the more stationary personal market freedoms, and the corresponding application of these provisions in situations where they would not have applied before Maastricht and b) the abolition of the requirement of cross-border specificity for all the personal

---

[137] G Davies, *Nationality Discrimination in the European Internal Market* (The Hague, Kluwer, 2003) 196–97; L Azoulai, 'The Court of Justice and the Social Market Economy: The Emergence of an Ideal and the Conditions for its Realization' (2008) 45 *Common Market Law Review* 1335, 1341; C Hublet, 'The Scope of Article 12 of the Treaty of the European Communities vis-à-vis Third-Country Nationals: Evolution at Last?' (2009) 15 *European Law Journal* 757, 759–61; S Weatherill, 'From Economic Rights to Fundamental Rights' in S de Vries, U Bernitz and S Weatherill (eds), *The Protection of Fundamental Rights in the EU After Lisbon* (Oxford, Hart Publishing, 2013) 17.
[138] K Lenaerts (n 23) 220.
[139] A Tryfonidou (n 90). See, also, E Spaventa (n 57) 28.
[140] AG Opinion in *Konstantinidis* (n 59), para 46.

market freedoms. The analysis in the remainder of this section, shall, therefore, focus on exploring the Court's post-Maastricht case-law which demonstrates these points.

i. The Addition of a Second Primary Right in the Material Scope of the More Stationary Personal Market Freedoms

The main aim of this subsection is to demonstrate that the Court—through its *Ritter-Coulais* saga[141]—appears to have gradually reconsidered its interpretation of the more stationary personal market freedoms, by reading them as granting a second primary right, additional to (and independent of) the only primary right originally considered to stem from them. This is the right to start pursuing an economic activity in a cross-border context, irrespective of whether there has been a prior exercise of the right to take-up an economic activity *in the territory of another Member State*. In other words, the requirement of a change in the economic base of the economic actor (ie where his/her business is permanently situated) and/or in the location of the economic activity (ie where the economic activity is permanently pursued), which persisted in the period before Maastricht, seems to have now been abandoned. Accordingly, *all* the personal market freedoms (and not just the freedom to provide services, as seen in the previous section) now also appear to be a source of the primary right to start pursuing an economic activity in a cross-border context, even in cases where there is no change in the location of the economic activity and/or the economic base of the economic actor; and, thus, the Court's ruling in *Werner*[142] appears to have been overruled. This new right is considered to be a primary right because its restriction suffices for establishing a breach of the personal market freedoms, even if the (traditionally only) primary right deriving from these provisions—the right to take-up an economic activity in *another* Member State—is not restricted; and, as will be explained in the next subsection, this is a fundamental right because its grant (and exercise) does not appear capable of contributing to the economic aims of these provisions and seems, therefore, that it is granted for its own sake and simply to further the interests of Union citizens.

In the *Ritter-Coulais* group of cases,[143] Union citizens who were economically active in their State of nationality, had moved to another Member State *for the purpose of taking-up residence* there, whilst they continued to permanently exercise an economic activity in their State of origin and nationality. The question which arose in this group of cases was whether the situation fell within the scope of the

---

[141] Case C-152/03 *Ritter-Coulais* [2006] ECR I-1711; Case C-470/04 *N* [2006] ECR I-7409; Case C-464/05 *Geurts* [2007] ECR I-9325; Case C-527/06 *Renneberg* [2008] ECR I-7735; Case C-379/11 *Caves Krier* ECLI:EU:C:2012:798; Case C-87/13 *X* ECLI:EU:C:2014:2459. For an article focusing on this saga, see A Tryfonidou, 'In Search of the Aim of the EC Free Movement of Persons Provisions: Has the Court of Justice Missed the Point?' (2009) 46 *Common Market Law Review* 1591.
[142] *Werner* (n 87).
[143] n 141.

more stationary personal market freedoms, given that the movement exercised had not been for an economic purpose and the contested measure would primarily affect the exercise of the right to move for the purpose of taking-up residence in another Member State, since the immediate cause of the loss of the more favourable treatment previously enjoyed was, exactly, the fact that the relevant economic actors were no longer resident in their State of origin, where they continued to be economically active.

In *Ritter-Coulais*,[144] the applicants were German nationals who were employed as teachers in a German State secondary school whilst they resided in a house they owned in France. The main question in the case was whether Article 48 EC (Article 45 TFEU) precluded German legislation which did not permit the applicants, who were assessable to tax on their total income in Germany, to request that account be taken, for the purposes of determining the rate of taxation applicable to them, of rental income losses relating to their own use of their house in France. After noting that

> any Community national who, irrespective of his place of residence and his nationality, has exercised the right to freedom of movement for workers and who has been employed in a Member State other than that of residence falls within the scope of Article 48 EC[145]

the Court concluded that 'the situation of the appellants in the main proceedings, who worked in a Member State other than that of their actual place of residence, falls within the scope of' that provision.[146] The Court then held that the freedom of movement for workers precludes national legislation such as that at issue, because it treated non-resident workers less favourably than workers who resided in Germany in their own home.

A similar approach was followed by the Court in the establishment case of *N*.[147] Mr N was a Dutch national who was, initially, residing in the Netherlands and was the sole shareholder of three limited liability companies established and managed in that Member State. In 1997 (ie at some point after he became the sole shareholder in the companies), he decided to move his residence to the UK where he did not exercise any economic activity until 2002, when he started running a farm with an apple orchard. As a result of the transfer of his residence to the UK, Mr N was treated less favourably under the Dutch taxation system as regards the assessment and methods of enforcing income tax on profits from his holdings in the Dutch companies. The Court in its judgment noted that Mr N was an EU national who 'since the transfer of his residence, has been living in one Member State and holding all the shares of companies established in another. It follows that, since that transfer, N has fallen within the scope of Article 43 EC' (Article 49 TFEU).[148] Following the same reasoning as that employed in *Ritter-Coulais*, the Court, thus,

---

[144] ibid.
[145] ibid, para 31.
[146] *Ritter-Coulais* (n 141), para 32.
[147] *N* (n 141).
[148] ibid, para 28.

accepted that the exercise of free movement (for the purpose of taking-up residence in another Member State) which results in a situation whereby a Member State national holds shares in a company which is established in a Member State different from his State of residence, suffices for bringing a situation within the scope of Article 49 TFEU. The Court expressly acknowledged that the contested legislation would subsequently discourage Mr N 'from transferring his residence outside the Netherlands', which was an aspect of the right provided by Article 49 TFEU ('a taxpayer wishing to transfer his residence outside Netherlands territory, in exercise of the rights guaranteed to him by Article 43 EC').[149]

In *N*, like in *Ritter-Coulais*, the movement that was to be directly impeded as a result of the application of the contested legislation (ie the movement from the Netherlands to the UK) was not, at least initially, connected with the taking-up of an economic activity: Mr N was just taking his shares with him and he would continue holding shares in the Dutch companies following the transfer of his residence to the UK; any negative impact on the pursuit of that economic activity would only be felt indirectly, whilst it would be the exercise of the right of residence that would be directly restricted as a result of the contested legislation. As noted by Advocate General Kokott, Mr N's economic activities in relation to the Dutch companies would be 'affected only by way of reaction to the change of residence'.[150]

The Court's aim in this saga may have, indeed, been to protect the right—of economically active Union citizens—to take-up *residence* in the territory of another Member State. And the Court may have chosen to use the personal market freedoms as a source of this right, in order to ensure that economically active Union citizens claiming this right would not be subjected to the economic self-sufficiency conditions that are imposed on economically inactive Union citizens who rely on Article 21 TFEU to enforce such a right.[151] This would, however, amount to an inappropriate extension of the scope of application of the personal market freedoms given that it appears to be the task of Article 21 TFEU (and not of the market freedoms) to grant the right to *reside* in the territory of another Member State to Union citizens.

An alternative explanation—and the one I am in favour of—is that the Court in the *Ritter-Coulais* saga wished to ensure that Union citizens can begin pursuing an economic activity (that was previously exercised in a purely internal context) *in a cross-border context*, which is the case, inter alia, when a Union citizen pursues an economic activity in one Member State whilst residing in the territory of another. In this way, the material scope of *all* the personal market freedoms is now drawn in exactly the same manner, since all of these provisions (and not just Article 56

---

[149] ibid, para 35.
[150] Paragraph 36 of the Opinion of AG Kokott in *N* (n 141). This reasoning was later confirmed in *Geurts* (n 141). See, however, the different approach followed by the Court in a case which involved a legal—as opposed to a natural—person: Case C-386/04 *Stauffer* [2006] ECR I-8203.
[151] C O'Brien, 'Social Blind Spots and Monocular Policy Making: The ECJ's Migrant Worker Model' (2009) 46 *Common Market Law Review* 1107, 1112.

TFEU, as was traditionally the case)[152] appear, now, to grant to Union citizens[153] (also) the primary right to start pursuing an economic activity in a cross-border context, irrespective of whether there has also been a change in the economic base of the economic actor and/or in the location of the economic activity.[154]

Hence, although the scope *ratione personae* of the personal market freedoms appears to have remained unaltered by the *Ritter-Coulais* saga[155] as regards their material scope, the Court seems to have increased the types of situations that are now covered by the more stationary personal market freedoms and, correspondingly, to have expanded the list of primary rights that Union citizens can derive from them.[156] As a result of this move, the rights granted by *all* the personal market freedoms appear, now, to be the same. It will be explored subsequently in this chapter what the possible rationale behind this move is and in chapter five it will be examined whether the move is legally warranted.

ii. Dispensing with the Requirement of Cross-Border Specificity

As already explained, the personal market freedoms appeared, initially, to be viewed merely instrumentally, as the tools to be used in the process of building an internal market. Given that this transnational market would be built mainly through negative harmonisation and, hence, the main responsibility for regulating it would continue to fall upon the Member States, these provisions would not be used on a mission to extinguish *all* national regulation but would, rather, be used as the tools to ensure that national legislation would not be used in a way which would impede the achievement of the EU's economic aims.

Accordingly, the basic regulatory schema initially employed was based on the principle that the Member States should maintain the power to regulate economic activities taking place in their own territory, whilst the EU should only interfere when the exercise of those regulatory powers could negatively affect the achievement of the aim of building an internal market, *by being biased against the initiation of a cross-border economic activity*. In other words, under this schema, the

---

[152] *Koestler* (n 83).
[153] The Court's case-law in this saga concerned situations which involved natural persons that were holding the nationality of a Member State (ie Union citizens) and, thus, this primary right seems to be only available to Union citizens. It should be noted that this right can be enforced both by the Union citizen himself, as well as—in situations involving employed (rather than self-employed) persons—by his/her employer—see *Caves Krier* (n 141).
[154] The above reading of the *Ritter-Coulais* saga has been recently confirmed in Case C-303/12 *Imfeld* ECLI:EU:C:2013:822, especially para 53.
[155] In order for the market freedoms to apply, the Union citizens who rely on them must (still) be engaged in an economic activity—see Case C-544/07 *Rüffler* [2009] ECR I-3389.
[156] In her Opinion in *X* (n 141) para 14, AG Kokott noted the following: 'It is true that, according to the wording of the first sentence of Article 43(1) EC, only the establishment "of nationals of a Member State in the territory of *another* Member State" is protected, which is not so in the case of the establishment of X, a Netherlands national, in the Netherlands. However, the Court has through its case-law extended the protective scope of freedom of establishment. Under that case-law, every citizen of the Union, irrespective of his nationality, falls within the scope of Article 43 EC in so far as he pursues a professional activity in a Member State other than that of residence.'

EU should not interfere at all in situations where the Member State that should regulate an economic activity (ie the rightful regulator), did this in an entirely neutral manner, by simply limiting the economic freedom of economic actors. As Advocate General Tizzano stressed in his Opinion in *CaixaBank*, allowing economic operators to abuse the personal market freedoms 'in order to oppose any national measure that, solely because it regulated the conditions for pursuing an economic activity, could in the final analysis narrow profit margins and hence reduce the attractiveness of pursuing that particular economic activity' 'would be tantamount to bending the Treaty to a purpose for which it was not intended: that is to say, not in order to create an internal market in which conditions are similar to those of a single market and where operators can move freely, but in order to establish a market without rules'.[157]

For this reason the Court had, traditionally, adopted a discrimination-based approach when delimiting the material scope of the personal market freedoms. Hence, until the 1990s, it was widely believed that only (directly or indirectly) discriminatory measures should be caught by these provisions. However, instead of considering discrimination in this context to be covering merely discrimination on the ground of nationality (which is what is made explicit in the Treaty text), a much broader approach has been followed, which has been summarised by Advocate General Poiares Maduro in his Opinion in *Vassilopoulos*, when he noted that the market freedoms should be considered to prohibit national measures that 'lead to cross-border situations being treated less favourably than purely national situations'.[158]

As explained in chapter one, the (pre-Maastricht) requirement that only discriminatory measures (in the broad sense mentioned above) should be caught by the personal market freedoms has been, in essence, a requirement of 'cross-border specificity', ie a requirement that only Member State measures which have a heavier impact on cross-border situations or non-nationals/migrants should be caught by these provisions. Accordingly, as we saw in the previous section, under the Court's traditional approach to the personal market freedoms, measures which were incapable of having cross-border specificity, were considered to fall altogether outside the scope of the personal market freedoms. Therefore, genuinely non-discriminatory measures which were merely 'the rules of the game' aiming, simply, to regulate an economic activity in a neutral manner, traditionally escaped the ambit of the personal market freedoms, if they were imposed by the (rightful)

---

[157] Paragraphs 62 and 63 of the Opinion of AG Tizzano in Case C-442/02 *CaixaBank* [2004] ECR I-8961.
[158] Paragraph 41 of the Opinion of AG Poiares Maduro in Joined Cases C-158 & 159/04 *Vassilopoulos* [2006] ECR I-8135. For commentators who are in favour of adopting a discrimination-based reading for all the market freedoms, albeit one that is based on a very wide concept of discrimination, see J Snell (n 80) 46; G Davies, 'Discrimination and Beyond in European Economic and Social Law' (2011) 18 *Maastricht Journal of European and Comparative Law* 7; S Enchelmaier, 'Always at your Service (within Limits): the ECJ's Case Law on Article 56 TFEU (2006–11)' (2011) 36 *European Law Review* 615, 630–33. For criticisms of a discrimination-based test in the context of any of the market freedoms see P Caro de Sousa (n 90) 89–98.

regulator (ie the State where the economic activity took place).[159] Although these might have been capable of limiting the freedom of economic actors to take-up and/or pursue a cross-border economic activity, they limited this freedom in the same manner for all economic actors, whether the economic activities that were taken-up were going to be pursued in the territory of another Member State/in a cross-border context or in a purely national setting.

In order to determine whether the facts of a case involve cross-border specificity, it is important to be clear about which State is the rightful regulator in that particular factual scenario.[160] As will be seen, a different answer to this question is given, depending on which personal market freedom is applicable on the facts and depending on the aspect of the economic activity that is sought to be regulated.

A Union citizen who—relying on the more stationary personal market freedoms—moves *permanently* to another Member State and severs all links with his/her State of nationality (ie takes-up an economic activity that is pursued permanently in the territory of the host Member State), becomes an integral part of the labour market of the host State and (s)he is, therefore, in the same position as national workers. The same is the case with a Union citizen who establishes a company in another Member State, in exercise of her freedom of establishment (irrespective of whether she also moves to reside in that Member State or not). Accordingly, the economic activity sought to be taken-up and pursued by that person (exclusively) in the host State can *only* be regulated by the latter. Hence, the host Member State—as the only regulator of the said economic activity—is entirely free to impose any rules it chooses in order to regulate that economic activity (both as regards access to it and its pursuit), as long as it does not discriminate against nationals of other Member States or, more broadly, situations which involve a cross-border element. Since genuinely non-discriminatory rules imposed by the host State are incapable of impeding the taking-up and pursuit of an economic activity in the territory of that State by nationals of another Member State *more than they can of its own nationals*, there is no cross-border specificity and, hence, *under a purely instrumental approach to the interpretation of the personal market freedoms*, such rules must fall altogether outside the scope of these provisions, even if they limit the freedom of economic actors.[161]

Conversely, if the home State (ie the State from which the person originates) decides to regulate the economic activity of workers and the self-employed *even* when they have taken-up an economic activity in another Member State which is permanently and exclusively pursued there, this will, automatically, amount to a discriminatory (on the grounds of migration) restriction, since it will impose a dual burden on the nationals of that Member State who have exercised the rights

---

[159] C Barnard, *The Substantive Law of the EU: The Four Freedoms* (Oxford, Oxford University Press, 2013) 253.
[160] RCA White (n 74) 264–65.
[161] L Daniele (n 65) 196–98; C Hilson, 'Discrimination in Community Free Movement Law' (1999) 24 *European Law Review* 445, 457.

they derive from the personal market freedoms, since they will (rightfully) be subject (also) to the regulations of the host State. In this case, the home State's rules will automatically amount to a restriction caught by the freedom of establishment or the free movement of workers provisions, and that State will have to justify them using the Treaty derogations or the objective justifications.

The situation with services is somewhat different, nonetheless, given that the permanent economic base of the service-provider remains the home State.[162] Accordingly, in this context the (rightful) regulator regarding *access* to an economic activity (ie the setting-up of an economic base from which services are to be provided either in a purely national setting or across borders) is the home State. Conversely, when it comes to the pursuit of the economic activity—ie the actual provision of the service—then in most instances[163] the appropriate regulator is the host State (because it is there that the economic activity takes place). This means that, under a purely instrumental approach, in the context of services—as is the case for goods from *Keck* onwards[164]—the home State should be free to (*neutrally*) regulate access to the provision of services (ie to lay down the rules that must be satisfied by economic actors who are established in its territory in order to be able to provide services from there), whilst the rules governing the *provision* of services as such (ie the pursuit of this economic activity), should be laid down by the host State.[165] Accordingly, the host State cannot impose on persons established in another Member State any rules regarding access to the provision of services—if it does so, this will, automatically, amount to a (indirectly discriminatory) restriction on the free movement of services/service-providers/service-recipients since it imposes a dual-burden on the provision of cross-border services, unless it can be proved that such rules are justified by a non-economic objective or if it is shown that the service provider has not complied with the rules of any other Member State.[166] Similarly, if the home State imposes any rules regarding the *provision* of services *in the territory of another Member State*, this will also amount to a dual burden measure which is, as such, indirectly discriminatory against cross-border services and will, therefore, amount to a violation of Article 56 TFEU, unless a justification can be made out.[167]

---

[162] EI Kaldellis, 'Freedom of Establishment versus Freedom to Provide Services: An Evaluation of Case-Law Developments in the Area of Indistinctly Applicable Rules' (2001) 28 *Legal Issues of European Integration* 23, 37 and 39.

[163] In essence, when the service is actually provided in the territory of the host State and not across borders (eg online).

[164] Joined Cases C-267 & 268/91 *Keck and Mithouard* [1993] ECR I-6097.

[165] For a similar view, see EI Kaldellis (n 162) 40–45. For an explanation of the division of regulatory competences between the home and the host State (as this was established until the early 1990s) see J Snell (n 80) Ch 2. For an explanation of the difference in approach as regards the division of competences in the context of the free movement of workers and the freedom of establishment, on the one hand, and the free movement of goods and services, on the other, see C Barnard (n 159) 243.

[166] Case C-58/98 *Corsten* [2000] ECR I-7919. J Snell (n 80) 61–62.

[167] This seems to be the reason why the measure in *Alpine Investments* (n 83) is not, on closer inspection, genuinely non-discriminatory. For an explanation see J Snell (n 80) 91–98. See also G Davies (n 137) 82–84.

Hence, until the early 1990s when it was considered that the personal market freedoms could only cover measures which had cross-border specificity, the above schema seems to have been the basis on which it was determined whether national regulations amounted to a restriction caught by the personal market freedoms. However, as we shall see in this subsection, this is not the case, anymore, as the Court appears—in the majority of its case-law[168]—to have broadened the scope of application of these provisions to catch genuinely non-discriminatory measures, ie measures which are applied in situations where there is no cross-border specificity and their effect is to merely limit the freedom of economic actors in a neutral manner. As will be seen, although the Court abandoned the requirement of cross-border specificity initially in cases involving direct restrictions on the primary rights stemming from the personal market freedoms (ie restrictions on the primary rights deriving from them), this requirement seems to have been also later abolished, in cases involving measures which restricted the exercise of secondary rights stemming from these provisions (ie measures which only indirectly restricted the exercise of the primary rights granted by these provisions).

(a) Abandoning the Requirement of Cross-Border Specificity: Direct Restrictions

The first sign of deciding to abandon the requirement of cross-border specificity, can be seen in *Säger*, where the Court pointed out that Article 59 EEC (Article 56 TFEU)

> requires not only the elimination of all discrimination against a person providing services on the ground of his nationality but also the abolition of any restriction, even if it applies without distinction to national providers of services and to those of other Member States, when it is liable to prohibit or otherwise impede the activities of a provider of services established in another Member State where he lawfully provides similar services.[169]

This, however, could not, conclusively, be taken as evidence that genuinely non-discriminatory restrictions would now be caught by the personal market freedoms—or, at least, by the above provision—given that the contested measure

---

[168] There have been cases decided after Maastricht where the Court ruled that a genuinely non-discriminatory restriction on the exercise of the rights stemming from the market freedoms could not be caught by these provisions—see eg Joined Cases C-51/96 and C-191/97 *Deliège* [2000] ECR I-2549; Case C-285/01 *Burbaud* [2003] ECR I-8219; and the Court's direct taxation case-law. It is widely accepted nonetheless, that the personal market freedoms no longer require cross-border specificity in order to apply in a situation.

[169] Case C-76/90 *Säger* [1991] ECR I-4221, para 12. Confirmed post-Maastricht in, inter alia, Case C-369/96 *Arblade* [1999] ECR I-8453, para 33; Case C-168/04 *Commission v Austria* [2006] ECR I-9041, para 36; Case C-515/08 *Santos Palhota* [2010] ECR I-9133, para 29.

on the facts of the case imposed a dual burden, in that services which were lawfully provided in the home Member State had, in addition, to comply with the requirements of the host State.[170]

It was, rather, in 1994, in the services case of *Schindler*,[171] that the Court found for the first time that the same provision can catch within its scope a genuinely non-discriminatory measure. In that case, the Court held that the UK prohibition on the holding of lotteries—clearly a non-discriminatory measure—amounted to a restriction on the freedom to provide services, albeit one which was justified.[172]

The following year, the Court made it clear that the provisions governing the rights of workers (*Bosman*) and the self-employed (*Gebhard*), prohibit *both* discriminatory *and* genuinely non-discriminatory restrictions on free movement, which are incapable of being justified by a non-economic objective. In these cases, the contested measures could in no way fit within a discrimination analysis: they were genuinely non-discriminatory and were capable of having exactly the same restrictive impact on access to the said economic activity, in cross-border and purely internal situations.[173] Thus, they lacked cross-border specificity.

Gebhard[174] concerned an Italian law which provided that in order for *anyone* to use the title *avvocato*, (s)he should enrol at the local bar. Mr Gebhard was a German lawyer working in Milan in a self-employed capacity, who used the title without having previously enrolled at the Milan Bar. When a case was brought against him, he tried to rely on the personal market freedoms in his defence. The ECJ, responding to a reference for a preliminary ruling, found that the measure was liable to hinder or make less attractive the exercise of the freedom of establishment but that it could, nonetheless, be justified. What is important to note is not the result of the case—ie that the Italian rules were justified and could, thus, continue to be applied to both Italian and non-Italian nationals—but, rather, that the Court had read Article 52 EC (Article 49 TFEU) broadly enough to cover measures which were genuinely non-discriminatory and had no cross-border specificity, in this way placing the burden on the Member States to justify their application to nationals of other Member States. This is, undoubtedly, an extension of the scope

---

[170] S O'Leary, 'The Free Movement of Persons and Services' in P Craig and G de Búrca (eds), *The Evolution of EU Law* (Oxford, Oxford University Press, 1999) 400.
[171] Case C-275/92 *Schindler* [1994] ECR I-1039.
[172] Note, however, that some commentators consider that the measure at issue in *Schindler* could be considered to be discriminatory—see J Snell (n 80) 83–86. Also, it is important to note that although in this case the freedom to provide services was invoked by Member State nationals (ie Union citizens) who were acting as agents promoting and selling the lottery tickets, it was a public body (ie a *legal* person) that would be prevented from providing cross-border services as a result of the impugned measure.
[173] It should be noted that there have not been many cases which involved measures which lacked cross-border specificity—EI Kaldellis (n 162) 32.
[174] *Gebhard* (n 65). See J Lonbay, 'Annotation of *Gebhard*' (1996) 33 *Common Market Law Review* 1073, for a comment that views the judgment favourably.

of application of the personal market freedoms and a corresponding diminution of the situations where the actions of the Member States remain free from EU intervention.

As Spaventa explains, in *Gebhard* there was no cross-border specificity—the rules were 'movement-neutral'.[175] Gebhard, just like every (Italian or non-Italian) lawyer, had to be registered as an avvocato in order to be able to practise on the Italian Bar; the rules were, simply, the 'rules of the game' and there was no hint of bias against cross-border economic activities or economic actors whose situation was cross-border in nature. After all, by seeking to establish in the host State as an avvocato on a permanent basis, Mr Gebhard was, in effect, in the same situation as that of the nationals of that State who were in a purely internal situation: Italy would be the only Member State that would have the competence to regulate Mr Gebhard's access to the profession of avvocato, as was the case with Italian nationals whose situation did not involve a cross-border element.[176]

Hence, from a (pre-Maastricht) approach whereby Member State measures completely escaped EU scrutiny when they merely regulated economic activities in a neutral manner, the Court with *Gebhard* moved to a situation whereby whenever a national measure is capable of restricting the freedom of a Union citizen to take-up an economic activity in the territory of another Member State, *even if this has the same restrictive impact on nationals of that Member State who are in a purely internal situation*, the measure amounts to a restriction caught by the personal market freedoms and the onus falls on the relevant Member State to prove that the said rule is necessary for achieving a valid non-economic aim (eg to ensure that the said economic activity is regulated).

It should, therefore, be highlighted here that what has changed is the presumption (ie now it is presumed that even national measures that do not have cross-border specificity can amount to restrictions contrary to Article 49 TFEU and need to undergo EU scrutiny) rather than the final result reached in each case, since many of the measures scrutinised for their compliance with the personal market freedoms are found to be justified.

The same can be said about *Bosman*.[177] Bosman was a Belgian footballer whose contract with a Belgian team had expired and was subsequently offered a job with a French team. The problem was that UEFA and the national football federations

---

[175] E Spaventa (n 21) 99.
[176] The same (final) conclusion had been reached in the earlier Case 292/86 *Gullung* [1988] ECR 111, where it was held that the requirement to register at the local Bar in order to practise as a lawyer in France was not prohibited by Art 52 EEC (Art 49 TFEU). However, unlike in *Gebhard*, the Court in that case did not find that there was a restriction caught by the freedom of establishment provisions which was, nonetheless, justified but, by applying a discrimination-based approach, it held that 'the requirement that lawyers be registered at a bar laid down by certain Member States must be regarded as lawful in relation to Community law provided, however, that such registration is open to nationals of all Member States without discrimination.' (para 29). This is one obvious example which demonstrates the change in the Court's approach from, originally, a discrimination-based approach which required the existence of cross-border specificity, to one where national measures which are genuinely non-discriminatory can, nonetheless, be caught by the personal market freedoms.
[177] *Bosman* (n 65).

had rules requiring the payment of transfer fees by the receiving team to the original team; and these rules applied to *any* transfers, whether between Member States or between one and the same Member State. In Bosman's case, the receiving team refused to pay these transfer fees and, as a result, Bosman remained without a job. He, therefore, sought to challenge the rules claiming that they were in violation of a number of Treaty provisions, including of Article 48 EEC (Article 45 TFEU). In its submissions, UEFA sought to draw a parallel between the rules that were challenged and 'selling arrangements', which, according to *Keck*, fall outside the scope of the free movement of goods provisions, given that they are neutral rules, which merely seek to regulate an economic activity.[178] The Court, however, held that the contested rules were different, in that they 'directly affect players' access to the employment market in other Member States and are thus capable of impeding freedom of movement for workers'.[179] Despite the fact that the impugned rules were, indeed, capable of restricting access to the market of another Member State, these rules were—like the rules in *Gebhard*—'movement-neutral', in that they would restrict in exactly the same way access to the market in a purely national setting: if Mr Bosman wished to move to another Belgian team, he would be faced with exactly the same restriction.[180] Accordingly, under a purely instrumental reading of the personal market freedoms, these rules would escape the ambit of Article 48 EEC. The Court, however, in this case, like in *Gebhard*, chose to include these rules within the scope of that provision and, in this way, to activate the process of EU scrutiny, whereby it would need to be proved that the rules were justified.[181]

Apart from the expansion of the scope of the more stationary personal market freedoms to cover measures that lacked cross-border specificity, there are, also, a number of services cases where the Court subjected to EU scrutiny rules which were genuinely non-discriminatory and which, therefore, did not have cross-border specificity; and these rules—like in *Gebhard* and *Bosman*—were imposed by the rightful (and only) regulator of the economic activity (on the facts, the home State). The two most prominent examples are *SETTG*[182] and *Gourmet*.[183]

In *SETTG*,[184] at issue was the compatibility with Article 59 EC (Article 56 TFEU) of a Greek rule which provided that tourist guides *that were licensed by*

---

[178] ibid, para 102.
[179] ibid, para 103. Szydlo has considered that rules such as those in *Bosman*, which 'immobilize' the workers in question 'by not allowing them to be involved (deployed) in economic processes' are 'the most far-reaching restriction on the free movement of services and workers, but also on the freedom of establishment and the free movement of capital, even if it is of a non-discriminatory nature'—see M Szydlo, 'Export Restrictions within the Structure of Free Movement of Goods. Reconsideration of an Old Paradigm' (2010) 47 *Common Market Law Review* 753, 764.
[180] For a similar view see G Davies (n 137) 73–76.
[181] This approach of dispensing with the requirement of cross-border specificity was confirmed in subsequent case-law. See eg Case C-108/96 *Mac Quen* [2001] ECR I-837; Case C-196/96 *Lehtonen* [2000] ECR I-2681; Case C-294/00 *Gräbner* [2002] ECR I-6515; Case C-79/01 *Payroll* [2002] ECR I-8923.
[182] Case C-398/95 *SETTG* [1997] ECR I-3091.
[183] Case C-405/98 *Gourmet* [2001] ECR I-1795.
[184] *SETTG* (n 182).

the Greek State could only provide their services as *employees* of tourist and travel agencies, and not as self-employed service-providers. As the Court admitted, the rule was neutral between Greek and non-Greek tourist guides that were licensed by the Greek State.[185] In fact, practically speaking, the contested rule would—if at all—in only exceptional cases be capable of affecting tourist guides established in other Member States that wished to provide their services in Greece since, as made clear from the various submissions made to the Court, tourist guides from other Member States did not need such a licence in order to offer their services in Greece. Yet, neither the fact that the rule lacked cross-border specificity, nor that it appeared incapable, in practice, of impeding the provision of services in Greece by tourist guides established in other Member States, prevented the Court from finding a restriction caught by Article 59 EC.

In *Gourmet*[186]—a case where the freedom to provide services was relied on by a legal (as opposed to a natural) person—at issue was the compatibility with Article 59 EC (Article 56 TFEU) of Swedish rules which prohibited the advertising of alcoholic drinks in magazines, newspapers, on television, and on the radio. The claimant was a Swedish company (Gourmet International Products AB) which published a magazine which, in one of its issues, included an advertisement of an alcoholic drink, in contravention of those rules. When the Court was called to decide whether the advertising prohibition was contrary to the freedom to provide services, it noted that the rules restricted 'the right of press undertakings established in the territory of that Member State to offer advertising space in their publications to potential advertisers established in other Member States'.[187] In doing so, the Court tried—artificially—to point to the existence of cross-border specificity, by noting that

> A measure such as the prohibition on advertising at issue in the proceedings before that court, even if it is non-discriminatory, has a particular effect on the cross-border supply of advertising space, given the international nature of the advertising market in the category of products to which the prohibition relates, and thereby constitutes a restriction on the freedom to provide services within the meaning of Article 59 of the Treaty.[188]

There is no doubt that the measure was genuinely neutral as regards the provision of advertising services, whether these were provided to advertisers in Sweden or to advertisers in other Member States. Unlike the impact of this measure on the free movement of goods, which appeared to be different between goods imported from other Member States (which needed advertising in order to penetrate the Swedish market) and Swedish goods with which the Swedish consumer was, already, familiar, the restriction on the provision of advertising services was entirely neutral. As a result of the contested rule, Swedish publishers would be unable to sell

---

[185] ibid, para 15. It should be noted that tourist guides that were not licensed were free to provide their services in Greece as self-employed service-providers.
[186] *Gourmet* (n 183).
[187] ibid, para 38.
[188] ibid, para 39.

advertising space (for alcoholic products) to Swedish advertisers; in other words, there was *no market* in Sweden for these kinds of services.[189] In exactly the same way, publishers would be unable to sell advertising space to advertisers established in other Member States.[190]

Gourmet, therefore, illustrates that genuinely non-discriminatory rules of the State where the services are provided (ie the home State) which is the *only* regulator of this economic activity, can be challenged simply if they hinder service-providers established in its territory from providing their services to *potential* recipients in other Member States. Thus, this is another case where the decisions of the sole regulator are put under EU scrutiny in order to ensure the liberty of the economic actor as opposed to the free provision of services across borders, in the same way that services are provided within a purely domestic context.[191] Moreover, and more broadly, *Gourmet* demonstrates that the freedom to provide services provisions bestow on persons not merely the right to take-up and (then) to pursue an economic activity in the territory of another Member State/in a cross-border context, but, also, the right to pursue an economic activity *in their own Member State* and, thus, to *require* that Member State to permit them to do so, provided that they can point to an (*even merely potential*) cross-border element.

It can, therefore, be concluded that the personal market freedoms are no longer merely sources of the right to take-up and (then) pursue an economic activity in the territory of another Member State/in a cross-border context *under the same conditions as are imposed in situations which are purely internal to a Member State* (ie the traditional reading of these provisions), but rather, they are sources of the broader right to be free from any disproportionate and unjustified regulation when seeking to take-up and pursue an economic activity in the territory of another Member State/in a cross-border context.[192] Moreover, the Court's approach in *Gourmet* demonstrates that the personal market freedoms appear, now, to be also sources of the right not to be restricted in the taking-up and pursuit of an economic activity *in one's own Member State, provided the said economic activity is exercised or will be exercised potentially across borders*. By bringing *any* rules which in some way restrict the taking-up and pursuit of an economic activity within the scope of the personal market freedoms, and even where those rules are the only set of regulations which regulate an economic activity, the Court has effectively brought under EU scrutiny *all* national measures that seek to regulate an economic activity.

---

[189] E Spaventa (n 21) 101.
[190] For a similar case see Case C-6/98 *PRO Sieben Media* [1999] ECR I-7599, though it should be noted that this case did not involve a total ban on advertising a specific product but, rather, a national rule which merely restricted the number of interruptions for advertisements. Accordingly, unlike in *Gourmet* (n 183), in *PRO Sieben Media* there was a lawful market in advertising in Germany (the country which imposed the rules).
[191] For criticisms of this case see E Spaventa (n 21) 47.
[192] ibid, 109.

Commenting on cases such as *Gebhard* and *Gourmet*, Spaventa noted that the developments in these cases

> represent not only a step towards a considerable expansion of the scope of the free movement provisions, but also a *qualitative* leap in the content of the free movement rights. Thus, if previously the Court's interpretation of the persons' provisions was instrumental—or could be so explained and justified—to the achievement of the internal market, the move towards a non-discriminatory assessment adds a new dimension to the rights conferred upon individuals by the community.[193]

(b) Abandoning the Requirement of Cross-Border Specificity: Indirect Restrictions

In this part of the section, it will be demonstrated that the expansion of the scope of the personal market freedoms to catch measures which lack cross-border specificity, has also been effected in situations where the contested national measure amounts to only an indirect restriction on the primary rights stemming from these provisions. For this purpose, the Court's family reunification rights case-law of the last three decades will be analysed.[194]

Although the text of the personal market freedoms never included a reference to family reunification rights, the Community legislature, already back in the 1960s, was aware that the migrant's desire to move would be lessened, if not completely extinguished, if (s)he had to leave his/her family behind.[195] Hence, it has been recognised through secondary legislation (firstly, Regulation 1612/68,[196] and Directive 73/148,[197] the Residence Directives,[198] and, now, Directive 2004/38)[199] and via the Court's rulings, that Union citizens who move between Member States may derive an automatic right to family reunification from EU law and, hence, in such instances, Member States are precluded from applying their immigration laws for the purpose of refusing access to their territory to the third-country national family members of those Union citizens. Since family members that hold the nationality of a Member State are *themselves* entitled to free movement rights, Member States cannot apply their immigration laws to them and, hence, there is no need for EU law to apply and grant family reunification rights in such cases in order to preclude the application of national immigration legislation.

---

[193] ibid, 101.
[194] For an analysis of some of this case-law see A Tryfonidou, 'Family Reunification Rights of (Migrant) Union Citizens: Towards a Liberal Approach' (2009) 15 *European Law Journal* 634. For comments on the Court's approach to the issue of family reunification and its impact on federalism in the EU see S Adam and P Van Elsuwege, 'EU Citizenship and the European Federal Challenge Through the Prism of Family Reunification' in D Kochenov (n 90).
[195] The (traditional) rationale behind the grant of family reunification rights has been summarised in paragraph 46 of the Opinion of AG Sharpston in *O and B* and *S and G* (n 59).
[196] Reg 1612/68 (n 13), Art 10.
[197] Dir 73/148 (n 45), Art 1.
[198] 1990 Residence Directives (n 107), Art 1.
[199] Dir 2004/38 (n 10), Art 3.

Traditionally, the ECJ seemed to be of the view that EU law must step in (only) in order to 'compensate' moving EU citizens for the loss they incur as a result of the exercise of the primary rights stemming from the free movement of persons provisions and, hence, there was a requirement of cross-border specificity. Accordingly, it was considered that EU family reunification rights should be granted only in situations where a Member State national who used to live in his State of origin with his third-country national family members lost this right when he moved.[200] This view seems to be best reflected in the Opinion of Advocate General Tesauro in *Singh*, where he noted that 'the simple exercise of the right of free movement within the Community is not in itself sufficient to bring a particular set of circumstances within the scope of Community law; there must be some connecting factor between the exercise of the right of free movement and the right relied on by the individual'.[201]

Thus, traditionally, EU law sought to ensure that mobile Member State nationals who had been living with their family members in their home State and subsequently decided to move to another Member State were treated in the same manner as Member State nationals who had *not* moved and whose family members had lawfully lived with them in their home State. This was because in such situations, the position of the two categories of persons was the same, bar from the exercise of free movement rights. Hence, just like the latter could continue living with their family members in their home State, the former should, also, be able to continue living with their family members after moving to the host State. Similarly, just as Member State nationals who were in a purely internal situation could only be *joined* (for the first time) by their third-country national family members if the latter satisfied the immigration requirements of their home State, in the same manner it was thought that mobile Member State nationals who wished to be joined (for the first time)—rather than accompanied after having lived with them in their home State—in the host Member State by their third-country national family members, could only do so if the requirements laid down in national immigration legislation (in this case of the *host* State) were satisfied.

A clear reflection of the above approach is the 2003 judgment in *Akrich*,[202] where the Court established that a right to family reunification in the territory of the destination State should only be derived from EU law, if the family member had been lawfully resident in the territory of a Member State *from which* she moved to the host State together with the migrant. This is known as 'the condition of prior lawful residence' and the reason behind it appears to be that the personal market freedoms (and Article 21 TFEU) should only interfere with the application of national immigration rules, if the latter creates (intentionally or unintentionally) a bias against persons who have made use of their free movement

---

[200] G Barrett, 'Family Matters: European Community Law and Third-Country Family Members' (2003) 40 *Common Market Law Review* 369, 375–76; P Caro de Sousa (n 90) 195.
[201] Paragraph 5 of the Opinion of AG Tesauro in *Singh* (n 37).
[202] *Akrich* (n 123).

rights. Accordingly, only if the refusal of the host Member State—in application of its immigration rules—to admit within its territory the family members of the migrant led to the loss of rights previously enjoyed in another Member State could it be considered to amount to a breach of the personal market freedoms (or Article 21 TFEU, in case the migrant was economically inactive).[203]

Nonetheless, this condition was abolished in subsequent case-law where *Akrich* was confined to its own special facts, and where it was also made clear that family reunification rights can now be granted by EU law in a broader range of circumstances than it was originally thought.[204]

The case where the Court explicitly stated that the 'prior lawful residence condition' can no longer be applied by the Member States under any circumstances, is *Metock*,[205] where the Court explained that 'if Union citizens were not allowed to lead a normal family life in the host Member State, the exercise of the freedoms they are guaranteed by the Treaty would be seriously obstructed'.[206] In other words, depriving Union citizens of the chance to lead a normal family life in the host State by not allowing them to live there with their close family members (whether the latter were their family members prior to the move to the host State or not), *in itself*, according to the Court, amounts to a sufficient disincentive for the exercise of the rights deriving from the free movement of persons provisions *and* suffices for a finding of a breach of these provisions even in the absence of *cross-border specificity* (ie if it is obvious that the inability to enjoy family life in the host State does not relate in any way to the exercise of the rights stemming from those provisions).

The *Metock* reasoning appears, in fact, to be also offering an explanation for the Court's decision in the previous case of *Jia*,[207] where family reunification rights were derived from one of the personal market freedoms in a scenario which clearly lacked cross-border specificity. In that case, at issue was the refusal of a Member State (Sweden) to grant a right of residence to Ms Jia, the Chinese mother-in-law (who had come to Sweden *directly from China*) of a German national who had moved to Sweden from Germany in order to exercise her freedom of establishment. The Court held that if Ms Jia was not allowed to join her daughter-in-law in Sweden, this would amount to a breach of the provisions governing the freedom of establishment. In this case it is clear that there was no link between the refusal to grant family reunification rights and the exercise of the right to move to another Member State for the purpose of taking-up an economic activity there. Given that the migrant Union citizen had never, previously, lived with her mother-in-law, it is clear that

---

[203] ibid, paras 50–54.
[204] Case C-1/05 *Jia* [2007] ECR I-1; and, more clearly, Case C-127/08 *Metock* [2008] ECR I-6241.
[205] *Metock* (n 204). For comments, see S Peers, 'Free Movement, Immigration Control and Constitutional Conflict' (2009) 5 *European Constitutional Law Review* 173; N Cambien, 'Annotation of *Metock*' (2009) 15 *Columbia Journal of European Law* 321; C Costello, '*Metock*: Free Movement and "Normal Family Life" in the Union' (2009) 46 *Common Market Law Review* 587.
[206] *Metock* (n 204), para 62.
[207] *Jia* (n 204). For comments see A Tryfonidou, 'Jia or Carpenter II: The Edge of Reason' (2007) 32 *European Law Review* 908.

the Swedish refusal to admit the latter in its territory, did not create a disadvantage related to the exercise of free movement rights; it was, rather, the result of an entirely neutral application of Swedish immigration legislation, which *happened* to disadvantage a migrant Union citizen, and would disadvantage a Swedish national in a comparable situation in exactly the same way (ie a Swedish national who sought to be joined in Sweden by a third-country national family member who had never previously lived with him). Moreover, had Ms Jia's daughter-in-law stayed in Germany (and, thus, had not exercised free movement rights), it is likely that the same disadvantage would be suffered, as a result of the application of the German immigration rules. Accordingly, looked at from any angle, there was no cross-border specificity on the facts of the case and, yet, this did not prevent the Court from concluding that the contested refusal of family reunification rights amounted to a restriction caught by the provisions governing the freedom of establishment.[208]

The same approach has also been followed in cases involving Union citizens who sought to rely on EU law to claim family reunification rights *in their State of nationality*.

The first group of cases we shall see is that involving Union citizens who sought to rely on family reunification rights under EU law in their State of nationality, after returning from another Member State where they had moved in exercise of their rights under the free movement of persons provisions (the 'returnees' case-law).

Singh[209]—a case decided in the 1990s—involved a couple who, after moving from the UK to Germany where the wife had been employed, wished to return to the UK. The Singhs got married in the early 1980s and were lawfully residing in the UK together. Mr Singh was an Indian national and Mrs Singh was a British national. In 1983, the couple decided to move to Germany where Mrs Singh was employed (ie she was a 'worker'). After a couple of years in Germany, the Singhs decided to return to the UK, where Mrs Singh established a business. Soon after their return to the UK, Mr Singh was given limited leave to remain which, however, was subsequently cut short because the couple had filed for divorce; the UK authorities proceeded to issue a deportation order against Mr Singh when he continued residing in the UK after his leave had expired. The issue was referred to the ECJ which held that the contested deportation amounted to a breach of 52 EEC (Article 49 TFEU) and Directive 73/148. Although the Court's decision to employ the above provisions seems to indicate that the measure was prohibited because it was capable of impeding Mrs Singh's *return* to the UK *for the purpose of setting-up a business* there,[210] the Court's reasoning, quite confusingly, points to a different rationale, this being that the contested action was contrary to EU law

---

[208] The Court took the same approach in the recent Case C-423/12 *Reyes* ECLI:EU:C:2014:16.
[209] *Singh* (n 37).
[210] This was also the view of the AG in the case.

because it was capable of impeding the original exercise of free movement from the UK to Germany:

> A national of a Member State might be deterred from leaving his country of origin in order to pursue an activity as an employed or self-employed person as envisaged by the Treaty in the territory of another Member State if, on returning to the Member State of which he is a national in order to pursue an activity there as an employed or self-employed person, the conditions of his entry and residence were not at least equivalent to those which he would enjoy under the Treaty or secondary law in the territory of another Member State[211]

Examining the first scenario (ie that it is the movement back to the UK that would be impeded), would the right of Mrs Singh to return from Germany to the UK be impeded if she was aware that, on her return, UK immigration law would apply to her husband and thus she would lose the right to live with him? In theory,[212] yes. Such a reading of the judgment accords also with an instrumental approach to the market freedoms, as there is, in such a scenario, cross-border specificity: the loss of the right to be with family members emerged as a result of the exercise of the right to move back to the UK given that the couple had previously lived together in Germany.[213] Conversely, there appears to be no cross-border specificity, when the refusal of family reunification rights on the facts of the case is considered to amount to an impediment to the original movement from the UK to Germany: Mr Singh's right of residence in the UK would be regulated by English immigration law if Mrs Singh had not moved, as was the case after she moved back to the UK from Germany; it was merely the *result* to which the application of English immigration legislation led in these two different situations that differed. When Mr Singh originally joined Mrs Singh in the UK he satisfied national immigration requirements, whereas when he sought to continue residing in the UK after the couple had filed for a divorce, he did not satisfy those requirements anymore. Accordingly, the exercise of the right to move from the UK to Germany did not give rise to fewer rights for the Singhs than they would have been granted had they not moved.

Until recently, it was not clear which of the Court's line of reasoning in *Singh* represented the law. Nonetheless, subsequent case-law (*Eind* and *O and B*) has shown that what the Court seems to be aiming to protect in cases involving facts like those in *Singh* is the original movement from the UK to Germany, despite the fact that in that context there is no cross-border specificity.

Eind[214] concerned a Dutch national who had left the Netherlands and went to the UK in order to work. He was subsequently joined by his 11-year-old daughter (a national of Surinam), who joined him there directly from her country of

---

[211] *Singh* (n 37), para 19.
[212] I say 'in theory' because bearing in mind that the reason for cutting short Mr Singh's residence permit was that the couple applied for a divorce, in practice, this would not seem to be the case.
[213] G Davies (n 7) 165; G Barrett (n 200) 379; E Spaventa (n 21) 23–24.
[214] Case C-291/05 *Eind* [2007] ECR I-10719.

nationality, and who was granted by the UK authorities a right to reside there. After a year in the UK, Mr Eind decided to return to the Netherlands (where he would not be working) and his daughter accompanied him there; the Dutch authorities, however, refused to issue the latter with a residence permit and it was claimed that this amounted to a breach of the free movement of persons provisions. The ECJ held that Mr Eind derived a right of family reunification from Regulation 1612/68,[215] and, thus, his daughter should be allowed to reside in the Netherlands. According to the Court, if Mr Eind was not given this right, he would be deterred from leaving the Netherlands to move to the UK as a worker—this would result

> simply from the prospect ... of not being able, on returning to his Member State of origin, to continue living together with close relatives, a way of life which may have come into being in the host Member State as a result of marriage or family reunification.[216]

Accordingly, in this case, the Court found that the right to free movement from a Union citizen's State of nationality and origin (the home State) to another Member State (the host State), can be impeded if that person will not be able to take back with him to the home State his family members who are lawfully resident with him in the host State (and who have firstly entered the EU via the latter). However, in such a scenario there is, clearly, no cross-border specificity—the right to be with close family members is only lost *as a result* of the movement *back* to the home State but is entirely unrelated to the original exercise of free movement rights. Thus, although the result of the case (ie a finding that the contested refusal of family reunification rights is, prima facie, a breach of EU law) accords even with an instrumental reading of the personal market freedoms given that the contested refusal will *cause* persons who *return* to their home State to lose the right to be with their family members and, thus, there is cross-border specificity, the Court's reasoning according to which it is the original movement from the home State to the host State that will be impeded and which needs to be protected by these provisions, does not accord with such a reading since such a scenario lacks cross-border specificity.

The same can be said about the Court's recent ruling in *O and B*.[217] The reference for a preliminary ruling emerged from two separate cases which involved the refusal of the Dutch authorities to grant the right to reside within the Netherlands to the third-country national spouses of Union citizens, who had lived with the latter in another Member State before they sought to return with them in the latter's State of nationality and work (ie the Netherlands). The Court held that family reunification rights should be granted in these cases since, otherwise, the right of the Union citizens to enter into and reside in the *host* Member State (ie the State where they had lived with their spouses) would be impeded; it pointed out that it is necessary to guarantee that a migrant Union citizen 'will be able, in his Member

---

[215] Reg 1612/68 (n 13).
[216] *Eind* (n 214), paras 35–36.
[217] Case C-456/12 *O and B* ECLI:EU:C:2014:135.

State of origin, to continue the family life which he created or strengthened in the host Member State'.[218]

If it is accepted—as appears to be the case—that the Court in both *Eind* and *O and B* considered that the movement that would be impeded as a result of the contested refusal of family reunification rights, was the original movement from the State of origin/nationality to the host Member State, it is clear, once more, that Member State actions which lack cross-border specificity can be subjected to EU scrutiny. It is, indeed, true that if a person is aware that (s)he will not be able to live with his or her close family members in a particular Member State, (s)he is, likely, not to move to that Member State; or, if (s)he is already resident in that Member State, this may be a sufficient reason to leave. Accordingly, in *all* of the above cases there *is* an impediment to the exercise of the rights stemming from the free movement of persons provisions. Nonetheless, for the reasons explained earlier, not all cases involve cross-border specificity and, in particular, there is no cross-border specificity if the movement that is sought to be protected is the original movement from the State of origin to the host State. This is because, in such cases, it is not the exercise of free movement from the home State to the host State that led to the loss of family reunification rights but, rather, it is the subsequent movement back to the State of origin.

The same observations can be made about *Carpenter* and the very recent *S and G* judgment, which involved, again, Union citizens seeking to claim family reunification rights in their State of nationality in order to side-step national immigration legislation. In these cases, however, the claimants had never moved their residence to another Member State but had, rather, taken-up and were pursuing an economic activity in a cross-border context.

Carpenter[219] is a case that has stirred so much reaction in the literature that makes it unnecessary to delve into it in detail here.[220] As is well-known, the case involved a British national, Mr Carpenter, who was providing services selling advertising space in the UK as well as to clients established in other Member States. He lived in the UK where he had his permanent establishment whilst he often travelled to other Member States for the purpose of providing his services. The problem arose when a deportation order was issued against Mr Carpenter's Filipina wife, because she had overstayed her visa. It was submitted that Mrs Carpenter facilitated Mr Carpenter's moves to other Member States because she was taking care of his children from a previous marriage whilst he was away—a factor

---

[218] ibid, para 49.
[219] Case C-60/00 *Carpenter* [2002] ECR I-6279.
[220] See, inter alia, S Acierno, 'The Carpenter Judgment: Fundamental Rights and the Limits of the Community Legal Order' (2003) 28 *European Law Review* 398; H Toner, 'Annotation of *Carpenter*' (2003) 5 *European Journal of Migration and Law* 163; A Tryfonidou, '*Mary Carpenter v Secretary of State for the Home Department*: The Beginning of a New Era in the European Union?' (2003) 14 *King's College Law Journal* 81; Editorial Comment: 'Freedoms Unlimited? Reflections on Mary Carpenter v. Secretary of State' (2003) 40 *Common Market Law Review* 537; E Spaventa, 'From *Gebhard* to *Carpenter*: Towards a (Non-)Economic European Constitution' (2004) 41 *Common Market Law Review* 743.

which was not discussed by the Court in its judgment. The question was whether Mr Carpenter could derive family reunification rights from EU law, which would, in effect, prevent the UK from applying its immigration legislation. The Court held that the contested deportation order amounted to a restriction caught by Article 49 EC (Article 56 TFEU) because

> it is clear that the separation of Mr and Mrs Carpenter would be detrimental to their family life and, therefore, to the conditions under which Mr Carpenter exercises a fundamental freedom. That freedom could not be fully effective if Mr Carpenter were to be deterred from exercising it by obstacles raised in his country of origin to the entry and residence of his spouse.[221]

The above statement says, in essence, that because the third-country national wife of Mr Carpenter would be deported, he would be unable to continue providing his services across borders and, hence, the exercise of UK immigration powers on the facts would lead to a violation of the right of Mr Carpenter to provide services across borders, unless justified.

It is clear that in this case, there was no cross-border specificity and, to borrow the words of Gormley (said in a different context), 'the integrationist merit is thin beyond belief'.[222] The loss of the right to be with his wife in his State of nationality, was in no way related to the decision of Mr Carpenter to provide services in a cross-border context. Moreover, the refusal to permit Mrs Carpenter to continue living with Mr Carpenter and his children in the UK would not affect Mr Carpenter's cross-border economic activity differently (worse) than it would have affected it had it been pursued in a purely domestic context. Accordingly, in this case, again, there was no cross-border specificity and, in fact, there appeared not to be even an (genuinely non-discriminatory) obstacle to the provision of services across borders.

In the more recent *S and G* case,[223] the Court applied the same reasoning in a case which involved frontier workers—ie Union citizens who maintained their residence in their State of nationality whilst they took-up employment in the territory of another Member State to which they were travelling on a daily or weekly basis. The Court, again, held that the refusal of their State of nationality and residence to permit their close family members to reside with them, could prevent them from continuing to pursue their cross-border economic activities, but in this case, the Court noted that this was so because those family members helped with childcare and, thus, enabled them to pursue those activities. Again, nonetheless, there appears to be a complete lack of cross-border specificity: the loss of the right to be with close family members was in no way related to the exercise of the rights stemming from Article 45 TFEU, nor would the refusal of family reunification

---

[221] *Carpenter* (n 219), para 39.
[222] LW Gormley, 'Free Movement of Goods and their Use—What is the Use of it?' (2009–10) 33 *Fordham International Law Journal* 1589, 1599.
[223] Case C-457/12 *S and G* ECLI:EU:C:2014:136.

rights on the facts specifically disadvantage frontier workers and treat them worse than workers in a purely internal situation.

Accordingly, a pure internal market/free movement rationale appears incapable of supporting the Court's recent family reunification rights case-law, analysed in this subsection. Instead of seeking merely to ensure that Union citizens will not be disadvantaged as a result of exercising their free movement rights by guaranteeing to them that when they do so they will not *lose* the right to live with their close family members, the Court appears, now, to be granting Union citizens who have exercised such rights a 'bonus right' to family reunification; in other words, they are not treated in the same manner as they would have been treated had they not exercised free movement rights, but they are, in fact, treated better.[224] The reason behind this is the Court's recognition that any disturbance in the family life of the Union citizen may have an impact on his or her ability to continue residing and/or pursuing an economic activity in another Member State/in a cross-border context and this—as made clear earlier in cases involving direct restrictions on the exercise of the primary rights stemming from the personal market freedoms—appears now to suffice for finding a restriction caught by the personal market freedoms; it is no longer necessary—as was the case traditionally—to show, in addition, that this disturbance has emerged as a result of the exercise of free movement rights which have led to the loss of rights that were enjoyed prior to this exercise.

Accordingly, as a general conclusion from the analysis in subsection C (ii), it can be noted that Union citizens no longer derive from the personal market freedoms merely the right to take-up and to pursue an economic activity in another Member State or in a cross-border context *under the same conditions* that are imposed on Union citizens who take-up an economic activity in a purely national context. Rather, more broadly, Union citizens now have the right to take-up an economic activity in another Member State or in a cross-border context and they should be free to exercise this right in all instances, even in situations where the right to take-up a similar economic activity in a purely national context is restricted or, simply, does not exist. Hence, potentially, Member States can be required to justify *any* regulation, measure or action, which appears capable of restricting—directly or indirectly—the primary rights stemming from the personal market freedoms.

D. The Reconceptualisation of the Personal Market Freedoms as (Also) Sources of Fundamental Economic Rights for the Union Citizen

As can be deduced from the preceding analysis, although, originally, only one primary right appeared to have been considered as stemming from the more

---

[224] M Poiares Maduro, 'The Scope of European Remedies: The Case of Purely Internal Situations and Reverse Discrimination' in C Kilpatrick, T Novitz and P Skidmore (eds), *The Future of European Remedies* (Oxford, Hart Publishing, 2000) 125. Poiares Maduro used this term when criticising the Court's judgment in *Singh* (n 37).

stationary personal market freedoms—the right to take-up an economic activity in the territory of another Member State that is to be permanently pursued there or in a cross-border context—the Court's recent case-law seems to be indicating that *all* the personal market freedoms are, now, the source of two primary— independent of each other—rights:

a) the right to *take-up* an economic activity *in another Member State* that is going to be (permanently *or* temporarily, depending on the freedom) pursued there or in a cross-border context; *and*
b) the right to *start pursuing* an economic activity (that had already been taken-up and was pursued in a purely national context) in a cross-border context (which presupposes the *continuation* of an economic activity that had already been taken-up in a single State context, but the *mode of pursuit* of which is subsequently changed).

Although it is beyond the scope of this chapter to consider whether the personal market freedoms *can* and *should* be interpreted as granting to Union citizens both of the above rights (this will be considered in chapter five), I shall consider, here, whether such a reading of these provisions is compliant with an instrumental approach which views them, merely, as tools to be used for the construction of an internal market.

My view is that it is not, when it comes to the more stationary personal market freedoms. A purely instrumental reading of these provisions considers that they have as their sole aim to ensure that Member State nationals can leave their home Member State and take-up and pursue an economic activity for an indefinite duration *in another Member State*; or that they can maintain their residence in their home State but that they can take-up and indefinitely pursue an economic activity *in another Member State*. This is what is required for an internal market to be *built*, where (employed or self-employed) workers can *work* anywhere they want (here, meaning, in any *other* Member State) and where entrepreneurs can establish a company in any (other) Member State. Accordingly, the grant of the first primary right mentioned above by *all* the personal market freedoms can be fully justified by an internal market rationale.

However, the second primary right that seems, now, to stem from *all* the personal market freedoms (and not just from the freedom to provide services provisions, as used to be the case traditionally) cannot be justified by such a rationale in the context of the more stationary market freedoms. By expanding the scope of the more stationary personal market freedoms to cover situations where there has been no *initiation* of an *economic activity in another Member State*, the Court seems to have stretched the scope of these provisions in a manner which is not required by their (economic) *raison d'être* (ie to build an internal market). Does the ability of Member State nationals to choose where to live in the EU whilst *continuing to pursue an economic activity permanently in their home State* contribute in any way to building an internal market by removing obstacles to the initiation of an economic activity *in another Member State*? The answer is, clearly, 'no'. The broadening of the material scope of the more stationary personal market freedoms in the broader manner seen in the *Ritter-Coulais* saga, therefore, can be read as providing an (implicit) hint that these provisions are no longer viewed by the Court merely as the tools for building an internal market. On the other hand, even a purely economic rationale can justify the grant of this right by the freedom to provide services provisions, given that the aim of building an internal market in services requires that both service-providers/recipients *and* the services themselves can freely move between Member States (without requiring a change in the location of the economic base of the provider).

Having in mind the Court's express admission of the need to take into account, when interpreting the personal market freedoms, of the fact that (some of) their beneficiaries are Union citizens, the most plausible rationale—in my view—for the broader reading of the more stationary personal market freedoms in the *Ritter-Coulais* saga, is the need to (re-)interpret these provisions in the light of Union citizenship; a rationale that has, also, been considered by Spaventa, as the main normative explanation for the Court's case-law which cannot be explained if the personal market freedoms are read as having as their sole aim to ensure that an internal market is built.[225]

However, how exactly is the (new primary) right sought to be protected in *Ritter-Coulais* and its progeny, connected with the status of Union citizenship? From the Court's reasoning in the *Ritter-Coulais* saga, it seems that the rationale behind this broadening of the scope of application of the personal market freedoms, is that these provisions no longer seek merely to protect the right of Member State nationals to *take-up an economic activity* in the territory of another Member State in furtherance of the economic aims of the Treaty, but they also aim to protect the right of Union citizens to pursue an economic activity *in a crossborder context*, an aspect of this—the only one explored in ECJ case-law so far—being to pursue an economic activity in one Member State whilst residing in the territory of another. In this line of case-law, in particular, the Court seems to have wished to protect the right of Union citizens who have moved to another Member State for the purpose of taking-up *residence* there to (continue to) pursue an economic activity in the territory of another Member State. In other words, the Court has considered that it is the job of the personal market freedoms to protect not merely the right of Union citizens to *take-up* an economic activity that is going to be pursued in the territory of another Member State or in a cross-border context, but, also, the right to pursue an economic activity in a cross-border context, even if the cross-border element in the situation has emerged as a result of the Union citizen's exercise of the fundamental (citizenship) right to take-up residence in the territory of another Member State. Accordingly, from this case-law it seems that the Union citizen is, no longer, merely viewed as a tool to be used in the process of building an internal market, but is now, also, viewed as a citizen-worker, who can be assured that (s)he will be able to continue pursuing an economic activity, if

---

[225] E Spaventa (n 21).

112 *Citizenship and Persons Market Freedoms*

(s)he decides to exercise his/her (fundamental citizenship) right to transfer his/her residence to another Member State. Moreover, given that this new primary right is granted in situations where there is no contribution to the internal market aims of the Treaty, it seems that it is no longer an instrumental right, bestowed for the purpose of furthering the economic aims of the Treaty, but is granted to Union citizens for its own sake and, thus, can be considered a *fundamental* right.

The other novelty in the Court's post-Maastricht case-law, which also appears to be incongruous with a purely instrumental reading of the personal market freedoms, is the abandonment of the requirement of cross-border specificity.[226] In order for a national measure or action to be prohibited by the personal market freedoms, it is no longer necessary to prove that the measure itself or its application is biased against the initiation or pursuit *of a cross-border* economic activity. It suffices that the said measure simply restricts one of the primary rights stemming from these provisions, and it does not matter if the contested national measure or action simply seeks to regulate an economic activity in an entirely neutral manner without drawing any distinction between purely internal and cross-border situations.

As explained already in different parts of this book, the requirement of cross-border specificity was a central aspect of the Court's instrumental reading of the personal market freedoms. This is due to the fact that this requirement served as the main mechanism which reconciled the need, on the one hand, to identify and put under EU scrutiny national measures that impeded the achievement of the aim of building an internal market, with the need, on the other, to ensure that the internal market would be a smoothly-functioning, *regulated*, market, since this requirement would ensure that only national measures which did not seek to regulate an economic activity *in a neutral manner* would be caught by the market freedoms.

Accordingly, and in light of the abolition of the requirement of cross-border specificity, a different *raison d'être* must now be sought for the personal market freedoms; in other words, it must be considered which other—or which additional—aim may be capable of justifying the Court's decision to expand the scope of the personal market freedoms to cover *all* national measures that limit in some way the freedom of Union citizens to exercise the primary rights stemming from the personal market freedoms. In my view the rationale behind this move can, again, be considered to be the need to ensure that the personal market freedoms are read in the light of Union citizenship. More specifically, and taking into account the Court's post-Maastricht approach in its case-law—and its express admission that the personal market freedoms must be re-read in the light of Union citizenship—these provisions appear now to be aiming not, merely, to contribute

---

[226] To date, there has been no case where the second primary right now considered to be derived from the personal market freedoms was found to be breached in a situation which lacked cross-border specificity since all the cases where this right was recognised as stemming from the personal market freedoms (ie the *Ritter-Coulais* saga) did involve cross-border specificity.

to the process of building a properly-functioning market (the economic aim) but also to grant to Union citizens[227] *fundamental* economic rights (the citizenship aim) that *exist* in all instances and not, merely, when they are enjoyed in situations which do not involve the exercise of the rights stemming from the Treaty.[228] If the personal market freedoms were read as still only prohibiting measures that have cross-border specificity, this would mean that the said rights would only come to exist if and when the host Member State provided them to its own nationals or if and when the home State granted them to Union citizens who did not exercise their rights under the said provisions; in other words, their existence would become conditional on their availability in a purely internal context.

But this is a reading which is incongruous with a reading of these provisions as sources of *fundamental* rights.[229] Just as it sounds utterly absurd to say that a person visiting a country which is a signatory to the ECHR has the right to be free from torture only if this same right is granted to the nationals of that State, it is equally illogical to say that a Union citizen has the (EU) right to have access to, say, employment in the territory of the host Member State, only if this same right is given by the latter to its own nationals. Accordingly, the aim now appears to be not merely to create a cross-border market in, inter alia, labour, but also to ensure that Union citizens who are economically active enjoy a number of fundamental rights in all instances, and the violation of these rights is contrary to EU law, irrespective of whether such rights are also granted to Union citizens who escape the ambit of these provisions.[230]

Accordingly, the ECJ no longer merely acts as a 'mediator' between EU citizens and the Member States, merely stepping in to require the latter to extend the rights and freedoms they already afford to their own nationals (or to persons who pursue an economic activity in a purely domestic context) to migrant economic actors. In line with its case-law in the citizenship context, the ECJ has now read the personal market freedoms as granting to all Union citizens the two primary (and fundamental) economic rights noted at the beginning of this sub-section. The latter, therefore, are rights which do not originate from national law but they are rights that the EU has considered necessary to grant to all of its citizens. Hence, a direct relationship between the EU and its citizens has been created.

In order to 'survive', national measures or rules that restrict the exercise of the primary rights stemming from the personal market freedoms must be justified and must comply with the general principles of EU law and, in particular, the principle

---

[227] As will be discussed in more detail in chs 5 and 6 below, this citizenship-based rationale is incapable of explaining the broadening of the scope of application of the market freedoms in situations involving legal persons such as *Gourmet* (n 183) and, as will be suggested in those chapters, the Court should revert to its original, instrumental, approach to the interpretation of the personal market freedoms in such situations.

[228] M Szydlo (n 179) 777–78 (esp fn 67). For the opposite view, see RCA White (n 74) 207.

[229] Paragraph 203 of the Opinion of AG Lenz in *Bosman* (n 65).

[230] For a similar view, see J Snell, 'And then there were Two: Products and Citizens in Community Law' in T Tridimas and P Nebbia (eds), *European Union Law for the Twenty-First Century: Volume II* (Oxford, Hart Publishing, 2004) 70.

of proportionality. And, as pointed out by the Court, in view of the fact that these rights are now considered to be fundamental, citizenship, rights, a 'particularly restrictive' approach should be taken,[231] when deciding whether measures that limit their exercise are justified. In addition, the procedures followed at national level for determining whether and to what extent these rights can be restricted in certain circumstances, must be such as to reflect the *fundamental* nature of these rights. As Advocate General Ruiz-Jarabo Colomer stressed in *Petersen*,

> the concept of citizenship, which entails a *legal status for individuals*, means that the Member States must pay *particular attention to individual legal situations*. ... Holding their fundamental rights as prerogatives of freedom, citizens of the Union afford their claims greater legitimacy. ... That definition calls for the freedoms of movement to be reinterpreted where the individuals who are entitled to those freedoms hold the status conferred in Articles 17 and 18 EC.[232]

Accordingly, it is not surprising that the Court in its post-Maastricht case-law has emphasised that national authorities or courts must take into account the *individual situation* of the Union citizen, firstly, when examining whether there is a restriction on the exercise of the primary rights stemming from the free movement of persons provisions and, secondly, when deciding whether the recalcitrant Member State is justified in applying a measure or pursuing an action that restricts such rights. Hence, and in accordance with the suggestion of Advocate General Ruiz-Jarabo Colomer quoted above, in its case-law concerning the rights stemming from (all) the free movement of persons provisions, the Court has adopted a common 'hermeneutic technique',[233] which is based on the fact that the beneficiaries of these provisions are *citizens* (whether economically active or inactive) of the EU polity. This 'technique' requires an examination of the *specific* circumstances of the individual concerned and the impact that the contested measure or action has on the *specific* position of *that* individual. In addition, the Court often provides 'guidelines' which seek to ensure that certain 'procedural guarantees'[234] are safeguarded, when national courts or authorities determine whether there is an unjustified breach of the fundamental rights that Union citizens derive from the free movement of persons provisions.[235]

---

[231] *Orfanopoulos and Oliveri* (n 104), para 65.
[232] Opinion of AG Ruiz Jarabo Colomer in Case C-228/07 *Petersen* [2008] ECR I-6989, para 27.
[233] E Spaventa (n 21) 138.
[234] The term has been taken from S Prechal, 'Topic One: National Applications of the Proportionality Principle: Free Movement and Procedural Requirements: Proportionality Reconsidered' (2008) 35 *Legal Issues of Economic Integration* 201.
[235] Of course, the discretion of national authorities when exercising their administrative powers is, also, limited when there is a conflict with the more economic freedoms (goods) and or in more 'economic' situations, though the Court does not provide as detailed guidelines regarding how that discretion should be exercised as it does in cases involving persons. See eg Case C-205/99 *Analir* [2001] ECR I-1271; Case C-390/99 *Canal Satélite* [2002] ECR I-607; Case C-483/99 *Commission v France* [2002] ECR I-4781; Case C-250/06 *United Pan-Europe Communications* [2007] ECR I-11135.

Examples of this approach in the context of the personal market freedoms is the judgment in *Carpenter*,[236] where the Court examined the specific circumstances of Mr and Mrs Carpenter in order to determine whether the UK's decision to deport the latter could be justified, as well as the Court's rulings in its healthcare case-law, where it has provided detailed guidelines, which, in essence, require national authorities/courts to focus on the specific circumstances of the case before deciding whether the contested refusal to reimburse medical expenses was justified.[237] Similarly, in the context of the citizenship provisions, this 'technique' has been used in cases involving, inter alia, the deportation of an economically inactive Union citizen,[238] the withdrawal of Member State nationality,[239] and the refusal of the right of residence in the territory of another Member State due to the lack of economic self-sufficiency.[240] The need to focus on the particular circumstances of the individual concerned in order to decide whether—on the facts of the case—there is an unjustified breach of the fundamental rights stemming from the free movement of persons provisions (including the personal market freedoms) is also evident in a number of provisions in the 2004 Citizens' Rights Directive.[241]

As De Vries has noted, 'Member States in exercising their powers to pursue fundamental rights have to take account of principles of good governance',[242] and, hence, the Court's recent jurisprudence in this context 'not only impacts on the Member States' regulatory autonomy, but also on the Member States' regulatory practices, i.e. on the way the rules are applied to the particular circumstances of the case'.[243]

---

[236] *Carpenter* (n 219).
[237] See eg *Vanbraekel* (n 124), para 90; *Geraets Smits and Peerbooms* (n 124), para 104; *Müller Fauré* (n 124), para 90; *Inizan* (n 124), para 46; *Watts* (n 124), para 62; *Elchinov* (n 124), para 66; *Petru* (n 124), para 32. For comments see O Gerstenberg, 'The Question of Standards for the EU: From "Democratic Deficit" to "Justice Deficit?"' in D Kochenov, G de Búrca and A Williams (eds), *Europe's Justice Deficit?* (Oxford, Hart Publishing, 2015). Greer and Sokol have called the guidelines provided by the ECJ in its healthcare case-law 'rules for rights' (meaning, 'setting principles by which to judge the rules Member States use to make decisions about social rights' (p 77)) and this approach 'responds to the problem of establishing social citizenship rights in an EU where the diverse Member States, rather than the regulatory EU, must pay for and provide the actual content of rights' (p 85)—see SL Greer and T Sokol, 'Rules for Rights: European Law, Health Care and Social Citizenship' (2014) 20 *European Law Journal* 66.
[238] Case C-145/09 *Tsakouridis* [2010] ECR I-11979. See D Kostakopoulou and N Ferreira, 'Testing Liberal Norms: The Public Policy and Public Security Derogations and the Cracks in European Union Citizenship' (2013–14) 20 *Columbia Journal of European Law* 167, 170–71.
[239] Case C-135/08 *Rottmann* [2010] ECR I-1449, para 56.
[240] Case C-333/13 *Dano* ECLI:EU:C:2014:2358, para 80.
[241] See eg Art 28(1) and Recital 16 to the Preamble of the Directive (n 10).
[242] S De Vries, 'The Protection of Fundamental Rights within Europe's Internal Market after Lisbon—An Endeavour for More Harmony' in S de Vries, U Bernitz and S Weatherill (n 137) 68–69; see, also, pp 79 and 82.
[243] E Spaventa (n 21) 155.

V. CONCLUSION

The aim of this chapter was to examine how the interpretation of the personal market freedoms has been affected by the introduction of the status of Union citizenship.

It has been seen that following the establishment and development of Union citizenship, the Court reconsidered fundamental tenets of its earlier jurisprudence in the area of the personal market freedoms. The Court, therefore, took the opportunity to note expressly that the interpretation of the personal market freedoms had to be adjusted in order to take into account the fact that economic actors who bear the nationality of a Member State are now also—and, perhaps, primarily[244]—Union citizens.

What is more important, however, are the implicit steps that the Court has taken in its case-law, indicating that the personal market freedoms appear, now, to be part of the package of rights bestowed by the EU on its citizens. In particular, it has been seen that the Court has departed from its traditional position under which the (more stationary) personal market freedoms were viewed as merely sources of instrumental rights and, in particular, of only one primary right—the right to move to another Member State *for the purpose of taking-up* an economic activity that is going to be pursued there or in a cross-border context. Now, these provisions—as has always been the case with the freedom to provide services—appear to also grant to Union citizens the right to start pursuing an economic activity in a cross-border context (irrespective of whether there has been a change in the location of the economic activity); a right the grant of which cannot be explained under an internal market-based rationale. In addition, the Court seems to have abandoned the requirement of cross-border specificity, in this way broadening the scope of the market freedoms to catch any measure which restricts the exercise by Union citizens of the rights stemming from the personal market freedoms, *irrespective of whether* the measure *simply* regulates *in a neutral* manner an economic activity and as such *merely* limits the *economic freedom* of Union citizens. This is, also, significant because it shows that the personal market freedoms are, now, read in a manner which cannot be justified by a market-building rationale.

Accordingly, the Court's post-Maastricht rulings seem to support the view that the personal market freedoms are no longer merely the tools for building an internal market but they are, also (and perhaps primarily), the sources of *fundamental* economic rights for Union citizens, which are protected and respected for their own sake and not in order to further the achievement of a certain objective. Adopting the words of Advocate General Poiares Maduro, the aim of the personal market freedoms appears, now, to be to establish 'an internal market in which the rights of European citizens are protected'.[245] Thus, the role of these provisions

---

[244] S Currie, 'The Transformation of Union Citizenship' in M Dougan and S Currie (eds), *50 Years of the European Treaties: Looking Back and Thinking Forward* (Oxford, Hart Publishing, 2009) 381.
[245] Case C-446/03 *Marks and Spencer* [2010] ECR I-10837, para 37.

as market-building tools continues to exist, but is coexistent with the other aim of the EU which appears to be to grant certain fundamental economic rights to Union citizens.

Whether the current position with regards to the interpretation of the personal market freedoms can be sustained under either a literal or a teleological approach to their interpretation, will be examined in chapter five. Before moving there, however, we shall explore what may have been the impact of Union citizenship on the interpretation of the free movement of goods provisions. The next chapter is devoted to this issue.

4

Union Citizenship and the Free Movement of Goods

I. INTRODUCTION

IN THIS CHAPTER, the focus will be placed on the rights that *individuals* derive from the free movement of goods provisions, as the question that is sought to be answered is whether the introduction of Union citizenship has had any impact on the interpretation of these provisions.[1] Although the provisions that seek to remove obstacles to the free movement of goods target both tariff[2] and non-tariff[3] barriers to trade, and there are also a number of provisions which deal with barriers to trade that emerge from aid granted by a Member State to a specific industry ('State aid'),[4] from monopolies of a commercial character,[5] or from action taken by private parties which restricts competition in the internal market,[6] this chapter will be focusing on the provisions prohibiting non-tariff barriers to the free movement of goods and, in particular, on Article 34 TFEU. This is for the simple reason that it is only through the case-law interpreting this provision that any evidence can be gathered that the provisions governing the free movement of goods may have now been read as sources of rights—and, even, fundamental rights—for individuals, which may form the basis for an argument that these provisions have been affected by the introduction of Union citizenship.

The structure of the chapter will be as follows. The first main section (II) will seek to illustrate how Article 34 TFEU has *traditionally* been interpreted. It will be explained that the Court's orthodox case-law in this area demonstrates that this provision has been considered as having as its sole aim to ensure that goods can move freely between Member States whilst Member States should remain

---

[1] This chapter explores in more detail some of the ideas firstly presented in A Tryfonidou, 'Further Steps on the Road to Convergence among the Market Freedoms' (2010) 35 *European Law Review* 36.
[2] Arts 30 and 110 TFEU.
[3] Arts 34 and 35 TFEU.
[4] Arts 107–09 TFEU.
[5] Art 37 TFEU.
[6] Arts 101 and 102 TFEU.

free to regulate neutrally economic activities taking place in their territory. Any rights that individuals have derived from Article 34 TFEU have, therefore, traditionally been instrumental in the achievement of this aim. Moreover, the section will highlight the Court's (traditional) insistence on the existence of cross-border specificity, according to which only national measures that *specifically* affect inter-State trade should be considered to be restrictions caught by this provision. This will be followed by a section (III) which will explore the Court's stance on the nature of the free movement of goods provisions: has the Court in its case-law attributed a (fundamental) rights-nature to these provisions, as it seems to have done in its personal market freedoms case-law that we saw in the previous chapter? The next section (IV) will then examine some (sporadic) case-law where the Court appears to have read Article 34 TFEU as a source of direct rights for individuals, whilst it will also consider recent case-law where the classic market-building rationale that has traditionally been applied in this context appears incapable of explaining the Court's approach in its rulings. The last section (V) will conclude.

Through the analysis in this chapter, it will be seen that, (probably) due to the fact that re-conceptualising the free movement of goods provisions as sources of (fundamental) rights for persons is much more controversial and, as such, less well-entrenched than arguing the same thing for the personal market freedoms, the Court has been much less forthcoming in its case-law about the position of individuals in this context and about whether they derive any (fundamental) rights from these provisions. Moreover, unlike with the personal market freedoms, the Court has nowhere explicitly admitted (or even hinted at) the need to re-interpret the free movement of goods provisions in the light of Union citizenship. Accordingly, although—as we saw in the previous chapter—the process of transformation of the personal market freedoms into sources of fundamental rights for the Union citizen appears to be now well underway, the same cannot be said about the free movement of goods provisions. Rather, it can merely be argued that the Court's case-law provides us with certain scattered indications that we *may* be heading in the same direction in this context as well, although, if we do, we are still clearly in the very early stages of this process.

II. THE TRADITIONAL INTERPRETATION OF THE FREE MOVEMENT OF GOODS PROVISIONS

Article 34 TFEU provides that '[q]uantitative restrictions on imports and all measures having equivalent effect shall be prohibited between Member States'. The prohibition is not absolute since Article 36 TFEU provides an exhaustive list of grounds which can be used to justify any measures that amount to a restriction that is prima facie contrary to this provision and, when it comes to indistinctly applicable measures that are MEQRs (measure having equivalent effect to quantitative restrictions), the Court established in its famous *Cassis de*

Dijon ruling,[7] an additional, non-exhaustive, list of non-economic grounds (the 'mandatory requirements')[8] that can be used to provide a justification for them. Unlike the personal market freedoms, Article 34 TFEU is not accompanied by much secondary legislation,[9] and, hence, the burden has fallen almost exclusively on the Court of Justice to develop the law in this context.

This section aims to illustrate two things. Firstly, that Article 34 TFEU has been traditionally read as merely seeking to ensure the free circulation of goods within the EU, whilst permitting the Member States to continue regulating trade *in a neutral manner* (ie without drawing any distinction between cross-border trade and trade between Member States); for this reason, it will be explained, there has, traditionally, been a requirement of cross-border specificity, in order for this provision to apply.[10] Secondly, that this provision has traditionally been viewed as solely aiming to liberalise the inter-State movement of *goods*,[11] and, as such, any rights that Member State nationals (and persons, more broadly) have traditionally derived from it have been merely instrumental and enforceable solely for the purpose of ensuring that the goods produced, marketed, or simply owned by them, can move freely between Member States.

The analysis in this section will begin by considering what is a 'good' within the meaning of Article 34 TFEU and how the personal scope of this provision has traditionally been differentiated from that of the personal market freedoms (and the rationale behind this). The greatest part of the analysis, however, will be devoted to a consideration of the Court's traditional jurisprudence interpreting the term MEQR for the purposes of this provision.[12] The reason for choosing the above

---

[7] Case 120/78 *Rewe-Zentral AG v Bundesmonopolverwaltung für Branntwein* ('*Cassis de Dijon*') [1979] ECR 649.

[8] For more on the terminology, see P Oliver and S Enchelmaier, 'Free Movement of Goods: Recent Developments in the Case-Law' (2007) 44 *Common Market Law Review* 649, 689–90.

[9] For an early overview of secondary legislation in this area, see AWH Meij and JA Winter, 'Measures having an Effect Equivalent to Quantitative Restrictions' (1976) 13 *Common Market Law Review* 79, 82–84.

[10] The existence of cross-border specificity is, still, required for the other Treaty provisions seeking to remove obstacles to the free movement of goods. Art 30 TFEU prohibits customs duties and charges having equivalent effect to customs duties, which are, in essence, dues that are imposed *by reason of the fact that goods have crossed borders*; Art 110 TFEU prohibits (only) discriminatory taxation on goods; Art 35 TFEU had traditionally been read as only prohibiting measures which are directly discriminatory against goods destined for exports (Case 15/79 *Groenveld* [1979] ECR 3409), but more recently its scope has been expanded to catch, also, indirectly discriminatory measures (Case C-205/07 *Gysbrechts* [2008] ECR I-9947), though it has not been stretched to also cover genuinely non-discriminatory measures.

[11] HD Jarass, 'A Unified Approach to the Fundamental Freedoms' in M Andenas and W-H Roth (eds), *Services and Free Movement in EU Law* (Oxford, Oxford University Press, 2002) 143.

[12] Note that the same prohibition as that provided in Art 34 TFEU with regards to imports is provided in Art 35 TFEU with regards to exports. Although a common interpretation has been adopted for the notion of 'quantitative restrictions' for the purposes of both provisions (see Case 2/73 *Geddo* [1973] ECR 865), a different approach has been followed towards the interpretation of the term 'MEQR'. For more on the interpretation of Art 35 TFEU see, inter alia, A Dawes, 'A Freedom Reborn? The New Yet Unclear Scope of Article 29 EC' (2009) 34 *European Law Review* 639; M Szydlo, 'Export Restrictions within the Structure of Free Movement of Goods. Reconsideration of an Old Paradigm' (2010) 47 *Common Market Law Review* 735; A Tryfonidou (n 1).

issues as the focus of the analysis is that it is mainly through the Court's (recently) differentiated approach towards them (to be seen in section IV below) that we can discern the first signs of a possible move towards the re-interpretation of the free movement of goods provisions as sources of rights (and, even, of fundamental rights) for persons; hence, an explanation of the Court's traditional approach to these issues is necessary in order to enable a comparison to be drawn between that approach and the Court's recently differentiated approach.

A. The Court's Traditional Approach to the Personal Scope of Article 34 TFEU

In order for the provisions governing the free movement of goods to apply, the first issue to consider is whether the product at issue is a 'good'. 'Goods' have been defined by the Court as products which 'can be valued in money and which are capable, as such, of forming the subject of commercial transactions'.[13] The free movement of goods provisions have been held to apply to goods in transit,[14] as well as to goods moving from one Member State to another with the purpose of staying put in the latter State. Conversely, with the exception of Article 30 TFEU,[15] these provisions do not apply to situations which involve goods that move within one and the same Member State, which are, therefore, deemed to be in a purely internal situation.[16]

The Court has made it clear that it makes no difference whether goods are imported or exported for commercial or personal use.[17] In other words, a situation does not need to involve a commercial transaction in order to fall within the scope of the free movement of goods provisions: an individual who merely wishes to move his or her goods across borders can rely on these provisions, just as much as a trader who wishes to move goods between Member States as part of his/her economic activities.[18] This must be contrasted with the personal market freedoms which—as we saw in the previous chapter—require the presence of an economic

---

[13] Case 7/68 *Commission v Italy (the art treasures case)* [1968] ECR 423, 428–29.
[14] *Geddo* (n 12), para 7 (for quantitative restrictions). For MEQRs see, inter alia, Case 266/81 *SIOT* [1983] ECR 731, para 16; Case C-173/05 *Commission v Italy* [2007] ECR I-4917, para 31.
[15] See, inter alia, Joined Cases C-363 & 407-411/93 *Lancry* [1994] ECR I-3957; Joined Cases C-485 & 486/93 *Simitzi v Kos* [1995] ECR I-2655; Case C-72/03 *Carbonati Apuani* [2004] ECR I-8027; Case C-293/02 *Jersey Produce Marketing Organisation v States of Jersey and Jersey Potato Export Marketing Board* [2005] ECR I-9543. For more on this see A Tryfonidou, 'Resolving the Reverse Discrimination Paradox in the area of Customs Duties: The *Lancry* Saga' (2011) 22 *European Business Law Review* 311.
[16] Case 286/81 *Criminal Proceedings against Oosthoek's Uitgeversmaatschappij BV* [1982] ECR 4575, para 9.
[17] Case 215/87 *Schumacher* [1989] ECR 617; Case C-62/90 *Commission v Germany* [1992] ECR I-2575; Case C-387/01 *Weigel* [2004] ECR I-4981. For an early argument supporting this, see the Opinion of AG Warner in Case 34/79 *Henn and Darby* [1979] ECR 3795, 3827. See, also, the (second) Opinion of AG Jacobs in Case C-2/90 *Commission v Belgium* [1992] ECR I-4431, para 15.
[18] J Snell, *Goods and Services in EC Law: A Study of the Relationship between the Freedoms* (Oxford, Oxford University Press, 2002) 5.

element (ie remuneration) in order to apply.[19] As Barnard has explained, this is an element that brings the free movement of goods closer to the free movement of capital, given that in order for the latter to apply, there is no need to prove that a commercial transaction is involved.[20]

Traditionally, it has been considered that the sole aim of the free movement of goods is to ensure that *goods* can move freely between Member States whilst Member States can continue to regulate economic activities involving the production and sale of goods in a neutral manner. And although these provisions have been held to be directly effective and, as such, can be relied on by individuals before national courts,[21] this seemed—at least traditionally—to have been recognised merely in order to ensure that goods can move freely between Member States and not for the purpose of protecting any rights that individuals are supposed to derive from these provisions:[22] since goods themselves cannot enforce their 'right' to move freely between Member States (if, indeed, it can be said that goods are holders of rights), the next best thing is to allow individuals affected by obstacles to the free movement of goods to enforce these provisions. Hence, any rights derived by persons from the free movement of goods provisions have traditionally been considered as merely instrumental to the aim of ensuring the free movement of goods between Member States. In fact, the complete lack of interest (on the part of the EU) in the rights of the persons affected by the free movement of goods, has been one of the main differentiating elements drawn between these provisions and the personal market freedoms, and one of the reasons preventing convergence between them.[23]

This lack of interest, in this context, in the rights of individuals, is due to the fact that the aim of building an internal market in goods does not require that traders (in addition to goods) can move between Member States, as is often[24] the case in the context of the freedom to provide services. The sale of goods is normally located geographically at the place of the buyer—not the seller—and, hence, in a single market, what appears imperative to be protected is the ability of goods to move

---

[19] See Art 57 TFEU for services. The other personal market freedoms do not make express reference to the notion of remuneration, but the need for this has been established in the case-law.

[20] C Barnard, *The Substantive Law of the EU: The Four Freedoms* (Oxford, Oxford University Press, 2013) 35. For an example of a movement of capital which was not for an economic purpose, see Case C-133/13 Q ECLI:EU:C:2014:2460.

[21] Case 74/76 *Iannelli* [1977] ECR 557, para 13.

[22] As Enchelmaier has noted '[i]t is the goods that count; the treatment of the trader is only a proxy for the treatment of the goods'—S Enchelmaier, 'Moped Trailers, Mickelsson & Roos, Gysbrechts: The ECJ's Case Law on Goods Keeps on Moving' (2010) 29 *Yearbook of European Law* 190, 203. For a similar view see C Krenn, 'A Missing Piece in the Horizontal Effect "Jigsaw": Horizontal Direct Effect and the Free Movement of Goods' (2012) 49 *Common Market Law Review* 177, 199.

[23] J Snell, 'And then there were Two: Products and Citizens in Community Law' in T Tridimas and P Nebbia (eds), *European Union Law for the Twenty-First Century: Volume II* (Oxford, Hart Publishing, 2004) 49; P Oliver, 'Of Trailers and Jet Skis: Is the Case Law on Article 34 TFEU Hurtling in a New Direction?' (2009–10) 33 *Fordham International Law Journal* 1423, 1426.

[24] Though, admittedly, there are many services which do not require the provider to move with them, and this is the case especially in recent years as a result of the increase in the use of the Internet for the provision of services.

to the buyer.[25] This, together with the fact that the production and sale of goods are, in the vast majority of cases, entirely separated, and thus, in order for goods to be sold it is not necessary that their producer moves with them, explains why the free movement of goods provisions (as reflected in their wording which does not make any reference to persons) only seek to protect the free inter-State movement of goods and are not concerned at all with the free movement of traders. Unlike services which are, usually, of a non-storable nature and thus require the simultaneity of provision and use,[26] the production and provision (in this context, retail) stages in commercial transactions involving goods, can—in most instances—be easily separated.[27] Accordingly, unlike the provisions governing services which have always been read as involving, also, a personal element, envisaging the movement of natural persons,[28] the free movement of goods provisions have traditionally only been read as covering the free movement of goods (and not that of persons).[29] Thus, traditionally, if the goods involved on the facts of a case had not moved between Member States, this led to the situation being immediately classified as purely internal to a Member State and, thus, as falling outside the scope of Article 34 TFEU;[30] unlike in the context of services, the Court would not examine whether a person 'related' to those goods had exercised free movement which could, instead, bring the situation within the scope of the free movement of goods provisions.[31]

A corollary of the above is that, unlike the personal market freedoms which are primarily concerned with the free movement of economically active *Union citizens* and which, hence, can only be *relied on by persons holding the nationality of a Member State*, the free movement of goods have (at least traditionally) not been concerned at all with ensuring that Member State nationals can move freely between Member States and they, thus, have not required that the person relying on them holds the nationality of a Member State;[32] the same is, of course, the case with the

---

[25] C Barnard and S Deakin, 'Market Access and Regulatory Competition' in C Barnard and J Scott, *The Law of the Single European Market: Unpacking the Premises* (Oxford, Hart Publishing, 2002) 203.
[26] TP Hill, 'On Goods and Services' (1977) 23 *Review of Income and Wealth* 315. See, also, J Snell (n 18) 20; V Hatzopoulos, 'Turkish Service Recipients under the EU-Turkey Association Agreement: Demirkan' (2014) 51 *Common Market Law Review* 647, 660–61.
[27] '[T]he marketing of a product on a domestic market may entail a number of stages between the time when the product is manufactured and the time when it is ultimately sold to the end consumer'— Case C-322/01 *DocMorris* [2003] ECR I-14887, para 70.
[28] J Snell (n 18) 9 and 16–17.
[29] RCA White, *Workers, Establishment, and Services in the European Union* (Oxford, Oxford University Press, 2004) 221–22; P Caro de Sousa, 'Quest for the Holy Grail—Is a Unified Approach to the Market Freedoms and European Citizenship Justified?' (2014) 20 *European Law Journal* 499, 505.
[30] *Oosthoek's* (n 16).
[31] HD Jarass (n 11) 143.
[32] P Oliver, 'Non-Community Nationals and the Treaty of Rome' (1985) 5 *Yearbook of European Law* 57, 61; HD Jarass (n 11) 144; J Snell (n 18) 5; P Oliver and S Enchelmaier (n 8) 667; S Kadelbach, 'Union Citizenship' in A von Bogdandy and J Bast (eds), *Principles of European Constitutional Law* (Oxford, München, Hart Publishing, CH Beck, Nomos, 2011) 452. As Gormley has noted, '[i]t is particularly important that producers outside the Community realize that they can and should seek to enforce their basic right to engage in inter-State commerce within the Community'—see LW Gormley, '"Actually or Potentially, Directly or Indirectly"? Obstacles to the Free Movement of Goods' (1989) 9 *Yearbook of European Law* 197, 204.

provisions governing the free movement of capital.[33] Accordingly, the nationality of the owner of the products or of the producer/importer/retailer/consumer is irrelevant when it comes to the application of the free movement of goods provisions; the only requirement is that the goods, the movement of which has been impeded, originate in a Member State or are in free circulation in the EU.[34]

B. The Court's Traditional Approach to 'Restrictions' Caught by Article 34 TFEU: *Dassonville*, *Cassis*, and *Keck*, and the Requirement of Cross-Border Specificity

As seen above, Article 34 TFEU is the Treaty provision which prohibits quantitative restrictions and MEQRs on imports.

Quantitative restrictions have been defined by the Court in *Geddo* as 'a total or partial restraint of, according to the circumstances, imports, exports or goods in transit'.[35] There has not been much case-law on quantitative restrictions,[36] given that defining this term has been a rather straightforward exercise and that Member States, being aware of this prohibition and of the fact that it is overly easy to spot a quantitative restriction, have refrained from introducing such measures following the coming into force of the EEC Treaty.[37]

However, things have not been as simple with the other type of measures prohibited by Article 34 TFEU: MEQRs.[38] Following an attempt to provide a definition of this term via secondary legislation (Directive 70/50[39]), it mostly fell to the Court of Justice to elucidate its meaning, mainly through its preliminary rulings jurisprudence.

The process of defining the term 'MEQR' began in the early 1970s—in 1974, to be more accurate, with the case of *Dassonville*[40]—and continues to the present day. This constant need to (re-)define this term is attributable to two factors. Firstly, the term is hugely significant because it can encompass a (much) wider array of national measures than quantitative restrictions (QRs), and, in particular, measures which

---

[33] S Kadelbach (n 32) 452; N Nic Shuibhne, *The Coherence of EU Free Movement Law* (Oxford, Oxford University Press, 2013) 67.
[34] Joined Cases 2 & 3/69 *Diamantarbeiders* [1969] ECR 211, paras 24/26. For comments see J Snell (n 18) 5 and 11 and G Davies, *European Union Internal Market Law* (London, Routledge, 2003) 205.
[35] *Geddo* (n 12).
[36] See, inter alia, *Henn and Darby* (n 17); Case 288/83 *Commission v Ireland* ('*Cyprus Potatoes*') [1985] ECR 1761.
[37] Textbooks only devote, at most, a couple of pages to quantitative restrictions. See eg P Craig and G de Búrca, *EU Law: Text, Cases and Materials* (Oxford, Oxford University Press, 2011) 638–39; C Barnard (n 20) 72–73. See, also, the comments by EL White, 'In Search of Limits to Article 30 of the EEC Treaty' (1989) 26 *Common Market Law Review* 235, 239–42.
[38] EL White (n 37) 242.
[39] Dir 70/50 on the abolition of measures which have an effect equivalent to quantitative restrictions on imports and are not covered by other provisions adopted in pursuance of the EEC Treaty [1970] OJ L13/29.
[40] Case 8/74 *Dassonville* [1974] ECR 837.

are 'innocent' and hence not *intended* at all to impede *inter-State* trade (though they do have such an effect),[41] and, thus, it is through this term that the Court determines the limits that EU law can place on the exercise of Member State regulatory competence in the context of trade.[42] Secondly, the process of building an internal market is an ongoing one and the goalposts keep shifting; accordingly, it is only natural that as the aims of the process of internal-market building evolve, so should the interpretation of the main term that is used for determining the scope of application of the central provision that is used for achieving those aims.

In *Dassonville*, MEQRs were defined as 'all trading rules enacted by Member States which are capable of hindering, directly or indirectly, actually or potentially, intra-Community trade'.[43] This is known as 'the *Dassonville* formula' which is—to the present day—the Court's starting point in cases where it seeks to establish whether a national measure amounts to an MEQR contrary to Article 34 TFEU: in such cases, the Court usually begins its reasoning by repeating this definition, albeit with some minor modifications in some instances.[44] However, the *Dassonville* formula 'is strikingly, almost insanely, broad',[45] and hence the root of the lack of legal certainty in this area and the reason for the cascade of case-law that has followed since then. This may, however, be, at the same time, its virtue and the reason that it has survived almost unscathed for more than 40 years, since it is, in essence, an open, imprecise, definition for the term 'MEQRs', which has left a large amount of leeway for fine-tuning, in order to reflect the priorities of the Community and, later, the EU, at any particular time. As Davies has very characteristically put it, if 'all philosophy since the Greeks is merely footnotes to Plato, then goods law is not much more than footnotes to *Dassonville*'.[46] The ease with which it could be established, following *Dassonville*, that a measure amounted to an MEQR was further enhanced by the fact that the Court did not 'seek to establish whether a State measure *actually* has an effect which is economically equivalent to a quantitative restriction on imports (requiring it to make an economic analysis) but rather examines whether a measure is *capable of hindering* imports'.[47]

The next significant step in the process of defining the term 'MEQR', was the Court's ruling in *Cassis de Dijon*, which was delivered in 1979.[48] The judgment is

---

[41] J Steiner, 'Drawing the Line: Uses and Abuses of Article 30 EEC' (1992) 29 *Common Market Law Review* 749, 750.
[42] AWH Meij and JA Winter (n 9) 81.
[43] *Dassonville* (n 40), para 5.
[44] eg the word 'rules' has been replaced by 'measures' in order to enable measures emanating from the State which, however, are not binding laws, to be caught by Art 34 TFEU—Case 104/75 *de Peijper* [1976] ECR 613, para 12. See, moreover, the facts in Case 249/81 *Commission v Ireland* [1982] ECR 4005 ('*Buy Irish* case') and paragraph 28 of the Court's judgment in that case.
[45] G Davies (n 34) 22.
[46] ibid.
[47] EL White (n 37) 236. See also, LW Gormley, 'The Definition of Measures Having Equivalent Effect' in A Arnull, P Eeckhout and T Tridimas (eds), *Continuity and Change in EU Law* (Oxford, Oxford University Press, 2008) 191.
[48] *Cassis de Dijon* (n 7).

significant for two reasons. Firstly, it made it clear that Article 34 TFEU does not, only, prohibit distinctly applicable measures but it catches, also, indistinctly applicable measures[49]—something which does not contradict the *Dassonville* formula but which also could not be conclusively inferred from the judgment in *Dassonville*, given that the facts in that case involved a distinctly applicable rule.[50] Secondly, the Court confirmed the application of the principle of mutual recognition and the home State principle in this context: it noted that provided the goods are lawfully produced in their home State (ie they comply with the laws of that State) they should be free to move to any other Member State, without having to also comply with the host State's requirements. This was the Court's response to the menace of dual-burden regulation, which emerged from the possibility that goods which crossed borders could be subjected to two sets of regulations (ie the rules of the home State *and* the rules of the host State), whereas goods that stayed put in a single Member State would merely have to satisfy one set of regulations. Rules which impose a dual burden are, therefore, indirectly discriminatory measures, since they treat imported goods worse than domestic goods and they have cross-border specificity since they particularly (and only) affect goods that move and, hence, are obviously capable of (specifically) impeding the free movement of goods.[51]

Cassis itself involved such a measure, ie an indistinctly applicable, indirectly discriminatory, measure which, when applied to imported products which had already complied with the product requirements of their own State, imposed a dual burden. In particular, it concerned a German rule which required fruit liqueurs to contain a minimum of 25 per cent alcohol in order to be sold on the German market. Hence, from this judgment it was only clear that the term MEQRs can catch indistinctly applicable measures *which are indirectly discriminatory in fact*, by imposing an additional burden on goods that move between Member States.[52] It was not clear, however, whether the Article 34 TFEU prohibition went even further and caught genuinely non-discriminatory indistinctly applicable measures, ie equal-burden measures (ie measures that regulated economic activities in an entirely neutral manner and which under no circumstances impeded cross-border trade more than trade in goods confined within a single Member State).[53]

---

[49] In this chapter, the following terminology is employed: 'directly discriminatory measures' or 'distinctly applicable measures' refer to measures which discriminate in law and in fact against imported goods; indirectly discriminatory measures are indistinctly applicable measures which do not discriminate in law but discriminate in fact against imported goods; genuinely non-discriminatory measures are indistinctly applicable measures which discriminate neither in law nor in fact against imported goods.

[50] C Hilson, 'Discrimination in Community Free Movement Law' (1999) 24 *European Law Review* 445, 446. Art 3 of Dir 70/50 (n 39) explicitly provides that indistinctly applicable measures can amount to MEQRs.

[51] Wilsher considers the argument that *Cassis* and its progeny are based on the need to prevent dual-burden measures to be unconvincing—see D Wilsher, 'Does *Keck* Discrimination Make Any Sense? An Assessment of the Non-Discrimination Principle within the European Single Market' (2008) 33 *European Law Review* 3, 12–13.

[52] For subsequent cases where this was confirmed see, inter alia, Case 788/79 *Gilli and Andres* [1980] ECR 2071, para 10; Case 261/81 *Rau* [1982] ECR 3961, para 13; Case 16/83 *Prantl* [1984] ECR 1299, para 23.

[53] C Hilson (n 50) 446.

During the decade that followed *Cassis de Dijon* (ie the 1980s), the Court's approach was ambivalent, and giving mixed signals as regards the outer limits to the scope of Article 30 EEC (Article 34 TFEU).[54] In particular, in its judgments in cases involving national regulations that imposed an equal burden on domestic and imported goods—so-called 'market circumstances' rules or, as they later came to be known, 'selling arrangements'—the Court sometimes held that such measures fell altogether outside the scope of Article 30 EEC,[55] whilst in others—most prominently the 'Sunday Trading saga'—it found that the measure was caught by that provision and it was up to the relevant Member State to justify it.[56] Given that selling arrangements are, in most instances, regulations that target the trader rather than the goods themselves, they can also be challenged under the freedom of establishment or the free movement of services provisions.[57] Nonetheless, since in most instances traders are established in the State which imposes these rules and from which they engage in trade in goods, the situation is found to be purely internal for the purposes of these provisions and, hence, falls outside their scope. It is exactly for this reason that in such cases, traders seek to rely on the only extraneous factor in the case—imported goods—even though the contested measure may in no way affect—*specifically*—the free movement of goods but may merely (neutrally) limit the commercial freedom of traders.[58]

It is true that equal burden rules may have an impact on the overall volume of trade. However, they lack cross-border specificity since, as their name suggests, they have no greater or worse impact on cross-border trade than they have on domestic trade.[59] In other words, equal burden rules merely limit the freedom of traders and, with it, possibly the volume of *all* trade, but they do not impede *specifically* the *inter-State* movement of goods. As Weatherill has pointed out, in some of its post-*Cassis* jurisprudence where equal-burden measures were brought within the scope of Article 30 EEC (Article 34 TFEU),

> the Court had lost sight of the link between Article 30 and internal market building by pushing it too far in the direction of general review of national market regulation disassociated from a need to show a hindrance to trading activities aimed at the realization of the internal market.[60]

---

[54] For an excellent analysis of this period see LW Gormley (n 47) 192–95.
[55] See eg Case 155/80 *Oebel* [1981] ECR 1993; Case 75/81 *Blesgen* [1982] ECR 1211; Case 148/85 *Forest* [1986] ECR 3448.
[56] See eg Joined Cases 60 & 61/84 *Cinetheque* [1985] ECR 2605; and the 'Sunday Trading cases' C-145/88 *Torfaen* [1989] ECR 765 and C-312/89 *Conforama* [1991] ECR I-997.
[57] M Poiares Maduro, 'Harmony and Dissonance in Free Movement' in M Andenas and W-H Roth (n 11) 68.
[58] See eg Case 20/87 *Gauchard* [1987] ECR 4879, especially the Opinion of AG Da Cruz Vilaça; Joined Cases C-418-421/93, 460-462/93, 464/93, 9-11/94, 14-15/94, 23-24/94 and 332/94 *Semeraro Casa Uno Srl* [1996] ECR I-2975; and, more recently, Case C-483/12 *Pelckmans* ECLI:EU:C:2014:304. See also, paragraph 27 of the Opinion of AG Tesauro in Case C-292/92 *Hünermund* [1993] ECR I-6787.
[59] EL White (n 37) 246.
[60] S Weatherill, 'After *Keck*: Some Thoughts on how to Clarify the Clarification' (1996) 33 *Common Market Law Review* 885, 904.

The Court's ambivalent attitude towards measures which in all instances imposed an equal burden on domestic and imported goods, led to a large section of the literature[61] critiquing the emerging lack of clarity and predictability in this area and pointing to the resultant dangers of deregulation and of overstepping the boundaries between EU and Member State competence in the area of trade.[62] It also led to a number of Advocates General criticising the Court's approach and making their own suggestions as to how the scope of Article 30 EEC (Article 34 TFEU) should be delimited.[63] Advocate General Tesauro, in his landmark Opinion in the *Hünermund* case,[64] which was delivered in the early 1990s, posed the following question: 'Is Article 30 of the Treaty a provision intended to liberalize intra-Community trade or is it intended more generally to encourage the unhindered pursuit of commerce in individual Member States?' In his view, this should be answered by saying that the above provision merely aims

> to ensure the free movement of goods in order to establish a single integrated market, eliminating therefore those national measures which in any way create an obstacle to or even mere difficulties for the movement of goods; its purpose is not to strike down the most widely differing measures in order, essentially, to ensure the greatest possible expansion of trade.[65]

This is a view which Advocate General Tesauro repeated when writing extra-judicially in 1995.[66] His Opinion in that case is, in fact, a clear expression of the requirement that there must be cross-border specificity in order for the free movement of goods provisions to apply.[67]

---

[61] See eg R Barents, 'New Developments in Measures Having Equivalent Effect' (1981) 18 *Common Market Law Review* 271; EL White (n 37); K Mortelmans, 'Article 30 of the EEC Treaty and Legislation Relating to Market Circumstances: Time to Consider a New Definition?' (1991) 28 *Common Market Law Review* 115; J Steiner (n 41); WPJ Wils, 'The Search for the Rule in Article 30 EEC: Much Ado about Nothing' (1993) 18 *European Law Review* 475; D Chalmers, 'Free Movement of Goods within the European Community: An Unhealthy Addiction to Scotch Whisky?' (1993) 42 *International and Comparative Law Quarterly* 269.

[62] These problems were exacerbated as a result of the fact that the Court in its case-law had 'certainly meant to confirm that the qualification of State measures as measures of equivalent effect to quantitative restrictions does not depend on the furnishing of proof that it *effectively* restricts intra-Community trade'—AWH Meij and JA Winter (n 9) 97; see also D Chalmers (n 61) 275. For cases see, inter alia, Case 12/74 *Commission v Germany* [1975] ECR 181, para 14; *Buy Irish* case (n 44) para 25; Case 124/85 *Commission v Greece* [1986] ECR 3935, para 7.

[63] See eg AG Slynn in *Cinetheque* (n 56) 2611; AG Van Gerven in *Torfaen* (n 56); AG Tesauro in *Hünermund* (n 58).

[64] *Hünermund* (n 58).

[65] Paragraph 28 of the Opinion of AG Tesauro in ibid.

[66] G Tesauro, 'The Community's Internal Market in the Light of the Recent Case-Law of the Court of Justice' (1995) 15 *Yearbook of European Law* 1, 4.

[67] See, especially, paragraph 10 of the Opinion of AG Tesauro in *Hünermund* (n 58), where he appears to equate a 'barrier to trade between Member States' with 'a hindrance, *a difficulty of access to the market such as to affect imports in particular*' (emphasis in the original).

In 1993, the Court—as predicted,[68] and suggested,[69] by Eric White—responded to the above calls, and attempted 'to remove some of the confusion created by the contradictions in the previous case-law'.[70] In *Keck*,[71] after noting that

> in view of the increasing tendency of traders to invoke Article 30 of the Treaty as a means of challenging any rules whose effect is to limit their commercial freedom even where such rules are not aimed at products from other Member States, the Court considers it necessary to re-examine and clarify its case-law on this matter,[72]

it proceeded to provide a refinement to the law governing non-tariff import restrictions. In particular, the Court held that

> Contrary to what has previously been decided, the application to products from other Member States of national provisions restricting or prohibiting certain selling arrangements is not such as to hinder directly or indirectly, actually or potentially, trade between Member States within the meaning of the *Dassonville* judgment ... so long as those provisions apply to all relevant traders operating within the national territory and so long as they affect in the same manner, in law and in fact, the marketing of domestic products and of those from other Member States.[73]

The Court then went on to explain that

> Provided that those conditions are fulfilled, the application of such rules to the sale of products from another Member State meeting the requirements laid down by that State is not by nature such as to prevent their access to the market or to impede access any more than it impedes the access of domestic products. Such rules therefore fall outside the scope of Article 30 of the Treaty.[74]

As noted elsewhere,[75] if there were a prize for the free movement judgment which has attracted the largest amount of interest from academic commentators and members of the Court alike, this would have been won by *Keck*.[76] Therefore, I will not try to provide another detailed analysis of this important case, here. Rather, I will confine my comments to an explanation of the importance of this judgment for the purposes of the development of the law on the free movement of goods.

---

[68] EL White (n 37) 238 and 279.
[69] For the suggestion which seems to have been the inspiration behind the Court's response to these calls, see EL White (n 37) 246–47. Similarly, see the Opinion of AG Tesauro in *Hünermund* (n 58).
[70] Paragraph 34 of the Opinion of AG Jacobs in Case C-412/93 *Leclerc-Siplec* [1995] ECR I-179.
[71] Joined Cases 267 & 268/91 *Keck and Mithouard* [1993] ECR I-6097.
[72] ibid, para 14.
[73] *Keck and Mithouard* (n 71), para 16. This is the '*Keck* formula'.
[74] ibid, para 17.
[75] A Tryfonidou (n 1) 47.
[76] For literature on *Keck* see, inter alia, M Poiares Maduro, '*Keck*: The End? The Beginning of the End? Or Just the End of the Beginning?' (1994) 1 *Irish Journal of European Law* 30; D Chalmers, 'Repackaging the Internal Market—The Ramifications of the *Keck* Judgment' (1994) 17 *European Law Review* 385; S Weatherill (n 60); LW Gormley, 'Two Years after *Keck*' (1996) 19 *Fordham International Law Journal* 866; I Higgins, 'The Free and Not so Free Movement of Goods Since *Keck*' (1997) 6 *Irish Journal of European Law* 166; P Koutrakos, 'On Groceries, Alcohol and Olive Oil: More on Free Movement of Goods after *Keck*' (2001) 26 *European Law Review* 391; S Enchelmaier, 'The Awkward Selling of a Good Idea, or a Traditionalist Interpretation of *Keck*' (2003) 22 *Yearbook of European Law* 249; A Tryfonidou, 'Was *Keck* a Half-Baked Solution After All?' (2007) 34 *Legal Issues of Economic Integration* 167.

The judgment in *Keck* appears to be a conscious decision on the part of the Court to clarify that in order for Article 34 TFEU to bite, the contested national measure must be discriminatory against imported goods.[77] In other words, the Court appears to have been determined to confine the scope of application of that provision to measures that have cross-border specificity, ie measures that treat goods that move between Member States worse than goods that are produced and marketed within one and the same Member State. Following *Keck*, Article 34 TFEU catches only a) quantitative restrictions (which are, obviously, discriminatory measures);[78] b) distinctly applicable measures (which are directly discriminatory measures); and indirectly discriminatory indistinctly applicable measures akin to those challenged in *Cassis de Dijon* (ie rules that imposed a dual burden on goods that move). Conversely, measures regulating selling arrangements which—in most instances—impose an equal burden on imported and domestic goods, fall altogether outside the scope of Article 34 TFEU, unless they are discriminatory.

However, what is the rationale behind the Court's approach in *Keck*? It is clear that what the Court wanted to do with the clarification it provided in that judgment was to ensure that economic activities involving trade in goods remained regulated by *one* Member State (in this way ensuring that the internal market is a *regulated* market) and to establish that it is only when such regulations have cross-border specificity by making the conduct of inter-State trade in goods less attractive than the conduct of trade in goods in a purely national setting, that they should be prohibited.

But let me explain this a bit better. As we saw in chapter one, the basic model traditionally used for building the internal market has been negative integration. Under this model, it is presumed that economic activities should be regulated by Member States (unless there is EU secondary legislation which exclusively harmonises the matter), and the EU should only intervene when national rules impede *specifically* the free—inter-State—movement of products and factors of production (ie where there is cross-border specificity).[79] As we saw above, the major type of measures that affect *specifically* the inter-State movement of goods—apart from, of course, quantitative restrictions and distinctly applicable measures—are measures which give rise to a double burden: measures that require products which have already complied with the requirements of one Member State to comply, in addition, with the requirements of a second State which serve the same purpose. The Court's response to such rules has been to apply the principle of mutual

---

[77] Paragraph 39 of the Opinion of AG Jacobs in *Leclerc-Siplec* (n 70). See, also, inter alia, C Hilson (n 50) 451; G Davies, *Nationality Discrimination in the European Internal Market* (The Hague, Kluwer, 2003) 65; G Infantino and P Mavroidis, 'Inherit the Wind: A Comment on the *Bosman* Jurisprudence' in M Poiares Maduro and L Azoulai (eds), *The Past and Future of EU Law: The Classics of EU Law Revisited on the 50th Anniversary of the Rome Treaty* (Oxford, Hart Publishing, 2010) 503.

[78] See eg J Snell (n 18). For a different view, see S Enchelmaier, 'Four Freedoms, How Many Principles' (2004) 24 *Oxford Journal of Legal Studies* 155, 159.

[79] N Bernard, 'Discrimination and Free Movement in EC Law' (1996) 45 *International and Comparative Law Quarterly* 82, 103.

recognition, according to which products which comply with the requirements of one State should be free to move anywhere within the EU without having to comply, in addition, with the requirements of another State, unless the latter are justified. Since, however, the principle of mutual recognition requires that goods are subjected to only *one set of regulations*, there must be a rule to guide the determination as to which State should be responsible for regulating an economic activity involving goods.

As in the context of the personal market freedoms, seen in the previous chapter, the rule that has been adopted for allocating competence to legislate in the area of trade, has been the home State rule: it is the State where the economic activity takes place (ie the home State) that should regulate it.[80] As seen in the previous chapter, the important point to note is that determining which is the home State in any particular situation, depends on the *type* of measure that is at issue and the type of economic activity that is pursued. When it comes to goods, when a measure concerns the production process of a good, the home State is the State of production of the good; if a measure concerns the marketing stage and, hence, how a product is sold (rather than produced), the home State is the State where the good is sold which, in the case of goods that have crossed State borders, differs from the State of production.[81]

The above mode of regulatory allocation among the Member States is reflected in the Court's (traditional) Article 34 TFEU case-law. *Cassis de Dijon* and *Keck* are both a faithful implementation of the home State principle. *Cassis de Dijon* is authority for the proposition that goods lawfully *produced* in their State of production should be free to move to any other Member State without having to comply, *also*, with the (production) rules of the host State; accordingly, if the host State tries to impose its own product requirements on goods that come from other Member States it will be found to be in violation of Article 34 TFEU, unless it can provide a valid justification. Conversely, it is the State where the goods are sold and marketed that should have the responsibility (and the freedom) to regulate how these goods are sold and marketed. In other words, when it comes to goods that have moved between Member States, it is the State of destination that has the power to regulate how these goods are going to be sold and marketed in its territory. This is why selling arrangements should be regulated by the State where the goods have moved—the host State—which, for the purpose of sale and marketing of goods, becomes the home State.[82] With *Keck*, the Court excluded such rules (provided they are non-discriminatory and they are imposed by the State where the goods are sold) from the scope of Article 34 TFEU. Since the receiving State

---

[80] Bernard uses the term 'country of establishment' instead—see ibid, 106.
[81] For a similar view, see D Chalmers (n 61) 280–81; J Snell, 'Who's Got the Power? Free Movement and Allocation of Competences in EC Law' (2003) 22 *Yearbook of European Law* 323, 330. See also, paragraphs 73 and 74 of the Opinion of AG Bot in Case C-110/05 *Commission v Italy (mopeds)* [2009] ECR I-519.
[82] P Oliver and W-H Roth, 'The Internal Market and the Four Freedoms' (2004) 41 *Common Market Law Review* 407, 420.

is the only State that can and should regulate the marketing of goods sold in its territory, the application of its marketing rules to all goods (whether imported or domestic), does not amount to a violation of Article 34 TFEU. *Keck* has made it clear that traders who wish to sell their products in another Member State have to comply with the selling arrangements of that State; to paraphrase Advocate General Fennelly, they have to take the market (and its rules regarding the sale and marketing of products) as they find it.[83]

Hence, with *Keck*, the Court appears to have answered the question asked by Advocate General Tesauro in *Hünermund*, by indicating that the aim of Article 34 TFEU is merely to ensure the liberalisation of *inter-State* trade and not to attack any national measures that merely (and neutrally) limit the commercial freedom of traders. Accordingly, after *Keck*, Article 34 TFEU did not prohibit 'every national measure, the repeal of which could bring about an increase in sales and in imports',[84] but, rather, only measures which affected imports *in particular*; ie measures that had cross-border specificity.[85]

The analysis in this section has demonstrated that the Court appears to have viewed the free movement of goods provisions purely instrumentally, as tools for the construction of an internal market in goods; an aim which—for the practical reasons explained earlier—merely requires the free movement of *goods* and not (also) the free movement of persons. This aim does not require that obstacles to the free movement of goods are removed at all costs. Rather, it requires Member States to be free to (neutrally) regulate economic activities involving the production and sale of goods, from which it follows that EU law can only step-in to require the non-application of national measures which are biased against *cross-border* trade. For this reason, any measures which do not *specifically* affect inter-State trade—ie they do not have cross-border specificity—but which merely limit the freedom of traders or persons who are in some way connected to goods, have traditionally been considered to be beyond the reach of Article 34 TFEU and, more broadly, of the provisions seeking to protect the free movement of goods between Member States.

III. THE COURT'S STANCE ON THE QUESTION OF WHETHER THE FREE MOVEMENT OF GOODS PROVISIONS ARE SOURCES OF (FUNDAMENTAL) RIGHTS FOR INDIVIDUALS

When it comes to the provisions governing the free movement of goods, the important question for the purposes of this book is not whether goods themselves can derive rights from these provisions and, hence, the philosophical question of

---

[83] Paragraph 32 of the Opinion of AG Fennelly in Case C-190/98 *Graf* [2000] ECR I-493. See also, paragraph 63 of the Opinion of AG Tizzano in Case C-442/02 *CaixaBank* [2004] ECR I-8961.
[84] Paragraph 10 of the Opinion of AG Tesauro in *Hünermund* (n 58).
[85] Opinion of AG Poiares Maduro in Joined Cases C-158 & 159/04 *Vassilopoulos* [2006] ECR I-8135, para 37.

whether inanimate objects such as goods, undertakings, or capital can be the bearers of rights, shall not concern us here. The main question for our purposes is, rather, whether Union citizens can, and do, derive any *fundamental* rights from the free movement of goods provisions—ie rights which are *protected for their own sake* and not in order to contribute to the achievement of a certain aim—and this section shall aim to explore the Court's stance to date on this question.

In its judgment in *Schul* back in 1982, after defining the concept of the 'common market', the Court proceeded to point out that '[i]t is important that not only commerce as such but also private persons who happen to be conducting an economic transaction across national frontiers should be able to enjoy the benefits of that market'.[86] This, however, does not clarify how, exactly, individuals are to enjoy these benefits. Does this emerge merely incidentally, as a side-effect of the achievement of what has traditionally been considered to be the only aim of the free movement of goods provisions, ie to remove obstacles to the free movement of goods in situations where there is cross-border specificity? Or should individuals be considered as themselves deriving rights from these provisions which are not granted to them merely in furtherance of the economic aim of these provisions?

This (persisting) lack of clarity with regards to this matter is, inter alia, obvious from the Opinion of Advocate General Trstenjak in *Danske Slangterier*. As we saw in the previous section, the Court has made it clear that Article 34 TFEU is directly effective and, as such, confers rights on individuals which can be enforced before national courts.[87] The Advocate General described the rights stemming from the market freedoms, including from the free movement of goods provisions, as 'individual public law rights',[88] which can be relied on by individuals against public authorities. She then proceeded to highlight that

> The mere fact that an individual derives an advantage from a legal rule does not, however, establish in itself a 'subjective' right, but provides at most a favourable legal effect by rebound. The doctrine relating to 'subjective' public law rights supports the existence of a 'subjective' right if a provision of mandatory law is intended to serve not only the public interest but in addition at least the interest of particular individuals.[89]

The Advocate General, nonetheless, did not explain whether the rights stemming from the free movement of goods provisions are, indeed, such 'subjective' rights (which seems to be, basically, another name for 'fundamental rights'), nor has the Court done so.[90] In fact, the Court has stopped short of using the term

---

[86] Case 15/81 *Gaston Schul* [1982] ECR 1409, para 33.
[87] *Iannelli* (n 21), para 13.
[88] Opinion of AG Trstenjak in Case C-445/06 *Danske Slangterier* [2009] ECR I -2119, para 75.
[89] ibid, para 72.
[90] For an explanation of why the judgments in Case C-228/98 *Dounias* [2000] ECR I-577 and Case 240/83 *ABDHU* [1985] ECR 531 (esp para 9) cannot be viewed—as suggested by some commentators—as examples where the Court presented Art 34 TFEU as a source of fundamental rights, see F de Cecco, 'Fundamental Freedoms, Fundamental Rights and the Scope of Free Movement Law' (2014) 15 *German Law Journal* 383, 390–91.

'fundamental rights' when referring to the free movement of goods provisions, although a wide range of other terms signifying the importance of these provisions for European (economic) integration, such as 'fundamental freedom'[91] and 'fundamental principle'[92] or 'one of the foundations of the' Union,[93] have been used. In addition, the Court has traditionally placed the emphasis on the protection of the free movement of goods, without making any reference to the persons involved in inter-State trade. For instance, in *Heinonen* the Court noted that 'the objective pursued by Articles 30 and 36 of the Treaty [34 and 36 TFEU] is to guarantee respect of the fundamental freedom which is the free movement of goods in the internal market'.[94]

Accordingly, it appears that the Court has, to date, avoided clarifying whether the free movement of goods provisions are sources of fundamental rights and, hence, at the moment, the formal position appears to be, still, that unlike the personal market freedoms which, as we saw in the previous chapter, appear to be viewed as sources of fundamental rights for the Union citizen, when it comes to the free movement of goods provisions, individuals do, indeed, derive rights from them, but this is only for the purpose of ensuring that goods can move freely between Member States. Nonetheless, despite the fact that, at the moment, it seems unlikely that the free movement of goods provisions will be expressly declared (by the Court) to be sources of (fundamental) rights, this does not mean that this may never happen.[95] In fact, in some of the Court's recent case-law there are some signs that the Court may now wish to read Article 34 TFEU as a source of rights (sometimes even fundamental rights) for individuals. It is to an analysis of this case-law that the next section is devoted.

IV. SOME SIGNS IN THE COURT'S CASE-LAW THAT THE FREE MOVEMENT OF GOODS PROVISIONS MAY NOW BE THE SOURCE OF INDIVIDUAL RIGHTS FOR PERSONS

This section shall aim to bring together all the 'evidence' that can be gathered in support of the argument that the Court may now be moving towards considering the free movement of goods provisions as (also) sources of rights—and, even, in some cases, fundamental rights—for persons. In particular, the section will examine all instances where Article 34 TFEU has been read as a source of rights for individuals and will consider whether any of these are *fundamental* rights,

---

[91] See, inter alia, Case C-390/99 *Canal Satélite* [2002] ECR I-607, paras 28–30; Case C-265/95 *Commission v France* [1997] ECR I-6959, para 32; Case C-112/00 *Schmidberger* [2003] ECR I-5659, paras 62 and 74.
[92] See, inter alia, Case C-205/89 *Commission v Greece* [1991] ECR I-1361, para 9; *Commission v France* (n 91), paras 24 and 27; *Schmidberger* (n 91), paras 59, 62, 66 and 67; Case C-573/12 *Ålands Vindkraft* ECLI:EU:C:2014:2037, para 65.
[93] Case C-194/94 *CIA* [1996] ECR I-2201, para 40.
[94] Case C-394/97 *Heinonen* [1999] ECR I-3231, para 38.
[95] F de Cecco (n 90) 391–92.

as well as—and in particular—whether they are fundamental rights for *Union citizens*.[96]

A. The Rights of Consumers Under Article 34 TFEU

Consumers of goods are passive economic actors.[97] In other words, they take part in an economic activity by purchasing goods but they do so only passively, the active economic actor in the transaction being the producer/wholesaler/retailer.

The question that interests us here is whether consumers—as passive economic actors—derive any rights from the free movement of goods provisions, in the same way that service-recipients (as we saw in the previous chapter) derive rights from the free movement of services provisions.

As will be explained below, in its free movement of goods case-law, the Court has had to balance two different, even opposite, rights of consumers: the right to be protected as the weaker party in economic transactions and the right to choice. The former right has been protected through its recognition by the Court as a mandatory requirement and, hence, as an *exception* from the prohibition of (indistinctly applicable) MEQRs on imports, whilst the latter right has been protected as a result of the Court's removal of obstacles to the free movement of goods (ie it has been protected *incidentally*, as a result of the Member States being required by Article 34 TFEU not to apply measures which impede the free movement of goods, this having as a consequence that goods from other Member States can reach the market of a Member State, thus increasing consumer choice).[98] What is more important for our purposes, however, is the Court's explicit recognition in the early 1990s, that consumers derive from the free movement of goods provisions the right to move to another Member State for the purpose of purchasing goods; a right akin to that recognised as deriving from Article 56 TFEU, for service-recipients.

We should now examine in more detail how and to what extent the above three (consumer) rights have been safeguarded in the Court's case-law.

As explained by Reich,

> the consumer as a passive market citizen, is only indirectly protected by the community system and does not enjoy rights of his or her own. Insofar as an increase in the free movement of goods, persons, services and capital will improve competitive conditions in

---

[96] Nic Shuibhne has wondered: 'the nationality of a trader importing goods from Member State A to Member State B was never relevant; will Union citizenship now make it (restrictively) relevant? The injection of *personal* protection into the scope of Article 34 TFEU could extend trade rights for EU nationals, but the consequences for those excluded are potentially problematic'—N Nic Shuibhne, 'EU Citizenship after Lisbon' in D Ashiagbor, N Countouris and I Lianos (eds), *The European Union after the Treaty of Lisbon* (Cambridge, Cambridge University Press, 2012) 150.

[97] The analysis here can be transposed, also, to consumers of cross-border services (as products which reach the consumer in his/her home State), to consumers of services which are provided by (natural or legal) persons in the consumer's home State, as well as to persons who move to another Member State to receive services there.

[98] This is obvious, inter alia, in Case C-456/10 *ANETT* ECLI:EU:C:2012:241, para 54.

the internal market, the consumer will also be placed at an advantage through increased choice. There is, however, no 'right to choice' which may be enforced in courts of law through the direct effect of Community legislation.[99]

Sharing similar views, Weatherill has pointed out that 'the effective application of the rules of the internal market game is a form of consumer policy'.[100]

This is, certainly, an accurate description of the Court's approach to the consumer's right to choice: although consumers do, indeed, indirectly,[101] benefit from the free movement of, inter alia, goods since they are—as a result—offered a greater variety of goods in their domestic market, the Court in its jurisprudence has always placed the focus on the protection of the free movement of goods and not on the protection of the right of the consumer to choose or, perhaps more specifically, on the right to purchase imported goods in his or her State of origin; the latter has, only, been protected incidentally, as a side-effect of protecting the free movement of goods.[102] This is specifically obvious in cases involving national measures that restrict the *use* of goods (ie 'use restrictions'), since although such measures affect, primarily, consumers (since they limit their ability to use a certain product, rather than the ability of traders to produce it, import it, or sell it), the Court adopts reasoning which demonstrates that the main question is whether the contested restriction impedes the free movement of goods and, by extension, the right of traders to import goods from other Member States.[103]

On the other hand, the Court has appeared more concerned with safeguarding the right of the consumer to be protected as the weaker party in economic transactions. In particular, the Court has recognised that (indistinctly) applicable Member State measures that amount to MEQRs may, nonetheless, be justified if their continued application is necessary in order to protect the consumer. In this way the Court *expressly* recognised the importance of protecting—in certain instances—the consumer, even if this comes at the expense of the free movement of goods.[104] Consumer protection has been one of the first mandatory requirements recognised by the Court and has, since Maastricht, gained Treaty recognition,[105]

---

[99] N Reich, 'A European Constitution for Citizens: Reflections on the Rethinking of Union and Community Law' (1997) 3 *European Law Journal* 131, 142–43.

[100] S Weatherill, 'Consumer Policy' in P Craig and G de Búrca (eds), *The Evolution of EU Law* 2nd edn (Oxford, Oxford University Press, 2011) 838.

[101] M Dani, 'Assembling the Fractured European Consumer' (2011) 36 *European Law Review* 362, 368.

[102] S Weatherill, 'Consumer Policy' in P Craig and G de Búrca (eds), *The Evolution of EU Law* (Oxford, Oxford University Press, 1999) 696–97. It should be noted that consumers have also benefited from the promulgation of legislation at EU level which seeks to remove obstacles to the creation and functioning of the internal market *whilst maintaining a high level of consumer protection*—for more on this see S Weatherill (n 100) 844–63.

[103] Case C-265/06 *Commission v Portugal* ('*tinted film*') [2008] ECR I-2245; *Commission v Italy* ('*mopeds*') (n 81); Case C-142/05 *Mickelsson and Roos* [2009] ECR I-4273.

[104] See, inter alia, *Cassis de Dijon* (n 7); *Oosthoek's* (n 16); Case 328/87 *Buet* [1989] ECR 1235.

[105] See (now) Art 169 TFEU. Moreover, Art 12 TFEU stipulates that 'Consumer protection requirements shall be taken into account in defining and implementing other Union policies and activities', hence, mainstreaming consumer protection into all EU policies.

although it is still *not* one of the Treaty derogations provided by Article 36 TFEU, and, hence—at least in theory[106]—a Member State cannot maintain a measure which is distinctly applicable, on the ground that it needs to protect the consumer.

Yet, the importance of the mandatory requirement of consumer protection (from the point of view of the consumer) has been tempered by the Court's view of the type of consumer that is populating the internal market: the 'reasonably circumspect' consumer.[107] More specifically, in a relatively long line of case-law—the most well-known being the judgments in *Cassis de Dijon*,[108] *3 Glocken*,[109] *Smanor*,[110] *Yves Rocher*,[111] *Clinique*[112] and *Mars*[113]—after finding that the contested measure could amount to an MEQR, the Court proceeded to consider possible justifications, and in all of these cases it accepted that the measure was *capable* of being justified on the ground of consumer protection (ie it found that the measure was *suitable* for achieving this objective). Nonetheless, the Member State's justification failed in the subsequent stage, where it was examined whether the measure was *necessary* for achieving that objective. The Court in all these cases found that the measure was *not* justified because it was not proportionate, either because the same objective (protection of the consumer) could be attained by less restrictive means (namely, labelling), or because the measure went too far in protecting the consumer at the expense of the free movement of goods. In doing so, the Court had assumed that markets are populated by the 'reasonably circumspect' consumer. This demonstrates that 'vulnerable consumers are sacrificed to the interests of self-reliant consumers in deregulation, market integration and wider choice'.[114]

Hence, when it comes to the rights to consumer protection and consumer choice *in their own State*, consumers have only *indirectly* benefited from the free movement of goods provisions: any benefits accruing to them with regards to these rights have been merely incidental, emerging simply as a consequence of the application of these provisions for the purpose of removing (or justifying) obstacles to the free movement of goods. Accordingly, these are, clearly, instrumental

---

[106] The general principle is that mandatory requirements cannot be used to justify distinctly applicable measures. However, in certain cases, the Court—without abandoning this principle—did accept that a measure which was distinctly applicable could be justified under a mandatory requirement. See, inter alia, *Commission v Belgium* (n 17); Case C-120/95 *Decker* [1998] ECR I-1831; Case C-379/98 *PreussenElektra* [2001] ECR I-2099; Joined Cases C-204-208/12 *Essent Belgium* ECLI:EU:C:2014:2192.

[107] This term was mentioned in, inter alia, Case C-470/93 *Mars* [1995] ECR I-1923, para 24; and, more recently, Case C-481/12 *Juvelta* ECLI:EU:C:2014:11, para 23. For a detailed discussion of the question as to how confused must consumers be before protective rules introduced by Member States are justified, see S Weatherill, 'Recent Case Law Concerning the Free Movement of Goods: Mapping the Frontiers of Market Deregulation' (1999) 36 *Common Market Law Review* 51, 60–70.

[108] *Cassis de Dijon* (n 7).
[109] Case 407/85 *3 Glocken* [1988] ECR 4233.
[110] Case 298/87 *Smanor* [1988] ECR 4489.
[111] Case C-126/91 *Yves Rocher* [1993] ECR I-2361.
[112] Case C-315/92 *Clinique* [1994] ECR I-317.
[113] *Mars* (n 107).
[114] S Weatherill (n 107) 58. For a similar view see M Dani (n 101) 367–69.

rights that are granted to *all* persons (not just Member State nationals) in furtherance of the aim of building an internal market in goods.

It was only in its judgment in *GB-INNO-BM*,[115] delivered in 1990, that the Court for the first time *expressly* recognised that Article 34 TFEU can be the source of a direct right *to move* for the consumer who wants to purchase goods from other Member States:

> Free movement of goods concerns not only traders but also individuals. It requires, particularly in frontier areas, that consumers resident in one Member State may travel freely to the territory of another Member State to shop under the same conditions as the local population. That freedom for consumers is compromised if they are deprived of access to advertising available in the country where purchases are made.[116]

The case arose from a dispute between CCL, a non-profit-making association which represented the interests of Luxembourg traders, and GB-INNO-BM, which operates supermarkets on Belgian territory. The latter had distributed advertising leaflets in Luxembourg and Belgium and CCL applied to the Luxembourg courts for an injunction against the company to stop the distribution of those leaflets because they violated the (applicable at the time) Luxembourgian law on unfair competition, which provided that sales offers involving a temporary price reduction may not state the duration of the offer or refer to previous prices. The injunction was granted and GB-INNO-BM appealed, relying on Article 30 EEC (Article 34 TFEU). The Court found that an obstacle to the free movement of goods arose as a result of the absence of common rules and the disparities between national laws concerning advertising. It then went on to consider whether 'national legislation which prevents the consumer from having access to certain information may be justified in the interest of consumer protection.'[117] After explaining that EU consumer policy 'establishes a close link between protecting the consumer and providing the consumer with information',[118] the Court concluded that under EU law

> concerning consumer protection the provision of information to the consumer is considered one of the principal requirements. Thus Article 30 cannot be interpreted as meaning that national legislation which denies the consumer access to certain kinds of information may be justified by mandatory requirements concerning consumer protection.[119]

Hence, *GB-INNO-BM* established that like Union citizens derive the right from Article 56 TFEU to move to another Member State to receive a service, in the same

---

[115] Case C-362/88 *GB-INNO-BM* [1990] ECR I-667.
[116] ibid, para 8.
[117] ibid, para 13.
[118] ibid, para 14. See also paras 14–17.
[119] ibid, para 18. See, however, the Court's narrower approach to the right to receive information regarding abortion services provided in other Member States in Case C-159/90 *Grogan* [1991] ECR I-4621.

way, persons derive from Article 34 TFEU the right to move to another Member State in order to purchase goods.[120] In addition, subsequent case-law established that Article 34 TFEU grants to consumers the right to purchase goods across borders, without any person moving, in the same way that Union citizens can rely on Article 56 TFEU to enforce their right to receive (without moving to another Member State) services from persons (whether natural or legal) established in other Member States.[121] However, this latter right has been recognised only indirectly, in litigation initiated by the trader who was prevented from selling his/her goods online, rather than by the consumer himself/herself.[122]

It should be highlighted that the Court has refrained from clarifying whether the above rights of consumers are only available to persons holding the nationality of a Member State who are, thus, Union citizens.[123] Accordingly, it cannot be argued that consumers benefit from Article 34 TFEU *qua* Union citizens, instead of, simply, as passive economic actors. Moreover, since—pragmatically speaking—mobile consumers who purchase goods from another Member State will obviously (most likely) bring them back with them to their State of origin, a national measure which impedes the right of consumers to move to another Member State will, clearly, also impede the free movement of goods between Member States. The same can be said about consumers who order goods online *from other Member States* and have them delivered to their home State. Therefore, the Court's recognition that persons who purchase goods from other Member States can rely on Article 34 TFEU, cannot be considered as a conclusive indication that persons can derive rights from the free movement of goods provisions *even in situations where there is no contribution to the aim of this provision*, ie to protect the free movement of goods between Member States. Only if the material scope of Article 34 TFEU was extended to cover the rights of consumers (also) in situations where there was no impediment to the free movement of goods, would these rights be considered genuine, fundamental, rights, which are granted to consumers for their own sake.

---

[120] The parallel that can be drawn between goods and services in this context is, also, obvious from the fact that just like the free movement of services can be relied on by Union citizens in order to receive healthcare services in the territory of another Member State (see eg Case C-158/96 *Kohl* [1998] ECR I-1931 and the other cases mentioned in that context in the previous chapter), the Court has made it clear in *Decker* (n 106), that persons can rely on Art 34 TFEU in order to challenge any national measures that limit their freedom to purchase healthcare products from other Member States.
[121] See eg Case 15/78 *Koestler* [1978] ECR 1971; Case C-384/93 *Alpine Investments* [1995] ECR I-1141.
[122] *DocMorris* (n 27); Case C-108/09 *Ker-Optika* [2010] ECR I-12213. For an annotation of the latter see P Caro de Sousa, 'Through Contact Lenses, Darkly: Is Identifying Restrictions to Free Movement Harder than Meets the Eye? Comment on Ker-Optika' (2012) 37 *European Law Review* 79.
[123] The issue of whether service-recipients must—like service-providers—hold the nationality of a Member State has, similarly, not been clarified (P Oliver (n 32) 87), though, from the Court's case-law to date, it would seem that they must hold the nationality of a Member State—G Davies (n 34) 206. We shall return to this point in ch 6.

B. The Right of Persons to *Move* to Another Member State for the Purpose of Selling Goods

Under the Court's orthodox approach, all that was needed for bringing a situation within the scope of the free movement of goods provisions was proof that the facts of the case involved goods that had moved, or were to move, between Member States.[124] If *this* cross-border element was not satisfied on the facts of the case, the situation was deemed to fall automatically outside the scope of EU law. For the same reason, even if the traders involved were nationals of the State which applied the contested legislation and had never moved between Member States, this did not make the situation purely internal, provided that the impugned measure affected the free movement of goods between Member States.[125] Finally, even if the contested national measure regulated the trader, as opposed to the goods themselves, and, hence, its direct impact appeared to be on the free movement of the trader and the impediment on the free movement of goods seemed to be merely a side-effect of this, the Court found a violation of Article 34 TFEU, if it could be established that the impugned legislation impeded the free movement of *goods* (the fact that the measure appeared to also impede the free movement of traders, did not appear to matter).[126]

Traditionally, and bearing in mind the market-building aim of this provision, it was assumed that Article 34 TFEU did not apply to situations where there was an impediment to the free movement of traders *but not* to the free movement of goods. Moreover, in cases where the facts of the case involved, in addition to the free movement of goods, the free movement of traders who had moved for the purpose of selling goods, the Court appeared to be concerned merely with removing obstacles to the free movement of goods. A clear example of this is *Burmanjer*.[127] In that case three Dutch nationals (who were self-employed vendors representing a German company) were prosecuted in Belgium for offering for sale on the public highway, without a prior authorisation, subscriptions to periodicals that were published by Dutch and German companies. In its judgment, when considering whether Article 28 EC (Article 34 TFEU) was applicable on the facts of the case, the Court took a number of factors into account, including the nationality of the vendors (and, hence, the fact that they were nationals of one Member State who had moved to another for the purpose of selling goods):

> So far as concerns, more particularly, the national rules on itinerant sales, they are intended to regulate, as regards subscriptions to periodicals, a certain selling arrangement, namely marketing through itinerant activities. It is not disputed that those

---

[124] See, *inter alia*, *Oosthoek's* (n 16) para 9.
[125] See eg the facts in *Ooesthoek's* (n 16) and *Buet* (n 104) and, for a post-*Keck* case, Case C-254/98 *TK-Heimdienst* [2000] ECR I-151.
[126] An example of this can be seen in Case C-239/90 *Boscher* [1991] ECR I-2023 (see, in particular, para 16).
[127] Case C-20/03 *Burmanjer* [2005] ECR I-4133.

periodicals are goods. So far as the main proceedings are concerned, they arise from a situation in which a company incorporated under German law sells or intends to sell in Belgium, through self-employed vendors *who are Dutch nationals*, subscriptions to periodicals published by companies established in the Netherlands and in Germany.[128]

Notwithstanding the above statement which shows that the Court might have taken into account the fact that nationals of one Member State had moved to another for the purpose of selling goods, the focus of the Court when determining whether there was an MEQR, was *merely* placed on whether the contested measure impeded the free movement of goods—and did not consider, at all, its impact on the free movement of the traders involved. Accordingly, although the Court's reference to the nationality of the vendors made us wonder whether the free movement of goods provisions could now be read as seeking, *also*, to protect the free inter-State movement of *Union citizens* if this is for the purpose of selling goods,[129] its actual reasoning was merely a confirmation of the traditional approach that Article 34 TFEU solely seeks to protect the free movement of *goods*.[130]

Nonetheless, in a case decided shortly after *Burmanjer*, the Court seems to have taken a step further towards recognising that traders may be deriving a right to free movement from Article 34 TFEU, and—importantly—even in situations where it is not clear that the goods involved have moved between Member States. However, for reasons to be explained below, the value of this case as a precedent is in doubt and, hence, the case cannot be taken as conclusive evidence that Article 34 TFEU is now the source of a right for traders to move freely between Member States, *irrespective of whether on the facts of the case the movement of goods between Member States is impeded*; a right which would be a fundamental right since extending the scope of Article 34 TFEU to protect the free movement of traders in situations where there is no obstacle to the free movement of goods, cannot be justified under the market-building rationale of that provision.

The case is *A-Punkt*.[131] This was a preliminary reference originating from an Austrian court and was made in proceedings between the Austrian company A-Punkt, on the one hand, and Ms Schmidt, who ran an undertaking with headquarters in Germany, on the other. A-Punkt relied on Austrian legislation, which prohibited collecting orders for or selling certain goods, including silver jewellery, at private homes in support of its argument that Ms Schmidt should stop selling silver jewellery door-to-door in Austria. In particular, Ms Schmidt organised a 'jewellery party' at a private house in Austria and following that party, A-Punkt, which had a competing business, brought proceedings against Ms Schmidt, seeking to stop her

---

[128] ibid, para 21. Emphasis added.
[129] For a discussion of this, see P Caro de Sousa, *The European Fundamental Freedoms: A Contextual Approach* (Oxford, Oxford University Press, 2015) 69–70.
[130] The traditional approach was, also, followed by AG Léger who, in his Opinion in *Burmanjer* (n 127), concluded that Art 34 TFEU applied to the facts of the case, in so far as the periodicals which would be affected by the contested measure had been imported from other Member States (see para 45).
[131] Case C-441/04 *A-Punkt* [2006] ECR I-2093.

142 *Union Citizenship and the Free Movement of Goods*

business on the ground that it was in breach of Austrian law. The main question was whether the Austrian legislation relied on by A-Punkt amounted to an MEQR.

From a quick perusal, someone could say that the judgment consists of a simple application of the *Keck* formula and, hence, has nothing worth noticing. However, a closer look at it reveals that the judgment may be adding something new to the Court's previous jurisprudence. In particular, a statement made by the Court in one of the early paragraphs of the judgment may be hinting that the latter may now wish to expand the scope of Article 34 TFEU to also include situations where the goods have not crossed borders, provided that the trader involved on the facts of the case has. This can be seen in paragraph 9 of the judgment, where the Court noted that

> the main proceedings arise from a situation where a person running an undertaking with headquarters in Germany organised the sale of jewellery at private homes in Austria. In such a situation, the body of national rules prohibiting the sale of jewellery at private homes falls within the scope of the principle of free movement of goods.[132]

This sentence illustrates that the fact that Ms Schmidt was running an undertaking established in Germany whilst she came to Austria in order to sell jewellery, may have been sufficient for bringing the situation within the scope of Article 28 EC (Article 34 TFEU): the Court did not move on to consider whether the goods involved on the facts of the case were goods originating in other Member States.[133] Yet, in the subsequent part of the judgment the Court highlighted that a violation of Article 34 TFEU would emerge if the contested legislation was applied to *imported* goods—a matter that was left to be decided by the referring court. This, clearly, weakens the value of this case as authority for the proposition that Article 34 TFEU seeks to grant to traders the right to move between Member States for the purpose of selling goods, *irrespective of whether the goods that are going to be sold are goods that have moved between Member States.*

Two further factors serve to make this judgment a questionable precedent. The first one is the obvious fact that the paragraph quoted above has not been affirmed in a subsequent judgment of the Court. The second is that the composition of the Court hearing the case (a three-judge chamber), makes it somewhat unlikely that the judgment was intended to be a ruling going against well-established principles. When the Court is confronted with a question that necessitates a reassessment of

---

[132] For a criticism of the Court's judgment see P Oliver and S Enchelmaier (n 8) 658.

[133] In *Keck and Mithouard* (n 71), the referring court also did not specify whether the goods which were resold at a loss contrary to the contested French legislation were imported goods—LW Gormley (n 32) 867. Moreover, even assuming that the goods affected on the facts of the case were imported goods, the fact that the impugned measure did not impede access to the market for imported goods more than for domestic goods but would affect, in exactly the same way, domestic goods and *imported goods that had already gained access to the market* and which, therefore, for the purposes of the free movement of goods were now domestic goods, meant that the situation was a purely internal one—see D Chalmers (n 76) 390. See also, C Barnard, 'Fitting the Remaining Pieces into the Goods and Persons Jigsaw?' (2001) 26 *European Law Review* 35, fn 57.

basic principles and the case is initially assigned to a small chamber, the latter usually refers it to the Grand Chamber or, even, the Full Court.[134] However, here no such referral was made.

Accordingly, it seems that although there are some signs that the free movement of traders themselves (even in the absence of the free movement of goods) may suffice for bringing a situation within the scope of Article 34 TFEU, the Court's formal stance is, still, that Article 34 TFEU is merely concerned with ensuring the free movement of goods and, thus, Article 34 TFEU cannot be considered to be a source of a fundamental right for persons (whether Union citizens or not) to move between Member States for the purpose of selling goods.

C. The Fundamental Right to Trade Goods in a Cross-Border Context Without Being Restricted by Unjustified National Regulation

As seen earlier in the chapter, by giving direct effect to Article 34 TFEU, the ECJ recognised that traders derived enforceable (instrumental) rights from that provision, and, in particular, the right to import goods from other Member States. And although traditionally the Court avoided making reference to this right, concluding that the impugned measure impeded the free movement of goods, in its most recent case-law, it has increasingly made express reference to this right. For instance, in *Fra.bo*, the judgment began by citing the *Dassonville* formula and then moved on to say that 'the mere fact that an importer might be dissuaded from introducing or marketing the products in question in the Member State concerned constitutes a restriction on the free movement of goods *for the importer*'.[135] The same statement was repeated shortly afterwards in *Elenca*.[136] This statement may be an indication that, together with ensuring the free movement of goods as such, the free movement of goods provisions now appear to be also seeking to ensure that the *right* of traders to import goods from other Member States is not impeded.

Yet, it should be noted that such a right remains an instrumental right if it is granted merely in order to ensure that goods can move between Member States and that national measures do not *specifically* impede cross-border trade in goods. In other words, if the right only emerges in case a national measure treats goods that move across borders worse than goods that stay put in a single Member State, it is obvious that it is not a genuine right that simply seeks to provide an entitlement to an individual—the trader; a fundamental right that is granted for its own sake should be granted to traders *in all instances* and its existence should not be subject to conditions.

---

[134] This is in accordance with Art 60 of the Rules of Procedure of the Court of Justice (25 September 2012) and Art 16 of the Statute of the Court of Justice.
[135] Case C-171/11 *Fra.bo* ECLI:EU:C:2012:453, para 22. Emphasis added.
[136] Case C-385/10 *Elenca* ECLI:EU:C:2012:634, para 22.

144 *Union Citizenship and the Free Movement of Goods*

This subsection will aim to demonstrate that in the two (relatively) recent Article 34 cases of *Commission v Italy (mopeds)*[137] and *Mickelsson and Roos*,[138] the Court seems to have broadened the scope of application of Article 34 TFEU to include genuinely non-discriminatory obstacles to the free movement of goods, ie measures which do not have cross-border specificity. As will be explained below, if this is indeed the case, this will mean that the right to import goods that traders derive from Article 34 TFEU may now be considered a fundamental right which exists in all instances and, thus, traders can challenge *any* national measures that deter them from importing goods from other Member States, even those which simply seek to neutrally regulate an economic activity and merely happen to limit the ability of goods from other Member States to be imported as they also happen to limit the ability of goods produced in that Member State to be marketed.

In the previous section, we saw that with *Keck* and its progeny, the Court returned to a discrimination-based approach in the context of Article 34 TFEU, requiring the existence of cross-border specificity in order for a measure to be caught by this provision, and established a clear formula for determining whether a measure regulating a selling arrangement is *not* an MEQR. Despite the fact that in the first years after *Keck*, the Court applied rather mechanically the *Keck* formula and the presumptions deriving therefrom, and, hence, once a measure was found to be a selling arrangement it was deemed to fall outside the scope of (what is now) Article 34 TFEU,[139] it progressively followed a more nuanced approach when determining whether a measure amounted to an MEQR, increasingly taking into account the effect of the contested measure on the access of goods to the market of the host State.[140] As Advocate General Stix-Hackl explained in her Opinion in *DocMorris*, 'an interpretation of such a central rule of Community law as free movement of goods ... cannot be limited to a mechanical application of the two traditional requirements laid down in the *Keck* formula'.[141] Accordingly, as explained elsewhere,[142] recognising the problems with a mechanical application of the *Keck* formula, the Court in a number of cases—starting in the late 1990s—adopted a less formalistic approach, focusing more on the question of whether the contested national legislation had a substantially negative impact on the free movement of goods and on their access to the market of the host State, rather than on whether it was a measure regulating selling arrangements or a product requirement.

---

[137] *Commission v Italy (mopeds)* (n 81).
[138] *Mickelsson and Roos* (n 103).
[139] Hence, the Court did not take into account any other considerations such as the actual impact of the measure on the free movement of goods although, admittedly, it did consider (briefly) whether the *Keck* conditions were satisfied—see eg the Court's approach in Case C-63/94 *Belgapom* [1995] ECR I-2467. This was clearly conducive to legal certainty—see P Eeckhout, 'Recent Case-law on Free Movement of Goods: Refining *Keck and Mithouard*' (1998) 9 European Business Law Review 267.
[140] Paragraphs 19–20 of the Opinion of AG Fennelly in *Graf* (n 83). For an analysis of the Court's post-*Keck* case-law see M Poiares Maduro (n 57) 54–60; LW Gormley (n 47) 198–202.
[141] Paragraph 73 of the Opinion of AG Stix-Hackl in *DocMorris* (n 27).
[142] A Tryfonidou (n 76) 175–80.

The move towards a less formalistic approach, taking into account the actual impact of the measure on the access of goods to the market of another Member State, does not contradict *Keck*, given that paragraph 17 of the judgment in that case shows that 'the concept of market access informed *Keck*, and thus explains it to some extent'.[143] This, after all, according to Advocate General Stix-Hackl, is 'the—overriding—general criterion', of which the two *Keck* conditions are 'only expressions'.[144] A number of commentators took notice of this development,[145] which followed the suggestions of a section of the literature that advocated a move to a market access test instead of a strict adherence to the *Keck* formula.[146]

Nonetheless, even when *Keck* was transformed from a rigid formula based on a dry application of the two *Keck* conditions, to a more flexible test concerning the impact of the contested measure on market access, the (continued) importance attached to the proof of discrimination meant that there was, still, a requirement of cross-border specificity, in order for a measure to be caught by Article 34 TFEU. In other words, it was still only measures which had a different (detrimental) impact on cross-border trade than in purely domestic trade that could amount to a restriction that fell within the scope of this provision.

In some of its post-*Keck* case-law, however, the Court went further, and (*implicitly*) extended the scope of application of Article 34 TFEU to measures which appeared to be neutral between domestic and cross-border trade in goods. One such example is the action that was at issue in *Schmidberger*:[147] the contested permission granted by the Austrian authorities to the environmental organisation to demonstrate on the Brenner motorway would have had exactly the same impact on the free movement of goods irrespective of whether these were moving via that motorway merely within Austria or whether they were transiting via Austria, or moving from Austria, to another Member State. Another example of (implicitly) extending the scope of Article 34 TFEU to catch a measure which lacked cross-border specificity is the Court's judgment in *Commission v Portugal*:[148] the Portuguese prohibition of affixing tinted film to the window of motor vehicles did not appear in any way capable of affecting imported tinted film more than its

---

[143] P Eeckhout (n 139) 270.
[144] Paragraph 74 of the Opinion of AG Stix-Hackl in *DocMorris* (n 27).
[145] See eg P Eeckhout (n 139); D O'Keeffe and A Bavasso, 'Four Freedoms, One Market and National Competence: In Search of a Dividing Line' in D O'Keeffe and A Bavasso (eds), *Liber Amicorum in Honour of Lord Slynn of Hadley: Judicial Review in European Union Law* (The Hague, Kluwer, 2000); P Koutrakos (n 76).
[146] See, inter alia, S Weatherill (n 60); J Snell and M Andenas, 'Exploring the Outer Limits—Restrictions on the Free Movement of Goods and Services' (1999) 10 *European Business Law Review* 252; JHH Weiler, 'The Constitution of the Common Market Place: Text and Context in the Evolution of the Free Movement of Goods' in P Craig and G de Búrca (eds), *The Evolution of EU Law* (Oxford, Oxford University Press, 1999); D O'Keeffe and A Bavasso (n 145); C Barnard (n 133). Members of the Court of Justice have, also, advocated different approaches to determining what an MEQR is—for the most well-known examples see paragraphs 38–55 of the Opinion of AG Jacobs in *Leclerc-Siplec* (n 70); paras 74–82 of the Opinion of AG Stix-Hackl in *DocMorris* (n 27); paras 108–38 of the Opinion of AG Bot in *Commission v Italy (mopeds)* (n 81).
[147] *Schmidberger* (n 91).
[148] *Commission v Portugal (tinted film)* (n 103).

domestic counterpart.[149] Moreover, in another case the Court—quite confusingly and contrary to what seems to have been implied in *Keck*—hinted that national measures which apply to all goods in the same manner and they merely reduce the volume of sales (of domestic *and* imported goods) can amount to MEQRs, although the comment is *obiter*, since the contested measure on the facts was an import licence requirement which is, by nature, discriminatory against imported goods.[150]

The Court has, nonetheless, gone even further in the (relatively) recent 'sister' use restrictions cases of *Commission v Italy ('mopeds')* and *Mickelsson and Roos*, where it (seems to have) *expressly* extended the scope of Article 34 TFEU in a principled manner, to catch, also, *genuinely non-discriminatory* obstacles to the free movement of goods.[151] Accordingly, like in the context of the personal market freedoms, in its case-law concerned with the interpretation of Article 34 TFEU, the Court seems—albeit in a limited number of cases so far—to have abandoned the requirement of cross-border specificity.[152]

Starting with *Commission v Italy (mopeds)*,[153] the case arose from an enforcement action brought by the Commission against Italy, claiming that Italy was in violation of Article 28 EC (Article 34 TFEU), because it prohibited the use of trailers with mopeds, motorcycles, tricycles, and quadricycles. This was, clearly, a measure which lacked cross-border specificity: 'From what one can gather, there was no uneven factual impact, never mind a total ban of importing and marketing trailers, that is, of trading them across the borders between Member States'.[154]

Yet, despite this, the Court found that the measure amounted to an MEQR and then proceeded to consider whether it was justified.

The Court began its analysis by (re-)stating the law under a section entitled 'preliminary observations'. It began by recalling the *Dassonville* formula,[155] as well

---

[149] See also, Case C-65/05 *Commission v Greece* [2006] ECR I-10341.

[150] Case C-434/04 *Ahokainen* [2006] ECR I-9171, para 18: 'All trading rules enacted by Member States which are capable of hindering, directly or indirectly, actually or potentially, intra-Community trade must be considered to be measures having an effect equivalent to quantitative restrictions and are thus prohibited by Article 28 EC .... Even rules applied without distinction to domestic and imported products, the application of which to imported products is likely to reduce their sales volume, constitute in principle measures having equivalent effect prohibited by Article 28 EC.'

[151] For comments on the cases see, inter alia, E Spaventa, 'Leaving Keck Behind? The Free Movement of Goods after the Rulings in Commission v Italy and Mickelsson and Roos' (2009) 34 *European Law Review* 914; S Enchelmaier (n 22); A Tryfonidou (n 1).

[152] This also appears to be the case in the context of the free movement of capital—E Spaventa, *Free Movement of Persons in the European Union: Barriers to Movement in their Constitutional Context* (TheHague, Kluwer, 2007) 147; J Snell, 'Free Movement of Capital: Evolution as A Non-Linear Process' in P Craig and G de Búrca (eds), *The Evolution of EU Law* 2nd end (Oxford, Oxford University Press, 2011) 554–63. In a number of cases a restriction caught by Art 63 TFEU was found in situations where there clearly was no cross-border specificity—see eg Case C-367/98 *Commission v Portugal ('Golden Shares')* [2002] ECR I-4732; Case C-483/99 *Commission v France ('Golden Shares')* [2002] ECR I-4781; Case C-98/01 *Commission v UK ('BAA Golden Shares')* [2003] ECR I-4641; Joined Cases C-282-283/04 *Commission v Netherlands ('Golden Shares')* [2006] ECR I-9141.

[153] *Commission v Italy (mopeds)* (n 81).

[154] S Enchelmaier (n 22) 194.

[155] *Commission v Italy (mopeds)* (n 81), para 33.

Source of Individual Rights for Persons 147

as the principles established in *Cassis*[156] and *Keck*.[157] Most importantly, however, the Court went on to conclude that

> measures adopted by a Member State the object or effect of which is to treat products coming from other Member States less favourably are to be regarded as measures having equivalent effect to quantitative restrictions on imports within the meaning of 28 EC, as are the measures referred to in paragraph 35 of the present judgment [ie dual-burden measures]. *Any other measure which hinders access of products originating in other Member States to the market of a Member State is also covered by that concept.*[158]

The Court then concluded that the contested prohibition 'has a considerable influence on the behaviour of consumers' and thus 'prevents a demand from existing in the market at issue for such trailers and therefore hinders their importation',[159] but found that it was justified by reasons relating to the protection of road safety.

As Enchelmaier has rightly observed, in *Commission v Italy (mopeds)*, 'the ECJ gives the apparently "catch-all" category of "any other measures" no contours whatsoever. The Court's failure to do so came back to haunt it shortly thereafter, in the *Mickelsson & Roos* judgment'.[160]

The reference in *Mickelsson and Roos*,[161] arose from criminal proceedings brought by the Swedish Public Prosecutor's Office against the eponymous defendants, for failing to comply with a prohibition on the use of personal watercraft laid down by Swedish legislation. The main question referred was whether the contested legislation, which provided that jet-skis may be used only in general navigable waterways and in waters that would be designated by a local authority, amounted to an MEQR.

The Court began its analysis be recalling the paragraph summarising the law in this area, which was firstly laid down in *Commission v Italy (mopeds)*.[162] It then considered whether the contested measure hindered access to the market for jet-skis originating in other Member States. It noted that because—since no waters had been designated by a local authority as open to navigation by personal watercraft—jet-skis were permitted on only general navigable waterways which were intended for heavy traffic of a commercial nature, making the use of such watercraft dangerous, 'the actual possibilities for the use of personal watercraft in Sweden are, therefore, merely marginal'.[163] The Court then noted—possibly wishing to be clearer than it was in *Commission v Italy (mopeds)* regarding discrimination—that

> Even if the national regulations at issue do not have the aim or effect of treating goods coming from other Member States less favourably, which is for the national court to ascertain, the restriction which they impose on the use of a product in the territory of a

---

[156] ibid, para 35.
[157] ibid, para 36.
[158] ibid, para 37. Emphasis added.
[159] ibid, paras 56 and 57.
[160] S Enchelmaier (n 22) 205.
[161] *Mickelsson and Roos* (n 103).
[162] ibid, para 24.
[163] ibid, para 25.

Member State may, depending on its scope, have a considerable influence on the behaviour of consumers, which may, in turn, affect the access of that product to the market of that Member State.[164]

The Court then pointed out that since consumers know that the use permitted by the contested legislation is very limited, they 'have only a limited interest in buying that product'[165] and, hence, the contested measure may amount to an MEQR—a matter that was left to the national court to decide, together with the question of whether the measure was justified. It is important to underline that in this case (and in most of the recent case-law on Article 34 TFEU), the Court seems to have avoided any reference to the *Keck* formula.

The importance of the two use restrictions cases analysed above lies in the fact that it is the first time that the Court *expressly* adopted a (*non-discriminatory*) restrictions-based test in the context of Article 34 TFEU.[166] Accordingly, national rules regulating trade which have no cross-border specificity but which are capable of impeding the free movement of goods, *may* now be found to be contrary to Article 34 TFEU. I say 'may', because the majority of the cases that came after this duo of cases, involved (directly or indirectly) discriminatory measures and, hence, the Court has not had the opportunity after the above rulings, to make it clear that the scope of this provision has, indeed, been extended in this manner.[167]

If the way forward is, indeed, for genuinely non-discriminatory measures to be caught by Articles 34, this illustrates that the Court may now be in the process of completing an economic constitution for the European Union through which traders (or should it be merely Union citizens?—a point to be considered subsequently in the book) have the right to participate in the market without any unreasonable restrictions standing in their way.[168] Indeed, it seems that the Court

---

[164] ibid, para 25.
[165] ibid, para 27.
[166] For a different view see P Wenneras and KB Moen, 'Selling Arrangements, Keeping *Keck*' (2010) 35 *European Law Review* 387. It is true that—as already explained—in previous case-law (most prominently the 1980s Sunday Trading cases (n 56)) the Court did follow an approach which did not require proof of discrimination of any kind in order for a measure to be caught by Article 34 TFEU. Nonetheless, it did not *expressly* admit that there is no need for proof of discrimination, as it has done in these recent cases.
[167] See eg Case C-443/10 *Bonnarde* [2011] ECR I-9327; Case C-639/11 *Commission v Poland* ECLI:EU:C:2014:173; Case C-61/12 *Commission v Lithuania* ECLI:EU:C:2014:172; *Ålands Vindkraft* (n 92); Case C-423/13 *UAB Vilniaus Energija* ECLI:EU:C:2014:2186; *Essent Belgium* (n 106). Note, however, that in *ANETT* the contested legislation (when looked at as a whole) appeared to be genuinely non-discriminatory and this was expressly noted by the Court: 'In the main proceedings, nothing indicates that the national legislation at issue has the object or effect of treating tobacco coming from other Member States less favourably. Nor does it concern the requirements that those products must meet. However, it is still necessary to examine whether this legislation hinders the access of tobacco products coming from other Member States to the Spanish market'—*ANETT* (n 98) paras 36–37. The Court concluded that the prohibition on the direct importation by tobacco retailers of tobacco products from other Member States hinders access of tobacco products from other Member States into the Spanish market.
[168] For a similar argument made in relation to the personal market freedoms, see E Spaventa, 'From *Gebhard* to *Carpenter*: Towards a (Non-)Economic European Constitution' (2004) 41 *Common Market Law Review* 743.

may have decided to revisit the question posed by Advocate General Tesauro at the beginning of his Opinion in *Hünermund* (seen in section II (B) above), this time (implicitly) answering that Article 34 TFEU is intended 'to encourage the unhindered pursuit of commerce in individual Member States'.[169] According to Barnard, *Keck* had 'refocused the emphasis of the enquiry away from "has there been an impact on trade in general" to whether there has been a sufficient impact on *cross-border* trade'.[170] With *Commission v Italy (mopeds)* and *Mickelsson and Roos*, however, we seem to be moving in the opposite direction, the aim of Article 34 TFEU appearing to be redefined as being—in addition to ensuring the free movement of goods as such—to also ensure that traders can engage in commerce in a cross-border context without being subjected to any national regulations which disproportionately restrain that right.[171] This means that national measures which are entirely neutral and, merely, seek to regulate an economic activity would now be subjected to EU scrutiny in order to ensure that individuals are not impeded from exercising the above right.

With these cases, therefore, the Court may have decided to transform Article 34 TFEU 'into a kind of "economic due process" clause'[172] which does not only aim at ensuring the free movement of goods between Member States but which seeks to protect, also, the right of traders (and consumers) to freely conduct cross-border transactions involving the sale of goods, undisturbed by national regulations (unless, of course, Member States can prove that the latter are justified). Since there does not appear to be an ulterior motive behind the protection of this right in such instances (since it does not contribute to the market-building aim of this provision, which merely requires the removal of measures *that have cross-border specificity*), and the Court seems to be simply wishing to ensure that traders (and consumers) enjoy this right *in all instances* and not, merely, when its restriction impedes *specifically* the free movement of goods between Member States, it seems that Article 34 TFEU may, therefore, now be considered as a source of a *fundamental* right to take-up and pursue an economic activity that involves the sale or purchase of goods in a cross-border context, without being limited by disproportionate regulation.[173]

Such a right appears to be granted for its own sake—simply because it is considered that traders and consumers should enjoy this right—and not for an ulterior

---

[169] Paragraph 1 of the Opinion of AG Tesauro in *Hünermund* (n 58).

[170] C Barnard (n 133) 42. For a similar view see J Baquero Cruz, *Between Competition and Free Movement: The Economic Constitutional Law of the European Community* (Oxford, Hart Publishing, 2002) 134.

[171] For a similar view see S Enchelmaier, 'The ECJ's Recent Case-Law on the Free Movement of Goods: Movement in all Sorts of Directions' (2007) 26 *Yearbook of European Law* 115, 132.

[172] M Poiares Maduro (n 76) 61.

[173] This can, in fact, be considered an aspect of the fundamental freedom to conduct a business which has been recognised as a general principle of EU law and is, also, enshrined in Article 16 EU Charter of Fundamental Rights. For more on this see A Usai, 'The Freedom to Conduct a Business in the EU, its Limitations and its Role in the European Legal Order: A New Engine for Deeper and Stronger Economic, Social, and Political Integration' (2013) 14 *German Law Journal* 1868.

purpose (ie to ensure that an internal market in goods is built). If this is, indeed, the case, the same right should be read as stemming from Article 35 TFEU, since it would appear absurd to grant to traders the fundamental right to import goods from other Member States whilst giving them merely the (instrumental) right to export their goods to other Member States.

Such a fundamental rights-based reading of Article 34 would find proponents in academia, such as Eeckhout, who has explained:

> In legal terms the internal market is not merely an abstract notion referring to a set of economic transactions, but also a concrete asset to which citizens and companies are entitled. Hence rulings on Art 30 should also have a concrete dimension, concentrating on the specific position in which traders and consumers are found and examining whether they are faced with unjustified hurdles when attempting to benefit from intra-Community trade—ie to have access to the market of another Member State.[174]

Moreover, it accords with the views of some of the members of the Court of Justice itself. For instance, Advocate General Bot in his Opinion in *Commission v Italy (mopeds)* suggested that the criterion that should be used for determining whether a measure amounts to an MEQR should be whether 'it prevented, impeded or rendered more difficult access to the market for products from other Member States',[175] and then explained that the adoption of 'a single and simple criterion based on access to the market' would lead to convergence among the market freedoms which 'is necessary, having regard, in particular, to the requirements relating to construction of the single European market and the emergence of European citizenship'.[176]

Although it is still not possible to say with certainty whether the aim of Article 34 TFEU has been redefined in the above manner, it should be noted that if the rights stemming from that provision are, now, *fundamental* rights for individuals, which are unrelated to the economic aim of that provision, this will bring to the fore a number of important questions. Are these fundamental rights now granted to traders by virtue of their possession of Union citizenship, in which case, Article 34 TFEU will be interpreted in such a broad manner only when the said traders (or consumers) possess the nationality of a Member State? What outer limits can and should be placed on the scope of application of Article 34 TFEU? Is such a broadening of the scope of application of this provision legally warranted? These questions will be explored in the subsequent two chapters.

---

[174] P Eeckhout (n 139) 270.
[175] Paragraph 111 of the Opinion of AG Bot in *Commission v Italy (mopeds)* (n 81).
[176] ibid, para 118. For a commentator who considers that convergence among the market freedoms has been achieved and explores (from a political science perspective) the reasons that led to this see S Schmidt, 'Who Cares about Nationality? The Path-Dependent Case Law of the ECJ from Goods to Citizens' (2012) 19 *Journal of European Public Policy* 8.

V. CONCLUSION

The chapter's aim has been to examine whether it can be argued that the status of Union citizenship has had any impact on the free movement of goods provisions. For this purpose, the chapter sought to consider which rights individuals appear, now, to derive from these provisions and the Court's Article 34 TFEU case-law was examined for this purpose. It has been seen that, although the Court has never referred to this provision or, as a matter of fact, to any of the free movement of goods provisions, as sources of fundamental *rights*, it has, nonetheless, always recognised their importance as fundamental principles of the EU legal system. Moreover, the Court in its case-law has, indeed, recognised that individuals can derive rights from these provisions (eg rights to move to another Member State to sell or purchase goods, rights to sell or purchase goods in a cross-border context, rights to (simply) move goods across-borders). Until recently, however, in all cases where individuals sought to enforce one of the above rights when invoking Article 34 TFEU, the contested measure amounted to an obstacle to the free movement of goods between Member States (in addition to limiting the exercise of one of the above rights) *and* it (specifically) *impeded the free movement of goods between Member States* (ie it had cross-border specificity); in other words, the rights were granted in situations where their bestowal contributed to the economic aim of this provision, which has traditionally been to build an internal market in goods whilst permitting Member States to neutrally regulate economic activities. Hence, it was not possible to claim with certainty that the rights granted by the free movement of goods provisions to individuals were anything more than instrumental rights simply granted for the purpose of furthering the achievement of the aim of Article 34 TFEU.

Nonetheless, the Court's recent case-law in the context of Article 34 TFEU seems to have extended the scope of application of that provision by bringing within it genuinely non-discriminatory measures which simply appear to be limiting the commercial freedom of traders. This demonstrates that the Court may now wish to re-read this provision as not merely aiming to ensure the free movement of goods between Member States whilst ensuring that Member States can continue to (neutrally) regulate economic activities (the traditional aim of this provision), but, also, to grant to persons the (fundamental) right to trade in a cross-border context, without being inhibited by disproportionate regulation. As explained, if this has, indeed, been the intention of the Court, we are immediately faced with a series of all-important (but as yet unanswered) questions. In particular, it remains unclear whether this right—as a fundamental right which is *not* granted merely instrumentally in order to further the economic aim of this provision—is only available to Union citizens. However, only if this is the case will it be possible to argue that this (fundamental) right is an EU citizenship right and, thus, that the broadening of the material scope of this provision to encompass this right can be attributable to the introduction of the status of Union citizenship and to the impact the latter has had on the interpretation of the free movement of goods provisions.

In addition, there is isolated 'evidence' that the Court may be willing to bring within the scope of Article 34 TFEU situations which involve a restriction on the exercise of the right of traders to *move* between Member States for the purpose of selling goods, even though the goods involved are produced and marketed within one and the same Member State (ie there is no free movement *of goods*). If this is, indeed, the case, this is another right, the grant of which cannot be justified under a purely market-building rationale for this provision and, for this reason, should be considered to be a fundamental right. However, for the reasons explained earlier, the value as a precedent of the Court's case where the existence of this right was hinted, is limited and, hence, it cannot yet be said that this right, indeed, stems from Article 34 TFEU.

Accordingly, the analysis in this chapter has demonstrated that although there have been recent signs in the Court's Article 34 case-law that some of the rights stemming from this provision are not instrumental to the market-building aim of this provision, and, thus, that they are fundamental rights that are granted to individuals for their own sake, many important questions (including the question of whether these fundamental rights are reserved for Union citizens) remain unanswered and, thus, it is not possible to say with certainty whether the introduction and development of the status of Union citizenship has had any impact on the interpretation of the free movement of goods provisions.

Part III

The Future

5

(Re-)Interpreting the Market Freedoms in the Light of Union Citizenship: Emerging Questions

I. INTRODUCTION

IN CHAPTER THREE, it was seen that the Court's post-Maastricht case-law shows that the introduction and development of the status of Union citizenship has had a significant impact on the interpretation of the personal market freedoms: these provisions appear, now, to be viewed as (also) sources of *fundamental* economic rights for Union citizens, and they can apply even in situations that are not sufficiently connected to their market-building aim. As regards the free movement of goods provisions, on the other hand, things have not been as clear, although there are undeniably some signs in the case-law that demonstrate that the Court may now be in the early stages of a process of re-reading these provisions as sources of fundamental rights for individuals. The current chapter and the next will focus on exploring the broader implications of the above developments. The aim of this chapter will be to consider the questions that emerge once we accept that the interpretation of the market freedoms has been affected in the way seen in the previous chapters. In particular, it will be examined whether the Court *can* interpret the market freedoms in that way, taking into account both the text of these provisions as well as what appears to be their current aim. The chapter will, also, seek to offer a suggestion as to *what* should now be considered to amount to a restriction in the context of the market freedoms, as well as *how* it must now be decided whether a national measure amounts to a restriction caught by these provisions and whether it can be justified.

II. CAN THE MARKET FREEDOMS BE (RE-)INTERPRETED IN THE MANNER DOCUMENTED IN THE PREVIOUS TWO CHAPTERS?

The first question that arises following the conclusions reached in the previous two chapters is whether the market freedoms are *capable* of bearing the meaning that the Court has attributed to them in some of its post-Maastricht case-law. In other words, has the Court interpreted these provisions in a manner which is compliant with their natural meaning and/or purpose? Or has it exceeded its powers and engaged in judicial activism?

In the literature, judicial activism is treated as synonymous with judicial law-making: judges are supposed to—simply—interpret and apply the law; they are not supposed to interpret it in such a liberal way that they are, in effect, engaging in law-making.[1] Of course, the line dividing law-application from law-making is perilously thin and this is obvious from the literature, which demonstrates that commentators fail to agree not only on whether specific judgments are examples of judicial activism, but also, and more fundamentally, on a definition of—and even on the question of whether as a matter of principle, the ECJ can indeed be accused of (ever) engaging in—'judicial activism'.[2]

According to Hartley,[3] rulings *within* the text of a provision (ie judgments which adopt 'an interpretation within the possible range of meaning that the text might reasonably be said to have') are, clearly, not examples of judicial activism. Conversely, rulings *outside* the text (ie where 'the court's ruling, though ostensibly based on the text, is not supported by it') or rulings *contrary* to the text (ie a ruling 'which contradicts the text on the basis of any reasonable interpretation of it') can be examples of judicial activism.[4] The same commentator, however, acknowledged that despite the fact that one may argue that the Court is judicially active when delivering such rulings, another view could be that the Court is acting within its jurisdiction, since it seeks to fulfil its duty 'in developing the law in the desired direction' which is to develop the Treaties 'into the constitution of a fully-fledged federation'; the Treaties 'are not static instruments but were intended from the beginning to be dynamic: they are "genetically coded" … to develop into the constitution of a fully-fledged federation'.[5] Tridimas,[6] on the other hand, is much more sceptical about the use of the phrase 'judicial activism', pointing out a number of problems associated with it.[7] He, rather, prefers to view the Court's rulings

---

[1] This appears to be only one of several definitions of 'judicial activism'. Kmiec has identified five different definitions used in the US—see K Kmiec, 'The Origin and Current Meanings of "Judicial Activism"' (2004) 92 *California Law Review* 1441. Space precludes a detailed analysis of the issue of judicial activism and of the various approaches to it in the literature. For a thorough literature review regarding this topic, see G Conway, *The Limits of Legal Reasoning and the European Court of Justice* (Cambridge, Cambridge University Press, 2012) Ch 2. For an examination of judicial activism from a number of different angles, see M Dawson, B de Witte and E Muir (eds), *Judicial Activism at the European Court of Justice* (Cheltenham, Edward Elgar, 2013).

[2] The obvious examples here are the (related) articles by TC Hartley, 'The European Court, Judicial Objectivity and the Constitution of the European Union' (1996) 112 *Law Quarterly Review* 95 and T Tridimas, 'The Court of Justice and Judicial Activism' (1996) 21 *European Law Review* 199.

[3] TC Hartley (n 2) 95.

[4] ibid, 96.

[5] ibid, 107. For another commentator who is also of the view that the Court 'has sought to "constitutionalise" the Treaty, that is to fashion a constitutional framework for a federal-type structure in Europe' see GF Mancini, 'The Making of a Constitution for Europe' (1989) 26 *Common Market Law Review* 595, 596.

[6] T Tridimas (n 2) 199.

[7] T Tridimas (n 2). See, also, A Arnull, 'The European Court and Judicial Objectivity: A Reply to Professor Hartley' (1996) 112 *Law Quarterly Review* 411.

where an interpretation was adopted which would not have been warranted under a literal interpretation of their text, as examples of—legitimately—applying the so-called 'teleological approach' to interpretation, which 'seeks to interpret a rule taking account, in particular, of the purpose, the aim and the objective which if [sic] pursues'.[8]

Despite the many significant differences in the views of the above commentators, two common—related—conclusions can be drawn from their analyses: the first is that the constituent EU Treaties are dynamic and, hence, their interpretation has to be constantly adapted in order to reflect their revised priorities and aims;[9] and the second is that if the interpretation of a provision does not—strictly speaking—fall *within* its text but is such as to further the aims attributed to it at the time, the Court cannot be accused of engaging in judicial activism but is, merely, using a teleological approach to interpretation.[10] The above points are, according to da Cruz Vilaça and Piçarra, a reflection of the constitutional nature of the Treaties given that

> the term 'constitutionalisation' refers, in the Anglo-American literature, to a circular or spiral process in which a treaty such as the EC Treaty is interpreted by a court such as the Court of Justice in accordance with a systematic, teleological and, above all, dynamic method, similar to that used by the constitutional courts of the Member States and different from that characterising the approach usually taken by international courts and arbitrators for the interpretation of an international convention.[11]

Bearing the above points in mind, this section will seek to consider two questions: firstly, whether the interpretation of the market freedoms by the Court in its recent case-law documented in the previous chapters falls *within* the text of these provisions, under a literal interpretation of it; and secondly, whether the market freedoms have been interpreted in a way which is necessary for ensuring the achievement of their *current* aim. As will be seen, although answering the first question is a relatively straightforward exercise, the same is not the case for the second, since, for the reasons explained below, neither the travaux préparatoires of the Treaty nor the Court's jurisprudence can offer much help with this.

---

[8] T Tridimas (n 2) 204. For an explanation of the various types of judicial interpretation see G Conway (n 1) 19–21.

[9] As da Cruz Vilaça and Piçarra have noted '[t]he final destination of European integration is not defined once and for all in the EU Treaty. It is for future generations to decide, at each moment, which steps to take and which advances to accept.'—see JL da Cruz Vilaça and N Piçarra, 'Are there Substantive Limits to the Amendment of the Treaties?' in JL da Cruz Vilaça, *EU Law and Integration: Twenty Years of Judicial Application of EU Law* (Oxford, Hart Publishing, 2014) 41. For a similar view see J Snell, '"European Constitutional Settlement", an ever Closer Union, and the Treaty of Lisbon: Democracy or Relevance?' (2008) 33 *European Law Review* 619, 623–31.

[10] Of course, '[t]he ECJ relatively rarely expressly articulates in depth the interpretative method it adopts, quite often leaving this implicit or briefly stating, for example, that a broad or purposive approach to interpretation is appropriate'—G Conway (n 1) 22.

[11] JL da Cruz Vilaça and N Piçarra (n 9) 18. For a study the starting point of which is the fact that the European Court of Justice (ECJ) is a *constitutional* court, see N Nic Shuibhne, *The Coherence of EU Free Movement Law* (Oxford, Oxford University Press, 2013); see also, in particular, pp 8–21, for an explanation of why the ECJ is a constitutional court and for the responsibilities it has as a constitutional court.

158 *Emerging Questions*

Accordingly, the attempt to provide a positivist answer to this question will be intermingled with a normative exercise, exploring what the current aims of the market freedoms *should* be considered to be.

A. Is the Expansion of the Scope of the Market Freedoms in the Manner Documented Warranted Under a Literal Interpretation of their Text?

The text of the market freedoms was quoted in the previous chapters and, hence, will not be repeated here, apart from specific parts of it, where deemed necessary.

The personal market freedoms are now found in Title IV of the Treaty on the Functioning of the European Union (TFEU),[12] which is headed 'Free movement of persons, services and capital'. A close perusal of their text provides a mixed response to the question of whether a literal interpretation of these provisions would support the Court's recent rulings analysed in chapter three.

Starting with the freedom of movement for workers, the relevant provisions are found in Chapter 1 of the Title. The text of Article 45 TFEU—which is the core provision of the Chapter—concentrates on ensuring the free *movement* of workers. The provision does not only begin by providing that '[f]reedom of movement for workers shall be secured within the Union'—which seems to be the core aim of this provision—but in the remainder of it, it is shown that any rights derived from this provision are related to *this* freedom (see, in particular, the second and third paragraphs of this Article which begin, respectively, with the words '*[s]uch freedom of movement* shall entail' and '*[i]t* shall entail').[13] Moreover, all the rights explicitly listed in this provision and which must be related to the exercise of the said movement, are either economic in nature (eg 'to accept offers of employment actually made' or 'to move freely within the territory of Member States for this purpose')[14] or are related to the pursuit of an economic activity as an employed person (eg nationality discrimination must, according to Article 45(2), be abolished as regards employment, remuneration and other conditions of work and employment, and, importantly, the rights to free movement and 'to stay in a Member State' must be for the purpose of employment).[15]

Accordingly, it would seem that under a literal interpretation of Article 45 TFEU, the only (primary) right that workers can derive, is the right to take-up an economic activity as a 'worker' in the territory of *another* Member State. In other words, the focus is on ensuring that Member State nationals can move freely between Member States *for the purpose of taking-up an economic activity*, and, hence, in order for this provision to apply there must be a change in the economic base of the economic actor and the location of the economic activity.

---

[12] Consolidated Version of The Treaty on the Functioning of the European Union (TFEU) [2008] OJ C326/47.
[13] Emphasis added.
[14] Art 45(3)(a) TFEU.
[15] Arts 45(3)(b) and 45(3)(c) TFEU, respectively.

This means that reading this provision as being the source of the other right that has been (implicitly) held to stem from this provision by the Court (in its *Ritter-Coulais* saga)[16]—the right to start pursuing an economic activity in a cross-border context, *without this entailing a change in the economic base of the economic actor and in the location of the economic activity*—is not compliant with a literal interpretation of its text. Conversely, the text of Article 45 TFEU appears sufficiently broad to be able to cover (genuinely) non-discriminatory restrictions and, hence, an interpretation which does not require cross-border specificity to exist in order for a situation to fall within its scope, does not appear to be contrary to or (even) outside its text.

Establishment is governed by Chapter 2, which is entitled '*Right* of establishment'.[17] The main provision in this Chapter (Article 49 TFEU) prohibits 'restrictions on the freedom of establishment of nationals of a Member State in the territory of another Member State'. The provision states that 'freedom of establishment' shall *include* the right to take-up and pursue activities as self-employed persons under the conditions laid down for its own nationals by the country where such establishment is exercised, and, hence, measures which are discriminatory on the ground of nationality in relation to the exercise of this freedom are prohibited. However, the use of the word 'include' means that other rights which are not mentioned in its text can be derived from this provision, though a literal interpretation of it would require such rights to be related to the exercise of the freedom of establishment.

Accordingly, in the same manner that a literal interpretation of Article 45 TFEU requires that provision to be interpreted as granting only the primary right to take-up an economic activity in the territory of *another* Member State (and all other rights are secondary to it), a literal interpretation of Article 49 TFEU would seem to require the Court to read this provision as granting the right to take-up and (then) pursue a self-employed economic activity, in the territory of *another* Member State. Hence, as is the case with Article 45 TFEU, the text of Article 49 TFEU appears to be requiring a change in the economic base of the economic actor and the location of the economic activity and, hence, cases such as *N* (in the *Ritter-Coulais* saga),[18] where the facts involved merely a change in the location of the residence of the economic actor, whilst he maintained his economic activity in his State of origin, do not seem to accord with a literal interpretation of the text of this provision. Moreover, just as is the case with Article 45 TFEU, the text of Article 49 TFEU is, also, broad enough to cover measures which impede the exercise of this right irrespective of whether there is cross-border specificity.

---

[16] Case C-152/03 *Ritter-Coulais* [2006] ECR I-1711; Case C-470/04 *N* [2006] ECR I-7409; Case C-464/05 *Geurts* [2007] ECR I-9325; Case C-527/06 *Renneberg* [2008] ECR I-7735; Case C-379/11 *Caves Krier* ECLI:EU:C:2012:798; Case C-87/13 *X* ECLI:EU:C:2014:2459; Case C-303/12 *Imfeld* ECLI:EU:C:2013:822 (hereafter collectively called 'the *Ritter-Coulais* saga').
[17] Emphasis added.
[18] *N* (n 16).

As regards the freedom to provide services, the relevant Chapter is entitled 'Services' and Article 56 TFEU focuses on prohibiting 'restrictions on freedom to provide services within the Union' in situations where a national of a Member State wishes to provide such services to a person who is established in a different Member State. Although this appears to be focusing on the right of service-providers—who must hold the nationality of a Member State—to provide services to persons established in another Member State, it is not contrary to (or even outside) the text of this provision if it is read as also prohibiting restrictions on the receipt of services, since these, clearly, are the opposite side of the same coin of the restrictions that are, expressly, sought to be removed by this provision (ie restrictions on the *provision* of services).[19] Moreover, as seen in chapter three of the book, Article 56 TFEU has been read as also applying to situations where no person moves but the service itself moves across borders; such a reading is, also, compliant with a literal approach to the interpretation of this provision, given that its text simply refers to the freedom to provide services to persons established in a different Member State, without it being necessary that a person also moves for this purpose. A literal interpretation of Article 56 TFEU can, also, include within its scope even genuinely non-discriminatory measures and, hence, the provision can apply even in situations where there is no cross-border specificity, provided that there is an obstacle to the provision of services across borders.

However, as has been made clear in the Court's case-law, Article 56 TFEU covers, also, instances where the provider moves to another Member State and from there provides services to persons established in his or her own Member State who have, also, temporarily moved to that State;[20] an interpretation which would seem to be outside the text of this provision. In order to justify the extension of the scope of Article 59 EEC (Article 56 TFEU) to cover such situations, the Court made reference to the purpose of that provision, noting that

> [a]lthough Article 59 of the Treaty expressly contemplates only the situation of a person providing services who is established in a Member State other than that in which the recipient of the service is established, the purpose of that Article is nevertheless to abolish restrictions on the freedom to provide services by persons who are not established in the State in which the service is to be provided ... It is only when all the relevant elements of the activity in question are confined within a single Member State that the provisions of the Treaty on freedom to provide services cannot apply.[21]

Finally, it should be noted that the fact that the Court had (early on) read (what is now) Article 56 TFEU as the source of the right to start providing services in a cross-border context, even in situations where there had been no change in the economic base of the economic actor and the location of the economic activity

---

[19] J Snell, *Goods and Services in EU Law: A Study of the Relationship between the Freedoms* (Oxford, Oxford University Press, 2002 (reprinted 2005)) 14; J Baquero Cruz, 'The Case Law of the European Court of Justice on the Mobility of Patients: An Assessment' in F Benyon (ed), *Services and the EU Citizen* (Oxford, Hart Publishing, 2013) 89.
[20] Case C-154/89 *Commission v France (Tourist Guides)* [1991] ECR I-659.
[21] ibid, para 9.

and where the change that led to the service provision being pursued across borders was the change of residence of the recipient,[22] seems to accord with a literal interpretation of this provision which simply requires that the provider and the recipient of the services are established in different Member States, without requiring a change in the economic base (ie the establishment) of the economic actor.

Moving, now, to the free movement of goods provisions, as regards Article 34 TFEU, the position, again, is mixed. Tridimas has pointed out that this provision 'is overwhelming in its simplicity. It prohibits "quantitative restrictions on imports and measures having equivalent effect". But what is a measure having equivalent effect?'[23] The text of this provision allows much freedom to the Court when it interprets it. In particular, the wording of the prohibition is broad enough to catch genuinely non-discriminatory indistinctly applicable measures. If—as was suggested in the previous chapter—following the use restrictions cases, the prohibition in Article 34 TFEU has, now, been read as also catching such measures, this can, clearly, be considered an interpretation which is not contrary to or, even outside, the text of this provision.[24]

Things, however, become more complicated when Article 34 TFEU is read as a source of rights for individuals. Title II TFEU is entitled 'Free movement of goods' and, just like the Title which includes the personal market freedoms, it is found in Part Three of the Treaty ('Union Policies and Internal Actions'). Article 34 TFEU is placed in Chapter 3 of the Title, which is entitled 'Prohibition of quantitative restrictions between Member States'. The wording of the provision (which speaks only about goods and does not make any reference whatsoever to persons) taken together with its position in the Treaty and the fact that it has been separated from the personal market freedoms, illustrates that the drafters of the original Treaty (and, possibly, the drafters of the subsequent amending Treaties who have not made any changes to its wording) may have been of the view that this provision simply seeks to remove obstacles to the free movement of goods between Member States. Although an interpretation of this provision which brings within its scope situations where an impediment to the free movement of persons leads, also, to an obstacle to the free movement of goods does accord with a literal approach to its interpretation, an interpretation which brings within its scope *situations which do not involve an impediment to the free movement of goods between Member States*, appears to be outside or, even, contrary to its text, since the latter clearly requires that in order for a measure to be caught, it must amount to a quantitative restriction or a measure having equivalent effect to quantitative restrictions (MEQR) *on imports*.[25]

---

[22] For an example of such a scenario see Case 15/78 *Koestler* [1978] ECR 1971.
[23] T Tridimas (n 2) 205.
[24] As Snell has correctly noted, both a discrimination-based and an obstacle-based reading of the free movement of goods provisions are 'hermeneutically perfectly feasible'—J Snell (n 19) 2.
[25] The same points can be made about the literal interpretation of Art 35 TFEU.

B. What are the Current Aims of the Market Freedoms?

What is the *telos* of the market freedoms? What is their *current* aim or aims?

The travaux préparatoires of the Treaties can merely elucidate the intended meaning of their provisions at the time these were drafted, which means that they are merely of historical significance, given that, as explained earlier, the constituent EU Treaties are dynamic and hence their aims—and the aims of their provisions—are constantly subject to change. Moreover, the Court gives seldom indications as to what it believes to be the aims of the Treaty provisions, and it has never sought to state clearly and exhaustively what the aims of each of the market freedoms are.[26] Therefore, in the absence of more tangible evidence, the conclusions drawn here regarding the question of what is—and what should be—the aims of the market freedoms at the moment, are based on an observation of the overall development of EU law but are also, inevitably, influenced by the Court's approach in its recent case-law and, in particular, in the cases we saw in the previous two chapters.

However, (partly) relying on ECJ jurisprudence for identifying the current aims of the market freedoms suffers from a number of weaknesses.

First of all, it is unavoidably based on pure speculation as to what the intentions of the Court may have been, rather than on any concrete evidence, in this way creating a wide margin of error.

Secondly, it is based on circular reasoning, which leads to an instance of a 'chicken or the egg' type of dilemma. This is because in order to discern what—in the Court's view—is or are the current aim(s) of the market freedoms, the only guidance available is the Court's jurisprudence which is, however, what needs to be judged against these aims, in order to provide an answer to the question examined in this subsection. In other words, the interpretation of the market freedoms by the Court will be used for establishing what appear to be the current aims of these provisions; and the latter will then be used to judge the correctness of this interpretation.

A third weakness of this approach is that it makes assumptions about the Court and the way it operates which do not appear to hold true. In particular, it tends to ignore the fact that the Court does not act as a single, unified, actor but it meets in many different formations and is comprised of (at the moment) 28 judges who, often, have significantly different views on fundamental issues: it would be a distortion of reality to assume that the Court has a single mind (in the same way that it has to speak with a single voice) or that it has a settled and clearly-formed view on various important matters, including on the question of what the current aims of the market freedoms are.[27] In addition, practice has, so far, illustrated that the

---

[26] One such rare example is the judgment in Case C-371/08 *Ziebell* [2011] ECR I-12735.

[27] For an article arguing that ECJ rulings demonstrate that judges do not share uniform preferences and that 'judges' preferences lie on a continuum from Europhilia to Euroscepticism', see M Malecki, 'Do ECJ Judges all Speak with the Same Voice? Evidence of Divergent Preferences from the Judgments of Chambers' (2012) 19 *Journal of European Public Policy* 59.

Court does not, usually, have a plan as to how a particular policy area should be developed; instead, it often operates in a rather intuitive fashion and delivers judgments which seek to achieve the best result on the facts of the case (according to the group of judges who hear the case), rather than to follow a particular line of thought and reasoning laid down beforehand.[28]

Bearing the above points in mind, we should now proceed to consider what are/should be the current aims of the market freedoms and whether these aims can justify the re-interpretation of these provisions in the manner seen in the previous two chapters.

Before the establishment of the EEC, which had as its core aim to build a common market shared by the EEC Member States, markets in Europe remained divided along national lines. With the coming into force of the EEC Treaty, therefore, the focus was placed on *building* a common market in goods, services, labour and—at a later time—capital. Given that there were not yet (m)any traders or economic actors who were pursuing an economic activity in the territory of another Member State or in a cross-border context, the focus had to be placed initially on encouraging traders and workers to *take-up* such cross-border economic activities. Hence, traders should be encouraged to start exporting or importing their goods to/from other Member States, Member State nationals should be encouraged to look for work or to set-up a self-employed economic activity in other Member States, legal persons (ie corporate entities) should be free to start pursuing their economic activities in a cross-border context, and economic actors should be encouraged to start providing services to persons established in other Member States; only in this way would a common market be *built*. The main tools that would be used for building this transnational market would be the market freedoms, which would be used for requiring Member States not to act in ways which could impede corporate entities, economic actors, and traders from *taking-up* an economic activity in another Member State/in a cross-border context.[29]

Hence, the market freedoms were considered originally to have as their aim to ensure that an internal market would be built and, thus, they merely aimed to ensure that economic actors would be free to *take-up* an economic activity that would be pursued in the territory of *another* Member State or in a *cross-border* context. Of course, the aim was not, simply, to build an internal market, but to build a *smoothly-functioning market*. And in order for a market to operate smoothly, there must be—at least some minimum—regulation. The extent of the regulation will depend on the specific type of market that is sought to be built, but

---

[28] S Wernicke, 'Au nom de qui? The European Court of Justice between Member States, Civil Society and Union Citizens' (2007) 13 *European Law Journal* 380, 381. For the limitations of research based on case-law, see N Nic Shuibhne (n 11) 4–6.

[29] As Davies has noted, 'competition law and state aids are to do with the functioning, or maintenance, or operation of the internal market, by contrast with the free movement articles and the rules on taxation, which are to do with its creation or establishment'—G Davies, *European Union Internal Market Law* (London, Routledge, 2003) 137.

the EU has espoused agnosticism in relation to this matter, not showing preference for any specific type of market economy.[30]

A decentralised system of regulation seemed to have been chosen, whereby rules for the operation of economic activities would be laid down by Member States and, only as a last resort, by the EU itself. This, in combination with the fact that the internal market should be a regulated market in order to be a properly-functioning market, and, thus, economic activities would have to be regulated somewhere (in the 'home State', as explained in previous chapters), meant that national rules which merely limited the freedom of traders or economic actors by regulating an economic activity, without *specifically* seeking to limit their ability to start working or trading *in another Member State or in a cross-border context*, had traditionally been deemed to be automatically excluded from the scope of application of the market freedoms. Conversely, when national rules regulating an economic activity appeared to be concealing a 'bias' against economic transactions conducted in a cross-border context or against persons that wished to take-up an economic activity in the territory of another Member State, they needed to be assessed for their compatibility with the market freedoms. This is why, as we saw in the two preceding chapters, the Court had, traditionally, employed a requirement of cross-border specificity in order for the market freedoms to apply: national rules should remain untouched if they were applied by the rightful regulator and if they neutrally regulated an economic activity, and this was so even if they, as a side-effect, limited the freedom of traders and economic actors; it was only when national legislation regulating an economic activity was not neutral, and discouraged (*only*) the initiation of a *cross-border* economic activity or *specifically* impeded the freedom of Member State nationals to take-up an economic activity in the territory of another Member State, that should be subjected to EU scrutiny.

Accordingly, as we saw in the previous chapters, the pre-1993 interpretation of the market freedoms appeared to be a clear reflection of the fact that these provisions had as their sole aim to build a common market.

The question that will be considered now, however, is whether the aims of the market freedoms have changed in recent years and, in particular, during the period that the Court appears to have differentiated its approach towards their interpretation (ie after Maastricht).

Within the context of the EU's internal market policy, after Maastricht, the aim appears no longer to be merely to *build* an internal market but, also, to ensure that the newly-built—smoothly-functioning—market is *maintained*.[31]

As seen in chapter one, the Single European Act sought to inject new impetus to the process of building an internal market, as a response to the sluggishness of the

---

[30] C Kaupa, 'Maybe not Activist Enough? On the Court's Alleged Neoliberal Bias in its Recent Labor Cases' in M Dawson, B de Witte and E Muir (eds), *Judicial Activism at the European Court of Justice* (Cheltenham, Edward Elgar, 2013) 59–61. This does not appear to be problematic; in fact, it has been argued that the EU lacks the democratic legitimacy to impose a certain type of market economy on its Member States. See, generally, J Snell (n 9).

[31] A Tryfonidou, *Reverse Discrimination in EC Law* (The Hague, Kluwer, 2009) Ch 5.

1970s and early 1980s, which followed the Luxembourg accords. In fact, this was done in a concrete manner, by setting a deadline for the completion of the internal market, this being the end of 1992. Although the deadline was, clearly, not legally binding,[32] and although—practically speaking—the construction of the internal market is a never-ending process,[33] it was important to set a specific deadline for achieving at least the basics regarding the creation of the internal market. The deadline, however, was also important in that it signalled the (symbolic) completion of the internal market and the beginning of another—more mature—phase for the EU's internal market policy, where the focus would no longer be merely on building an internal market by removing obstacles *to the initiation* of cross-border economic activities, but also and perhaps to a greater extent, on ensuring that the internal market built so far would be maintained,[34] ie that cross-border economic activities that had been initiated after making use of the right to take-up an economic activity that was pursued in another Member State or in a cross-border context would continue to be pursued in the same way.

Can this broader economic aim, nonetheless, justify the inclusion within the scope of application of the market freedoms, of situations which lack cross-border specificity? Moreover, does it justify the re-interpretation of these provisions as sources of the additional rights that appear to have been (implicitly) read as stemming from them in recent years? For the reasons to be explained below, it does not.

Maintaining the internal market that has been built requires that the economic activities that have already been taken-up and are pursued in the territory of another Member State/in a cross-border context can *continue* to be so pursued. The emphasis is, therefore, on the *continuation* of the status-quo, in contrast to the aim of building an internal market, which places the focus on encouraging a *change* in the status quo, by enabling economic actors to *change* the location of their economic activity or the mode in which an economic activity is pursued. Nonetheless, it should be kept in mind that this aim is interlinked with the aim of building an internal market—hence, it can only justify the extension of the personal market freedoms to cover situations where there has been a prior initiation of a cross-border economic activity, and it is the continuation of *this* activity that needs to be safeguarded. Hence, the aim of *maintaining* the internal market appears, for instance, to be the rationale behind the Court's rulings in cases involving frontier workers, including the family reunification rights cases of *S and G*[35] and *Carpenter*,[36] where the aim of the Court was to prevent Member States from

---

[32] P Craig, 'The Evolution of the Single Market' in C Barnard and J Scott (eds), *The Law of the Single European Market: Unpacking the Premises* (Oxford, Hart Publishing, 2002) 16.
[33] K Mortlemans, 'The Common Market, the Internal Market and the Single Market, What's in a Market?' (1998) 35 *Common Market Law Review* 101, 102; K Armstrong and S Bulmer, *The Governance of the Single European Market* (Manchester, Manchester University Press, 1998) 14; P Craig (n 32) 15; RCA White, *Workers, Establishment, and Services in the European Union* (Oxford, Oxford University Press, 2004) 4.
[34] J Snell (n 19) 77.
[35] Case C-457/12 *S and G* ECLI:EU:C:2014:136.
[36] Case C-60/00 *Carpenter* [2002] ECR I-6279.

(unjustifiably) impeding the exercise of the right of Union citizens to continue pursuing an economic activity that had (previously) been taken-up and was pursued in a cross-border context.

The aim of maintaining the internal market can, however, not justify the expansion of the scope of the market freedoms to cover situations which do not involve cross-border specificity. Since this aim requires that the internal market that is sought to be maintained is functioning smoothly, in the sense that it must be sufficiently regulated, it would seem that the abandonment of the requirement of cross-border specificity and the resultant opening of the scope of the market freedoms to all sorts of measures, would go against this aim, and against the principle of subsidiarity, introduced by the Treaty of Maastricht.[37] As Horsley has rightly argued, subsidiarity should not be viewed merely 'as a restraint on the Union legislature' but, rather, it 'should also be considered to operate as an important source of restraint on the *exercise* of the Court's own interpretative authority'.[38] A smoothly functioning internal market is not a market where obstacles to the initiation and pursuit of an economic activity in the territory of another Member State/across borders are removed at all costs,[39] but a market where such obstacles are removed in a way which respects the other values of the EU legal system, including the value of maintaining a (sufficiently) regulated market. Hence, the aim of building and maintaining such a market cannot, in my view, justify the inclusion within the scope of the market freedoms of situations which lack cross-border specificity.

Similarly, the expansion of the material scope of the more stationary personal market freedoms, by adding the primary right to start pursuing an economic activity in a cross-border context even when the economic base of the economic actor and the location of the economic activity does not change—ie as in the *Ritter-Coulais* saga[40]—cannot be justified under an internal market rationale, given that it does not contribute to the aim of building an internal market (since there is no *initiation* of a cross-border *economic* activity), nor does it contribute to the aim of maintaining the internal market that has been built (as there is no prior initiation of an economic activity *in another Member State* which needs to be maintained). In addition, the re-interpretation of Article 34 TFEU as a source of the right for traders to move between Member States for the purpose of engaging in trade in situations where the goods that are involved have not moved between Member States, cannot be justified under such an economic rationale. If, say, a Belgian

---

[37] Consolidated Version of The Treaty on European Union [2012] OJ C326/13.
[38] T Horsley, 'Unearthing Buried Treasure: Art. 34 TFEU and the Exclusionary Rules' (2012) 37 *European Law Review* 734, 752. For an analysis of the role that subsidiarity can play as a restraint on the Court's own interpretative functions, see T Horsley, 'Subsidiarity and the European Court of Justice: Missing Pieces in the Subsidiarity Jigsaw?' (2012) 50 *Journal of Common Market Studies* 267. See, also, GA Bermann, 'Taking Subsidiarity Seriously: Federalism in the European Community and the United States' (1994) 94 *Columbia Law Review* 331, 402.
[39] A Tryfonidou (n 31) Ch 5.
[40] *Ritter-Coulais* saga (n 16).

farmer who lives, and has a farm, in Belgium near the border with Luxembourg, is prevented from going to the latter State twice a week to sell there door-to-door from his van *goods produced in Luxembourg and which are sold to him by Luxembourgian wholesalers*, this does not appear capable of impeding the aim of ensuring the free movement of *goods* between Member States or the aim of maintaining an internal market where *goods* can move freely between Member States.

Accordingly, the important question is whether the market freedoms now have another (additional) objective, which is capable of justifying the expansion of their scope of application in the manner described in chapters three and four of the book. In particular, does the fact that (some) of their beneficiaries are now Union citizens, justify the expansion of the scope of these provisions to cover situations, the inclusion of which is not justified by their internal market rationale?

The introduction of the status of Union citizenship at Maastricht demonstrated that the internal market policy—although still very central to the EU project—would no longer be *the* single most important policy of the EU. Post-Maastricht, and equally high on the EU's agenda is the development of the status of EU citizenship, the creation of an area of freedom, security, and justice, the achievement of a social market economic, and the promotion of a high level of employment, to give just a few examples of the EU's post-1993 mandate. The internal market policy of the EU, therefore, is no longer the focus of the attention of the EU legislator and judges, and is not the policy that defines all the other policies pursued in the EU's name;[41] instead, it has to work and blend harmoniously with its other policies and aims.[42] In addition, and perhaps more importantly, other (non-economic) policy interests—such as consumer protection and the protection of public health—have gained increasing importance *within* the EU's internal market policy.[43] After all, Article 26(2) TFEU—which is the (second) successor of Article 7a EEC, introduced by the Single European Act (SEA)—provides that '[t]he internal market shall comprise an area without internal frontiers in which the free movement of goods, persons, services and capital *is ensured in accordance with the provisions of the Treaties*'.[44]

---

[41] This is, after all, obvious from the changes to the structure of the EC Treaty made by the Treaty of Maastricht. Although in the original EEC Treaty, the market freedoms fell within Part Two which was entitled 'Foundations of the Community', in the EC Treaty (as amended by Maastricht), they were demoted by being moved to two of the Titles comprising 'Community policies'. The Treaty of Lisbon has—more or less—maintained the post-Maastricht structure.

[42] J Snell (n 19) 78; L Azoulai, 'The Court of Justice and the Social Market Economy: The Emergence of an Ideal and the Conditions for its Realization' (2008) 45 *Common Market Law Review* 1335, 1336–38; A Tryfonidou, 'Further Steps on the Road to Convergence among the Market Freedoms' (2010) 35 *European Law Review* 36, 39; C Barnard, *The Substantive Law of the EU: The Four Freedoms* (Oxford, Oxford University Press, 2013) 28–29; C Barnard, 'The Protection of Fundamental Social Rights in Europe after Lisbon: A Question of Conflicts of Interests' in S de Vries, U Bernitz and S Weatherill (eds), *The Protection of Fundamental Rights in the EU After Lisbon* (Oxford, Hart Publishing, 2013) 38 and 51; NJ de Boer, 'Fundamental Rights and the EU Internal Market: Just how Fundamental are the EU Treaty Freedoms? A Normative Enquiry Based on John Rawls Political Philosophy' (2013) 9 *Utrecht Law Review* 148, 159.

[43] P Craig (n 32) 38.

[44] Emphasis added.

Following the latest Treaty amendment in 2009—effected by the Treaty of Lisbon[45]—the personal market freedoms are found in Title IV ('Free movement of persons, services and capital') of Part Three ('Union policies and internal actions') of the TFEU. The provisions governing the rights of Union citizens are, nonetheless, found in a separate part (Part Two: 'Non-discrimination and citizenship of the Union'). This illustrates that the drafters of the Treaty of Lisbon wished to indicate that the personal market freedoms are to continue to be used as tools for pursuing the EU's internal market policy. Hence, and as argued above, it is still the aim of the personal market freedoms to ensure that Member State nationals—now Union citizens—as well as legal persons, are free to take-up and (then) (continue to) pursue an economic activity in a cross-border context/in another Member State. The same, of course, is the case for the free movement of goods provisions, which have also remained in the same Part (ie Part Three) of the Treaty and which, as we saw in the previous chapter, seek merely to safeguard the free movement of *goods* between Member States.

However, since 1993 and the introduction of the citizenship provisions into (what is now) the TFEU, further considerations must be taken into account when interpreting the provisions of the Treaties. In particular, (what is now) Article 20(2) TFEU provides, in its first sentence, that '[c]itizens of the Union shall enjoy the rights and be subject to the duties provided for in the Treaties'. This appears to suggest that, inter alia, the market freedoms should be re-read as part of the package of rights that the Union seeks to provide to its citizens.[46] As Advocate General Poiares Maduro had pointed out in his Opinion in the *Vassilopoulos* case,

> It is important that the freedoms of movement fit into the broader framework of the objectives of the internal market and European citizenship. At present, the freedoms of movement must be understood to be one of the essential elements of the 'fundamental status of nationals of the Member States'.[47]

Accordingly, the internal market should no longer merely be a market where goods, services, capital and economic actors can move between Member States and where cross-border economic activities can be freely taken-up and continue to be pursued, but it should, now, also, be an internal market where Union citizens can freely exercise the fundamental rights they derive from the Treaty *qua* Union citizens. As Spaventa has pointed out,

> [n]ot only Europe has progressed towards an integrated economy, but the European project has evolved to create a new constitutional dimension which "puts the individual at the heart of its activities". The Union citizen is then not merely instrumental to the

---

[45] Treaty of Lisbon [2007] OJ C306/1.
[46] Currie has noted that 'Citizenship in a European sense, therefore, stretches further than its articulation in Articles 17 to 22 EC, so as also to incorporate the traditional "economic" free movement provisions, read alongside the extensive interpretation provided by the ECJ of the social rights of economic migrants'—S Currie, 'The Transformation of Union Citizenship' in M Dougan and S Currie (eds), *50 Years of the European Treaties: Looking Back and Thinking Forward* (Oxford, Hart Publishing, 2009) 369–70. See, also, A Tryfonidou (n 42).
[47] Paragraph 40 of the Opinion in Joined Cases C-158 & 159/04 *Vassilopoulos* [2006] ECR I-8135.

economic welfare of the Community—rather, she achieves an additional status, and with that, an additional layer of fundamental rights protection.[48]

In my view, therefore, when the market freedoms are invoked by Union citizens, they should now be *read together with the citizenship provisions* and—in such a case—they must be considered to have as their aim to grant to Union citizens certain fundamental economic rights.[49] Moreover—and rather circularly—it is only when the market freedoms are read in conjunction with the citizenship provisions, that they can include within their scope the situations, the inclusion of which cannot be justified under their market-building rationale. Accordingly, although the inclusion of these situations within the scope of EU law is not unwarranted, a different (set of) provisions should, nonetheless, be employed for this purpose: a market freedom plus a citizenship provision.

More specifically, when the free movement of goods provisions are read in conjunction with Article 21 TFEU, they can cover the situation of *Union citizens* that move to another Member State for the purpose of selling (or purchasing) goods. Accordingly, Union citizens should, now, be considered to be deriving the primary, fundamental right to move to another Member State for the purpose of selling or purchasing goods and if either the home State (Article 35 TFEU read together with Article 21 TFEU) or the host State (Article 34 TFEU read together with Article 21 TFEU) restricts this right, this should amount to a restriction caught by these provisions and the Member State actions that create this restriction will have to be subjected to EU scrutiny. And, given that this will be a fundamental right, it will exist in all instances and, thus, cross-border specificity will not be required in order for any restriction on its exercise to be caught by these provisions. Nonetheless, given that Articles 34 and 35 TFEU explicitly require that goods move between Member States, traders will only be able to rely on either of these provisions read together with Article 21 TFEU to prevent obstacles to their own movement if the goods they intend to sell are goods that move between Member States; if not, Article 21 TFEU should be read together with Article 16 of the EU Charter of Fundamental Rights (EUCFR) which recognises the freedom to conduct a business.

Moreover, traders (or consumers of goods) who are Union citizens should now be able to rely on Article 34 TFEU read together with Article 20 TFEU, in order to challenge *any* measures which impede them from importing or bringing within their home State goods purchased from another Member State. Since this right is, now, a fundamental, citizenship right, its *existence* is not dependent on proof that it exists and is enjoyed, also, in purely internal situations (which is the case when

---

[48] E Spaventa, *Free Movement of Persons in the European Union: Barriers to Movement in their Constitutional Context* (The Hague, Kluwer, 2007) xv.

[49] For a discussion of whether the market freedoms should be considered as sources of fundamental rights, see S De Vries, 'The Protection of Fundamental Rights within Europe's Internal Market after Lisbon—An Endeavour for More Harmony' in S de Vries, U Bernitz and S Weatherill (n 42) 83–86.

there is a requirement of cross-border specificity). Hence, cases like *Commission v Italy (mopeds)* and *Mickelsson and Roos*[50] where the situation lacked cross-border specificity, should be resolved with the use of this combination of Treaty Articles, as opposed to Article 34 TFEU on its own. The same rationale can be used for reading Article 35 TFEU (in conjunction with Article 20 TFEU) as catching within its scope genuinely non-discriminatory measures of the home State which can impede the fundamental right of Union citizens to trade their goods in the territory of another Member State.

Accordingly, Articles 34 and 35 TFEU—*when read alone*—should still be read as only prohibiting national measures which impede the free movement of goods between Member States, and a breach of them should only be found in situations where there is cross-border specificity. This means that *any* traders (including non-Union citizens and legal persons) who are impeded from trading their goods in a cross-border context—and any consumers who are impeded from purchasing goods from other Member States—should be able to rely on either of these provisions, *provided* that the contested measure specifically disadvantages goods that move between Member States. Measures, on the other hand, which do not have cross-border specificity but which limit the right of *Union citizens* to trade their goods (or purchase goods) in a cross-border context, will require the use of Article 34 or 35 TFEU together with Article 20 TFEU. Similarly, national measures which impede Union citizens from *moving* to another Member State for the purpose of selling or purchasing goods, should now be covered by Article 21 TFEU read together with Article 34 TFEU or Article 35 TFEU.

The various primary, fundamental rights that should now be derived from the free movement of goods provisions—when these are read together with the citizenship provisions—can, in fact, also be reduced to the two primary, fundamental, rights that, as explained in chapter three, appear to stem from the personal market freedoms (and which, as will be suggested below, *should* continue to stem from them, but only when they are read with the citizenship provisions). In particular, the free movement of goods provisions should—when read in conjunction with the citizenship provisions—be considered to grant to Union citizens: a) the right to take-up an economic activity in another Member State for the purpose of selling goods there or in a cross-border context (this will, basically, include the right to move to another Member State temporarily for the purpose of selling goods as well as its passive reflection, ie the right to move to another Member State temporarily for the purpose of purchasing goods); and b) the right to start selling goods in a cross-border context, whilst maintaining their economic base in the home State, and the right to start purchasing goods in a cross-border context (eg to sell or purchase goods over the Internet).

Like the free movement of goods provisions, the expansion of the scope of the personal market freedoms to cover situations where this is not warranted by the

---

[50] Case C-110/05 *Commission v Italy (mopeds)* [2009] ECR I-519 and C-142/05 *Mickelsson and Roos* [2009] ECR I-4273.

internal market rationale of these provisions, can be justified by a re-reading of these provisions in conjunction with the citizenship provisions of the Treaty.

As regards the expansion effected to the material scope of the more stationary personal market freedoms by the *Ritter-Coulais* saga,[51] this appears to be justified if—as it should—the internal market is viewed in a more holistic manner, as the market of a polity which has its own citizens who must be free to exercise all the rights (economic and non-economic) stemming from that status. Hence, the fact that Member State nationals are now also Union citizens, means that they should be free to exercise the fundamental economic rights they derive from EU law in conjunction with the other (non-economic) fundamental rights they derive from the citizenship provisions. Since, as we saw in chapter two, Union citizens derive the fundamental right to reside in the territory of another Member State from Article 21 TFEU, it would be absurd if Member States were permitted to apply a less favourable regime to economic actors who have decided to exercise this right *and* as a result of this and the fact that *they work in one Member State whilst residing in the territory of another*, they are disadvantaged when compared to persons who work and reside in the same Member State. In other words, economically active Union citizens should not be disadvantaged if they pursue an economic activity in a cross-border context and *if the pursuit of the economic activity in this manner has been the result of them exercising one of their fundamental citizenship rights*. Accordingly, Union citizens should now be considered to derive from the Treaty a hybrid citizenship-economic fundamental right to pursue an economic activity in one Member State whilst residing in the territory of another, irrespective of whether their economic base and the location of the economic activity has changed (ie irrespective of whether they have moved for the purpose of taking-up an economic activity).

Nonetheless, instead of stemming from the personal market freedoms when they are read *alone*,[52] this right should be derived from these provisions read together with Article 21 TFEU. In particular, since it is the exercise of the right to reside in the territory of another Member State which appears to have 'brought about' the situation which is the cause of the less favourable treatment complained of (the pursuit of an economic activity whilst being resident in the territory of another Member State), it is Article 21 TFEU (which is the source of this right) that should be used for bringing the situation within the scope of EU law. However, it is a breach of the personal market freedom applicable on the facts (depending on the type of the economic activity pursued) that should be found to have been established as a result of the less favourable treatment suffered, *provided* that this treatment *directly* concerns the pursuit of the economic activity (if, for instance, the fact that the Union citizen resides in a Member State different from the one

---

[51] *Ritter-Coulais* saga (n 16).
[52] For a commentator who does not object to the use of the market freedoms alone in such situations, see D Kochenov, 'The Essence of EU Citizenship Emerging from the Last Ten Years of Academic Debate: Beyond the Cherry Blossoms and the Moon?' (2013) 62 *International and Comparative Law Quarterly* 97, 111–14.

172 Emerging Questions

where (s)he pursues an economic activity results in higher income taxes—ie taxes charged for the income derived from the economic activity pursued).

Hence, if it is found that it is the fact that an economic activity is pursued in a cross-border context that is the cause of the less favourable treatment complained of (ie the fact that the economic activity is pursued in one Member State whilst the economic actor resides in the territory of another) *and* the less favourable treatment concerns the pursuit of *this* economic activity, the situation should be found to fall within the scope of EU law by virtue of Article 21 TFEU and the relevant market freedom. If, however, the treatment complained of does not concern the exercise of the economic activity at all but is, merely, affecting the right of residence that was exercised on the facts, then the personal market freedoms should not be used at all, but Article 21 TFEU should be employed for both bringing the situation within the scope of EU law *and* for establishing a breach of EU law.[53]

As regards situations which involve restrictions on the exercise of the right to take-up and/or pursue an economic activity in another Member State or in a cross-border context *which lack cross-border specificity*, these should be included within the scope of the personal market freedoms *read together with Article 20 TFEU*.

Given that the primary rights stemming from the market freedoms should now—when these provisions are read in conjunction with the citizenship provisions—be reconceptualised as fundamental, citizenship rights granted by the EU to its citizens simply because they hold Union citizenship and not for an ulterior (economic) purpose, their *existence* can under no circumstances become conditional (eg conditional on the existence of cross-border specificity), although, admittedly, their exercise can be limited, provided that this is done in a way which is acceptable and compliant with a number of specific requirements which are congruent with the fundamental nature of the right.[54] Hence, all Union citizens now *have* the primary fundamental rights to (actively or passively)[55] take-up an economic activity that is going to be pursued in another Member State or in a cross-border context and to start pursuing an economic activity in a cross-border context, and they should be able to rely on the market freedoms in order to challenge any national measure that limits the exercise of either of these rights; in each case, the onus will then fall on the recalcitrant Member State to prove that it has good reason for doing so and that it does so in a manner which is compliant with the fundamental rights-nature of the said right.

---

[53] An example of such a measure would be a law which provides that non-residents cannot have free access to museums. This would mean that nationals of that Member State who continue to work in that Member State and merely exercise the right to move to another Member State for the purpose of residing there would no longer be entitled to free access to museums. Such a measure is entirely unrelated to the exercise of the economic activity (and, of course, to the exercise of an economic activity in a cross-border context) and, hence, the only right that may be impeded as a result of it is the right to reside in the territory of another Member State. Of course, in practice, it is likely that the Member State will not apply a residence requirement *to its own nationals*.

[54] For a different view, see G Davies, *Nationality Discrimination in the European Internal Market* (The Hague, Kluwer, 2003), especially Ch 6.

[55] ie, as economic actors or as employers, consumers of goods, or recipients of services.

As da Cruz Vilaça and Piçarra have noted when explaining the process of constitutionalisation of the market freedoms,

> the notion that those fundamental freedoms express the fundamental rights of citizens of the Member States of the Community to carry out an economic activity and to choose the place and orientation of their occupation or vocational training entails recognition that the relevant provisions of the Treaty ensure the appropriate protection of those citizens against any undue interference from Member States.[56]

Hence, the EU should now *guarantee* to Union citizens the primary (economic) fundamental rights stemming from the market freedoms (when these are read in conjunction with the citizenship provisions) in all instances, and should espouse—what has been termed by Kingreen—'supranational legitimation', according to which these provisions intend 'to complement the national and supranational protection of the individual by fundamental rights and serve the purpose of a general liberalisation'.[57]

Conversely, when the market freedoms are read alone, they can only be used as the tools for 'transnational integration' and, thus, they can 'only serve to cover those specific gaps of protection in cross-border transactions'.[58] Accordingly, the Court must revert to its traditional interpretation of these provisions, when they are relied on alone, because they are enforced by a legal person or by a natural person who is not a Union citizen. Hence, in order for a measure to amount to a restriction caught by these provisions (when they are read alone), there should (again) be a requirement of cross-border specificity. In addition, the only primary (instrumental) right that can be derived from the more stationary personal market freedoms will be the original right to take-up an economic activity *in another Member State* that is going to be pursued there or in a cross-border context. And, the free movement of goods provisions will only catch within their scope measures that impede the free movement of goods between Member States (irrespective of whether they, also, impede the free movement of the persons that are associated with those goods).

III. HOW SHOULD THE MARKET FREEDOMS NOW BE INTERPRETED WHEN INVOKED BY UNION CITIZENS?

Contrary to the view of a long list of scholars, who have criticised the Court's decision to expand the scope of the market freedoms beyond discrimination and/or who have sought to fit the Court's interpretation of these provisions within a

---

[56] JL da Cruz Vilaça and N Piçarra (n 9) 21.
[57] T Kingreen, 'Fundamental Freedoms' in A von Bogdandy and J Bast (eds), *Principles of European Constitutional Law* (Oxford, München, Hart Publishing, CH Beck Nomos, 2011) 532.
[58] ibid.

discrimination-based approach,[59] it is my contention that the market freedoms (when read together with the citizenship provisions) must now be viewed as catching within their scope *all* measures which impede the exercise *by Union citizens* of the (fundamental) primary rights stemming from them.

Of course, when it comes to situations involving third-country nationals or corporations where, as explained, these provisions should—where applicable—continue to be applied alone as mere tools for market integration, the Court should revert to its traditional, instrumental, approach to the interpretation of these provisions, which requires the existence of cross-border specificity and a sufficient connection with the aim of building and maintaining an internal market.

Since the Court's traditional approach to the interpretation of the market freedoms was analysed in the previous two chapters, the remainder of this chapter will focus on the question of how the market freedoms should be interpreted when they are read together with the citizenship provisions of the Treaty, in situations where they are invoked by Union citizens.

When the market freedoms are relied on by Union citizens, they should be viewed as not merely the tools for building an internal market but also, and primarily, as sources of fundamental, economic, rights for the Union citizen. Accordingly, from these provisions, Union citizens should now be considered to derive the (traditional)—but in this context fundamental—right to take-up an economic activity in another Member State that is going to be pursued there/in a cross-border context, *as well as* the right to start pursuing an economic activity in a cross-border context, irrespective of whether there has been a prior change in the economic base of the economic actor and/or the location of the economic activity. In addition, they should be considered to derive the fundamental right to move to another Member State to receive a service or purchase goods, or to (simply) receive a service or purchase goods via cross-border transactions. Moreover, in this context, there should be no need to prove that the contested measure has cross-border specificity, and, thus, national rules, measures, or actions, which are entirely neutral and merely limit the freedom of Union citizens to exercise the above primary (fundamental) rights, should amount to a restriction caught by these provisions, and should require justification.

Obviously, this creates the potential for a very broad scope of application of these provisions since, as Gareth Davies has characteristically put it, '[o]nce we escape from the cage of discrimination into the high pastures of mere obstacles, it is hard to see any fences ahead'.[60] This means that the ability of the Member States (and, where relevant, of the EU) to limit the exercise of the primary rights stemming from these provisions, will be greatly circumscribed. In fact, as already seen in the previous two chapters of the book, this has already happened in the Court's

---

[59] eg N Bernard, 'Discrimination and Free Movement in EC Law' (1996) 45 *International and Comparative Law Quarterly* 82; J Snell (n 19); G Davies (n 54) Ch 6.
[60] G Davies (n 29) 56.

case-law,[61] and (wrongly) not merely in situations involving *Union citizens* relying on the market freedoms, but also in situations where these provisions have been relied on by corporations.[62]

Re-reading the market freedoms (in conjunction with the citizenship provisions) in a very broad manner can prove problematic in three respects.

Firstly, it is capable of bringing virtually *any* national measure within the scope of the personal market freedoms and, thus, to subject it to EU scrutiny. Hence, all national measures capable of impeding the exercise of the (fundamental) rights stemming from the market freedoms, will have to be examined for their compatibility with *EU* rules and principles and, most importantly, the balancing of the competing interests (ie the fundamental rights stemming from the market freedoms with other non-economic objectives that need to be protected for the common good) will have to be conducted by the (usually national) judiciary. Apart from the obvious practical problem of an inflated workload for the courts, this will also have the effect of 'reallocating choices which usually pertain to the legislature in the hands of the judiciary'.[63] Thus, although it is the job of the national legislature—an elected body usually comprised of persons with a variety of qualifications and different areas of expertise—to make choices as to how economic activities should be regulated and to what extent, as well as to determine how the various interests represented in society should be balanced against each other, these choices and decisions will, now, be made by (unelected) judges who are unlikely to possess the necessary (often) technical expertise required to make informed decisions in relation to these matters.

Secondly, the expansion of the scope of application of the market freedoms to cover virtually any national measure will, inevitably, lead to a corresponding reduction in the Member States' freedom to regulate economic activities.[64] Preventing the *unwarranted* expansion of the scope of these provisions to cover measures which do not, *in reality*, limit the exercise of the rights stemming from them is, therefore, not merely required in order to maintain an appropriate balance of powers between the EU and its Member States but, also, in order to prevent overcentralisation and a situation whereby the majority of regulations will be coming from Brussels. A finding that national measures amount to unjustified restrictions in breach of the market freedoms will mean that the Member States will not be able to apply them, and in case they are not replaced with rules which

---

[61] This is the so-called 'high impact' approach which, according to Barnard, is the approach followed in the EU (as opposed to the US) context, and which 'requires intense intervention by the federal authorities'—C Barnard, 'Restricting Restrictions: Lessons for the EU from the US' (2009) 68 *Cambridge Law Journal* 575, 590–91.

[62] See eg Case C-405/98 *Gourmet* [2001] ECR I-1795, where the Court interpreted Art 59 EC (Art 56 TFEU) very broadly, as catching within its scope a measure that lacked cross-border specificity, even though the provision on the facts was relied on by a legal person.

[63] T Kingreen (n 57) 521.

[64] For a discussion of the impact that different interpretations of the market freedoms can have on the balance of powers between the EU and its Member States, see J Snell (n 19), especially Ch 2.

comply with the market freedoms, a regulatory gap will ensue. Moreover, if the measures are found to be restrictions which are, nonetheless, justified on non-economic grounds, this means that they will be able to continue to be applied. In order to remedy these regulatory gaps or the justified restrictions that persist, the EU may, then, decide to take it upon itself to regulate the matter, which will lead to an increase in the matters that are regulated at EU level which, in the longer term, may lead to excessive centralisation.[65] This is, obviously, something that goes against the principle of subsidiarity which—when introduced together with the status of Union citizenship by Maastricht—sought to ensure that decisions are taken as closely as possible to the citizen, thus creating a presumption that in areas of shared EU and Member State competence (such as the internal market policy), legislation should be made at national or, even regional, level unless the aims of the measure cannot be achieved in this manner, in which case legislation will need to be promulgated by the EU.[66]

Thirdly, the expansion of the scope of the market freedoms to cover *any* measures that appear to limit the freedom of Union citizens to take-up or pursue a cross-border economic activity, will perpetuate—and perhaps—aggravate the lack of certainty surrounding the notion of 'restriction',[67] which has always been unclear in the internal market context, especially following the post-Maastricht expansion of the market freedoms to encompass genuinely non-discriminatory measures.[68] Apart from the practical problems which ensue as a result of the lack of clarity in this respect, it appears to be incompatible with the principle of legal certainty, which is recognised as one of the general principles of EU law.[69] Although it is only in a case involving the application of Article 63 TFEU that the Court explicitly referred to this requirement (ie to ensure legal certainty),[70] it is clear that it is applicable to all the market freedoms. In fact, ensuring that there is legal certainty as regards the rights that Union citizens derive from the market freedoms is, also, particularly important when these provisions are—as they

---

[65] J Snell (n 19) 227.
[66] ibid, 76.
[67] A Tryfonidou, 'The Notions of "Restriction" and "Discrimination" in the Context of the Free Movement of Persons Provisions: From a Relationship of Interdependence to One of (Almost Complete) Independence' (2014) 33 *Yearbook of European Law* 385.
[68] Iliopoulou Penot has noted that 'the exact meaning and scope of the concept of "obstacle" to free movement is' one of the 'thorny issues' 'surrounding the law of the internal market'—A Iliopoulou Penot, 'The Transnational Character of Union Citizenship' in M Dougan, N Nic Shuibhne and E Spaventa (eds), *Empowerment and Disempowerment of the European Citizen* (Oxford, Hart Publishing, 2012) 16. Moreover, Barnard and Deakin have noted that the test for determining access to the market can be either formal or substantive, and that in the Court of Justice's jurisprudence, it is possible to detect 'albeit not clearly articulated, a spectrum of possibilities between these two senses of the test'—C Barnard and S Deakin, 'Market Access and Regulatory Competition' in C Barnard and J Scott (n 32) 204–05.
[69] For more on the principle of legal certainty, see T Tridimas, *The General Principles of EU Law* (Oxford, Oxford University Press, 2006) Ch 6.
[70] Case C-54/99 *Association Eglise de Scientologie de Paris* [2000] ECR I-1335, para 22.

should be—read together with the citizenship provisions of the Treaty and are, thus, reconceptualised as sources of fundamental rights.[71]

Hence, although it may, admittedly, be practically difficult—and too limiting—to provide a clear, positive, definition of what a restriction caught by the market freedoms *is*, the Court should, nonetheless, provide clear guidance as to what is *not* such a restriction.[72]

It is, therefore, for this reason that the main filtering mechanisms—which have traditionally been used together with the requirement of cross-border specificity—for determining what *cannot* amount to a 'restriction', should now be used by the Court and by the national courts or authorities assessing possible breaches of the market freedoms (when read with the citizenship provisions), in order to exclude from EU scrutiny *ab initio* measures that do not—on closer inspection—appear to be capable of amounting to a restriction on the exercise of the fundamental rights stemming from these provisions.

The aim of the analysis in the remainder of this section, therefore, will be to consider which filtering mechanisms should be utilised (and how) for ensuring that the scope of application of the market freedoms will not be inordinately broadened by including within it measures which, on closer inspection, do not, *in reality*, impede the exercise of the fundamental rights stemming from these provisions.

A. A *De Minimis* Test?

It is well-known that in the area of EU competition law, a *de minimis* test has always been considered as one of the most significant mechanisms used to filter out agreements or actions of undertakings which appear incapable of having a *sufficiently* negative impact on the competitive process in the internal market. This test has been particularly important in that context, in view of the fact that the purely internal rule—which is one of the filtering mechanisms that has always been used in the market freedoms context—does not apply in that area.[73]

In a number of cases involving the free movement of goods, the Court was confronted with the question of whether a *de minimis* test could or should also be

---

[71] As Iglesias Sánchez has noted, '[c]larity in itself is already a citizen-friendly attribute, mostly when it comes to the definition of the framework for the protection of individual rights in a multi-layered system whose contours are neither obvious nor even decipherable to the eyes of the common citizen'— S Iglesias Sánchez, 'Fundamental Rights and Citizenship of the Union at a Crossroads: A Promising Alliance or a Dangerous Liaison' (2014) 20 *European Law Journal* 464, 471–72.

[72] For a recent article emphasising that the 'threshold for the application of EU free movement law is low' see S Weatherill, 'From Economic Rights to Fundamental Rights' in S de Vries, U Bernitz and S Weatherill (n 42) 16 (see the whole chapter for examples of case-law where the Court has overstretched the scope of application of the market freedoms).

[73] A Tryfonidou (n 31) 67–69.

applied when delimiting the scope of these provisions.[74] Despite the suggestions of commentators[75] and members of the Court[76] that a *de minimis* test should be adopted in this context, the Court rejected this:

> Article 30 [34 TFEU] of the Treaty does not distinguish between measures having an effect equivalent to quantitative restrictions according to the degree to which trade between Member States is affected. If a national measure is capable of hindering imports it must be regarded as a measure having an effect equivalent to a quantitative restriction, even though the hindrance is slight and even though it is possible for imported products to be marketed in other ways.[77]

Judged from a purely practical perspective, a *de minimis* test in this context would be problematic due to the uncertainty it would beget.[78] For instance, would this require a quantitative assessment—as is the case in competition law—or would a qualitative assessment have to be conducted? If the former, what would be the basis of the calculation? If the latter, what would be the qualitative element that would determine which situations should or should not be included within the scope of these provisions?

Moreover, and given that 'as a consequence of its special position, the State bears a higher duty than private bodies',[79] a *de minimis* rule should not be applied in the

---

[74] For a recent article devoted to the question of whether a *de minimis* test has been, or could be, used by the ECJ in its free movement case-law, see MS Jansson and H Kalimo, 'De Minimis Meets "Market Access": Transformations in the Substance—and the Syntax—of EU Free Movement Law?' (2014) 51 *Common Market Law Review* 523.

[75] See eg C Barnard, 'Fitting the Remaining Pieces into the Goods and Persons Jigsaw' (2001) 26 *European Law Review* 35.

[76] Mainly, AG Jacobs in Case C-412/94 *Leclerc Siplec* [1995] ECR I-179. For the opposite view see paragraph 21 of the Opinion of AG Tesauro in Case C-292/92 *Hünermund* [1993] ECR I-6787, where he noted that 'to apply a *de minimis* rule in the field of trade in goods … is, it seems to me, very difficult if not downright impossible: quite apart from anything else, proving the degree of hypothetical effects would be a *probation diabolica*'.

[77] Joined Cases 177 & 178/82 *Van de Haar* [1984] ECR 1797, para 13. See also, Case 103/84 *Commission v Italy* [1986] ECR 1759, para 18; Case C-126/91 *Yves Rocher* [1993] ECR I-2361, para 21; Case C-463/01 *Commission v Germany* [2004] ECR I-11705, para 63; Case C-309/02 *Radlberger* [2004] ECR I-11763, para 68; Case C-315/13 *De Clercq* ECLI:EU:C:2014:2408, para 6. In a handful of cases, however, the Court seems to have implicitly adopted such a test—see eg Case C-20/03 *Burmanjer* [2005] ECR I-4133; Case C-134/03 *Viacom Outdoor* [2005] ECR I-1167. Moreover, an (indirect) *de minimis* test appears to have been employed by the Court in its use restrictions cases seen in the previous chapter (*Commission v Italy (mopeds)* (n 50) para 56 and Case C-142/05 *Mickelsson and Roos* (n 50), para 25), whereby it required that the contested use restriction had a 'considerable influence' on the behaviour of consumers in order to amount to an MEQR. It should be noted, however, that in subsequent case-law, the requirement for a *considerable* influence was dropped, merely requiring a measure to have an 'influence on the behaviour of consumers'—see Case C-443/10 *Bonnarde* [2011] ECR I-9327, para 30. For comments see S Weatherill, 'Free Movement of Goods' (2012) 61 *International and Comparative Law Quarterly* 541, 542–43. For the free movement of persons and a similar (indirect) *de minimis* test, see Case C-168/91 *Konstantinidis* [1993] ECR I-1191, para 15; Case C-353/06 *Grunkin-Paul* [2008] ECR I-7639, para 23; Case C-208/09 *Sayn-Wittgenstein* [2010] ECR I-13693, paras 66–71; Case C-391/09 *Runevic-Vardyn* [2011] ECR I-3787, para 76.

[78] P Oliver, 'Some Further Reflections on the Scope of Articles 28-30 (Ex 30-36) EC' (1999) 36 *Common Market Law Review* 783, 792; J Snell (n 19) 101–02; A Tryfonidou (n 42) 51; S Enchelmaier, 'Moped Trailers, *Mickelsson & Roos, Gysbrechts*: The ECJ's Case Law on Goods Keeps on Moving' (2010) 29 *Yearbook of European Law* 190, 193 and 215–16.

[79] P Oliver (n 78) 791.

context of the market freedoms, since in the vast majority of cases these are relied on to challenge Member State measures, unlike the provisions of competition law which are mainly used to challenge the acts of undertakings.[80]

Such a test is, nonetheless, also inappropriate as a filtering mechanism for the market freedoms, especially when they are relied on by Union citizens and they are, thus, reconceptualised as the sources of fundamental citizenship rights. Just as it is entirely absurd to say that the breach of a fundamental human right has not been made out because the contested action which leads to it can only affect a limited number of persons, in the same way it is not possible to say that a breach of the fundamental rights stemming from the market freedoms is not established if the contested measure affects only a handful of Union citizens.[81]

Accordingly, the introduction of a *de minimis* test as a limiting factor for determining which national measures can, in the first place, be brought within the scope of the market freedoms, would be inappropriate.[82]

B. A Remoteness Test?

On the other hand, the adoption—and clearer application—of a remoteness test, would be much more suited in this context.

Although the Court has in a number of cases[83] employed what academics call[84] the notion of remoteness, in order to exclude from the scope of application of the market freedoms measures, the effect of which on the exercise of rights stemming from these provisions was 'too uncertain and indirect', a precise 'remoteness test' has never been articulated by the Court.[85] As explained by Nic Shuibhne,

---

[80] ibid.

[81] As Oliver has put it 'it would be virtually inconceivable in any jurisdiction where the rule of law prevails for *habeas corpus* to be subject to any kind of *de minimis* rule. Precisely the same reasoning applies—albeit with less force—to the four freedoms enshrined in the Treaty of Rome. To take a relatively clear case, it would be hard to imagine the Court finding a national measure discriminating against workers from other Member States to be compatible with Article 39 (ex 48) EC, on the basis that only a small class of persons were affected: for those individuals, the severity of the restriction is in no way lessened by the circumstance that their plight is shared by a relatively insignificant number in terms of the host State taken as a whole'—P Oliver (n 78) 791–92.

[82] For a view that certain aspects of an appreciability test have, actually, been adopted and used sporadically by the Court in its case-law, see N Nic Shuibhne (n 11) 158–69.

[83] eg Case 75/81 *Blesgen* [1982] ECR 1211; Case C-69/88 *Krantz* [1990] ECR I-583; Case C-93/92 *Baskiciogullari* [1993] ECR I-5009; Case C-379/92 *Peralta* [1994] ECR I-3453; Case C-266/96 *Corsica Ferries* [1998] ECR I-3949; Case C-190/98 *Graf* [2000] ECR I-493; Case C-282 & 283/04 *Commission v Netherlands (Golden Shares)* [2006] ECR I-9141; Case C-256/06 *Jäger* [2008] ECR I-123; Case C-211/08 *Commission v Spain* [2010] ECR I-5267;Case C-602/10 *SC Volksbank România SA* ECLI:EU:C:2012:443.

[84] The Court has not used this label in its case-law.

[85] P Oliver (n 78) 788–89; A Biondi, 'In and Out of the Internal Market: Recent Developments on the Principle of Free Movement' (1999–2000) *Yearbook of European Law* 469, 488; J Snell (n 19) 124–125. For a detailed explanation as to how the remoteness test has so far been used by the Court and as to how it can best be used, see D Doukas, 'Untying the Market Access Knot: Advertising Restrictions and the Free Movement of Goods and Services' (2006–07) 9 *Cambridge Yearbook of European Legal Studies* 177, 205–15.

'*de minimis* would apply when a situation is connected to EU law but is too minor for EU law to bother with; but remoteness is about situations that are not connected to EU law in the first place'.[86]

The problems with the exact definition of such a test in other areas of law, such as tort law, are well-known,[87] and there is no reason to believe that similar difficulties will not be encountered in the context of the market freedoms, should the Court decide to precisely define such a test.[88] Yet, the fact that the scope of application of the market freedoms will be infinitely broadened when these provisions are read together with the citizenship provisions, deems the use of strong filtering mechanisms imperative and, thus, the Court should establish a clear and precise remoteness test in order to ensure that only national measures that, indeed, lead to a restriction on the exercise of the rights stemming from these provisions, are caught by them.

The test should, in essence, be one of causation,[89] and the question that should be asked is the following: is the contested measure the cause (or, at least, a sufficiently proximate cause) of the restriction on the exercise of a primary right stemming from the market freedoms? Or, as Kingreen has put it, would the impediment 'have occurred in the absence of the measure in dispute'?[90] In fact, in its relatively recent case-law, the Court seems to have explicitly adopted a causation-based test for establishing remoteness when, in *Guarnieri & Cie*, it noted that the criterion of 'effects too uncertain and indirect' is intended to ensure that there is a 'causal link between the possible distortion of intra-Community trade and the difference in treatment at issue'.[91]

Such a causation-based test will have to be applied in *all* situations where there is no cross-border specificity,[92] since 'discriminatory restrictions are *never* too uncertain and indirect'.[93] However, different presumptions will have to apply,

---

[86] N Nic Shuibhne (n 11) 157. It should be noted that—quite confusingly—there has been a 'conceptual spillage' of the remoteness and *de minimis* doctrines in some of the Court's recent case-law—see N Nic Shuibhne (n 11) 169–71. Perhaps this is why some commentators consider that remoteness is, in fact, an aspect of the *de minimis* test, though, admittedly, in such a case, they view the *de minimis* test rather broadly, and not as something that only employs quantitative criteria for determining whether a certain measure is capable of leading to a restriction on the exercise of the rights stemming from the market freedoms—see MS Jansson and H Kalimo (n 74) 541–44.

[87] J Snell (n 19) 124.

[88] AG Kokott in her Opinion in *Mickelsson and Roos* suggested that instead of applying the remoteness criteria which are 'difficult to clarify and thus do not contribute to legal certainty', the Court should extend the *Keck* formula to measures that amount to use restrictions when deciding whether the latter are caught by Art 34 TFEU—see paragraphs 46 and 47 of the Opinion in *Mickelsson and Roos* (n 50). Jansson and Kalimo have pointed out that 'the fact that the remoteness test may have been abandoned in US trade law, would speak for not giving relevance to the directness of the causality in EU trade law'—MS Jansson and H Kalimo (n 74) 543.

[89] This has been the view, also, of a number of Advocates General. See eg Opinion of AG Fennelly in Case C-67/97 *Bluhme* [1998] ECR I-8033, para 19; Opinion of AG La Pergola in Case C-44/98 *BASF* [1998] ECR I-6269, para 18.

[90] T Kingreen (n 57) 532.

[91] Case C-291/09 *Guarnieri & Cie* [2011] ECR I-2685, para 17.

[92] This is, after all, also quite obvious in the Court's case-law—see eg *Peralta* (n 83) paras 24–25.

[93] N Nic Shuibhne (n 11) 179. See also, T Horsley, 'Unearthing Buried Treasures' (n 38).

depending on the type of restriction (direct or indirect) to which the contested measure gives rise.

It should be recalled that the market freedoms (when read together with the citizenship provisions) should be considered as granting to all Union citizens two primary fundamental rights: the right to take-up an economic activity in another Member State that is going to be (actively or passively) pursued there or in a cross-border context; and the right to start pursuing an economic activity in a cross-border context, irrespective of whether an economic activity has been taken-up in the territory of another Member State. Any other rights deriving from these provisions should be considered secondary (and hence not fundamental) rights that *only* emerge in situations where their violation will lead to a breach of either (or both) of the above primary rights. When the contested national measure directly impedes the exercise of a primary right stemming from the market freedoms, this amounts to a *direct* restriction on the exercise of the relevant right and, of course, this should clearly suffice for finding a breach of the relevant provision, unless the measure is justified. Where, however, one of the primary rights deriving from these provisions will only be restricted as a result of a (direct) breach of another right, the latter right will—on the facts of the case—be deemed to be a secondary right stemming from these provisions and the contested measure should be considered to only amount to an *indirect* restriction on the exercise of the relevant primary right.

As explained in chapter one, identifying the secondary rights that can be derived from the market freedoms is a task which is fact-specific, given that a right, the violation of which, may lead to a restriction on the exercise of the primary rights stemming from these provisions *in a particular factual setting*, may not lead to such a restriction under different circumstances. Accordingly, whilst a direct restriction on the exercise of the primary rights stemming from the market freedoms undoubtedly amounts to a restriction under all circumstances (and, thus, there is no need to assess the exact impact that the contested measure will have on the exercise of these rights on the particular facts of the case), whether a measure can amount to an indirect restriction on the exercise of the primary rights deriving from these provisions, always depends on the particular facts of the case and on how the measure is applied in that particular factual context.

The following two presumptions should, therefore, be applied when determining whether the remoteness test is satisfied with regards to a particular measure.

On the one hand, whenever there is a direct restriction on the exercise of one of the primary fundamental rights that stem from the market freedoms (read together with the citizenship provisions), this should suffice to automatically establish causation and, hence, a remoteness test will not need to be applied. Of course, this is merely a presumption, and the Member State that is accused of breaching EU law will be able to claim in its defence that the contested measure does not lead to the alleged restriction and in that way rebut the above presumption, by establishing that the contested measure is too remote.

On the other hand, in situations that do not involve a direct restriction on the exercise of either of the primary fundamental rights stemming from the market freedoms (read in conjunction with the citizenship provisions), the Court will need to be satisfied that the contested measure does, indeed, lead to a (direct) restriction on a right, the violation of which, in its turn, leads to an indirect restriction on the primary fundamental rights stemming from these provisions. In other words, in such a case, it cannot be taken as a given that there is a restriction contrary to the relevant market freedom, but the ECJ or the national court/authority seeking to establish whether there is a prima facie restriction, must examine whether there is causation between the contested measure and the (alleged) restriction on the exercise of the primary right(s) stemming from these provisions. Only if it can be proved that this is the case *on the facts of the case*, will the contested measure be considered to amount to a restriction and will thus be caught by the relevant market freedom.[94]

C. The Purely Internal Rule

The other main filtering mechanism that should (continue to) be used—together with remoteness—for excluding from the scope of application of the market freedoms situations which are not sufficiently related to the aims of these provisions, is the purely internal rule.

As is well-known, the market freedoms do not apply to situations which are considered to be purely internal to a Member State.[95] This rule (the so-called 'purely internal rule') was first established by the ECJ in the late 1970s,[96] and is, still, one of the main limits placed on the scope of application of the market freedoms.[97] It is often (mistakenly) treated as synonymous with the problem of reverse discrimination, although the latter is merely a side-effect of the former. The two notions are, therefore, separate and, as such, deserve separate treatment, and any calls for prohibiting reverse discrimination should not be equated with calls for the abolition of the purely internal rule.[98]

---

[94] Spaventa has, similarly, suggested that there should be presumptions with regards to causation, depending on the type of measure, though the distinction she has drawn is between 'rules that regulate trade' and 'rules that do not regulate trade': 'It is in relation to those rules [ie rules which do not regulate trade] that the claimant will need to demonstrate the existence of a causal relationship between rule and alleged barrier; in relation to trading rules, however, the analysis will be exclusively focused on the existence of a barrier (however defined) since causation is taken for granted. Once the barrier is found to exist, there is no need for an investigation as to a causal relationship between that barrier and the situation at issue in the case under investigation'—E Spaventa, 'The Outer Limit of the Treaty Free Movement Provisions: Some Reflections on the Significance of *Keck*, Remoteness and *Deliège*' in C Barnard and O Odudu (eds), *The Outer Limits of European Union Law* (Oxford, Hart Publishing, 2009) 253; see also, 263–64.

[95] For a detailed analysis of the rule, see A Tryfonidou (n 31), Chs 1 and 2.

[96] Case 115/78 *Knoors* [1979] ECR 399; Case 175/78 *Saunders* [1979] ECR 1129.

[97] The rule, of course, also applies to Arts 20 and 21 TFEU, as we saw in ch 2. See eg Case C-34/09 *Ruiz Zambrano* [2011] ECR I-1177.

[98] In this book, we are only interested in the purely internal rule. As argued elsewhere (A Tryfonidou (n 31), Ch 4), reverse discrimination is, clearly, an incongruity in a Citizen's Europe and should, thus, no longer be considered a permissible difference in treatment under EU law. A book devoted to an assessment of the development of the status of Union citizenship and to an examination of the

The purely internal rule is one of the ways used by the Court for drawing a line between EU and Member State competence in the internal market policy area, which—as explicitly noted in the TFEU—is an area of *shared* competence between the EU and the Member States.[99] Accordingly, there is nothing problematic with the existence of the rule as such.[100] The rule is an empty shell which is instilled with life every time the Court (implicitly) defines its content and through it determines what amounts to a purely internal situation. Therefore, what *is* a purely internal situation is in constant flux and this notion expands or contracts depending on whatever approach the ECJ takes in its various decisions. This means that the rule, as such, is not problematic and its existence is, in fact, necessary for ensuring that the line dividing EU from Member State competence is not distorted. What *can* be problematic, nonetheless, is the way that the Court chooses to define what a purely internal situation is.

It is clearly not the place here to analyse in detail the purely internal rule and its development by the Court.[101] Rather, I shall consider how the content of the rule should, now, be (re-)defined, in order for it to operate as an effective filtering mechanism for excluding from the scope of the market freedoms situations which do not involve a violation of the rights stemming from them.

The basis of the rule—which is that national measures which are not connected in any way with the exercise of the (by nature cross-border) rights stemming from the market freedoms, should escape the ambit of these provisions—should remain intact. Accordingly, the requirement of a negative impact on the initiation or (the active or passive) exercise of a *cross-border* economic activity should be maintained. This is so even following the Court's rulings in the *Ruiz Zambrano* line of cases,[102] whereby the scope of Article 20 TFEU was extended to cover situations

---

question whether there are any elements that prevent Union citizenship from becoming a meaningful status would obviously require a consideration of whether reverse discrimination is currently an acceptable difference in treatment under EU law and, if not, it would seek to consider appropriate solutions. This book, however, focuses on the interpretation of the market freedoms as—now also—sources of fundamental rights. Reverse discrimination—as such—is not problematic in this context since in case it emerges in situations which are, indeed, purely internal to a Member State, then it has nothing to do with the exercise of the rights stemming from the market freedoms (though, admittedly, it can be contrary to other principles of EU law and, in particular, the general principle of equality, as I argued elsewhere). I will, therefore, not touch on reverse discrimination here but I will, rather, focus on the purely internal rule (which is its root cause).

[99] Art 4(2)(a) TFEU.
[100] As O'Leary has recently noted, '[t]here is something incoherent in demanding that the Court abandon a rule such as the purely internal rule, whose primary purpose is to patrol the division of competence between the EU and its members and delimit the scope of EU law, while castigating the Court for the inroads its citizenship case law continues to carve into areas of national competence in fields of, for example, taxation, immigration, social welfare, education, health care or the rules on the acquisition and loss of Member State nationality'—S O'Leary, 'The Past, Present and Future of the Purely Internal Rule in EU Law' in M Dougan, N Nic Shuibhne and E Spaventa (n 68) 63–64.
[101] For this see A Tryfonidou (n 31).
[102] See, inter alia, Case C-135/08 *Rottmann* [2010] ECR I-1449; *Ruiz Zambrano* (n 97); Case C-434/09 *McCarthy* [2011] ECR I-3375; Case C-256/11 *Dereci* [2011] ECR I-11315.

184 *Emerging Questions*

which did not involve a cross-border element: Article 20 TFEU—unlike the market freedoms and Article 21 TFEU—is not merely the source of rights which are of a cross-border nature but is, rather, the core citizenship provision which attaches to Union citizens a number of rights (of *both* a cross-border and a non-cross-border nature) and which requires the Treaties to be read in the light of Union citizenship. Accordingly, a purely internal situation under that provision does not necessarily equate with a situation which lacks a cross-border element, unlike the position with regards to the market freedoms and Article 21 TFEU.

What *should* change, however—and, in fact, as will be seen below, there are certain hints in the Court's (relatively recent) case-law that we may be heading towards this direction—is the way that it is determined that a situation is purely internal to a Member State. More specifically, in the analysis below, it will be suggested that the purely internal rule will have to (continue) to be applied as a substantive requirement in *all* cases, whereas it should be used as (also) a jurisdictional requirement in (only) certain situations—ie those where there is only an alleged *indirect restriction* on the exercise of the primary (fundamental) rights stemming from the market freedoms. As a jurisdictional requirement, the purely internal rule will simply take the form of a test checking whether the situation assessed involves the exercise (or the *definite* future exercise) of one of the primary rights stemming from the market freedoms (which, as noted above, are cross-border by nature); as a substantive requirement, on the other hand, the rule will be embodied in a test considering whether the contested measure is capable of impeding the exercise of one of the primary rights stemming from these provisions (which, as noted above, are cross-border by nature). The latter test seems to be what Advocate General Sharpston had in mind, when she noted that the question asked in order to determine whether a measure or rule amounts to a restriction caught by the market freedoms or Article 21 TFEU is 'does [the national rule] potentially have a "chilling effect" on any EU citizen contemplating exercising free movement rights within the EU as a worker, a self-employed person or simply as a citizen'?[103]

However, let us see in more detail the rationale behind the above suggestion.

In its traditional case-law, the Court used the purely internal rule *both* as a jurisdictional and as a substantive filtering mechanism in *all* cases. This meant that, traditionally, whenever the facts of the case did not involve a cross-border element such as a situation whereby a Member State national had *already* moved to another Member State for the purpose of taking-up an economic activity,[104] or a Member State national who had *already* been offered a contract of employment and would thus *certainly* exercise free movement rights in the near future had the contested measure not been applied,[105] the Court found that the situation was purely internal to a Member State and did not proceed to consider whether the contested measure could, nonetheless, impede the exercise of a right stemming

---

[103] Paragraph 38 of the Opinion in Joined Cases C-523 & 585/11 *Prinz* ECLI:EU:C:2013:524.
[104] See eg the facts in Case C-55/94 *Gebhard* [1995] ECR I-4165.
[105] See eg the facts in Case C-415/93 *Bosman* [1995] ECR I- 4921.

from the market freedoms.[106] The same approach has also been followed in cases involving the free movement of goods, although, as explained by Advocate General Cosmas in his Opinion in the *Belgapom* case, the approach taken in this latter context has been somewhat different.[107] Moreover, the importance attached to the existence of a cross-border element on the actual facts of the case had meant that—as the Court stressed—a purely hypothetical future exercise of the rights stemming from the market freedoms could not suffice for establishing a sufficient link with the market freedoms, and when confronted with such a factual background, the Court immediately classified the situation as purely internal without considering whether the contested measure could (potentially) impede the exercise of the rights stemming from the market freedoms.[108]

Nonetheless, the above one-size-fits-all approach has proved inappropriate, given that there are circumstances where it is obvious that the mere *existence* of a measure amounts to a (potential) restriction on the exercise of the primary rights stemming from the market freedoms and, hence, it is not necessary for the Court (or the national courts or authorities) to examine whether the application of that measure *on the particular facts of the case* will have a restrictive impact on the exercise of the said right; it is clear that such a restrictive impact arises simply as a result of the *existence* of the said measure. Moreover, in certain cases the way that a certain market operates is such that it is impossible for new entrants to obtain access to it and this, clearly, impedes the exercise of the right of Union citizens to move to that Member State for the purpose of taking-up an economic activity or, simply, to initiate and pursue an economic activity in its territory or with persons based in its territory. Accordingly, in those circumstances, the fact that on the particular facts of the case one of the primary rights stemming from the market freedoms has not been exercised, should not suffice for ruling that the situation is purely internal to a Member State. The Court or the national court/authority assessing the national measure must consider that it *does* amount to a (potential) restriction on the exercise of the rights stemming from the market freedoms and should then proceed to consider whether it is nonetheless justified.

Conversely, in circumstances where a neutral measure is involved, the mere *existence* of which does not amount to a restriction on the exercise of one of the primary rights stemming from the market freedoms but can only be transformed into such a restriction in certain factual circumstances, in order to make

---

[106] Case 180/83 *Moser* [1984] ECR 2539; Case C-299/95 *Kremzow* [1997] ECR I-2629; Case C-108/98 *RI.SAN* [1999] ECR I-5219.

[107] AG Cosmas in Case C-63/94 *Belgapom* [1995] ECR I-2467, para 13: 'There is no similar statement of principle in the case-law relating to Article [34] of the Treaty [ie that this provision does 'not apply to situations or activities which are confined in all respects within a single Member State'], which prohibits the Member States from imposing measures having an effect equivalent to quantitative restrictions on imports. It may none the less be inferred from the case-law on the matter as a whole that, according to the Court, the possibility that Article 30 applies cannot be ruled out on the basis of the purely internal nature of a given situation or activity unless the proceedings before the national court are governed by a domestic provision which exclusively concerns domestic products.'

[108] *Moser* (n 106), para 18; *Kremzow* (n 106), para 16.

186 *Emerging Questions*

an accurate assessment as to whether the said measure can, indeed, restrict the exercise of one of the primary rights stemming from the market freedoms, it is necessary to assess it taking into account its application in a particular factual scenario. Thus, it is important that such a measure is assessed in a factual background which includes the exercise (or an attempted exercise) of the rights stemming from the market freedoms.

This book, therefore, suggests that in situations where the contested national measure amounts to a *direct* restriction on a primary right stemming from the market freedoms, the Court should not use the purely internal rule as a jurisdictional requirement and should, thus, in all instances—irrespective of the facts of the case—rule that the contested measure is a prima facie breach of the relevant market freedom. This is because the *mere existence* of the said measure amounts to an actual or potential restriction on the exercise of one of the primary rights stemming from the market freedoms; the measure is fundamentally flawed from the point of view of EU law and thus, unless it can be justified, it should no longer be in force or should be amended in order to ensure that it does not impede the exercise of the primary rights stemming from the market freedoms.

On the other hand, when the right that is allegedly going to be directly violated by the impugned national measure is not one of the primary rights stemming from the market freedoms but another right which, it is argued, is capable of restricting, in its turn, such a primary right—in other words, when it is claimed that there is a breach of a secondary right (allegedly) stemming from these provisions—this requires the Court (or the national court) to analyse the particular facts of the case. Accordingly, in such cases, the purely internal rule should be used *both* as a jurisdictional *and* as a substantive requirement because if the facts of the case are purely internal to a Member State in the sense that one of the primary rights stemming from the market freedoms has not been exercised or is not (certainly) going to be exercised, then it will not be possible for the Court to assess whether the secondary right, the violation of which is claimed, does, indeed, emerge *on the facts of the case*; and whether its breach will, indeed, lead to an (indirect) restriction on the fundamental rights stemming from the market freedoms.[109]

The above suggested distinction may, actually, be capable of explaining the approach followed in a number of post-Maastricht cases.

Calfa[110] involved an Italian tourist who was convicted of drug-related offences whilst holidaying in Greece and, for that reason, was permanently expelled from that Member State. Although, in that case, the right that was capable of being (potentially) impeded as a result of the contested measure had not yet been exercised on the facts of the case (the right to move (again) to Greece), and, in fact,

---

[109] This approach may be, actually, capable of explaining the Court's approach in the recent Case C-40/11 *Iida* ECLI:EU:C:2012:691. For comments on this see A Tryfonidou, '(Further) Signs of a Turn of the Tide in the CJEU's Citizenship Jurisprudence, Case C-40/11 *Iida*, Judgment of 8 November 2012, not yet reported' (2013) 20 *Maastricht Journal of European and Comparative Law* 302, 307–13.

[110] Case C-348/96 *Calfa* [1999] ECR I-11.

might never be exercised given that there were no special factors that indicated that there was more than a merely hypothetical possibility that Ms Calfa might wish to return to Greece in the future, the Court found that there was a violation of Article 59 EC (Article 56 TFEU). This may be capable of being explained by the distinction drawn in the previous paragraphs: because the (potential) future restriction that would ensue would be a direct restriction of one of the primary rights stemming from the above provision (the right to move to another Member State for the purpose of receiving a service), the situation was not purely internal, even though the facts of the case did not yet involve the exercise of the said right. The contested Greek legislation required Greek courts to order the expulsion for life from Greece of (non-Greek) persons convicted of certain offences. This amounted to a legal bar on a Union citizen's movement to Greece, which is, obviously, a *direct* restriction on the exercise of the right to move freely between Member States (on the facts of the case, the right to move for the purpose of receiving (tourist) services).

The same can be said for *Alpine Investments*,[111] where the Court held that Article 59 EEC (Article 56 TFEU) prohibits national measures that directly affect access to the market by service-providers in the territory of another Member State, and this is so even if these services are offered to potential (and thus unidentified) recipients. The right that would allegedly be restricted as a result of the contested national measure—to offer financial services (through cold-calling) to clients in another Member State—had not been exercised on the facts of the case; and the company seeking to rely on EU law against the impugned Dutch legislation was not claiming that a particular service contract with a particular service-recipient was in danger, as a result of the contested legislation. Yet, because the contested measure amounted to a direct, albeit potential, restriction on the provision of cross-border services—ie the mere *existence* of the measure amounted to a restriction on the exercise of the said right—the Court held that the legislation was contrary to Article 59 EEC.[112]

Moreover, in a number of cases where the contested measure protected the status quo on the market, the Court, again, did not rule out its jurisdiction where the facts before it did not involve the exercise of the primary rights stemming from the market freedoms. The Court's approach seems to have been based on the consideration that the mere existence of such measures has a direct impact on the exercise of the right to take-up and pursue a cross-border economic activity, in that traders from other Member States are—in effect—foreclosed from the market

---

[111] Case C-384/93 *Alpine Investments* [1995] ECR I-1141. Annotated by V Hatzopoulos (1995) 32 *Common Market Law Review* 1427.

[112] See also, inter alia, Case C-355/00 *Freskot* [2003] ECR I-5263, which concerned the compatibility with, inter alia, Art 59 EC (Art 56 TFEU), of a compulsory insurance scheme set up by the Greek state which appeared to be inherently discriminatory against insurance providers from other Member States who might be interested in providing the same insurance services to the Greek market; and Case C-367/12 *Sokoll-Seebacher* ECLI:EU:C:2014:68.

188 *Emerging Questions*

of the State applying the impugned measures.[113] In other words, their impact on cross-border trade or the taking-up or pursuit of an economic activity in a cross-border context is so obvious that they are—in effect—equivalent to direct restrictions on the primary, fundamental rights that appear to be stemming from the market freedoms.

Obvious examples of measures which have a foreclosing effect on the market and crystallise the status quo can be seen in situations where a Member State grants a contract for the provision of public services to a specific (national) economic operator without holding an open competition or where a limit is placed on the number of operators in a particular market. In *Parking Brixen*,[114] an Italian municipality (Brixen) had awarded a public service concession for the management of two car parks within that municipality to an Italian company (Stadtwerke Brixen AG), without putting it out to tender. Parking Brixen—the company that brought the action before an Italian court—was another Italian company which was interested in submitting a tender bid for the management of the car parks. It is clear that the facts which led to the case before the referring court did not involve a cross-border element: an Italian company was complaining that an Italian municipality awarded a concession to another Italian company, without putting it out to competition. Nonetheless, the Court held that Articles 43 and 49 EC (Articles 49 and 56 TFEU) *did* apply and concluded that the complete lack of any call for competition in the case of the award of a public service concession such as that at issue in the main proceedings was contrary to, inter alia, the above provisions. The Court rejected the argument that the above provisions did not apply to the situation before it because it was a purely internal one, noting that

> [i]t is possible that, in the main proceedings, undertakings established in Member States other than the Italian Republic might have been interested in providing the services concerned ... In the absence of advertising and the opening to competition of the award of a public service concession such as that at issue in the main proceedings, there is discrimination, at least potentially, against undertakings of other Member States which

---

[113] The Court recognised early on the importance of removing national measures which 'crystallize given consumer habits so as to consolidate an advantage acquired by national industries concerned to respond to them'—Case 170/78 *Commission v UK* [1983] ECR 2265, para 8. As Enchelmaier has explained in an article on the development of the law on the free movement of services, '[t]he whole point of the internal market is that anyone from whatever Member State is in principle allowed to try to find new customers in other Member States. To use a metaphor from the early case law on the prohibition of protectionist taxation ... Member States must not "crystallise" consumer habits to the benefit of domestic providers. It does not, therefore, matter that presently no one does engage in any cross-border provision of services: the market must be kept open for those who might at any point in time venture to do so. This would also explain the other paradigm mentioned by the Court, namely that a situation ceases to be wholly internal if traders from other Member States have been or would be interested in providing the services concerned. Here again, it is the potential for market entry that counts and that Member States must maintain at all times'—S Enchelmaier, 'Always at your Service (within Limits): The ECJ's Case Law on Article 56 TFEU (2006-11)' (2011) 36 *European Law Review* 615, 618.

[114] Case C-458/03 *Parking Brixen* [2005] ECR I-8585.

are prevented from making use of the freedom to provide services and of the freedom of establishment provided for by the Treaty.[115]

As Advocate General Kokott explained in her Opinion in this case,

> in public procurement law, any failure to fulfil the obligation of transparency has an impact not only on domestic undertakings ... but on all potential candidates, including any tenderers from other Member States. Consequently, any lack of publicity always simultaneously affects the fundamental freedoms of potential candidates from other Member States as well.[116]

In the subsequent case of *Europa 7*, which involved national legislation which limited the number of traders that can operate in a particular market, the Court was more forthcoming, stressing that '[t]he finding of a link with intra-Community trade will be presumed if the market in question has a certain cross-border interest'.[117] As Advocate General Poiares Maduro pointed out in his Opinion in this case,

> National measures which limit the number of operators in a particular market sector are liable to restrict free movement, since such measures carry the risk that they may solidify domestic market structures and protect the position of operators who have obtained a stronghold in that sector. Such operators, moreover, are likely to be domestic operators. Restrictions on the number of operators in a sector of the national market must therefore be justified.[118]

The same rationale can also be applied to explain a number of free movement of goods cases, where the Court ignored the fact that the case did not involve goods that had moved or were to move between Member States, and proceeded to consider whether the contested measure could amount to a potential restriction on the right to import or export goods. In these cases, *it was clear* that the mere existence of the contested measure was capable of impeding the free movement of goods and, hence, the Court did not need to assess the measure within a specific factual background in order to find a violation of the free movement of goods provisions.

---

[115] *Parking Brixen* (n 114), para 55. For similar rulings (though not as explicit as this one) see Case C-231/03 *Coname* [2005] ECR I-7287, paras 17–19; Case C-410/04 *ANAV* [2006] ECR I-3303; Case C-347/06 *ASM Brescia* [2008] ECR I-5641, paras 59–63. This approach is also implicit in a slightly older case: Case C-94/99 *ARGE* [2000] ECR I-11037. See also, more recently, Joined Cases C-357–359/10 *Duomo* ECLI:EU:C:2012:283, where the facts, again, did not involve a cross-border element and, yet, the Court proceeded to consider whether the specific requirements laid down by the contested Italian legislation in order for someone to be able to participate in a tender amounted to a restriction on the freedom of establishment and the freedom to provide services. Although the measure was not discriminatory against non-national companies, it was, nonetheless, capable of giving rise to a direct restriction on the exercise of the primary fundamental right to take-up an economic activity stemming from these freedoms since the requirement laid down was a prerequisite for taking part in the tender procedure which was the only way to have access to the said economic activity.
[116] Paragraph 39 of the Opinion of AG Kokott in *Parking Brixen* (n 114).
[117] Case C-380/05 *Europa 7* [2008] ECR I-349, para 67.
[118] Paragraph 33 of the Opinion of AG Poiares Maduro in *Europa 7* (n 117).

190 *Emerging Questions*

The most well-known example of this is *Pistre*,[119] where four French nationals were criminally prosecuted for using—without authorisation and, thus, contrary to French legislation—the label and description 'mountain' for meat products manufactured and marketed by them in France. According to French law, this was liable to mislead consumers as to the qualities of provenance of products and was, thus, prohibited. Given that the facts clearly did not involve a cross-border element, one would have expected the Court—applying its traditional approach to the purely internal rule—to rule out the application of EU law, stating that it did not have jurisdiction to consider the question whether the French law which was relied on to prosecute the traders was contrary to Article 30 EC (Article 34 TFEU). Nonetheless, the Court did not do so and, instead, proceeded to examine whether the measure amounted to a restriction on the importation of goods from other Member States. It justified its decision to do so by noting that 'Article 30 cannot be considered inapplicable simply because all the facts of the specific case before the national court are confined to a single Member State';[120] and

> In such a situation, the application of the national measure may also have effects on the free movement of goods between Member States, in particular when the measure in question facilitates the marketing of goods of domestic origin to the detriment of imported goods. In such circumstances, the application of the measure, even if restricted to domestic producers, in itself creates and maintains a difference of treatment between those two categories of goods, hindering, at least potentially, intra-Community trade.[121]

The Court then concluded that the measure amounted to a breach of Article 30 EC. This was because it 'discriminates against goods imported from other Member States in so far as it reserves use of the description "mountain" to products manufactured on national territory and made from domestic raw materials'[122] and

> in order for the description 'mountain' or specific geographical references to mountain areas to be used in relation to a product, its production, preparation, manufacture and packaging must be carried out in mountain areas situated on French territory. It is thus apparent that the legislation does not enable imported products to fulfil the conditions to which authorization to use the description 'mountain' is subject.[123]

Accordingly, the contested legislation directly impeded the importation of goods from other Member States, since it did not permit—under any circumstances—goods produced in other Member States to be marketed as 'mountain products'. The mere existence of the law, therefore, created an obstacle to the importation of goods from other Member States and, hence, it was not necessary for the Court to consider the effects of the contested legislation on a particular (cross-border)

---

[119] Joined Cases C-321-324/94 *Pistre* [1997] ECR I-2343.
[120] ibid, para 44.
[121] ibid, para 45.
[122] ibid, para 49.
[123] ibid, para 50.

factual setting—in all instances, the contested legislation amounted to a direct restriction on the importation of goods from other Member States.[124]

Similarly, there appear to be a number of cases where the Court held that it had no jurisdiction to consider whether the contested measure amounted to a breach of the market freedoms, because the facts of the case from which the preliminary reference arose were purely internal to a Member State. These cases involved measures which could—if at all—merely amount to *indirect* restrictions on the exercise of the primary rights stemming from the market freedoms and this may have been the reason that the Court did not proceed to consider whether there was a breach of these provisions.[125]

Accordingly, and to summarise what has been concluded in this section, it is argued here that in order to prevent an overly broad scope of the market freedoms (when read in conjunction with the citizenship provisions) and in order to avoid the subjection to EU scrutiny of national measures which, in reality, do not impede the exercise of the rights stemming from the market freedoms, the (two) main filtering mechanisms traditionally employed by the Court in the market freedoms context should, now, be used more effectively.[126] It has been suggested that the Court should establish a clear remoteness test, which should be based on causation, and it should require that the test is applied whenever a measure lacks cross-border specificity and/or amounts to an indirect restriction on the exercise of one of the primary rights stemming from the market freedoms. As regards the purely internal rule, its use should differ depending on the type of restriction that is created by the measure: for measures amounting to direct restrictions, the rule should only be used as a substantive requirement, requiring the ECJ or national court to simply consider whether the contested measure is, indeed, capable of

---

[124] For comments on the case, see G Davies (n 29) 170–72. A similar approach can be observed in, inter alia, Case C-379/98 *PreussenElektra* [2001] ECR I-2099; Case C-573/12 *Ålands Vindkraft*, ECLI:EU:C:2014:2037 and Joined Cases 204-208/12 *Essent Belgium* ECLI:EU:C:2014:2192, though the issue of purely internal situations was not expressly discussed there. Also, in the Art 258 TFEU action Case C-184/96 *Commission v France (Foie Gras)* [1998] ECR I-6197, it is obvious that the Court recognised that Art 34 TFEU can be used to outlaw national measures (here French laws regarding foie gras) which—although in reality do not have an impact *at the moment* on cross-border trade given that a certain (traditional) product is only produced in one Member State—they are capable of *potentially* impeding the importation of such goods produced in other Member States. On the facts, the contested French measure which laid down the production requirements that must be satisfied in order for foie gras to be marketed in France, did not include a mutual recognition clause and, thus, it was obvious that whenever this rule was applied to imported goods which did comply with the requirements of their home State but did not comply with the French requirements, there would be an obstacle to the importation of goods.

[125] See eg Joined Cases C-162 & 163/12 *Airport Shuttle Express* ECLI:EU:C:2014:74; Case C-139/12 *Caixa d'Estalvis i Pensions de Barcelona* ECLI:EU:C:2014:174.

[126] For a similar argument made specifically in the context of Art 34 TFEU, see T Horsley, 'Unearthing Buried Treasure' (n 38). Nic Shuibhne has noted that these filtering mechanisms 'are not properly defined, worked out, or distinguished in conceptual terms; they are not consistently applied; their application creates particular risks for subjective or arbitrary decision-making; and the impact of appreciability thresholds, in particular, has not been reconciled with apparently contradictory lines of authority that reject the relevance of *de minimis* concerns in free movement law'—N Nic Shuibhne (n 11) 193.

impeding the exercise of the (by nature cross-border) primary rights stemming from the market freedoms; for measures that may amount to indirect restrictions, the rule should be used *both* as a jurisdictional and as a substantive requirement, in this way requiring that measures which can only indirectly impede the exercise of the primary rights stemming from the market freedoms, are only assessed in a specific factual context which involves the exercise of the primary right which is, allegedly, impeded as a result of the contested measure.

IV. HOW SHOULD THE ASSESSMENT AS TO WHETHER THERE IS A BREACH OF THE MARKET FREEDOMS NOW BE MADE?

The re-conceptualisation of the market freedoms as provisions which—when they are read together with the citizenship provisions—also aim to be the source of fundamental economic rights for the Union citizen, will not merely require a change in the way that the personal and material scope of application of these provisions is delimited. It also appears to necessitate a change in the way that the assessment is conducted for the purpose of determining, first, whether there is a restriction contrary to these provisions, and, second, whether the measure which gives rise to this restriction is, nonetheless, justified.

In particular, what will be important now will be to determine whether the contested national measure (which will be a measure that will *not* have been excluded by the filtering mechanisms seen in the previous section), *when applied to the individual circumstances of the Union citizen that seeks to rely on these provisions*, gives rise to a restriction on the exercise of the right sought to be enforced, and whether its application is justified on the particular facts of the case and the particular situation of the individual concerned.

Accordingly, when assessing whether there is a breach of the market freedoms in situations where these provisions are relied on by Union citizens, the impugned measures should not be assessed in an abstract manner but they should, now, be assessed taking into account the individual circumstances of the Union citizen and it should be established whether the application of that particular measure in that particular factual scenario violates the fundamental rights that that particular Union citizen derives from the market freedoms. This approach—widely applied in the context of the Court's citizenship jurisprudence[127]—is also reflected in the Citizens' Rights Directive,[128] and has also been applied in the context of the personal market freedoms, as seen already in chapter three. Spaventa has also been of

---

[127] See, mainly, Case C-184/99 *Grzelczyk* [2001] ECR I-6193 and Case C-413/99 *Baumbast* [2002] ECR I-7091.

[128] See eg Arts 14 (3) and 28(1) of Dir 2004/38 on the right of citizens of the Union and their family members to move and reside freely within the territory of the Member States [2004] OJ L158/77.

the view that signs of this approach can also be discerned in the area of the free movement of goods.[129]

Moreover, in cases where there is no cross-border specificity and, hence, where it is clear that the contested measure is entirely neutral towards the initiation and pursuit of cross-border economic activities, the justification stage of the assessment should, now, always include an examination of whether the contested measure is justified by the need to ensure that the relevant activity is regulated. In other words, Member States should be given the chance to justify their measures which are entirely neutral and merely seek to regulate an economic activity (without being biased against cross-border economic activities) on the ground of the need to ensure that the EU internal market will not end up being an unregulated market.[130] Accordingly, a mandatory requirement/objective justification of protecting the collective interest in market regulation should be recognised. In this way, instead of the requirement that an economic activity is (neutrally) regulated being integrated into the definition of a 'restriction'—in which case a measure would be found to amount to a restriction only if it had cross-border specificity and, thus, if it regulated an economic activity in a biased manner—it should now be transformed into a mandatory requirement/objective justification which enables Member States to take measures which, although they do restrict the exercise of the fundamental rights stemming from the market freedoms, they do so in a justified and proportionate manner. In this way the Court will not only 'balance the Community interest in free trade against the national interest in regulation',[131] but also the EU's need to protect and respect the fundamental economic rights that Union citizens derive from the Treaty against the collective interest in regulation.[132]

Whether a measure will be found to be justified on this ground will depend on the particular measure that is contested and the way it is applied (ie on the type and degree of public intervention on the market) but, also, on the way that this particular measure affects the particular individual who is involved on the facts of the case.

---

[129] Citing as evidence *Commission v Germany* (n 77), para 75 and Case C-320/03 *Commission v Austria* [2005] ECR I-9871, para 90, Spaventa noted that 'in the field of goods, the court has held that rules which in principle might be justified according to the mandatory requirements doctrine, might still fall foul of the Treaty because of the way they have been adopted'—E Spaventa (n 48) 155. For an explanation of this approach, see C Barnard, 'Derogations, Justifications and the Four Freedoms: Is State Interest Really Protected?' in C Barnard and O Odudu (n 94) 286–87 and 294.

[130] As Maas has stressed, 'citizenship makes markets less free because it forces governments to regulate the markets in order to satisfy rights'—W Maas, *Creating European Citizens* (Lanham MD, Rowman & Littlefield, 2007) 6.

[131] J Snell (n 19) 2.

[132] Kaupa has noted that '[d]epending on the economic background assumptions, the outcome of the balancing test in internal market law will be very different. Neoclassical scholars who assume that individual economic action will generally lead to the most efficient outcomes, except in clearly defined areas of market failure, will tend to be critical about many forms of national regulation. Keynisians will tend to differentiate, *inter alia*, on the basis of the effects of the national measure on distribution, while institutionalist economists will oppose judgments that lead to the disintegration of a country's economically beneficial institutional structures. Depending on the economic standpoint, the economic (and not merely the social) worth of national regulations and institutions will be evaluated differently in a balancing test—C Kaupa (n 30) 63–64.

Therefore, an important part of the assessment will be to examine whether the said economic activity has been regulated somewhere (ie in the home State) and whether the guarantees provided by that regulation are equivalent to those afforded by the regulation of the host State. In other words, what Armstrong calls 'active mutual recognition', should now be considered an important part of the national court's or authority's assessment of whether the contested national action is justified by the need to ensure that the national and collective interest in regulation is respected; this 'requires the incorporation of the regulatory history of a product etc. into a contemporaneous regulatory process in the host state.'[133] Of course, this has always been considered a requirement imposed by EU law on Member State authorities,[134] but its effective application is now imperative given that it is necessary in order to differentiate between situations where a restriction on the exercise of the fundamental rights stemming from the market freedoms should be permitted, in order to ensure that an economic activity does not completely escape regulation.

It should here be highlighted, nonetheless, that the body or court making this assessment will have to bear in mind that there is—and there should be—*no* presumption in favour of market regulation.[135] As Snell has explained, 'in many circumstances public intervention is not an optimal solution. Even if there is a public interest at stake, it may be that measures will suffer from regulatory failures that are more serious than the original problem'.[136] Accordingly, it will have to be borne in mind that in certain instances, an economic activity may not need to be regulated at all.

V. CONCLUSION

In the first half of this chapter, the focus was placed on questions of legitimacy, examining whether the Court did have the competence to interpret the market

---

[133] K Armstrong, 'Mutual Recognition' in C Barnard and J Scott (n 32) 242.

[134] See eg Case 222/86 *Heylens* [1987] ECR 4097; Case 340/89 *Vlassopoulou* [1991] ECR 2357. It should be noted that in its judgment in *Commission v France (Foie Gras)* (n 124), the Court held that Art 34 TFEU was violated as a result of the fact that French legislation relating to preparations with *foie gras* as a base did not include in it a mutual recognition clause for products coming from a Member State and complying with the rules laid down by that State. As Armstrong explained, what is interesting in relation to this ruling is 'the idea that legislatures must also be "other-regarding" when legislating and ensure that products complying with equivalent rules or standards to that of the host state should be permitted market access.'—K Armstrong, ibid, 240.

[135] A somewhat different view was expressed by Bernard who asserted that the introduction of the principle of mutual recognition in *Cassis* 'was immediately neutralised by the mandatory requirements doctrine. The possibility for the host state to justify rules by reference to legitimate public interest objectives ensured that what was presented as the default principle, namely that products lawfully produced and marketed in one Member State should in principle be admitted in all other Member States, was confined to marginal situations, where no significant regulatory objectives were at stake.'— N Bernard, 'On the Art of Not Mixing One's Drinks: *Dassonville* and *Cassis de Dijon* Revisited' in M Poiares Maduro and L Azoulai (eds), *The Past and Future of EU Law: The Classics of EU Law Revisited on the 50th Anniversary of the Rome Treaty* (Oxford, Hart Publishing, 2010) 460.

[136] J Snell (n 19) 170–71.

freedoms in the way that was documented in chapters three and four of the book. It was seen that although some of the aspects of the Court's recent case-law in this context cannot be justified if a purely literal approach to the interpretation of these provisions is taken, they can, nonetheless, be considered to be compliant with a teleological approach to their interpretation. This, of course, required an examination of what the current aims of these provisions are.

It was concluded that the market freedoms should now be read as having two aims.

Firstly, when they are relied on by legal persons or natural persons that do not hold the nationality of a Member State, they should be viewed as merely the tools to be used in the process of building and maintaining a properly-functioning market. Accordingly, in such cases, they should be read alone and they should be viewed as having as their *sole* aim to ensure that a properly-functioning market is built and maintained. For this reason, the Court should revert to its traditional approach to their interpretation, always requiring cross-border specificity, and reading these provisions as merely sources of (instrumental) freedoms that are sufficiently related to the above aim.

Secondly, when the market freedoms are invoked by Union citizens, they should be read in conjunction with the citizenship provisions—either Article 20 TFEU or 21 TFEU, depending on the right sought to be enforced—and they should, thus, be reconceptualised as sources of fundamental economic rights for Union citizens. Accordingly, in such cases, the market freedoms should be viewed as having as their main aim to grant to Union citizens certain fundamental economic rights. The primary fundamental rights that should now be considered as stemming from these provisions are the right to take-up an economic activity in another Member State that is going to be pursued there or in a cross-border context and the right to start pursuing an economic activity in a cross-border context. Union citizens who seek to actively (as economic actors) or passively (as consumers of goods or recipients of services) exercise such rights can, clearly, rely on these provisions (read together with the citizenship provisions) to enforce either of these rights. Moreover, since the existence of fundamental rights cannot be subjected to conditions or limitations, the requirement of cross-border specificity must be abolished in this context.

Nonetheless, the (suggested) re-interpretation of the market freedoms in the above manner means that their scope of application is virtually unlimited, potentially bringing within that scope all national measures, even those which are entirely innocuous and simply seek to regulate an economic (or non-economic) activity or to protect certain valued non-economic interests without treating Union citizens who engage in cross-border economic activities in any way worse than those whose lives are organised in a purely national context. For this reason, it has been suggested that it is now imperative that the two main filtering mechanisms traditionally employed for excluding from the notion of 'restriction', measures which do not, when examined more closely, restrict the exercise of the measures stemming from the market freedoms (ie the notion of remoteness and the purely internal rule) are used more effectively. For this purpose, a suggestion has been made as to how, exactly, these mechanisms should be used, depending on the type of restriction (direct or indirect) that is at issue.

Finally, it has been suggested that the reconceptualisation of the market freedoms as sources of fundamental citizenship rights (when they are read together with the citizenship provisions), will require a change in the approach that is followed when determining whether a measure amounts to a restriction and whether it is justified. Firstly, it will always have to be examined whether the contested measure does, indeed, restrict one of the fundamental rights stemming from these provisions and whether the restriction of that right is, nonetheless, justified, *on the particular facts of the case*. Secondly, given that the requirement of cross-border specificity should—continue—to be inapplicable in situations involving Union citizens, the need to maintain a *regulated* internal market should be recognised as a mandatory requirement. In this way, national measures that limit the exercise by Union citizens of the fundamental rights they derive from the market freedoms will be able to be justified, when such measures merely seek to regulate an economic or non-economic activity in a neutral manner and when it is established that it is *necessary* that the said activity is regulated.

6

(Re-)Interpreting the Market Freedoms in the Light of Union Citizenship: Persisting Conundrums

I. INTRODUCTION

IN THE PREVIOUS chapter, the focus was on issues of competence and legitimacy and the aim was to consider whether the market freedoms can be interpreted in the manner analysed in chapters three and four of the book. It was concluded that the need to interpret these provisions in the light of Union citizenship, which has led to their reconceptualisation as sources of fundamental economic rights for the Union citizen, justifies the expansion of their scope—*when they are read together with the citizenship provisions*—to cover situations which under a purely economic-oriented, instrumental, reading of them, would be excluded. Accordingly, the Court has acted within the bounds of its jurisdiction when reading the market freedoms more broadly in recent years, but this has only been the case in situations where it was Union citizens (rather than legal persons or third-country nationals) that sought to enforce the rights stemming from these provisions. Moreover, it was explained that such a broader reading can only be employed in situations where the market freedoms are read in conjunction with the citizenship provisions, and, therefore, in the future, instead of applying the market freedoms alone (as it has done so far), the Court should employ the market freedoms *together with the citizenship provisions* in order to protect the (fundamental economic) rights of Union citizens.

The current chapter will take a broader approach and will concentrate on examining a number of difficult conundrums that persist in the area of EU free movement law and which appear to be either exacerbated or to simply emerge, as a result of the re-conceptualisation of the market freedoms as sources of fundamental economic rights for the Union citizen.

II. THE PERSISTING DISTINCTION BETWEEN UNION CITIZENS WHO ARE NATIONALS OF MEMBER STATES AND UNION CITIZENS WHO ARE NOT

The market freedoms have always been read as prohibiting, inter alia, restrictions on the exercise of the rights stemming from them, which are discriminatory on the ground of nationality. This has been the case both for the provisions which explicitly prohibit discrimination on the ground of nationality or which require that Member State nationals are treated in the same way as the nationals of the host State,[1] as well as for the provisions which do not make any reference to nationality discrimination or equality.[2] The reason behind this is obvious: if a national of another Member State will be treated in the host State worse than the latter's nationals, (s)he is likely to be discouraged from exercising the rights stemming from the market freedoms and this will amount to a restriction caught by these provisions.[3]

Nonetheless, despite the fact that national measures which are discriminatory against non-nationals do, obviously, amount to restrictions that should be caught by the market freedoms, since the beginning of the EU's existence it has been accepted that there are certain instances where the Member States are allowed to continue to treat nationals of other Member States differently from (ie less favourably than) their own nationals. This is reflected in a number of Treaty provisions and has been condoned by the Court in its judgments.

As regards economically inactive Union citizens, it was seen in chapter two that the Court appears to permit the differential treatment that emerges from national laws that grant certain benefits to nationals of the relevant Member State *automatically*, whilst requiring Union citizens who hold the nationality of another Member State to prove that they are sufficiently integrated into its society and that they have established a bond with it, in order to be able to claim those benefits.[4] Moreover, it seems that Member States are permitted to reserve certain political rights for their own nationals, given that the Treaty does not require them to open voting and candidacy in national elections to nationals of other Member States, although it does require this with regards to local and European Parliament elections.[5]

Since the focus of this book is on the market freedoms, this section will concentrate on examining the instances where the Court and/or the EU legislature have condoned differential treatment between nationals and non-nationals, in situations involving economically active persons. In particular, the main question will be whether it is still acceptable to permit such instances of differential treatment in a Citizens' Europe.

---

[1] Arts 18, 45 and 49(2), TFEU.
[2] Arts 56 and 63, TFEU.
[3] For an analysis of the relationship between the notions of 'restriction' and 'discrimination' in EU free movement law, see A Tryfonidou, 'The Notions of "Restriction" and "Discrimination" in the Context of the Free Movement of Persons Provisions: From a Relationship of Interdependence to one of (Almost Complete) Independence' (2014) 33 *Yearbook of European Law* 385. For an analysis of the ways in which nationality can be an obstacle to the enjoyment of EU citizenship, see M Szpunar and MEB López, 'Some Reflections on Member State Nationality: A Prerequisite of EU Citizenship and an Obstacle to its Enjoyment' in D Kochenov (ed), *Citizenship and Federalism in Europe* (Cambridge, Cambridge University Press, 2016, forthcoming).
[4] See, inter alia, Case C-158/07 *Förster* [2008] ECR I-8507 and Case C-123/08 *Wolzenburg* [2009] ECR I-9621, and see the comments in D Chalmers, G Davies and G Monti, *European Union Law* 2nd end (Cambridge, Cambridge University Press, 2010) 459.
[5] For comments on this see F Fabbrini, 'The Political Side of EU Citizenship in the Context of EU Federalism' in D Kochenov (n 3).

There are, mainly, two instances where such differential treatment has arisen in situations involving Union citizens seeking to exercise the rights they derive from the market freedoms. The first instance is when the host Member State reserves certain professions or posts for its own nationals, on the ground that these posts require a special bond of allegiance to it (ie the public service and official authority exceptions). The second is when Member States, by relying on the Treaty derogations, are allowed to apply different measures to nationals and non-nationals, to the detriment of the latter, the best example of this being cases where a Member State refuses to admit into its territory or deports a national of another Member State, although it can under no circumstances do the same with respect to its own nationals.[6] In both instances—as will be seen below—the differential treatment that emerges is permissible under EU law. It is not entirely clear, nonetheless, what the Court's or the EU legislature's exact rationale is for condoning such differential treatment: this could be either that although it is recognised that there is, indeed, discrimination based on nationality as regards the enjoyment of the rights stemming from the Treaty, this is, nonetheless, justified, or that the differential treatment that emerges does not qualify as discriminatory, since it is considered that in the relevant areas, nationals and non-nationals are not similarly situated and, hence, they must not be treated in the same manner.[7]

Article 45(4) TFEU (and before this, its predecessors) provides that Article 45 TFEU 'shall not apply to employment in the public service'. Similarly, according to Article 51 TFEU (and before this, its predecessors), the Treaty Chapter on Establishment 'shall not apply, so far as any given Member State is concerned, to activities which in that State are connected, even occasionally, with the exercise of official authority'. Article 62 TFEU extends the application of Article 51 TFEU to the Treaty Chapter on Services.[8]

Article 45(4) TFEU can justify only the refusal of Member States to give *access* to certain posts to nationals of other Member States and cannot be used to justify discriminatory conditions of employment against non-national workers once the latter have been admitted to the public service.[9] The Court has claimed a

---

[6] As seen in ch 2, after Maastricht, this instance of differential treatment also emerged in cases involving economically inactive Union citizens.

[7] As explained by Spaventa in a different context, which of these rationales is applicable does make a difference: 'It is important to stress that the non-comparability assessment differs from the justificatory assessment inherent in cases of indirect discrimination for two reasons: first of all, because if the two situations are deemed comparable, directly discriminatory rules can be justified, if at all, only having regard to the Treaty derogations. Secondly, because if the situations are not comparable, the matter is not affected by Article 12 EC [now Article 18 TFEU] and, since it does not need to be justified, there should be no need to scrutinize compliance with proportionality and fundamental rights. Thus, in cases of non-comparability, the personal circumstances of the migrant Union citizen should be immaterial'—E Spaventa, 'Seeing the Wood despite the Trees? On the Scope of Union Citizenship and its Constitutional effects' (2008) 45 *Common Market Law Review* 13, 29.

[8] For an explanation of the reasons behind the inclusion of these exceptions in the Treaty, see D Chalmers, G Davies and G Monti, *European Union Law* 3rd edn (Cambridge, Cambridge University Press, 2014) 937.

[9] Case 152/73 *Sotgiu* [1974] ECR 153, para 4; Joined Cases 389 & 390/87 *Echternach and Moritz* [1989] ECR 723, para 14.

hermeneutic monopoly over deciding whether a certain post or profession falls within this derogation,[10] as there is no secondary legislation providing any clarification regarding this matter. The test laid down by the Court is comprised of two, cumulative, limbs: a) whether the post involves direct or indirect participation in the exercise of powers conferred by public law and b) whether it is designed to safeguard the general interests of the State or of other public authorities.[11] As the Court has explained, only posts which 'presume on the part of those occupying them the existence of a special relationship of allegiance to the State and reciprocity of rights and duties which form the foundation of the bond of nationality' should be reserved for a Member State's own nationals.[12] This is, clearly, a rather restrictive approach from the point of view of the Member States.[13]

A similarly restrictive approach has been followed when interpreting the official authority exception from the freedom of establishment and the freedom to provide services. Although this exception has a similar role to play, it focuses on reserving certain activities which are connected with the use of official power to the nationals of a Member State, rather than on preventing access to professions or vocations within which official authority may be exercised.[14] The Court has underlined that although it is possible, in certain cases, to exclude a whole profession on the basis of Article 51 TFEU, in cases where the activities connected with the exercise of official authority are separable from the professional activity in question taken as a whole, the public authority exception will not apply.[15]

Even if, as a result of the Court's restrictive approach towards the interpretation of the public service/official authority exceptions, it is only rarely that the Member States are able to rely on them, their mere existence is symbolically significant because it perpetuates the traditional conception that nationals and non-nationals can (and perhaps should) be treated differently in certain circumstances, and also that the special relationship of allegiance between a State and its own nationals, can never be forged between a State and non-nationals, even if the latter have lived there for a large part of their lives. Agreeing with White, '[t]he future of these two

---

[10] *Sotgiu* (n 9), para 5.
[11] Case 149/79 *Commission v Belgium* [1980] ECR 3883, para 10.
[12] ibid.
[13] P Craig and G de Búrca, *EU Law: Text, Cases and Materials* (Oxford, Oxford University Press, 2011) 734. For a recent, detailed, analysis of the public service exception, see J Ziller's Report for the European Commission 'Free Movement of European Union Citizens and Employment in the Public Sector' (2010) available at ec.europa.eu/social/main.jsp?catId=465&langId=en. See, also, J Handoll, 'Article 48(4) EEC and Non-National Access to Public Employment' (1988) 13 *European Law Review* 223; D O'Keeffe, 'Judicial Interpretation of the Public Services Exception to the Free Movement of Workers' in D Curtin and D O'Keeffe (eds), *Constitutional Adjudication in European Community and National Law. Essays in Honour of Justice T F O'Higgins* (Dublin, Butterworths, 1992); B Wilkinson, 'Towards European Citizenship? Nationality, Discrimination and Free Movement of Workers in the European Union' (1995) 1 *European Public Law* 417, 425–29; RCA White, *Workers, Establishment, and Services in the European Union* (Oxford, Oxford University Press, 2004) 79–85.
[14] P Craig and G de Búrca (n 13) 769. For an explanation of the official authority exception see RCA White (n 13) 85–86.
[15] Case 2/74 *Reyners* [1974] ECR 631.

exceptions—or their ambit—might be considered to be in doubt following the introduction of citizenship of the European Union, since this provides some bond between nationals of all the Member States and the European Union'.[16]

Apart from the above (specific) exceptions, the Treaty derogations from the personal market freedoms (which, since Maastricht, also apply to justify restrictions caught by Article 21 TFEU) allow Member States to treat nationals of other Member States differently from their own nationals, provided that this is based on one of three grounds (public policy, public security, public health) and that the measure is proportionate and complies with the fundamental human rights protected under EU law. The use of these exceptions has been particularly prominent (and successful) in situations involving either the refusal of the host State to admit within its territory nationals of other Member States or their deportation. More specifically, the ECJ early on ruled that Member States can refuse access to their territory or deport nationals of other Member States, if this can be justified on any of the above grounds.[17] This, nonetheless, gives rise to differential treatment between nationals and non-nationals, since—under international law—States can never expel their own nationals, nor can they refuse to admit them within their territory.[18] It is likely that in such instances the Court considers that there is no discrimination, since the two categories of persons who are treated differently—nationals and non-nationals—are not considered similarly situated.[19]

Reflecting on the above situation, Kostakopoulou and Ferreira have observed that as far as security of residence is concerned, the position of migrant Union citizens approximates that of third-country national long-term residence status, and, thus, from this perspective, 'Union citizenship appears to be a lesser status than that of national citizenship'.[20] Yet, it should be noted that the Court has limited the permitted scope of differentiation in this context, by providing that a deportation or exclusion is justified only if it is due to conduct which will lead to repressive measures (short of exclusion or deportation) in situations involving the

---

[16] RCA White (n 13) 86.

[17] See eg Case 41/74 *Van Duyn* [1974] ECR 1337. For comments see M Meduna, '"Scelestus Europeus Sum": What Protection against Expulsion EU Citizenship Offers to European Offenders?' in D Kochenov (n 3).

[18] Case C-348/96 *Calfa* [2011] ECR I-11, para 20—for comments see C Costello, 'Annotation of *Donatella Calfa*' (2000) 37 *Common Market Law Review* 817, 823–824. See also, *Van Duyn* (n 17), paras 22–23; Case C-370/90 *Singh* [1992] ECR I-4265, para 22; Case C-65 & 111/95 *Shingara and Radiom* [1997] ECR I-3343, para 28.

[19] G Davies, *European Union Internal Market Law* (London, Routledge, 2003) 106–07. See also, A Evans, 'European Citizenship: A Novel Concept in EEC Law' (1984) 32 *American Journal of Comparative Law* 679, 700–01.

[20] D Kostakopoulou and N Ferreira, 'Testing Liberal Norms: The Public Policy and Public Security Derogations and the Cracks in European Union Citizenship' (2013–2014) 20 *Columbia Journal of European Law* 167, 176. Wollenschläger has also questioned the compatibility of this distinction with the status of Union citizenship—F Wollenschläger, 'A New Fundamental Freedom beyond Market Integration: Union Citizenship and its Dynamics for Shifting the Economic Paradigm of European Integration' (2011) 17 *European Law Journal* 1, 17.

Member State's own nationals.[21] Hence, conduct which does not lead to repressive measures against a Member State's *own* nationals, cannot form the basis for the exclusion or deportation of a Union citizen who holds the nationality of another Member State. Nonetheless, although this does, indeed, place some limits on when a Member State can deport or exclude nationals of other Member States from its territory, it still condones the differential treatment noted earlier between these two categories of Union citizens.

Moreover, in recognition of the links formed by the migrant with the host State as a result of the length of his/her residence in the host State, the EU legislature has ensured that the longer a Union citizen resides in the territory of the host State, the more difficult it becomes for the latter to deport him or her.[22] Yet, Kostakopoulou and Ferreira have rightly suggested that such long-term residents (and especially those that have lived in the host State for more than 10 years) should not be expellable at all, and that their position should become entirely assimilated to that of nationals of the host State, thereby abolishing the inherent distinction traditionally maintained between nationals and non-nationals in this context.[23]

The important question, of course, is whether the distinction drawn between Union citizens who hold the nationality of a Member State and Union citizens who do not, is acceptable in today's EU. Maintaining this distinction in certain contexts, such as those seen above, might appear acceptable and even well-suited in an organisation which merely seeks to establish and maintain an internal market. Although differential treatment which prejudices non-nationals is, generally, prohibited whenever this leads to an obstacle to building and/or maintaining such a market, it is, nonetheless, acceptable in certain situations to put the economic aims of the organisation to the side, in order to reserve certain benefits, entitlements, or privileges and even certain sensitive economic activities, to the State's own nationals. However, it is doubtful whether the same is the case in a Union which has developed—or aspires to develop—a meaningful status of citizenship.[24] In such a case, it would appear that discrimination on the grounds of nationality should under no circumstances be tolerated. As Mass has pointed out referring

---

[21] Joined Cases 115 & 116/81 *Adoui and Cornuaille* [1982] ECR 1665, para 8; Case C-268/99 *Jany* [2001] ECR I-8615, para 60; Case C-100/01 *Olazabal* [2002] ECR I-10981, para 42. For the same requirement in situations involving the different treatment of imported and domestic goods, see Case 121/85 *Conegate* [1986] ECR 1007.

[22] This is reflected in Articles 28(2) and 28(3) of Dir 2004/38/EC on the right of citizens of the Union and their family members to move and reside freely within the territory of the Member States [2004] OJ L158/77. This graded approach to deportation was suggested by AG La Pergola in the late 1990s, in his Opinion in Case C-171/96 *Pereira Roque* [1998] ECR I-4607, paras 46–48.

[23] D Kostakopoulou and N Ferreira (n 20) 177 and 187–89. For another commentator arguing that long-term residents in the host state (or 'virtual nationals', as she calls them) should not be expellable, see E Berry, 'The Deportation of "Virtual National" Offenders: The Impact of the ECHR and EU Law' (2009) 23 *Journal of Immigration, Asylum and Nationality Law* 11.

[24] For a discussion of the question whether the existence of the public service and official authority exceptions, and of the derogations from the free movement of workers which permit Member States to refuse access, or deport, nationals of other Member States, prevent the development of a meaningful notion of Union citizenship, see B Wilkinson (n 13) 420–21.

to the distinction between insiders and outsiders of a State, 'European Union (EU) citizenship supersedes this traditional distinction by removing the ability of European states to discriminate between their own citizens and those of other EU member states'.[25] Moreover, and in light of the fact that the rights stemming from the market freedoms (when these are read in the light of the citizenship provisions) should, now, be considered fundamental economic rights bestowed on Union citizens, it appears even less (if at all) acceptable, to permit the host Member State to treat nationals of other Member States worse than its own nationals with regards to the enjoyment of these rights.

As the Court itself noted in a number of cases,

> Union citizenship is destined to be the fundamental status of nationals of the Member States, enabling those who find themselves in the same situation to enjoy the same treatment in law irrespective of their nationality, subject to such exceptions as are expressly provided for.[26]

Accordingly, one of the important aims of Union citizenship as a fundamental status for Member State nationals is to ensure equality of treatment for all Union citizens.[27] Of course, the argument that would be made in response to this point would be that nationals and non-nationals are not similarly situated with regards to a number of issues. This, of course, may be true in certain instances. However, it cannot be *presumed* that nationals and non-nationals are *not* similarly situated; in fact, as noted by Spaventa, 'in the context of free movement ... there is usually (but not always) a presumption of comparability of situations between nationals and foreigners'.[28] Accordingly, before deciding whether—for a particular reason—nationals and non-nationals can be treated differently, it should be examined whether there is any factor that rebuts that presumption and demonstrates that nationals and non-nationals are *not* similarly situated for that particular purpose. Hence, what should now be examined is the position of the national of another Member State who has suffered discrimination, and compare this to the position of a national of that Member State whose situation is similar. If the only differentiating element is nationality, this should clearly not suffice for establishing that the position of the two Union citizens is different.

A possible solution to this is the one suggested by Gareth Davies,[29] according to which the factor determining whether someone should enjoy certain

---

[25] W Maas, *Creating European Citizens* (Lanham MD, Rowman & Littlefield, 2007) vii.
[26] Case C-184/99 *Grzelczyk* [2001] ECR I-6193, para 31 (emphasis added).
[27] This argument has been used elsewhere, in order to argue that reverse discrimination (which is a difference in treatment against Union citizens *who have not exercised the rights stemming from the market freedoms*) is no longer an acceptable difference in treatment in a Citizens' Europe'—see A Tryfonidou, *Reverse Discrimination in EC Law* (The Hague, Kluwer, 2009).
[28] E Spaventa, *Free Movement of Persons in the European Union: Barriers to Movement in their Constitutional Context* (The Hague, Kluwer, 2007) 17.
[29] G Davies, '"Any Place I Hang my Hat?" or: Residence is the New Nationality' (2005) 11 *European Law Journal* 43.

'special' rights or entitlements in a Member State should be the actual bond of the individual with the society of that State and not—as is currently the case—possession of its nationality. Long-term residence in a Member State may be a good factor to use as evidence of such a bond. It should be noted, nonetheless, that this should become the *only* factor to be taken into account for distinguishing persons who should be entitled to special rights or entitlements from persons who do not. In other words, long-term residence should not be used as a requirement for establishing a bond with the society of the host State *only* in situations involving non-nationals, whilst nationals (irrespective of their length of residence in their own Member State) are presumed to have a bond with that State merely by virtue of their nationality.[30] Hence, under such a solution, denizenship should, now, replace nationality in determining who should be considered a 'member' of the society of a Member State,[31] and, thus, in determining who should be entitled to certain 'special' advantages reserved only for persons belonging to that society.

III. SHOULD THERE STILL BE A NUMBER OF DIFFERENT FREE MOVEMENT OF PERSONS PROVISIONS?

One argument that is often tested in legal literature, is that in view of the perceived similarity currently existing between the material scope of Article 21 TFEU and that of the personal market freedoms,[32] and in light of the increasing blurring of the boundaries between the personal scope of these provisions, the maintenance of different Treaty Articles governing the position of Union citizens that wish to

---

[30] ibid, 52. An example of such legislation, which imposes a requirement for a sufficient link with the society of a Member State *on both its own nationals and nationals of other Member States* is the German legislation that was at issue in Joined Cases C-523 & 585/11 *Prinz* ECLI:EU:C:2013:524 and Case C-359/13 *B Martens* ECLI:EU:C:2015:118.

[31] For a similar view, see D Kostakopoulou, 'European Union Citizenship: The Journey Goes On' in A Ott and E Vos (eds), *Fifty Years of European Integration: Foundations and Perspectives* (The Hague, TMC Asser Press, 2009) 286. For a commentator who considered that the Court's 'real link' case-law demonstrated that 'European citizenship seems to evolve from a nationality citizenship to a residence citizenship', see J-Y Carlier, 'Annotation of *Zhu and Chen*' (2005) 42 *Common Market Law Review* 1121, 1131.

[32] O'Leary has pointed out that when writing about the free movement of persons provisions, '[s]eparating economically inactive migrants from their economically active counterparts results in a highly truncated analysis of the free movement of persons. Such a division is no longer tenable precisely because the Court's case law, and now secondary legislation, have meshed the foundations and treatment of the free movement and non-discrimination rights of the two categories.'—S O'Leary, 'Free Movement of Persons and Services' in P Craig and G de Búrca, *The Evolution of EU Law* (Oxford, Oxford University Press, 2011) 502. For a view that there is still an important difference as regards the rights granted by the market freedoms, on the one hand, and Art 21 TFEU, on the other, see C O'Brien, 'Social Blind Spots and Monocular Policy Making: The ECJ's Migrant Worker Model' (2009) 46 *Common Market Law Review* 1107; RCA White, 'Revising Free Movement of Workers' (2010) 33 *Fordham International Law Journal* 1563, 1564 and 1583–84.

move, reside, or take-up/pursue an economic activity in a cross-border context, appears to be redundant.[33] In the words of Davies,

> Since all workers and established people are also citizens, one can imagine that the specialised Treaty articles conferring their rights could then be done away with, and the same logic that allowed them to bring their families and gain social advantages could be applied to Art 18 [now Article 21 TFEU]. Then every EU citizen could go anywhere, and live anywhere, within the EU as if she was a national of that state. This is the Nirvana point, to which we are slowly headed. Not only will it have social benefits, but it will have legal ones; all of the Treaty rules on free movement of workers, established people, and service providers and recipients, may be abolished, and replaced by this nice, tidy, general, constitutional-looking combination of Arts 12 and 18 [now Articles 18 and 21 TFEU].[34]

Such a Treaty amendment would, in essence, mirror the development of secondary legislation in the area. As we have seen, Directive 2004/38[35] has consolidated a large number of pieces of secondary legislation which governed different categories of Union citizens depending on their status (worker, self-employed economic actor, economically inactive but self-sufficient Union citizen, student, retiree) and brought them under one umbrella which, inter alia, elucidates the meaning of the right to free movement and residence bestowed on all Union citizens by the Treaty. Nonetheless, the 2004 Directive maintains—to a certain extent—the distinction traditionally drawn among the different categories of Union citizens, and provides for different limitations and conditions that can legitimately be imposed on the exercise of the rights to free movement and residence, depending on the status of the Union citizen seeking to rely on these rights.

Although, at first glance, bringing all free movement of persons provisions under one umbrella provision appears to be an attractive move, both symbolically and practically, a more careful consideration of it reveals three problematic aspects.

Firstly, and perhaps most importantly, such a move gives rise to the danger of creating confusion as regards the role and aims of the personal market freedoms. As explained in the previous chapter, the personal market freedoms should be considered—and, from the Court's recent case-law it seems that they are considered—to have two equally important objectives: firstly, to serve as the tools for the construction and maintenance of a properly-functioning internal market *and* (when, as is suggested in this book, they are read together with the citizenship provisions) to act as sources of fundamental economic rights for the Union citizen. Moving the personal market freedoms to Part Two TFEU (ie the Citizenship Part) would create the danger that their economic aim will be downgraded or,

---

[33] In paragraph 49 of his Opinion in Case C-215/03 *Oulane* [2005] ECR I-1215, AG Léger noted that '[t]he development of Community law is undoubtedly towards the standardisation, or even the unity, of the rules on the freedom of movement of nationals of the Member States'.
[34] G Davies (n 19) 68; see also pp 121–22. This point was also, briefly, made by F Wollenschläger (n 20) 30.
[35] Dir 2004/38 (n 22).

worse, completely ignored.[36] This danger will, in fact, be greater if the provisions are not merely transferred to that Part but are completely abolished and subsumed within a single provision, the text of which will be along the lines of what is now Article 21 TFEU.

Secondly, and related to the above, is the point that transferring the personal market freedoms to Part Two TFEU, is particularly problematic because two of these provisions (Articles 49 and 56 TFEU) are not merely sources of fundamental rights for the Union citizen, but—as will be seen in the subsequent section—they are also sources of (non-fundamental) economic freedoms for artificial persons. In situations where, say, a corporation wishes to exercise its freedom of establishment to set-up a branch in another Member State, on which provision of the Treaty will it be able to rely in order to challenge obstacles to the exercise of this freedom? Surely, a provision which seeks to give to *Union citizens* the right to take-up and/or pursue an economic activity in another Member State/in a cross-border context, will not be the appropriate legal basis.

Thirdly, this move will widen the gap between the personal market freedoms, on the one hand, and the free movement of goods and capital, on the other. This appears to be going in the opposite direction of what seems to be the tendency in recent years, which points towards convergence of the market freedoms.[37] In addition, by taking the drastic step of repositioning the personal market freedoms and placing them within Part Two of the TFEU, whilst leaving the free movement of goods and capital provisions in Part Three ('Union Policies and Internal Actions'), the signal that will be given will be that the former should be treated, simply, as sources of fundamental economic rights for the Union citizen, whilst the latter will be merely tools for the construction and maintenance of the internal market. This, however, will provide a distorted picture of reality, since—as noted in the previous chapter—the personal market freedoms do still have as their aim (when they are read alone) to operate as tools in the process of building an internal market. Moreover, the free movement of goods and capital provisions have, in recent years, been interpreted in a manner which demonstrates that they may no longer have merely a market-building rationale of existence; and, as suggested in this book, these provisions should, also, be read together with the citizenship provisions and, in this way—like the personal market freedoms—be reconceptualised as sources of fundamental economic rights for the Union citizen.

Accordingly, and for the reasons cited above, the personal market freedoms should not be transferred to Part Two TFEU, and, even more so, should not be

---

[36] For a similar view, see P Caro de Sousa, *The European Fundamental Freedoms: A Contextual Approach* (Oxford, Oxford University Press, 2015) 82.

[37] D O'Keeffe and A Bavasso, 'Four Freedoms, One Market and National Competence: In Search of a Dividing Line' in D O'Keeffe and A Bavasso (eds), *Liber Amicorum in Honour of Lord Slynn of Hadley: Judicial Review in European Union Law* (The Hague, Kluwer, 2000); C Barnard, 'Fitting the Remaining Pieces into the Goods and Persons Jigsaw' (2001) 26 *European Law Review* 35; HD Jarass, 'A Unified Approach to the Fundamental Freedoms' in M Andenas and W-H Roth (eds), *Services and Free Movement in EU Law* (Oxford, Oxford University Press, 2002); A Tryfonidou, 'Further Steps on the Road to Convergence among the Market Freedoms' (2010) 35 *European Law Review* 36.

abolished and replaced by a provision akin to what is now Article 21 TFEU. The market freedoms should maintain their character—when read alone—as tools for the construction and maintenance of an internal market.

Perhaps the best option from the point of view of legal certainty, would be for the personal market freedoms to remain in Part III TFEU ('Union Policies and Internal Actions')—in this way confirming their role as internal market tools—whilst introducing in Part Two of the same Treaty a new provision granting to all Union citizens the fundamental rights to take-up an economic activity in another Member State which is going to be pursued there or in a cross-border context and to start pursuing an economic activity in a cross-border context. More specifically, the current Article 20 TFEU could be amended to include a general reference to the fundamental (economic) rights that Union citizens derive from EU law, whilst a new provision could be added after Article 21 TFEU, specifying which fundamental economic rights are granted by the Treaty to Union citizens.

IV. THE DISTINCTION BETWEEN NATURAL AND LEGAL PERSONS UNDER THE MARKET FREEDOMS

If one examines the Court's case-law where measures that lacked cross-border specificity were brought within the scope of the market freedoms, not all of those situations involved Union citizens who sought to exercise the (fundamental) rights that should now be considered to stem from the market freedoms, when—as suggested in this book—they are read together with the citizenship provisions. In some of that case-law, it was corporations that sought to rely on these provisions. Yet, the Court applied the same (broad) interpretation of these provisions, without specifying—as it should—that the measure (which lacked cross-border specificity) would only amount to a violation of the relevant provision in situations where it would restrict the exercise of the rights that *Union citizens* derive from these provisions.[38]

The freedom of establishment and the freedom to provide services provisions have, always, included within their personal scope *both* natural and legal persons.[39] In other words, the Treaty drafters recognised that *both* natural persons holding the nationality of a Member State as well as legal persons established in one of

---

[38] Baquero Cruz seems to also be advocating a different approach to the interpretation of the market freedoms, depending on whether they involve a Union citizen seeking to enforce a (fundamental) right or a legal person seeking to exercise its (purely instrumental) freedoms—J Baquero Cruz, 'The Case Law of the European Court of Justice on the Mobility of Patients: An Assessment' in F Benyon (ed), *Services and the EU Citizen* (Oxford, Hart Publishing, 2013) 103 and 105.

[39] Art 54(1) TFEU (which is within the Treaty Chapter on Establishment) provides that 'Companies or firms formed in accordance with the law of a Member State and having their registered office, central administration or principal place of business within the Union shall, for the purposes of this Chapter, be treated in the same way as natural persons who are nationals of Member States'. Art 62 TFEU which is part of the Services Chapter provides that 'The provisions of Articles 51 to 54 shall apply to the matters covered by this Chapter'.

the Member States should be free to provide services across borders or to set-up branches or take-up and pursue other types of economic activities falling within the scope of the freedom of establishment in the territory of another Member State. Moreover, *all* of the market freedoms can be *invoked* by legal persons. For instance, a company may rely on the free movement of goods provisions in order to ensure that it is not prevented from moving goods between Member States; a corporation can rely on the free movement of capital provisions to exercise its freedom to invest in another Member State or in a third-country; and a legal person may seek to rely on Article 45 TFEU as the employer of a 'worker' who is prevented from exercising the rights stemming from that provision.

One question which emerges is whether the same entitlements can be derived from the market freedoms by legal and natural persons. In other words, should these provisions be interpreted in the same manner, irrespective of whether they are invoked by natural or legal persons?

The text of the freedom of establishment and the freedom to provide services provisions and, in particular, Article 54(1) TFEU which is made applicable to services via Article 62 TFEU, appears to require that legal persons are treated in the same manner as natural persons when relying on these provisions. Such a reading is, of course, *to a certain extent*, plausible under a purely instrumental reading of these provisions (and of the market freedoms, in general): when the sole aim of these provisions was to ensure that economic actors would be able to have access to the market of another Member State by being free to take-up an economic activity in another Member State or across borders, this could and, actually, should also include legal persons. It goes without saying that the aim of building an internal market would not be able to be attained if only *natural* persons were able to exercise the economic freedoms granted to them by the Treaty; legal persons play an equally—if not more important—part in building an internal market.[40]

Yet, despite the fact that the main (primary) right traditionally granted to natural persons under a purely instrumental reading of the personal market freedoms—to take-up an economic activity in another Member State or in a cross-border context—can also easily be granted to legal persons, some of the (more personal) secondary rights that have been held to derive from these provisions cannot be extended to them.[41] For instance, it is quite obvious that the right to family reunification would be entirely irrelevant in a context involving, say, a corporate entity seeking to exercise its freedom to set-up a branch in the territory of another Member State. Moreover, as explained by Robin White, '[t]he free movement of business organizations remains subject to much greater limitations than the movement of individuals, even when the movement is for the same

---

[40] For the important role that companies play in the internal market, see J Snell, *Goods and Services in EU Law: A Study of the Relationship between the Freedoms* (Oxford, Oxford University Press, 2002) 26.
[41] RCA White (n 13) 260.

purpose'.[42] Accordingly, even under an *instrumental* reading of the market freedoms, a dichotomy exists in respect of the entitlements derived from these provisions: Member State nationals derive the primary (instrumental) right to take-up an economic activity in another Member State/in a cross-border context traditionally granted by these provisions but, also, some personal (albeit instrumental) secondary rights (family reunification rights, rights to social assistance benefits, and so on), whereas—as logic suggests—legal persons are only afforded the freedom to take-up and (then) pursue an economic activity in another Member State or in a cross-border context.[43]

One might, of course, question the appropriateness of this dichotomy, which results in a situation whereby the same Treaty provisions are used to grant different entitlements to different 'types' of beneficiaries.[44] The obvious response to this, however, is that it is not so much a matter of *excluding* a certain category of persons (ie legal persons) from entitlement to certain types of rights, but, rather, it is more that those rights are not of any interest or relevance to such persons. Hence, the dichotomy has ensued naturally, without this being the choice of the Treaty drafters.[45]

More difficult questions emerge, nonetheless, once it is accepted that the personal market freedoms should, now, be considered as not merely the tools for building an internal market but also, when read together with the citizenship provisions of the Treaty, as sources of fundamental rights for the Union citizen. Nic Shuibhne has wondered,

> We can assume that an EU citizen has a 'primary and individual right' to move and reside freely to provide or receive a service; but others (for example corporations or third country nationals established in one State providing services in another) have the 'freedom'

---

[42] RCA White (n 13) 260.

[43] J Snell, 'And then there were Two: Products and Citizens in Community Law' in T Tridimas and P Nebbia (eds), *European Union Law for the Twenty-First Century* (Oxford, Hart Publishing, 2004) Vol II, 61–62.

[44] An example of a market freedom which *is* interpreted differently depending on the situation (ie whether it is intra-EU or extra-EU) is Art 63 TFEU—for an explanation see J Snell, 'Free Movement of Capital: Evolution as A Non-Linear Process' in P Craig and G de Búrca (n 32) 564–73.

[45] As Countouris and Engblom have noted, 'over the years we have seen a growing—and fully justifiable—conceptual (and regulatory) separation between the sources regulating the freedom of establishment of *natural* persons, and the self-employed in particular, and that of legal persons, with the former category being progressively approximated to the "free movement of workers" regulatory scheme, at least in EU secondary legislation such as Directive 2004/38, and to a certain extent in provisions such as Article 15(2) of the Charter of Fundamental Rights of the EU (which crucially also refers to "citizens [that] provide services").' (p 10). However, the same authors argue that the same separation has not emerged in the context of the freedom to provide services where the Court has interpreted the free movement of services provisions in the same manner, irrespective of whether the service provider is a legal or natural person (p 17); on this point see also, J Snell (n 43). See N Countouris and S Engblom, '"Protection or Protectionism?"—A Legal Deconstruction of the Emerging False Dilemma in European Integration', UCL Labour Rights Institute On-Line Working Papers—LRI WP 1/2015 available at ucl.ac.uk/laws/lri/papers/1%20-2015%20-%20Protection%20or%20Protectionism.pdf.

so to do—does this matter? Does citizenship enhance the former set of rights within the context of economic activity beyond the standards of protection that the latter can expect?[46]

For the reasons given below, my answer to these questions is in the affirmative.[47]

As seen above, a distinction regarding the content of the material scope of the personal market freedoms has always existed, depending on whether it is natural or legal persons that are relying on these provisions. Member State nationals can always rely on these provisions to enforce primary economic rights *and* secondary rights of a more personal kind which are necessary for the exercise of the former. Conversely, legal persons can only rely on the same provisions in order to enforce purely economic freedoms—the freedom to provide and receive services across borders and the freedom of setting-up corporations in a different Member State or of setting-up branches in another Member State. Accordingly, there has always been a gap in entitlement between natural persons (who have been entitled to the full gamut of (instrumental) rights stemming from the personal market freedoms) and legal persons (who have only been entitled to the economic freedoms derived from these provisions).[48]

The reconceptualisation of the market freedoms as—also—sources of fundamental rights *for Union citizens* appears, nonetheless, liable to widen this gap.[49] Legal persons shall not merely receive just a portion of the full set of entitlements granted to Union citizens by these provisions (as has always been the case), but the freedoms derived by legal persons should, now, also, be interpreted differently from the fundamental economic rights derived from these provisions by Union citizens. More specifically, whilst the freedoms that legal persons derive from these provisions should only be found to be restricted if the purely economic aim of the market freedoms (to contribute to the construction and maintenance of the internal market) is impeded, the rights derived by Union citizens from these provisions

---

[46] N Nic Shuibhne, 'The Outer Limits of EU Citizenship: Displacing Economic Free Movement Rights?' in C Barnard and O Odudu (eds), *The Outer Limits of European Union Law* (Oxford, Hart Publishing, 2009) 185. See also, P Caro de Sousa, 'Quest for the Holy Grail—Is a Unified Approach to the Market Freedoms and European Citizenship Justified?' (2014) 20 *European Law Journal* 499, 514.

[47] De Cecco seems to have a different view. He has noted that one of the potential problems with a possible reconceptualisation of the free movement of goods provisions as sources of fundamental rights for the Union citizen is, exactly, that 'to treat these provisions as fundamental rights of *EU citizens* would introduce fragmentation in the internal market, because the same right would lose its fundamental status when relied on by non-EU nationals. Yet, it is practically unthinkable to separate cases that involve third country nationals from those that involve EU citizens'—see F de Cecco, 'Fundamental Freedoms, Fundamental Rights and the Scope of Free Movement Law' (2014) 15 *German Law Journal* 383, 397.

[48] For a somewhat similar view see RCA White (n 13) 130.

[49] ibid, 261. Caro de Sousa appears to be considering this problem and points out that '[a] better option would be to rationalize the case law on the protection of individuals under the market freedoms as relating to European Citizenship alone. In other words, the scope of European Citizenship should be distinguished from the scope of the market freedoms: the latter refer to economic rights and should be restricted to situations of inter-State movement with an economic purpose, while the former refers to a fundamental right of a more political nature which covers situations that may overlap with, but are more extensive than, those falling under the market freedoms.'—P Caro de Sousa (n 36) 217.

(when they are read in conjunction with the citizenship provisions) should be considered fundamental and, thus, must be interpreted in a way which reflects this.

Since the freedoms derived by legal persons should be considered to be purely instrumental, it should be necessary to prove cross-border specificity in order for a restriction of them to be established, since the aim, here, is not to ensure that legal persons are free to enforce these freedoms for their own sake but, only, to ensure that the relevant economic activity can be taken-up and (then) pursued in a cross-border context, without the person doing so being disadvantaged. Conversely, as explained in the previous chapter, when the rights stemming from the market freedoms are treated as fundamental rights—which is the case when these are enforced by Union citizens—a requirement of cross-border specificity can no longer be imposed. Moreover, there should be—and there are, already, in the context of the personal market freedoms—differences at the justification stage of the assessment: whilst it has always been required that a narrow approach to the interpretation of the limitations attached to the personal market freedoms should be taken, the Court stressed in *Orfanopoulos and Oliveri* that in cases involving Union citizens, a particularly strict approach to the interpretation of these limitations must be taken.[50]

The important question, of course, is whether the above distinction regarding a) the types of rights/freedoms that are derived from the personal market freedoms, b) the interpretation of these rights/freedoms, and c) the procedure that is followed when determining whether there is a breach of these provisions, would be legally warranted. In my view, the answer to this question is 'yes', though—as will be seen below—a Treaty amendment along the lines of the one proposed in the previous section, may be a good way of bringing further clarity in relation to this matter.

Practically speaking, it seems that there is nothing wrong with distinguishing between natural persons and legal persons, when it comes to the grant of entitlements under the market freedoms. As noted earlier, it is clear that considerations that must be taken into account in situations involving natural persons (eg the need to respect and protect fundamental human rights, the need to grant family reunification rights, etc) do not arise in situations involving artificial persons. Hence, these two categories of persons are differently situated and, accordingly, a difference in their treatment simply reflects their different position. In fact, it would appear plainly wrong to treat inanimate objects in the same manner as human beings, since it would be absurd to argue that corporations should—in the same way as natural persons—enjoy, for instance, the right to be accompanied by their family members in the territory of another Member State.

Yet, the distinction that has ensued between legal persons and Union citizens which is set to widen if the suggestions made in this book are followed, points to the main problem that is set to arise in this context, which is lack of clarity. Traditionally, it had been clear that although Member State nationals and legal

---

[50] Joined Cases C-482 & 493/01 *Orfanopoulos and Oliveri* [2004] ECR I-5257, para 65.

persons derived different entitlements from the market freedoms, the common entitlements were *interpreted* in the same way (eg the freedom of establishment was interpreted in the same, instrumental, manner for both legal and natural persons—there was a requirement of cross-border specificity). After Maastricht, nonetheless, not only do legal persons derive different entitlements from the market freedoms but the rights they derive—even when they are, in essence, the same as the fundamental rights granted to natural persons (eg the right to establish a branch in another Member State), *should be* (though, in practice, at the moment they are not) interpreted differently, in order to reflect their different nature. This, however, may prove problematic because it will create uncertainty and will give rise to the possibility of abuse since—being aware of the more extensive interpretation afforded to the rights stemming from the market freedoms when these are relied on by Union citizens than by legal persons—actions challenging national measures for their compatibility with these provisions may be (artificially) brought by natural persons (instead of—or in addition to—by legal persons), in order to secure a more favourable reading of these provisions.

Are there any solutions to this?

If, as suggested in chapter five, the market freedoms are read together with the citizenship provisions, in situations where they are invoked by Union citizens, whilst they continue to be applied alone when they are relied on by corporations, this will draw a natural distinction, making it clear that the interpretation of these provisions will differ in these two different contexts.

Alternatively, the solution suggested in the previous section could be adopted, in case the Treaty drafters would be willing to amend the Treaty in the way proposed: under this solution, the market freedoms would remain where they are in the TFEU (ie in Part Three) and would be interpreted as bestowing simply economic (instrumental) freedoms to legal persons in order to ensure that the latter can initiate economic activities in a cross-border context, whereas Part Two of the Treaty would be amended to expressly grant to all Union citizens the fundamental economic rights stemming from the market freedoms.[51]

V. SHOULD THE PERSONAL SCOPE OF THE PERSONAL MARKET FREEDOMS BE EXTENDED TO COVER THIRD-COUNTRY NATIONALS?

Another issue that needs to be considered once it is accepted that the market freedoms should—when read together with the citizenship provisions—be reconceptualised as sources of fundamental economic rights for the Union citizen,

---

[51] This solution is quite similar to the situation which exists with regards to the rights that non-EU citizens who are nationals of States which have an association agreement with the EU derive from EU law. It should be recalled that some of the association agreements signed by the EU with third countries include provisions which are similar in their wording to the personal market freedoms. Nonetheless, the Court—being aware that these provisions and the personal market freedoms have different aims—interprets the two sets of provision in a different manner. See eg Case C-371/08 *Ziebell* [2011] EC I-12735.

is the position of third-country nationals under these provisions. Should these provisions—when read alone and, thus, when they are used merely as tools for building an internal market—continue to exclude third-country nationals from their scope?

It is well-established that, when it comes to natural persons, the personal scope of the personal market freedoms only includes persons who hold the nationality of one of the Member States.[52] Although Article 45 TFEU only makes reference to 'workers' which could, easily, be read to also mean workers who are third-country nationals, the Court made it clear relatively early on that the personal scope of Article 45 TFEU can only include Member State nationals.[53] This had, after all, also been obvious in secondary legislation in the area, which has always specified that it is only Member State nationals that can benefit from the freedom of movement for workers.[54] Conversely, the exclusion of third-country nationals from the personal scope of Article 49 TFEU is obvious from the wording of the provision, which makes it clear that it is only 'nationals of a Member State' that can rely on it. The position with regards to the freedom to provide services is somewhat different: although the first paragraph of Article 56 TFEU grants the freedom to provide services to nationals of Member States, its second paragraph goes on to give competence to the EU legislature to 'extend the provisions of the Chapter to nationals of a third country who provide services and who are established within the Union'. Nonetheless, to date no action has been taken to this effect,[55] and, accordingly, the personal scope of Article 56 TFEU—like the other personal market freedoms—covers only Member State nationals.[56]

---

[52] Case C-230/97 *Awoyemi* [1998] ECR I-6781, para 29. See A MacGregor and G Blanke, 'Free Movement of Persons within the EU: Current Entitlements of EU Citizens and Third Country Nationals—a Comparative Overview' (2002) 8 *International Trade Law and Regulation* 173, 184; G Davies (n 19) 205–06; PJ Slot and M Bulterman, 'Harmonization of Legislation on Migrating EU Citizens and Third Country Nationals: Towards a Uniform Evaluation Framework?' (2005–06) *Fordham International Law Journal* 747, 767. For a criticism of this, see D Kochenov and M van den Brink, 'Pretending There is No Union: Non-Derivative *Quasi*-Citizenship Rights of Third-Country Nationals in the EU' in D Thym and M Zoetewij Turhan (eds), *Degrees of Free Movement and Citizenship* (The Hague, Martinus Nijhoff, 2015).

[53] Case 238/83 *Meade* [1984] ECR 2631. For a summary of the reasons which would justify the expansion of the scope of Art 45 TFEU to cover third-country nationals, see R Plender, 'An Incipient Form of European Citizenship' in FG Jacobs (ed), *European Law and the Individual* (North Holland, 1976) 43.

[54] This has been the case under both Reg 1612/68 on freedom of movement for workers within the Community [1968] OJ L257/2 and its successor Reg 492/2011 on freedom of movement for workers within the Union [2011] OJ L141/1.

[55] In the late 1990s, there was a proposal for a Directive granting to third-country nationals the freedom to provide cross-border services ([1999] OJ C67/17); this was, however, withdrawn by the Commission—see the Communication from the Commission, 'Withdrawal of Commission Proposals which are no Longer of Topical Interest' COM (2004) 542 final/2.

[56] This was confirmed in, inter alia, Case C-290/04 *Scorpio* [2006] ECR I-9461, paras 67–68. In addition, it should be noted that the citizenship provisions obviously apply only to Member State nationals. And, as pointed out by O'Leary, although Art 18 TFEU prohibits any discrimination on grounds of nationality and in this context 'Member State nationality is not specified, this provision is confined to the scope of application of the Treaty and is therefore taken to apply to nationals of Member States only'—S O'Leary (n 32) 35. See, also A Epiney, 'The Scope of Article 12 EC: Some Remarks on the Influence of European Citizenship' (2007) 13 *European Law Journal* 611, 614.

214 *Persisting Conundrums*

The exclusion of third country nationals from the personal scope of the personal market freedoms,[57] is also reflected in the EU Charter of Fundamental Rights (EUCFR) and, in particular, in its Article 15, which provides:

1. *Everyone* has the right to engage in work and to pursue a freely chosen or accepted occupation.
2. *Every citizen of the Union* has the *freedom to seek employment, to work, to exercise the right of establishment and to provide services in any Member State.*
3. Nationals of third countries who are authorised to work in the territories of the Member States are entitled to working conditions equivalent to those of citizens of the Union.[58]

As Maas has pointed out,

> The tension between rights for EU citizens and rights for others remained and is evident, for example, in the Charter's article on the freedom to choose an occupation and the right to work: everyone has the right to engage in work and to pursue a freely chosen or accepted occupation; only EU citizens have the freedom to seek employment, to work, to exercise the right of establishment, and to provide services in any member state; and third-country nationals authorized to work in the member states are entitled to working conditions equivalent to those of EU citizens. This makes three separate categories of rights holders within a single Charter article.[59]

Accordingly, although Union citizens should derive fundamental, economic, rights from the market freedoms (when these are read with the citizenship provisions), third-country nationals cannot derive *any* freedoms from the personal market freedoms (though, as already seen, they derive rights from these provisions via mobile Union citizens who are their family members).[60] It should be noted, nonetheless, that—as we saw in chapter four—third-country nationals derive enforceable rights from the free movement of goods and the free movement of capital provisions.

The question that will be explored in this subsection, therefore, is whether the exclusion of third-country nationals from the scope of application of the personal market freedoms is acceptable.

The first problematic aspect of the exclusion of third-country nationals from the personal scope of the personal market freedoms is that it does not make sense

---

[57] Of course, as seen earlier, third-country nationals who are family members of migrant Union citizens have—through the latter—derivative rights which stem from the personal market freedoms and the secondary legislation attached to them. Moreover, third-country nationals who are lawfully admitted into the EU can move between Member States as 'posted workers'. Finally, apart from certain third-country nationals who enjoy rights which are similar to the free movement rights granted to Union citizens by virtue of association agreements between their country of nationality and the EU (eg the EC-Switzerland Association Agreement on the free movement of persons [2002] OJ L114/6 and the EEA Agreement [1994] OJ L1/3), certain third-country nationals enjoy limited rights to reside in another Member State subject to certain provisos—A MacGregor and G Blanke (n 52) 186; M Bell, 'The Principle of Equal Treatment: Widening and Deepening' in P Craig and G de Búrca (n 32) 620.
[58] Emphasis added.
[59] W Maas (n 25) 71–72.
[60] S O'Leary (n 32) 35–38.

from an economic point of view.⁶¹ Although it was not illogical to consider that the immediate, first, step for building an internal market in labour and services would be to ensure that Member State nationals are free to move between Member States for the purpose of taking-up and pursuing an economic activity, this is, clearly, not sufficient for building a genuine internal market. As Article 26(2) TFEU provides, '[t]he internal market shall comprise an area without internal frontiers in which the free movement of goods, persons, services and capital is ensured in accordance with the provisions of the Treaties'. What is important for an internal market to be built and maintained is that goods, passive and active economic actors, services and capital can move freely within it, as if there are no borders. In fact, the free movement of goods provisions appear to reflect this, given that—as seen in chapter four—once goods have entered the EU, they enjoy free circulation and are assimilated to EU goods.⁶² From this it follows that any persons lawfully resident and/or established within the EU should be able to move freely as economic actors, irrespective of whether they hold the nationality of a Member State or not;⁶³ the aim of building and maintaining an internal market in labour is furthered just the same, whether the migrant economic actor is a Member State national or not.

As Wiesbrock has noted,

> the exclusion of TCNs from the citizenship rights of Union citizens has long been considered an anomaly within the EU internal market. It is considered to be inconsistent with the goals and functioning of the internal market to exclude third-country nationals from free movement in the EU, whereas they have long been permitted to fully participate in the Internal Market from the 'demand side', as recipients of services and purchaser [sic] of goods.⁶⁴

Becker has, even, noted that extending the rights stemming from the market freedoms to third-country nationals, is not merely desirable but may, actually, be required in order to enable the EU to have sufficient numbers of workers to 'satisfy

---

⁶¹ See T Hoogenboom, 'Integration into Society and Free Movement of Non-EC Nationals' (1992) 2 *European Journal of International Law* 36; S Iglesias Sánchez, 'Free Movement of Third Country Nationals in the European Union? Main Features, Deficiencies and Challenges of the new Mobility Rights in the Area of Freedom, Security and Justice' (2009) 15 *European Law Journal* 791, 792–94; D Kochenov and M van den Brink (n 52). In 1989, the European Parliament proposed that the personal scope of the market freedoms should be extended to cover third-country nationals (see European Parliament Resolution on the Joint Declaration Against Racism and Xenophobia and an Action Programme by the Council of Ministers [1989] OJ C69/40, 42 (para 5)). The proposal was, however, rejected by the Council of Ministers.

⁶² Case 41/76 *Donckerwolcke* [1976] ECR 1921.

⁶³ For a similar view see D Kochenov, 'Ius Tractum of Many Faces: European Citizenship and the Difficult Relationship between Status and Rights' (2009) 15 *Columbia Journal of European Law* 169, 224.

⁶⁴ A Wiesbrock, 'Granting Citizenship-related Rights to Third-Country Nationals: An Alternative to the Full Extension of European Union Citizenship?' (2012) 14 *European Journal of Migration and Law* 63, 90.

its labor markets and keep pension systems afloat', in view of its aging population and declining birth rates.[65]

Accordingly, an approach akin to that followed in the context of the free movement of goods would be more apt, which would mean that once third-country nationals have lawfully entered the EU, they should be able to move freely between Member States for an economic purpose.[66] In fact, as pointed out by O'Leary, granting the right to non-discrimination on the grounds of nationality only to workers holding the nationality of a Member State 'may have rendered third-country workers more attractive to prospective employers in the Community',[67] since the latter may be willing to work under conditions which are more beneficial from the point of view of the employer. This creates a situation of (reverse) discrimination against Union citizens which distorts competition in the internal market. It would, therefore, make much more economic sense to include within the personal scope of the personal market freedoms third-country nationals who have been lawfully admitted into the EU and who are lawfully resident in one of the Member States.[68] Of course, in case such a step was taken, third-country nationals would only be able to derive the economic *freedom* to have access to the market of another Member State and to pursue an economic activity in the territory of another Member State or in a cross-border context, and they would not be entitled to the more extensive fundamental economic rights that the EU (should) grant to its own citizens.

The argument for including third-country nationals within the personal scope of the personal market freedoms becomes even clearer, in contexts which are not so much concerned with the free movement of economic actors but, rather, with the free movement of commodities (goods, services, and capital). Since the aim of Article 56 TFEU is not, merely, to ensure that Member State nationals have the freedom to provide or receive services in a cross-border context but, also, to ensure that services (as such) can move between Member States, it is, obviously, not important who the provider (or the recipient) of the services is, but, simply, whether the services themselves can be provided across border. In other words, irrespective of whether the legal or natural person that is 'hiding' behind a service holds EU nationality, the aim of building an internal market is furthered just the same, if the services are freely provided between Member States. Hence, it would make much more economic sense if the EU legislature exercised the power given to it by Article 56 TFEU and made legislation extending the personal scope of that provision to third-country nationals. In fact, this would bring the personal scope of Article 56 TFEU (when it comes to services as products), in line with the personal scope of the provisions governing the free movement of goods. As seen

---

[65] MA Becker, 'Managing Diversity in the European Union: Inclusive European Citizenship and Third-Country Nationals' (2004) 7 *Yale Human Rights and Development Law Journal* 132, 170; see also, more broadly, 169–71 of the same article.
[66] For a similar argument see S O'Leary (n 32) 38.
[67] ibid, 37. See, also, R Plender (n 53).
[68] This has been suggested by, inter alia, T Hoogenboom (n 61).

in chapter four, the free movement of goods provisions—which do not make any reference to 'persons', 'traders' or 'Member States nationals'—can be relied on by *anyone* (ie Member State national or not, legal or natural person) who is involved in a situation which concerns goods that move between Member States. Accordingly, just as these provisions can be relied on by third-country nationals or non-EU corporate entities involved in the inter-State trade of goods (inter-State here referring to two or more Member States), Article 56 TFEU should be held to be applicable to anyone (even third-country nationals) involved in the cross-border trade in services.[69]

In fact, Advocate General Léger in his Opinion in *Scorpio* relied on a number of reasons in support of his argument that Article 56 TFEU should include within its personal scope third-country nationals who wish to provide or receive services across borders. Firstly, he noted that

> it does not follow either from the wording of Article 59 [now 56] of the Treaty or from the case-law of the Court that enjoyment by a service provider of the freedom provided for in that article is conditional upon the service provider showing that his contractual partner who is the recipient of the services is a national of a Member State.[70]

Secondly, he noted that it does not follow from the wording of that provision that a service provider must hold the nationality of a Member State.[71] Agreeing with the Commission's view, as expressed in its written observations in the case, the Advocate General pointed out that

> it is unjustified and unreasonable to distinguish according to the nationality of the service provider, because that would require the recipient of the service systematically to obtain, and check, information concerning the nationality of his trading partners established in another Member State.[72]

Finally, the Advocate General agreed with one of the submissions made in the case, that 'to accept that protection of a recipient of services depends on the nationality of his contractual partner would amount to depriving freedom to provide services of a significant part of its effects.'[73]

The second problematic aspect of the limitation of the personal scope of the personal market freedoms to Union citizens whilst excluding third-country

---

[69] The main provision which governs the free movement of capital (Art 63 TFEU) does not only apply in situations where third-country nationals wish to rely on it to move capital between Member States but also in situations involving the free movement of capital between Member States and third countries, though, the extension of the scope of the personal market freedoms in this manner is unnecessary if the economic aim of the personal market freedoms is, simply, to ensure that a properly-functioning *internal* market is built and maintained.

[70] *Scorpio* (n 56), Opinion of AG Léger, para 119.

[71] ibid, para 120.

[72] ibid, para 121. For a similar argument see Case C-484/93 *Svensson and Gustavsson* [1995] ECR I-3955, Opinion of AG Elmer, para 38, though it should be noted that the AG concluded that Art 56 can only be relied on by Member State nationals and, thus, the personal scope of that provision should not be extended to cover third-country nationals.

[73] *Scorpio* (n 56), para 122.

nationals, is that this creates a clear incentive for abuse. Entrepreneurs who are third-country nationals and wish to provide cross-border services within the EU internal market or to build a conglomerate operating within more than one Member State, will be advised to 'hide' behind a company established in accordance with the laws of a Member State which is active in the EU internal market. In this way, the economic actor is, in reality, a third-country national hiding behind the façade of a legal person who, through it, can take-up and pursue an economic activity in the European internal market. In view of the above and the ease with which, nowadays, legal persons can be established, it is questionable whether the exclusion of third-country nationals from the scope of some of the personal market freedoms—ie those which can be relied on by legal persons (Articles 49 and 56 TFEU)—makes any sense.

This is, also, rather problematic and leads to artificial choices when it comes to the market freedom that is relied upon. The free movement of capital can, '[r]emarkably and uniquely',[74] apply both to situations which involve the movement of capital within the EU *and* between an EU Member State and a non-EU country. Conversely, the freedom of establishment and the freedom to provide services can, only, be relied on by the former. The arbitrariness of the exclusion of third-country nationals from the scope of application of the latter freedoms whilst they are included within the scope of the free movement of capital provisions becomes obvious in cases where both the free movement of capital and one of the other market freedoms may be relevant.[75]

An obvious example of this is *Fidium Finanz*.[76] At issue was the compatibility with EU law of German rules which required companies to obtain an authorisation, before they could grant credit on a commercial basis to customers established in Germany. On the facts of the case, the German authorities denied a Swiss company the right to grant such credit, on the ground that it did not have the authorisation required by German law. The Swiss company brought an action against the German authorities for the annulment of the decision adopted against it, claiming that it amounted to a breach of the provisions governing the free movement of capital. The Court held that the impugned rules affected primarily the freedom to provide services and any restriction on the free movement of capital was merely a consequence of the restriction on the freedom to provide services; hence, it was only the former freedom that could apply to the facts. However, since Fidium Finanz was not established in a Member State and since the provisions governing the freedom to provide services are only applicable to companies established in an EU Member State, a violation of Article 49 EC (now Article 56 TFEU) could not be found on the facts of the case. Accordingly, Germany was able to continue

---

[74] J Snell (n 44) 551.
[75] See eg the situation in *Svensson and Gustavsson* (n 72) (though the Court did not deal with this issue); Case C-452/04 *Fidium Finanz* [2006] ECR I-9251.
[76] *Fidium Finanz* (n 75).

applying those rules to companies established in non-Member States. It should be highlighted that Fidium Finanz—possibly being aware of the more limited scope *ratione personae* of the provisions governing the freedom to provide services—argued its case based solely on the free movement of capital.

Accordingly, it is my contention that the personal scope of *all* the market freedoms should, now, be broadened to include third-country nationals. However, these provisions should be interpreted differently when invoked by third-country nationals (or legal persons) than when invoked by Union citizens (in which case they must be read together with the citizenship provisions). More specifically, third-country nationals—like legal persons—should be considered to derive mere instrumental—economic—freedoms from these provisions, which are afforded to them for the purpose of furthering the economic aims of the Treaty, and not the fundamental economic rights that Union citizens derive from them *qua* citizens. In addition, apart from the fact that different entitlements will be made available to third-country nationals than those granted to Union citizens, the market freedoms will have to be interpreted differently when they are relied on by third-country nationals than when they are relied on by Union citizens; for instance, the notion of 'restriction' should be interpreted differently in these two contexts.

VI. (FUNDAMENTAL) HUMAN RIGHTS vs (FUNDAMENTAL) ECONOMIC RIGHTS

An important question that emerges as a result of the reconceptualisation of the market freedoms as sources of fundamental rights for the Union citizen concerns the relationship between the latter and fundamental (human) rights,[77] as these are protected under the Charter and as general principles of EU law. In particular, in a case involving a clash between these two sets of rights—a 'clash of titans' as characterised by De Vries[78]—which of the two should prevail? How should these two categories of rights be balanced against each other? Should there be a presumption that one of the two should prevail, or should they be viewed as being of equal importance from the point of view of EU law?

In its early case-law, the Court had not been confronted with such a clash. This can possibly be explained by the fact that the market freedoms were originally viewed—as explained in earlier parts of this book—as merely sources of instrumental freedoms and rights which could, clearly, not be put on a par with fundamental human rights. The Court was, therefore, simply required—in some

---

[77] In this chapter, the term 'human rights' is broadly used as an umbrella term encompassing, inter alia, civil, political and social rights.
[78] S de Vries, 'The Protection of Fundamental Rights within Europe's Internal Market after Lisbon—An Endeavour for More Harmony' in S de Vries, U Bernitz and S Weatherill (eds), *The Protection of Fundamental Rights in the EU After Lisbon* (Oxford, Hart Publishing, 2013) 60.

cases—to decide whether national measures caught by the market freedoms which were, allegedly, justified by a non-economic objective, were (also) compliant with the fundamental human rights protected as general principles of EU law—an assessment which was, often, delegated to the referring national court.[79] The Court was not faced with a difficult dilemma, since the fundamental human rights protected under EU law and the freedoms and rights stemming from the market freedoms did not fight each other, but worked together to require the non-application of national measures which were contrary to both.[80]

The possibility of a clash between fundamental human rights and the rights stemming from the market freedoms has, however, become more real as a result of the expansion of the material scope of the market freedoms in recent years:

> Once EU free movement law is revealed to exert such a broad impact that it is likely to affect national measures protecting EU fundamental rights, there arises a tension. Pressure is loaded on the EU—most obviously, the Court—to take account of that fundamental rights context in assessing the justification advanced in support of trade-restrictive national measures ... EU economic law becomes porous in the sense that measures that appear to conflict with the free movement rules may nevertheless be saved with reference to their role in protecting or promoting fundamental rights.[81]

Moreover, the gradual metamorphosis of the market freedoms into sources of fundamental rights for the Union citizen has meant that EU law is no longer only seen as the source of certain fundamental *human* rights—in situations falling within its scope—but is also the source of fundamental *economic* rights. Although in most instances, the protection of the above sets of rights can go hand in hand and they can, therefore, coexist harmoniously, it is inevitable that in certain instances, a clash between them will emerge.

Accordingly, it is no surprise that in some of its post-Maastricht jurisprudence, the Court was confronted with a direct clash between fundamental human rights and the economic rights stemming from the market freedoms. In fact, the way that the Court responded to this challenge confirms one of the main arguments of this book, which is that the ECJ now views (some of) the market freedoms as sources of *fundamental* economic rights, which, as such, are in a position of equality with

---

[79] See eg Case C-260/89 *ERT* [1991] ECR I-2925 (national broadcasting monopoly—when assessing whether the monopoly was justified on the ground of public policy, it had to be examined whether it was not breaching the right to freedom of expression); and Case C-368/95 *Familiapress* [1997] ECR I-3689 (national measure which restricted the free movement of goods and was, allegedly, justified by the need to maintain press diversity had to be assessed for its compliance with the right to freedom of expression).

[80] Writing in the early 1990s, Coppel and O'Neill accused the Court of granting to the market freedoms a status equivalent to that of fundamental human rights which—according them—was inappropriate, as the latter should be given a higher status—J Coppel and A O'Neill, 'The European Court of Justice: Taking Rights Seriously?' (1992) 29 *Common Market Law Review* 669, especially 689–691.

[81] S Weatherill, 'From Economic Rights to Fundamental Rights' in S de Vries, U Bernitz and S Weatherill (n 78) 22–23.

(some of)[82] the *fundamental* human rights protected under EU law.[83] It should be noted, nonetheless, that as explained in the previous chapter, the market freedoms should only be viewed as sources of *fundamental* rights when they are relied on by Union citizens and when they are read together with the citizenship provisions. This means that the rights deriving from them should be considered as fundamental and, thus, as being on an equal footing with the fundamental human rights protected under EU law, only in situations where the market freedoms are invoked by Union citizens and not—as in the cases to be discussed below—when they are relied on by legal persons. The same is the case when the market freedoms are invoked by third-country nationals.

The first case where the Court was invited to balance fundamental human rights with fundamental economic rights was *Schmidberger*,[84] where the Court was faced with a direct conflict between the free movement of goods, on the one hand, and the fundamental rights to freedom of assembly and freedom of expression of individuals, on the other. The case emerged as a result of the authorisation granted tacitly by the Austrian authorities to a group of environmental protesters who wished to demonstrate on a part of the Brenner motorway, which is a main route for lorries carrying goods from northern to southern Europe. As a result of the demonstration, the motorway remained closed for nearly 30 hours, which meant that the movement of transport carrying goods was blocked. When an action was brought by a company against Austria claiming a violation of Article 30 EC (Article 34 TFEU) read in conjunction with Article 5 EC (Article 4(3) TEU) (the duty of cooperation), Austria relied on the need to protect the fundamental human rights of the demonstrators, as a mandatory requirement. The Court accepted that the need to protect or respect fundamental human rights is a legitimate interest which can be used as a justification for a restriction of one of the market freedoms,[85] and then it 'proceeded actively to assess the balance',[86] and found that the Austrian action was, indeed, justified. The Court, therefore, accepted that *on the particular facts of the case*, the protection of fundamental, human rights should prevail over the need to protect the free movement of goods between Member States.

Similarly, in the *Omega* case, which involved a conflict between the right to human dignity and the freedom to provide services, the Court, again, found that

---

[82] When it comes to the most fundamental human rights from which there can be no derogation under any circumstances (eg the right to life, the right to human dignity, the right to be free from torture), these should prevail under all circumstances, even over other *fundamental* rights (including fundamental economic rights like the ones stemming from the market freedoms). Accordingly, the term 'fundamental human rights' in the remainder of this section will not be taken to refer to such rights.

[83] E Spaventa, 'Federalisation Versus Centralisation: Tensions in Fundamental Rights Discourse in the EU' in M Dougan and S Currie (eds), *50 Years of the European Treaties: Looking Back and Thinking Forward* (Oxford, Hart Publishing, 2009) 361.

[84] Case C-112/00 *Schmidberger* [2003] ECR I-5659.

[85] ibid, para 74.

[86] S Weatherill (n 81) 25.

the need to protect the former prevailed over the latter and, thus, a German measure which amounted to a restriction on the free movement of services from other Member States into Germany was justified by the need to protect the human dignity of individuals.[87] This case is also important because

> Germany could rely on its particular conception of human dignity, shaped by its history and political culture and enshrined in its constitution, in order to justify a restriction to the free movement of services, even though this conception was not shared by other Member States.[88]

Moreover, like in *Schmidberger*, the Court in this case left a wide margin of appreciation to the relevant Member State (Germany) when deciding whether it could restrict the exercise of the fundamental rights stemming from the market freedoms in order to protect a fundamental human right. This demonstrates that 'greater deference to Member State choices is shown where the countervailing values to those of the market relate to what might be described as moral choices of a state.'[89]

Despite the fact that in the above two cases, the protection of fundamental human rights appeared to be treated on a par with the economic rights stemming from the market freedoms, and, on the facts of the case, it was decided that the former should prevail, the subsequent rulings in *Viking*[90] and *Laval*[91] have been criticised for being 'contaminated by an economic bias',[92] demonstrating a clear preference for the protection of the economic rights stemming from the market freedoms, at the expense of the collective social rights of workers.

Viking involved the question whether the collective action by the Finnish seamen's trade union which aimed to prevent an Estonian company from reflagging one of its vessels was in violation of the freedom of establishment, whilst in *Laval*, at issue was whether the collective action by Swedish labour unions which aimed to require a Latvian company that had posted its workers from Latvia to Sweden to comply with the more burdensome (for the employer) terms and conditions laid down in Sweden, was contrary to the free movement of services provisions. The conflict in both cases was, thus, between the economic freedoms of establishment and to provide services (invoked by *legal* persons) on the one hand, and, on the other, the fundamental social right to take collective action (which was a collective right of workers, in this instance). The Court began its analysis by stressing

---

[87] Case C-36/02 *Omega* [2004] ECR I-9609.
[88] A Iliopoulou Penot, 'The Transnational Character of Union Citizenship' in M Dougan, N Nic Shuibhne and E Spaventa (eds), *Empowerment and Disempowerment of the European Citizen* (Oxford, Hart Publishing, 2012) 22.
[89] D Ashiagbor, 'Unravelling the Embedded Liberal Bargain: Labour and Social Welfare Law in the Context of EU Market Integration' (2013) 19 *European Law Journal* 303, 315–16.
[90] Case C-438/05 *Viking* [2007] ECR I-10779.
[91] Case C-341/05 *Laval* [2007] ECR I-11767.
[92] S Weatherill (n 81) 26. For a similar view see P Syrpis and T Novitz, 'Economic and Social Rights in Conflict: Political and Judicial Approaches to their Reconciliation' (2008) 33 *European Law Review* 411; C Barnard, 'Social Dumping or Dumping Socialism?' (2008) 67 *Cambridge Law Journal* 262, 264; C Barnard, 'The Protection of Fundamental Social Rights in Europe after Lisbon: A Question of Conflicts of Interests' in S de Vries, U Bernitz and S Weatherill (n 78).

that 'the protection of fundamental rights is a legitimate interest which, in principle, justifies a restriction of the obligations imposed by Community law, even under a fundamental freedom guaranteed by the Treaty',[93] and underlined that the EU now has 'not only an economic but also a social purpose'.[94] It then left it to the referring courts to conduct the assessment as to whether the collective action which impeded the above market freedoms was justified or not.

The Court's approach in *Viking* and *Laval* has—as noted above—been criticised for privileging the economic fundamental rights stemming from the Treaty, at the expense of the fundamental social rights protected under EU law. This has been because the Court seems to have avoided presenting the conflict as being between two fundamental rights—one economic (the freedom of establishment and the freedom to provide services) and one social (the right to collective action)—and, instead, it presented the issue as one involving the breach of the rights stemming from the market freedoms and the need to rely on an objective justification (the protection of workers) in order to justify this. As Advocate General Trstenjak (writing extrajudicially) and Beysen noted, although in *Viking* the Court began its analysis by recognising that

> the collective actions at issue restricted the freedom of establishment of the ferry operator, the CJEU refrained from examining whether the EU fundamental right to take collective action was, as such, apt to justify this restriction on the freedom of establishment by the actions of the trade unions. Instead, the CJEU focused on the notion of protection of workers, which is inherent in the fundamental right to take collective action and which had already been recognised in settled case law as an overriding reason in the public interest ... A similar scheme of analysis was adopted by the CJEU in *Laval un Partneri*.[95]

Commenting on this aspect of the case, De Vries argued that instead of being considered a form of mandatory requirements or objective justifications, fundamental human rights should, instead, be considered as self-standing justification grounds similar to the Treaty derogations since, otherwise, they will not be able to be used to justify directly discriminatory measures and this will 'seriously jeopardise the idea that no a priori hierarchy exists between them [ie between fundamental human rights and the rights stemming from the market freedoms]'.[96] The approach that De Vries supports is, in fact, the approach that the Court had followed in *Schmidberger*.[97]

---

[93] *Laval* (n 91) para 93; *Viking* (n 90) para 45.
[94] *Laval* (n 91), para 105; *Viking* (n 90), para 79.
[95] V Trstenjak and E Beysen, 'The Growing Overlap of Fundamental Freedoms and Fundamental Rights in the Case-Law of the CJEU' (2013) 38 *European Law Review* 293, 312.
[96] S de Vries (n 78) 90. As AG Trstenjak noted in paragraph 198 of her Opinion in Case C-271/08 *Commission v Germany (occupational pensions)* [2010] ECR I-7091, in the subsequent Case C-346/06, *Rüffert* [2008] ECR I-1989, 'the Court considered, at least implicitly, the possibility that the fundamental social right to freedom of association, in itself, could justify a restriction on fundamental freedoms'.
[97] The Court's approach in *Omega* was not as clear, since in some of the paragraphs of the judgment, it treated the right to human dignity as an aspect of the public policy exception, rather than as a self-standing justification.

Advocate General Cruz Villalón in his Opinion in *Santos Palhota*, seems to have gone even further, by stressing that the protection of workers should not be treated as a mere derogation from the market freedoms—an argument which can, clearly, be extended to all fundamental rights protected under the Charter or as general principles of EU law:

> As a result of the entry into force of the Treaty of Lisbon, when working conditions constitute an overriding reason relating to the public interest justifying a derogation from the freedom to provide services, they must no longer be interpreted strictly. In so far as the protection of workers is a matter which warrants protection under the Treaties themselves, it is not a simple derogation from a freedom, still less an unwritten exception inferred from case-law. To the extent that the new primary law framework provides for a mandatory high level of social protection, it authorises the Member States, for the purpose of safeguarding a certain level of social protection, to restrict a freedom, and to do so without European Union law's regarding it as something exceptional and, therefore, as warranting a strict interpretation.[98]

Accordingly, the Advocate General seems to be of the view that instead of focusing on the fundamental right, the exercise of which appears to be restricted as a result of the contested measure and to treat the other fundamental right sought to be protected as a derogation from this right, the Court should treat both rights equally and should simply engage in a balancing exercise, without adopting a strict interpretation of either.

Hence, in an EU which *equally* values its economic and non-economic objectives and, with them, the fundamental economic and human rights it grants to its own citizens, there should not be a hierarchy of such rights.[99] As Advocate General Trstenjak has explained in her Opinion in *Commission v Germany (occupational pensions)*, '[i]n the case of a conflict between a fundamental right and a fundamental freedom, both legal positions must be presumed to have equal status'[100] and the best approach is to conduct an individual assessment in each case applying the principle of proportionality:[101]

> Therefore, if in an individual case, as a result of exercising a fundamental right, a fundamental freedom is restricted, a fair balance between both of those legal positions must be sought. In that regard, it must be presumed that the realisation of a fundamental freedom constitutes a legitimate objective which may limit a fundamental right. Conversely,

---

[98] Opinion of AG Cruz Villalón in Case C-515/08 *Santos Palhota* [2010] ECR I-9133, para 53.
[99] See eg the Opinion of AG Trstenjak in *Commission v Germany* (n 96), para 187. See, also, V Skouris, 'Fundamental Rights and Fundamental Freedoms: The Challenge of Striking a Delicate Balance' (2006) 17 *European Business Law Review* 225; A Usai, 'The Freedom to Conduct a Business in the EU, its Limitations and its Role in the European Legal Order: A New Engine for Deeper and Stronger Economic, Social, and Political Integration' (2013) 14 *German Law Journal* 1868.
[100] Opinion of AG Trstenjak in *Commission v Germany* (n 96), para 81.
[101] It should be noted that the AG uses the term 'fundamental freedoms' when referring to the rights stemming from the market freedoms, but from her analysis it is obvious that she considers fundamental freedoms to have the same qualities as fundamental rights (unlike the approach followed in this book—see ch 1 for an explanation of the terminology used in the book)—the reader should bear this in mind in order to avoid any confusion.

however, the realisation of a fundamental right must be recognised also as a legitimate objective which may restrict a fundamental freedom.[102]

The Advocate General then explained that a 'double proportionality test' should be applied for determining whether on the particular instance before the Court, the claimed fundamental right should prevail:

> if a conflict between such fundamental freedoms and fundamental rights is established, it must be determined whether, having regard to all the circumstances of the case, fundamental freedoms may justify a restriction on the fundamental right to bargain collectively and the fundamental right to autonomy in that process or conversely, whether those fundamental rights demand that the scope of those fundamental freedoms and the secondary law based thereupon must be limited.[103]

Accordingly, the correct approach *in situations where the market freedoms are invoked by Union citizens* is to consider that fundamental human rights are on a par with fundamental economic rights and, thus, the starting point must be that these are equally important from the point of view of EU law. The particular facts of the case must, then, be taken into account in order to decide which set of rights should prevail *in that particular instance*, applying the double test of proportionality suggested by Advocate General Trstenjak and quoted above. Yet, and following the practice of the European Court of Human Rights (ECtHR), the balancing exercise between the various fundamental rights that are invoked in the case should be left to the national courts and Member States should be given a *wide* margin of appreciation.[104] As the ECtHR noted in *Chassagnou v France*,[105]

> The balancing of individual interests that may well be contradictory is a difficult matter, and Contracting States must have a broad margin of appreciation in this respect, since the national authorities are in principle better placed than the European Court to assess whether or not there is a 'pressing social need' capable of justifying interference with one of the rights guaranteed by the Convention.

The preceding analysis, therefore, leads us to the following conclusions.

Firstly, it should be remembered that—for the reasons explained in the previous chapter—the market freedoms can only be considered as the sources of *fundamental* economic rights when they are invoked by Union citizens and are, thus, read together with the citizenship provision. Hence, when they are relied on by legal persons or natural persons who do not hold the nationality of a Member State (third-country nationals), they should only be viewed as sources of instrumental freedoms having as their aim simply to build and maintain an internal market. What this means is that a clash between *fundamental* economic rights

---

[102] Opinion of AG Trstenjak in *Commission v Germany* (n 96), para 188.
[103] ibid, para 84.
[104] For a comparison of the use of the margin of appreciation in the context of the EU and ECHR, see JA Sweeney, 'A "Margin of Appreciation" in the Internal Market: Lessons from the European Court of Human Rights' (2007) 34 *Legal Issues of Economic Integration* 27.
[105] *Chassagnou and others v France* App nos 25088/94, 28331/95 and 28443/95 (ECtHR, 24 April 1999), para 113.

226 Persisting Conundrums

(stemming from the market freedoms) and *fundamental* human rights protected under EU law, should only be considered to emerge in situations where the market freedoms are invoked by Union citizens; a clash between *fundamental* rights does not emerge when the market freedoms are invoked by corporations or third-country nationals in order to challenge the actions of Member States or (where applicable) individuals, seeking to protect the fundamental human rights of other persons.

Secondly, and relating to the above point, whether the person relying on the market freedoms (together with the citizenship provisions) in a case is a Union citizen or not, will have an important impact on the relationship of the rights invoked. In situations where Union citizens rely on the market freedoms, the two sets of rights that clash (ie fundamental economic rights and fundamental human rights) should be considered equal and, thus, the answer to the question of which set of rights should prevail on the facts of the case will require an individual assessment of the situation and a clear application of the principle of proportionality, along the lines proposed by Advocate General Trstenjak, as seen above. Conversely, in situations where the market freedoms are not invoked by Union citizens and, thus, the freedoms and rights stemming from them are purely instrumental, the presumption should be that fundamental human rights should prevail and, thus, any actions of Member States (or, where applicable, individuals) which seek to protect such rights should be presumed to be lawful and it is the need to protect the rights and freedoms stemming from the market freedoms that should be treated as an exception (and, as such, interpreted strictly).

Thirdly, in situations where the market freedoms (together with the citizenship provisions) are invoked by Union citizens, the double proportionality test suggested by Advocate General Trstenjak should be applied. Taking into account the fact that both sets of rights that are invoked are fundamental and that national courts and authorities are in a better position to balance them and to make the proportionality assessment, the matter should be left to the national court to decide, and a wide margin of appreciation should be left to Member States when determining either ex ante (national authorities) or ex post (the courts) which of the two rights should prevail in a specific situation. For the same reason, a soft proportionality approach should be taken, considering, in essence, whether it is reasonable to limit one of the two fundamental rights at issue, in order to prevent a breach of the other.

VII. INDIVIDUAL RIGHTS vs COLLECTIVE RIGHTS

Another difficult issue that has emerged as a result of the broadening of the scope of application of the market freedoms in the manner seen in the previous chapters, is that in certain instances, the fundamental *individual* rights stemming from these provisions are privileged over *collective* interests. In other words, the elevation of the market freedoms into sources of fundamental rights for the Union citizen creates the possibility of a clash between individual fundamental rights and collective rights/interests. This conflict can be seen in a number of different contexts but in this section—and for reasons of space—the focus will only be on three.

The first 'conflict' that emerges is that between the individual fundamental (economic) rights stemming from the market freedoms and the collective interest in sufficient market regulation (and regulation, more broadly). In particular, as noted in the previous chapter, given that the market freedoms apply, now, also in situations where there is no cross-border specificity and, hence, these provisions appear to be prohibiting *any* kind of measure—even those that simply regulate an activity or a situation in a neutral manner—this means that the collective interest of Union citizens in regulation is now constantly pitted against the fundamental economic rights of individual Union citizens. As explained in chapter five, it is now necessary for the Court to explicitly recognise a mandatory requirement/ objective justification of the protection of the collective interest in regulation.

This, however, does not, in itself, guarantee that the right balance between individual fundamental rights and the collective interest in regulation will be achieved.

It is well-established that any exceptions to the market freedoms must be read restrictively, and this has become even more pronounced after the introduction of the status of Union citizenship.[106] Moreover, apart from certain areas which are considered particularly sensitive from the point of view of the Member States where the Court conducts a soft proportionality assessment,[107] in the majority of situations in EU free movement law, the Court applies this principle rigorously, seeking to establish whether there is a less restrictive alternative which can achieve the same objective by impeding—or impeding to a lesser extent—the exercise of Treaty rights. In other words, the need to protect other interests (including the collective interest in market regulation) which interfere with the exercise of the rights stemming from the market freedoms is, in effect, valid only as a weapon of last resort. This, unavoidably, creates a bias in favour of individual rights and against national market regulation.

Accordingly, not only is (the majority) of national market regulation now potentially capable of needing to be justified under EU law, but the balance—when the justification assessment will be conducted—is likely to tilt in favour of individual rights.

A possible solution to this conundrum is that when it comes to Member State market-regulation measures that lack cross-border specificity and are, thus, neutral between intra-State and cross-border economic transactions/activities, the Court (or national court deciding the case) should consider whether they are justified by the need to ensure that the internal market is a regulated market *and* in

---

[106] *Orfanopoulos and Oliveri* (n 50) para 65.
[107] As explained elsewhere, there are certain (sensitive) areas where the Court does not wish to second-guess the choices of the Member States and, thus, applies a (very) light touch when assessing whether a national measure is proportionate—see A Tryfonidou, 'The Federal Implications of the Transformation of the Market Freedoms into Sources of Rights for the Union Citizen' in D Kochenov (n 3).

doing so, it must apply a soft proportionality test which will, in essence, simply check whether the measure is 'manifestly inappropriate'—ie a measure will not be stricken down unless it is manifestly inappropriate for the purpose of achieving its objectives.[108] This will also mean that the fact that there is a less restrictive alternative must not count against the impugned regulation, given that Member States must remain free to (*neutrally*) regulate their markets in whichever way they consider best, taking into account the specific characteristics of *their own* market. An obvious example of this is the Court's approach in *Schmidberger*, seen in the previous section.[109] The Court in that case applied proportionality with a light touch and did not consider whether there was a less restrictive alternative which would impede the free movement of goods to a lesser extent.[110] Of course, in situations where there *is* cross-border specificity, the stricter 'less restrictive alternative' proportionality test should be applied. As noted by Tridimas, '[t]he more tenuous the restriction on free movement, the more lax the standard of proportionality'.[111]

The second example of a 'clash' is that between the individual economic (fundamental) rights and the collective rights of workers. In cases such as *Viking*[112] and *Laval*,[113] there is an underlying conflict 'between the individual rights of the employer to free movement and the collective rights of the trade union workers to strike to protect the interests of their (individual) members'.[114] Judging from the Court's case-law to date—seen in the previous section—it seems that the Court has been biased in favour of protecting the individual rights of Union citizens (or, on the facts, of a company!). As Ashiagbor has pointed out,

> In relation to strike action, the Court of Justice in *Laval* and *Viking* offered a clear recognition of the right to strike in EU law, but subjected this right to potentially debilitating limitations. In particular, while accepting that the market rights under the Treaty must be balanced against the objectives pursued by social policy, the proportionality assessment applied to judge the legality of collective action was such that it is difficult to envisage strike action that interferes with exercise of a free movement right being readily justified. To satisfy the requirement that its resort to strike action was proportionate, a trade union would need to show that it had pursued alternative forms of action that were less restrictive of freedom of establishment.[115]

---

[108] Tridimas has explained that when wide discretion is left to the legislature (which, admittedly, should be the case in situations involving the promulgation of *neutral* national legislation which sets to balance a private (individual) insterest vis-à-vis a public (collective) interest), a soft proportionality test is applied—T Tridimas, *The General Principles of EU Law* (Oxford, Oxford University Press, 2006) 138. For an explanation of the 'manifestly inappropriate' test, see pages 142–49 of the same book.

[109] *Schmidberger* (n 84).

[110] A Biondi, 'Free Trade, a Mountain Road and the Right to Protest: European Economic Freedoms and Fundamental Individual Rights' (2004) 1 *European Human Rights Law Review* 51, 58–61.

[111] T Tridimas (n 108) 215. See, also, p 216, where the same author noted that 'a soft proportionality test may be the *quid pro quo* for extending the scope of free movement'.

[112] *Viking* (n 90).

[113] *Laval* (n 91).

[114] C Barnard, 'The Protection of Fundamental Social Rights in Europe after Lisbon' (n 92) 45. See, also, P Syrpis and T Novitz (n 92) 412–13.

[115] D Ashiagbor (n 89) 312–13.

Accordingly, and as suggested earlier in this section, a more balanced approach will need to be taken, whereby the individual (fundamental) right of Union citizens to take-up or pursue an economic activity in another Member State and the collective (fundamental) rights of workers will be placed on an equal footing—this being the starting point of the enquiry—and the principle of proportionality will have to be used effectively in order to judge which of these two sets of rights should prevail on the particular situation that is before the Court (or the national court, if the matter is referred back to it). As suggested earlier, a soft proportionality approach should be followed, under which the Court should consider whether restricting the rights of workers on the facts of the case in order to ensure respect of the rights of individuals is manifestly inappropriate, and vice-versa. Yet, as explained earlier, in situations where the market freedoms are invoked by legal persons and, thus, where the entitlements stemming from these provisions should be considered to be instrumental freedoms, the starting point of the enquiry should be different: it should be considered that the collective fundamental rights of workers should prevail unless the need to protect the individual freedoms of legal persons is necessary on the particular facts of the case. Hence, the need to protect the individual economic freedoms of legal persons should be considered a derogation from the fundamental collective rights of workers (eg to strike, etc) and a strict proportionality assessment should be conducted.

Finally, the third example of clash that has increasingly materialised in recent years is that between the individual economic rights stemming from the market freedoms and collective solidarity at the national level. Such a clash, of course, had already emerged even before the introduction of Union citizenship, when the Court interpreted the personal market freedoms and, in particular, the free movement of workers provisions, in an overly expansive manner, by bringing within their personal scope persons who earned much less than what they needed to be able to live in the host State and, thus, needed to supplement their income by having recourse to the social assistance system of the host State.[116]

Such a clash has, however, become even more prevalent following the introduction of Union citizenship. As seen in chapter two, although Directive 2004/38[117] provides that economically inactive Union citizens can only exercise their (fundamental) right to reside in the territory of another Member State (stemming from Article 21 TFEU) if they do not pose an unreasonable burden on the social assistance system of the host State, the Court held that there is 'a certain degree of financial solidarity between nationals of a host Member State and nationals of other Member States, particularly if the difficulties which a beneficiary of the right of residence encounters are temporary.'[118] Accordingly, and as seen in a number of cases, nationals of other Member States may, by virtue of their status as Union

---

[116] See Case 139/85 *Kempf* [1986] ECR 1741.
[117] Dir 2004/38 (n 22).
[118] Case C-184/99 *Grzelczyk* [2001] ECR I-6193, para 44.

citizens, claim social assistance benefits in the territory of another Member State, at least until the host State can prove that they pose an unreasonable burden on its social assistance system, taking into account all the specific circumstances of the particular case. Yet, the recent *Dano* judgment[119] demonstrates that the extent to which (economically inactive) Union citizens may claim social assistance benefits in the territory of another Member State, may have now been tempered by being confined to (rather) exceptional cases, given that persons who are not economically self-sufficient from their arrival in the host State cannot be considered to be able to exercise that right *ab initio*.

Moreover, when it comes to such a clash in situations involving the rights granted by the market freedoms, the obvious example that can be used is the ECJ's healthcare case-law, which we saw in chapter three. In that context, the Court has made it clear that healthcare cannot be entirely excluded from the scope of application of the market freedoms and Union citizens can rely on these provisions in order to challenge any national measures, including requirements of prior authorisation, which impede the (fundamental) right of Union citizens to move to another Member State in order to receive healthcare services. Of course, the Court has accepted, in principle, that there is a risk that the receipt of healthcare services in another Member State which requires the home State to foot the bill may seriously undermine the financial balance of the social security system of the latter, and, hence, this has been considered a ground on which a Member State— the home State—may rely in order to refuse to authorise one of its nationals to move to another Member State for the receipt of such services or to refuse—once someone has received such services abroad without a prior authorisation—to pay the bill. Yet, a quick glance at the justification assessment of the Court so far has demonstrated an unwillingness to accept that such a justification is made out on the particular facts of the case, in this way privileging the individual right to cross-border healthcare over the collective interest in national solidarity.[120] A change of approach at this justification assessment stage, however, according to which a soft proportionality assessment would be conducted when considering whether the above justification is made out, would lead to a more balanced approach between these individual rights and collective interests, in this context.

VIII. CONCLUSION

This chapter aimed to take the analysis further, beyond the focus of the previous chapters on the actual and normative interpretations of the market freedoms. As explained at the beginning of this chapter, the aim was to consider a number of conundrums that persist, and which have either been exacerbated or have (firstly) arisen as a result of the reconceptualisation of the market freedoms as sources

---

[119] Case C-333/13 *Dano* ECLI:EU:C:2014:2358.
[120] D Ashiagbor (n 89) 322–23.

of fundamental rights for the Union citizen. Without a doubt, the Court's—and, more broadly, the EU's—focus in the near future should, inter alia, be placed on resolving these conundrums. This chapter has, in fact, proposed a number of possible solutions to these conundrums. Nonetheless, before any action for resolving these issues can be taken, a clearer stance needs to be taken on a number of issues: on the exact delimitation of the personal and (especially) material scope of the market freedoms; on the interpretation of the notion of 'restriction'; on the application of the various filtering mechanisms when determining whether a national measure does amount to a restriction in the first place; on the assessment of justifications (including proportionality); and on *how*—if the suggestions made in this book are followed—the interpretation of the market freedoms should differ when these provisions are invoked by Union citizens, on the one hand, and when they are relied on by legal persons or third-country nationals, on the other. Only once these issues are clarified, will it be possible for the conundrums identified in this chapter to be effectively resolved.

Part IV

Conclusion

7
Conclusions

AS EXPLAINED IN chapter one, this book had a threefold objective: firstly, to consider how the introduction and development of the status of Union citizenship has (and may have) affected the interpretation of the market freedoms (chapters three and four); secondly, to assess whether the way that these provisions are now interpreted is legally warranted, taking into account both their text and their current aims (chapter five); and, thirdly, to identify any conundrums or problems that have emerged or are likely to emerge as a result of the re-interpretation of the market freedoms in the light of Union citizenship, and to consider how, if at all, these can best be (re)solved (chapter 6).

This final chapter will summarise the conclusions drawn from the analysis in this book and, in particular, from each of the main chapters.

The analysis in chapters three and four demonstrated that whilst it is clear that the interpretation of the personal market freedoms has, indeed, been affected by the introduction of Union citizenship, the same cannot be said with certainty about the free movement of goods and, even more so, about the free movement of capital which, for this reason, has been left outside the scope of this book.

In chapter three it was explained that although the market freedoms had, even before Maastricht, been interpreted as sources of *rights* for Member State nationals, the Court's approach to their interpretation demonstrated that these rights were purely instrumental, merely granted in order to enable and encourage individuals to contribute to the aim of building an internal market. The only primary right traditionally granted by these provisions was—for the more stationary personal market freedoms—the right to take-up an economic activity *in another Member State* which would be permanently pursued there or in a cross-border context; and—for the freedom to provide services provisions—the right to start providing (or receiving) services across borders, either by moving between Member States for this purpose or, simply, by staying in the home State and providing or receiving services across borders (eg via the internet). It was also explained that before Maastricht, measures had to have cross-border specificity in order to be caught by these provisions, since in this way it was ensured that the aim of building a smoothly-functioning (ie regulated) internal market would be furthered: national measures which *neutrally* regulated economic activities should not be caught by the market freedoms and only national measures which *specifically* affected cross-border economic activities should be subjected to EU scrutiny.

The chapter then proceeded to consider how the personal market freedoms have been interpreted in the period after Maastricht (ie after the status of Union citizenship was introduced). It was explained that during this period the Court in some of its case-law explicitly noted the need to re-interpret the personal market freedoms in light of the fact that (some of) their beneficiaries (ie natural—but not legal—persons) are Union citizens. Moreover, the Court *continued* interpreting broadly the scope *ratione personae* of these provisions, as was the case even before the introduction of Union citizenship. Most importantly, however, after the Treaty of Maastricht came into force, the Court began to expand the material scope of the personal market freedoms in a number of different ways.

Firstly, in the Court's citizenship case-law it was indicated that the situations falling within the material scope of the personal market freedoms include those involving the exercise of the rights stemming from these provisions. This demonstrated that it would no longer be necessary to establish that the specific entitlement, benefit or advantage claimed falls within the material scope of these provisions and, thus, any national measures capable of impeding the exercise of the rights stemming from the market freedoms would, now, automatically fall within the scope of these provisions, and this would be so even if those measures touched on areas that were supposed to be wholly regulated at national level. Secondly, in its post-Maastricht case-law, the Court (implicitly) abolished the requirement of cross-border specificity when assessing whether a measure amounts to a restriction caught by these provisions in this way bringing within the scope of these provisions even measures which neutrally regulate an economic activity. Thirdly, a cluster of ECJ rulings demonstrated that the more stationary personal market freedoms would no longer be merely the source of the primary right to take-up an economic activity *in the territory of another Member State* but they would now also grant the primary right to start pursuing an economic activity in a cross-border context, even in situations where that economic activity had not, prior to that, been taken-up *in the territory of another Member State*. Hence, it was concluded that the material scope of *all* the personal market freedoms was, now, delimited in the same manner and the primary rights stemming from them could be consolidated to the following two: a) the right to take-up an economic activity in the territory of another Member State, which will be pursued in that Member State or in a cross-border context; b) the right to start pursuing an economic activity in a cross-border context.

The discussion then proceeded to examine whether stretching the material scope of these provisions in this manner is compliant with a purely instrumental-based reading of them and it was explained that it is not. It was, therefore, concluded that the most plausible rationale that could explain the expansion of the material scope of the personal market freedoms in the manner described earlier in the chapter, was the need to re-read these provisions in the light of Union citizenship and, in particular, to re-interpret them as sources of *fundamental* economic rights for the Union citizen.

Chapter four was devoted to the free movement of goods and focused on the interpretation of Article 34 TFEU. The starting point of the analysis was that the Court in this context has been much less forthcoming, and in none of its judgments did it make any reference to the relationship between the free movement of goods and the status of Union citizenship, and to the impact that the latter has had (or should have had) on the former. It was concluded that, although until recently the Court's case-law in this context demonstrated that there was a requirement of cross-border specificity in order for a measure to amount to a restriction caught by the free movement of goods provisions, recent ECJ rulings have demonstrated that such a requirement may have now been abolished in the context of Article 34 TFEU. This, it was suggested, offers an indication that the Court may have wished to re-read this provision as a source of the fundamental right to do business (involving the sale of goods) anywhere in the EU, without being restricted by unjustified and disproportionate regulation. Moreover, from being originally considered as a provision seeking, merely, to ensure the free movement of *goods* between Member States, Article 34 TFEU has been, gradually, read more broadly, as the source of a number of rights for individuals: the right of consumers to move to another Member State for the purpose of purchasing goods; the right to import goods from other Member States; and the right of traders to move to another Member State for the purpose of engaging in trade in goods there. The Court has, nonetheless, nowhere clarified whether these rights are granted to individuals *merely in situations which involve goods that move between Member States* (in which case they appear to be simply reflecting the Court's traditional interpretation of this provision as seeking to ensure the free movement of *goods*), nor has it made it clear whether the persons that can rely on these rights are *only those that hold the nationality of a Member State* (ie they are Union citizens) and thus that they are entitled to them *because* of that status and not in order to further the economic aims of the Treaty. Accordingly, many important questions remain unanswered in relation to Article 34 TFEU and, hence, it is still not possible to assess with certainty the impact that Union citizenship has had on the interpretation of this provision and on the free movement of goods provisions in general.

Chapter five aimed to consider whether the interpretation of the market freedoms in the manner seen in chapters three and four was legally warranted. For this purpose, the text of the market freedoms was, firstly, analysed, and it was concluded that *some* of the changes made by the Court to the interpretation of these provisions in recent years *can* be accommodated even under a literal approach to their interpretation. It was, then, considered whether the post-Maastricht changes made to the scope of application of the market freedoms could be justified by a teleological approach to the interpretation of these provisions. Hence, an examination of what appear to be—and what should be considered to be—the current aims of these provisions followed. It was explained that these provisions *should* continue to be considered as having as their sole aim to build (and maintain) a (properly-functioning) internal market. This aim, nonetheless, is incapable of justifying the inclusion within the scope of these provisions of situations which do not contribute to this aim. Hence, some of the changes made to the scope of the market freedoms in recent years and especially after Maastricht, are not warranted when the (sole) economic aim of these provisions is taken into account. It was, nonetheless, argued that these changes *can* be justified when these provisions are read *together with the citizenship provisions,* in which case the aim of this combination of Treaty Articles is to grant to Union citizens fundamental economic rights.

Accordingly, and since the changes that this book has identified as having been made to the market freedoms in recent years cannot be supported when these provisions are read alone, it has been suggested that a different approach should be taken in the future: when the grant of a right does not contribute to the achievement of the economic aim of the market freedoms, it should be read as stemming not from the market freedoms *alone,* but from the market freedoms *read in conjunction with the citizenship provisions.* This, however, also means that the broader interpretation of the market freedoms which cannot be justified by their economic rationale can only be adopted in situations where these provisions are invoked by Union citizens. Conversely, and since the citizenship provisions do not apply to legal persons and third-country nationals, the latter can only rely on the market freedoms *alone.* In this latter scenario, it has been argued, the Court should revert to its traditional, instrumental, approach, whereby the market freedoms are read merely as seeking to serve as the tools for building (and maintaining) an internal market, and, thereby, exclude from their scope any situations not contributing to this aim.

The second half of the chapter sought to make suggestions as to how the scope of the market freedoms (read in conjunction with the citizenship provisions) should now be delimited when these provisions are invoked by Union citizens and, thus, when the (broader) approach to their interpretation can be applied. It was argued that due to the fact that their broader scope now means that virtually *all* national measures can be caught by these provisions as 'restrictions' which require justification, the two main filtering mechanisms (remoteness and the purely internal rule) traditionally applied for filtering out measures which do not, on closer inspection, restrict the exercise of the rights stemming from these provisions, should be clarified and used more effectively by the Court; in fact, particular suggestions for the adoption of certain presumptions when applying these filtering mechanisms, have been made. It was also suggested that in *all* cases where measures which lack cross-border specificity are challenged, the Court (or the national court hearing the case) should consider whether the measure at issue is, nonetheless, justified by the need to ensure that the internal market is a regulated market.

The final main chapter of the book (chapter six) took the analysis further and beyond the exploration of the actual and normative interpretations of the market freedoms. The chapter sought to identify the various conundrums that have emerged or will emerge when it becomes clearer that the market freedoms are, indeed, sources of fundamental economic rights for the Union citizen. The analysis in the chapter also took into account the suggestions that have been made in this book and considered the difficulties that will emerge if these are adopted.

The first issue which becomes particularly problematic once it is accepted that the market freedoms are sources of fundamental rights for the Union citizen, is the fact that in certain circumstances, a distinction as to the enjoyment of the rights stemming from the market freedoms persists between EU citizens who are nationals of a Member State and EU citizens who are not. In particular, the TFEU itself (and its predecessors) and the Court of Justice through its case-law, have condoned such instances of differential treatment exercised by Member States between their nationals and the nationals of other Member States. Such examples are the public service and official authority exceptions from the personal market freedoms and the Treaty derogations which can be relied on to justify even (directly) discriminatory measures, and, in particular, the use of these derogations to justify the decision of Member States to deport from their territory (or to refuse to admit within their territory) nationals of other Member States, whereas it is clear that under international law, they cannot do so with regards to their own nationals. The differentiation between nationals and non-nationals is also condoned by the citizenship provisions of the Treaty (in particular, the provisions on political rights) and by (some) of the ECJ's citizenship case-law, which has allowed Member States to assume that their nationals automatically have a bond with their society, whereas non-nationals need to positively prove this. It was explained that this automatic differentiation between Union citizens, which is based simply on nationality, is unacceptable in a Citizens' Europe where Union citizens should under no circumstances be impeded from exercising the fundamental economic rights they derive from EU law *simply* because of their nationality.

Accordingly, it was explained that in all instances, there should be a presumption that nationals and non-nationals are similarly situated and the onus should, therefore, be on the Member States to prove that—for a particular reason—these two categories of Union citizens are not comparable. Moreover, a possible solution to this issue is to replace nationality with residence as the factor that should be taken into account in determining whether a person has a sufficient link with the society of a Member State, which would be a (more) acceptable ground of differentiation in a Citizens' Europe.

The second issue that was examined was whether the personal market freedoms should be removed from Part Three TFEU and a new provision along the lines of Article 21 TFEU should replace all of them and be the source of the rights currently stemming from them. It was explained that this would be problematic for a number of reasons and, thus, it was concluded that such a step would not be recommended. The best option from the point of view of legal certainty would, rather, be for the personal market freedoms to remain in Part Three of the TFEU, in this way confirming their role as market-building tools, whilst a new provision should be introduced in Part Two of the Treaty which would grant to all Union citizens the fundamental economic rights stemming from the market freedoms when—as suggested in this book—these provisions are read together with the citizenship provisions.

Next, it was examined whether the distinction that should be drawn between legal persons and Union citizens regarding the entitlements that they can derive from the market freedoms is legally warranted. In particular, it was examined whether it is problematic for these two categories of beneficiaries of the market freedoms to receive different entitlements from the *same* provisions, as has been suggested in this book. It was concluded that it is not, since the distinction in entitlement is based on the simple fact that these two categories of persons are not similarly situated.

The next issue that was considered was the distinction that the market freedoms have, always, drawn between Member State nationals and third-country nationals. Whilst third-country nationals can benefit from the free movement of goods and capital provisions, since—just like Union citizens—they can enforce the directly effective rights they derive from these provisions to move their goods between Member States or to move their capital between Member States and between Member States and third countries, they have, always, been excluded from the personal scope of the personal market freedoms. It was explained that the latter is problematic because it does not make sense from an economic point of view and it encourages third-country nationals to (artificially) 'hide' behind a company in order to be able to benefit from the freedom to provide services and the freedom of establishment provisions, whilst, leading to artificial choices when it comes to the market freedom that is relied upon. It was suggested that once third-country nationals have lawfully entered the territory of the EU, they should be able to rely on (all) the market freedoms (although they should only be considered to derive instrumental economic freedoms from them).

The clash between fundamental human rights and fundamental economic rights was the next conundrum that was considered. As explained, the broader delimitation of the scope of application of the market freedoms, together with their reconceptualisation as sources of fundamental economic rights for the Union citizen, means that the likelihood of a clash between fundamental economic rights and fundamental human rights is increased. It was suggested that when Union citizens rely on the market freedoms (read in conjunction with the citizenship provisions) in order to enforce the fundamental economic rights they derive from them, these rights and fundamental human rights (from which there can be a derogation) should be considered to be equal. This will require that an individual assessment—having as its basis the equality between the two rights that clash—should be conducted, where a double (soft) proportionality test (examining whether the restriction on each of these rights is justified) is applied. This individual assessment should be left to be conducted by the national court which should, also, be left a wide margin of appreciation.

Finally, another clash was examined—that between fundamental individual rights (eg the economic rights stemming from the market freedoms) and fundamental collective rights (eg the collective rights of workers to strike and the right to collective solidarity at Member State level). A solution along the lines of the one proposed for the previous conundrum was suggested for this issue: ie the rights should be placed on an equal footing without either of them being presumed to be on higher level and a double (soft) proportionality test should be applied.

The chapter concluded by noting that before these conundrums can be resolved, a clearer stance should be taken on a number of issues such as the exact delimitation of the personal and (especially) material scope of the market freedoms, the interpretation of the notion of 'restriction', the application of the various filtering mechanisms when determining whether a national measure does amount to a restriction in the first place, and the assessment of justifications.

Bibliography

Acierno, S, 'The Carpenter Judgment: Fundamental Rights and the Limits of the Community Legal Order' (2003) 28 *European Law Review* 398

Adam, S and Van Elsuwege, P, 'EU Citizenship and the European Federal Challenge through the Prism of Family Reunification' in D Kochenov (ed), *Citizenship and Federalism in Europe* (Cambridge, Cambridge University Press, 2016, forthcoming)

Armstrong, K, 'Mutual Recognition' in C Barnard and J Scott (eds), *The Law of the Single European Market: Unpacking the Premises* (Oxford, Hart Publishing, 2002)

—— and Bulmer, S, *The Governance of the Single European Market* (Manchester, Manchester University Press, 1998)

Arnull, A, 'The European Court and Judicial Objectivity: A Reply to Professor Hartley' (1996) 112 *Law Quarterly Review* 411

Ashiagbor, D, 'Unravelling the Embedded Liberal Bargain: Labour and Social Welfare Law in the Context of EU Market Integration' (2013) 19 *European Law Journal* 303

Athanassiou, P and Laulhé Shaelou, S, 'EU Accession from Within?—An Introduction' (2014) 33 *Yearbook of European Law* 335

Azoulai, L, 'The Court of Justice and the Social Market Economy: The Emergence of an Ideal and the Conditions for its Realization' (2008) 45 *Common Market Law Review* 1335

Baquero Cruz, J, *Between Competition and Free Movement: The Economic Constitutional Law of the European Community* (Oxford, Hart Publishing, 2002)

——, 'The Case Law of the European Court of Justice on the Mobility of Patients: An Assessment' in F Benyon (ed), *Services and the EU Citizen* (Oxford, Hart Publishing, 2013)

Barents, R, 'New Developments in Measures Having Equivalent Effect' (1981) 18 *Common Market Law Review* 271

Barnard, C, 'Fitting the Remaining Pieces into the Goods and Persons Jigsaw?' (2001) 26 *European Law Review* 35

——, 'Social Dumping or Dumping Socialism?' (2008) 67 *Cambridge Law Journal* 262

——, 'Restricting Restrictions: Lessons for the EU from the US' (2009) 68 *Cambridge Law Journal* 575

——, 'Derogations, Justifications and the Four Freedoms: Is State Interest Really Protected?' in C Barnard and O Odudu (eds), *The Outer Limits of European Union Law* (Oxford, Hart Publishing, 2009)

——, *The Substantive Law of the EU: The Four Freedoms* (Oxford, Oxford University Press, 2013)

——, 'The Protection of Fundamental Social Rights in Europe after Lisbon: A Question of Conflicts of Interests' in S de Vries, U Bernitz and S Weatherill (eds), *The Protection of Fundamental Rights in the EU After Lisbon* (Oxford, Hart Publishing, 2013)

—— and Deakin, S, 'Market Access and Regulatory Competition' in C Barnard and J Scott (eds), *The Law of the Single European Market: Unpacking the Premises* (Oxford, Hart Publishing, 2002)

Barrett, G, 'Family Matters: European Community Law and Third-Country Family Members' (2003) 40 *Common Market Law Review* 369

Becker, MA, 'Managing Diversity in the European Union: Inclusive European Citizenship and Third-Country Nationals' (2004) 7 *Yale Human Rights and Development Law Journal* 132

Bell, M, 'The Principle of Equal Treatment: Widening and Deepening' in P Craig and G de Búrca (eds), *The Evolution of EU Law* (Oxford, Oxford University Press, 2011)

Bermann, GA, 'Taking Subsidiarity Seriously: Federalism in the European Community and the United States' (1994) 94 *Columbia Law Review* 331

Bernard, N, 'Discrimination and Free Movement in EC Law' (1996) 45 *International and Comparative Law Quarterly* 82

——, 'On the Art of Not Mixing One's Drinks: *Dassonville* and *Cassis de Dijon* Revisited' in M Poiares Maduro and L Azoulai (eds), *The Past and Future of EU Law: The Classics of EU Law Revisited on the 50th Anniversary of the Rome Treaty* (Oxford, Hart Publishing, 2010)

Berry, E, 'The Deportation of "Virtual National" Offenders: The Impact of the ECHR and EU Law' (2009) 23 *Journal of Immigration, Asylum and Nationality Law* 11

Biondi, A, 'In and Out of the Internal Market: Recent Developments on the Principle of Free Movement' (1999–2000) *Yearbook of European Law* 469

——, 'Free Trade, a Mountain Road and the Right to Protest: European Economic Freedoms and Fundamental Individual Rights' (2004) 1 *European Human Rights Law Review* 51

Borgmann-Prebil, Y, 'The Rule of Reason in European Citizenship' (2008) 14 *European Law Journal* 328

Cambien, N, 'Annotation of *Metock*' (2009) 15 *Columbia Journal of European Law* 321

Carlier, J-Y, 'Annotation of *Zhu and Chen*' (2005) 42 *Common Market Law Review* 1121

Chalmers, D, 'Free Movement of Goods within the European Community: An Unhealthy Addiction to Scotch Whisky?' (1993) 42 *International and Comparative Law Quarterly* 269

——, 'Repackaging the Internal Market—The Ramifications of the *Keck* Judgment' (1994) 17 *European Law Review* 385

——, 'The Single Market: From Prima Donna to Journeyman' in J Shaw and G More (eds), *New Legal Dynamics of European Union* (Oxford, Clarendon Press, 1995)

——, Davies, G and Monti, G, *European Union Law: Cases and Materials* 2nd edn (Cambridge, Cambridge University Press, 2010) 459

——, Davies, G and Monti, G, *European Union Law: Cases and Materials* 3rd edn (Cambridge, Cambridge University Press, 2014)

Closa, C, 'The Concept of Citizenship in the Treaty on European Union' (1992) 29 *Common Market Law Review* 1137

Condinanzi, M, Lang, A and Nascimbene, B, *Citizenship of the Union and Freedom of Movement of Persons* (The Hague, Martinus Nijhoff, 2008)

Conway, G, *The Limits of Legal Reasoning and the European Court of Justice* (Cambridge, Cambridge University Press, 2012)

Coppel, J and O'Neill, A, 'The European Court of Justice: Taking Rights Seriously?' (1992) 29 *Common Market Law Review* 669

Costello, C, 'Annotation of *Donatella Calfa*' (2000) 37 *Common Market Law Review* 817

——, '*Metock*: Free Movement and "Normal Family Life" in the Union' (2009) 46 *Common Market Law Review* 587

Craig, P, 'Constitutions, Constitutionalism, and the European Union' (2001) 7 *European Law Journal* 130

──, 'The Evolution of the Single Market' in C Barnard and J Scott (eds), *The Law of the Single European Market: Unpacking the Premises* (Oxford, Hart Publishing, 2002)

──, 'The Treaty of Lisbon: Process, Architecture and Substance' (2008) 33 *European Law Review* 137

── and de Búrca G, *EU Law: Texts, Cases and Materials* (Oxford, Oxford University Press, 2011)

Currie, S, 'The Transformation of Union Citizenship' in M Dougan and S Currie (eds), *50 Years of the European Treaties: Looking Back and Thinking Forward* (Oxford, Hart Publishing, 2009)

Da Cruz Vilaça, JL and Piçarra, N, 'Are there Substantive Limits to the Amendment of the Treaties?' in JL da Cruz Vilaça, *EU Law and Integration: Twenty Years of Judicial Application of EU Law* (Oxford, Hart Publishing, 2014)

Dani, M, 'Assembling the Fractured European Consumer' (2011) 36 *European Law Review* 362

Daniele, L, 'Non-Discriminatory Restrictions to the Free Movement of Persons' (1997) 22 *European Law Review* 191

Dashwood, A, 'The limits of European Community Powers' (1996) 21 *European Law Review* 113

Davies, G, *European Union Internal Market Law* (London, Routledge, 2003)

──, *Nationality Discrimination in the European Internal Market* (The Hague, Kluwer, 2003)

──, '"Any Place I Hang my Hat?" or: Residence is the New Nationality' (2005) 11 *European Law Journal* 43

──, 'Understanding Market Access: Exploring the Economic Rationality of Different Conceptions of Free Movement Law' (2010) 11 *German Law Journal* 671

──, 'Discrimination and Beyond in European Economic and Social Law' (2011) 18 *Maastricht Journal of European and Comparative Law* 7

Dawes, A, 'A Freedom Reborn? The New Yet Unclear Scope of Article 29 EC' (2009) 34 *European Law Review* 639

Dawson, M, de Witte B and Muir E (eds), *Judicial Activism at the European Court of Justice* (Cheltenham, Edward Elgar, 2013)

De Boer, NJ, 'Fundamental Rights and the EU Internal Market: Just how Fundamental are the EU Treaty Freedoms? A Normative Enquiry Based on John Rawls Political Philosophy' (2013) 9 *Utrecht Law Review* 148

De Cecco, F, 'Fundamental Freedoms, Fundamental Rights and the Scope of Free Movement Law' (2014) 15 *German Law Journal* 383

De Sousa, P Caro, 'Through Contact Lenses, Darkly: Is Identifying Restrictions to Free Movement Harder than Meets the Eye? Comment on Ker-Optika' (2012) 37 *European Law Review* 79

──, ──, 'Quest for the Holy Grail—Is a Unified Approach to the Market Freedoms and European Citizenship Justified?' (2014) 20 *European Law Journal* 499

──, ──, *The European Fundamental Freedoms: A Contextual Approach* (Oxford, Oxford University Press 2015)

De Vries, S, 'The Protection of Fundamental Rights within Europe's Internal Market after Lisbon—An Endeavour for More Harmony' in S de Vries, U Bernitz and S Weatherill (eds), *The Protection of Fundamental Rights in the EU After Lisbon* (Oxford, Hart Publishing, 2013)

De Waele, H, 'EU Citizenship: Revisiting its Meaning, Place and Potential' (2010) 12 *European Journal of Migration and Law* 319

De Witte, B, 'Direct Effect, Supremacy and the Nature of the Legal Order' in P Craig and G de Búrca (eds), *The Evolution of EU law* (Oxford, Oxford University Press, 1999)

Di Federico, G, 'Access to Healthcare in the Post-Lisbon Era and the Genuine Enjoyment of EU Citizens' Rights' in L Serena Rossi and F Casolari (eds), *The EU after Lisbon: Amending or Coping with the Existing Treaties?* (Heidelberg, Springer, 2014)

Dinan, D, *Europe Recast: A History of European Union* (Basingstoke, Palgrave Macmillan, 2014)

D'Oliveira, HU Jessurun, 'European Citizenship: Its Meaning, Its Potential' in Dehousse (ed), *Europe after Maastricht: An Ever Closer Union* (Munich, CH Beck, 1994)

——, ——, 'Union Citizenship: Pie in the Sky?' in A Rosas and E Antola (eds), *A Citizens' Europe? In Search of a New Order* (London, Sage Publications, 1995)

Dougan, M, 'The Treaty of Lisbon 2007: Winning Minds, Not Hearts' (2008) 45 *Common Market Law Review* 617

Doukas, D, 'Untying the Market Access Knot: Advertising Restrictions and the Free Movement of Goods and Services' (2006–07) 9 *Cambridge Yearbook of European Legal Studies* 177

Durand, A, 'European Citizenship' (1979) 4 *European Law Review* 3

Editorial Comment: 'Freedoms Unlimited? Reflections on Mary Carpenter v. Secretary of State' (2003) 40 *Common Market Law Review* 537

Editorial Comment: 'Two-Speed European Citizenship? Can the Lisbon Treaty Help Close the Gap?' (2008) 45 *Common Market Law Review* 1

Eeckhout, P, 'Recent Case-Law on Free Movement of Goods: Refining *Keck* and *Mithouard*' (1998) 9 *European Business Law Review* 267

Enchelmaier, S, 'The Awkward Selling of a Good Idea, or a Traditionalist Interpretation of *Keck*' (2003) 22 *Yearbook of European Law* 249

——, 'Four Freedoms, How Many Principles' (2004) 24 *Oxford Journal of Legal Studies* 155

——, 'The ECJ's Recent Case-Law on the Free Movement of Goods: Movement in All Sorts of Directions' (2007) 26 *Yearbook of European Law* 115

——, '*Moped Trailers, Mickelsson & Roos, Gysbrechts*: The ECJ's Case Law on Goods Keeps on Moving' (2010) 29 *Yearbook of European Law* 190

——, 'Always at Your Service (within Limits): The ECJ's Case Law on Article 56 TFEU (2006–11)' (2011) 36 *European Law Review* 615

Epiney, A, 'The Scope of Article 12 EC: Some Remarks on the Influence of European Citizenship' (2007) 13 *European Law Journal* 611

Evans, A, 'European Citizenship' (1982) 45 *Modern Law Review* 497

——, 'European Citizenship: A Novel Concept in EEC Law' (1984) 32 *American Journal of Comparative Law* 679

Everson, M, 'The Legacy of the Market Citizen' in J Shaw and G More (eds), *New Legal Dynamics of European Union* (Oxford, Clarendon Press, 1995)

Fabbrini, F, 'The Political Side of EU Citizenship in the Context of EU Federalism' in D Kochenov (ed), *Citizenship and Federalism in Europe* (Cambridge, Cambridge University Press, 2016, forthcoming)

Fries, S and Shaw, J, 'Citizenship of the Union: First Steps in the European Court of Justice' (1998) 4 *European Public Law* 533

Gerstenberg, O, 'The Question of Standards for the EU: From "Democratic Deficit" to "Justice Deficit?"' in D Kochenov, G de Búrca and A Williams (eds), *Europe's Justice Deficit?* (Oxford, Hart Publishing, 2015)

Golynker, O, 'Annotation of *Förster*' (2009) 46 *Common Market Law Review* 2021

246 Bibliography

Gormley, LW, '"Actually or Potentially, Directly or Indirectly'? Obstacles to the Free Movement of Goods' (1989) 9 *Yearbook of European Law* 197

——, 'Two Years after *Keck*' (1996) 19 *Fordham International Law Journal* 866

——, 'The Definition of Measures Having Equivalent Effect' in A Arnull, P Eeckhout and T Tridimas (eds), *Continuity and Change in EU Law* (Oxford, Oxford University Press, 2008)

——, 'Free Movement of Goods and their Use—What is the Use of it?' (2009–10) 33 *Fordham International Law Journal* 1589

Goudappel, F, *The Effects of EU Citizenship: Economic, Social and Political Rights in a Time of Constitutional Change* (The Hague, TMC Asser Press, 2010)

Greer, SL and Sokol, T, 'Rules for Rights: European Law, Health Care and Social Citizenship' (2014) 20 *European Law Journal* 66

Handoll, J, 'Article 48(4) EEC and Non-National Access to Public Employment' (1988) 13 *European Law Review* 223

Hansen, JL, 'Full Circle: Is there a Difference between the Freedom of Establishment and the Freedom to Provide Services?' in M Andenas and W-H Roth (eds), *Services and Free Movement in EU Law* (Oxford, Oxford University Press, 2002)

Hartley, TC, 'The European Court, Judicial Objectivity and the Constitution of the European Union' (1996) 112 *Law Quarterly Review* 95

Hatzopoulos, V, 'Turkish Service Recipients under the EU-Turkey Association Agreement: *Demirkan*' (2014) 51 *Common Market Law Review* 647

Higgins, I, 'The Free and Not so Free Movement of Goods since *Keck*' (1997) 6 *Irish Journal of European Law* 166

Hill, TP, 'On Goods and Services' (1977) 23 *Review of Income and Wealth* 315

Hilson, C, 'Discrimination in Community Free Movement Law' (1999) 24 *European Law Review* 445

——, 'What's in a Right? The Relationship between Community, Fundamental and Citizenship Rights in EU Law' (2004) 29 *European Law Review* 636

Hoogenboom, T, 'Integration into Society and Free Movement of Non-EC Nationals' (1992) 2 *European Journal of International Law* 36

Horsley, T, 'Subsidiarity and the European Court of Justice: Missing Pieces in the Subsidiarity Jigsaw?' (2012) 50 *Journal of Common Market Studies* 267

——, 'Unearthing Buried Treasure: Art. 34 TFEU and the Exclusionary Rules' (2012) 37 *European Law Review* 734

Hublet, C, 'The Scope of Article 12 of the Treaty of the European Communities vis-à-vis Third-Country Nationals: Evolution at Last?' (2009) 15 *European Law Journal* 757

Iglesias Sánchez, S, 'Free Movement of Third Country Nationals in the European Union? Main Features, Deficiencies and Challenges of the new Mobility Rights in the Area of Freedom, Security and Justice' (2009) 15 *European Law Journal* 791

——, 'Fundamental Rights and Citizenship of the Union at a Crossroads: A promising Alliance or a Dangerous Liaison' (2014) 20 *European Law Journal* 464

Iliopoulou, A Penot, 'The Transnational Character of Union Citizenship' in M Dougan, N Nic Shuibhne and E Spaventa (eds), *Empowerment and Disempowerment of the European Citizen* (Oxford, Hart Publishing, 2012)

Infantino, G and Mavroidis, P, 'Inherit the Wind: A Comment on the *Bosman* Jurisprudence' in M Poiares Maduro and L Azoulai (eds), *The Past and Future of EU Law: The Classics of EU Law Revisited on the 50th Anniversary of the Rome Treaty* (Oxford, Hart Publishing, 2010)

Jacobs, FG, 'Citizenship of the European Union—A Legal Analysis' (2007) 13 *European Law Journal* 591

Janssens, C, Annotation of *Wolzenburg* (2010) 47 *Common Market Law Review* 831

Jansson, MS and Kalimo, H, '*De Minimis* Meets "Market Access": Transformations in the Substance—and the Syntax—of EU Free Movement Law?' (2014) 51 *Common Market Law Review* 523

Jarass, HD, 'A Unified Approach to the Fundamental Freedoms' in M Andenas and W-H Roth (eds), *Services and Free Movement in EU Law* (Oxford, Oxford University Press, 2002) 143

Kaczorowska, A, 'A Review of the Creation by the European Court of Justice of the Right to Effective and Speedy Medical Treatment and its Outcomes' (2006) 12 *European Law Journal* 345

Kadelbach, S, 'Union Citizenship' in A von Bogdandy and J Bast (eds), *Principles of European Constitutional Law* (Oxford, München, Hart Publishing, CH Beck Nomos, 2011)

Kaldellis, EI, 'Freedom of Establishment versus Freedom to Provide Services: An Evaluation of Case-Law Developments in the Area of Indistinctly Applicable Rules' (2001) 28 *Legal Issues of Economic Integration* 23

Kaupa, C, 'Maybe not Activist Enough? On the Court's Alleged Neoliberal Bias in its Recent Labor Cases' in M Dawson, B de Witte and E Muir (eds), *Judicial Activism at the European Court of Justice* (Cheltenham, Edward Elgar, 2013)

Kingreen, T, 'Fundamental Freedoms' in A von Bogdandy and J Bast (eds), *Principles of European Constitutional Law* (Oxford, München, Hart Publishing, CH Beck Nomos 2011)

Kmiec, K, 'The Origin and Current Meanings of "Judicial Activism"' (2004) 92 *California Law Review* 1441

Kochenov, D, '*Ius tractum* of Many Faces: European Citizenship and the Difficult Relationship between Status and Rights' (2009) 15 *Columbia Journal of European Law* 169

——, 'Annotation of *Rottmann*' (2010) 47 *Common Market Law Review* 1831

——, 'Regional Citizenships and EU Law: The Case of the Åland Islands and New Caledonia' (2010) 35 *European Law Review* 307

——, 'A Real European Citizenship: A New Jurisdiction Test: A Novel Chapter in the Development of the Union in Europe' (2011) 18 *Columbia Journal of European Law* 55

——, 'The Citizenship Paradigm' (2012–13) 15 *Cambridge Yearbook of European Legal Studies* 196

——, 'The Essence of EU Citizenship Emerging from the Last Ten Years of Academic Debate: Beyond the Cherry Blossoms and the Moon?' (2013) 62 *International and Comparative Law Quarterly* 97

——, 'The Right to Have What Rights? EU Citizenship in Need of Clarification' (2013) 19 *European Law Journal* 502

—— and Pirker, B, 'Deporting the Citizens within the Euroepan Union: A Counter-Intuitive Trend in Case C-348/09, P.I. V Oberbürgermeisterin der Stadt Remscheid' (2012–13) 19 *Columbia Journal of European Law* 369

—— and Plender, R, 'EU Citizenship: From an Incipient Form to an Incipient Substance? The Discovery of the Treaty Text' (2012) 37 *European Law Review* 369

—— and Van den Brink, M, 'Pretending There is No Union: Non-Derivative *Quasi*-Citizenship Rights of Third-Country Nationals in the EU' in D Thym and M Zoetewij

Turhan (eds), *Degrees of Free Movement and Citizenship* (The Hague, Martinus Nijhoff, 2015)

Konstadinides, T, 'La fraternite europeene? The Extent of National Competence to Condition the Acquisition and Loss of Nationality from the Perspective of EU Citizenship' (2010) 35 *European Law Review* 401

Kostakopoulou, D, 'Ideas, Norms and European Citizenship: Explaining Institutional Change' (2005) 68 *Modern Law Review* 233

——, 'European Union Citizenship: Writing the Future' (2007) 13 *European Law Journal* 623

——, 'European Union Citizenship: The Journey Goes On' in A Ott and E Vos (eds), *Fifty Years of European Integration: Foundations and Perspectives* (The Hague, TMC Asser Press, 2009)

——, 'When EU Citizens become Foreigners' (2014) 20 *European Law Journal* 447

—— and Ferreira, N, 'Testing Liberal Norms: The Public Policy and Public Security Derogations and the Cracks in European Union Citizenship' (2013–14) 20 *Columbia Journal of European Law* 167

Koutrakos, P, 'On Groceries, Alcohol and Olive Oil: More on Free Movement of Goods after *Keck*' (2001) 26 *European Law Review* 391

Krenn, C, 'A Missing Piece in the Horizontal Effect "Jigsaw": Horizontal Direct Effect and the Free Movement of Goods' (2012) 49 *Common Market Law Review* 177

Lang, J Temple, 'The Development of European Community Constitutional Law' (1991) 25 *International Lawyer* 455

Leleux, P, 'Recent Decisions of the Court of Justice in the field of Free Movement of Persons and Free Supply of Services' in FG Jacobs (ed), *European Law and the Individual* (Amsterdam, North-Holland, 1976)

Lenaerts, K, 'Constitutionalism and the Many Faces of Federalism' (1990) 38 *American Journal of Comparative Law* 205

Lonbay, J, 'Annotation of *Gebhard*' (1996) 33 *Common Market Law Review* 1073

Maas, W, *Creating European Citizens* (Lanham MD, Rowman & Littlefield Publishers, 2007)

MacGregor, A and Blanke, G, 'Free Movement of Persons within the EU: Current Entitlements of EU Citizens and Third Country Nationals—a Comparative Overview' (2002) 8 *International Trade Law and Regulation* 173

Maduro, M Poiares, '*Keck*: The End? The Beginning of the End? Or Just the End of the Beginning?' (1994) 1 *Irish Journal of European Law* 30

——, *We, The Court* (Oxford, Hart Publishing, 1998)

——, 'The Scope of European Remedies: The Case of Purely Internal Situations and Reverse Discrimination' in C Kilpatrick, T Novitz and P Skidmore (eds), *The Future of European Remedies* (Oxford, Hart Publishing, 2000)

——, 'Harmony and Dissonance in Free Movement' in M Andenas and W-H Roth (eds), *Services and Free Movement in EU Law* (Oxford, Oxford University Press, 2002)

Malecki, M, 'Do ECJ Judges all Speak with the Same Voice? Evidence of Divergent Preferences from the Judgments of Chambers' (2012) 19 *Journal of European Public Policy* 59

Maletic, I, *The Law and Policy of Harmonisation in Europe's Internal Market* (Cheltenham, Edward Elgar, 2013)

Mancini, GF, 'The Making of a Constitution for Europe' (1989) 26 *Common Market Law Review* 595

——, 'The Free Movement of Workers in the Case-Law of the Court of Justice' in D Curtin and D O'Keeffe (eds), *Constitutional Adjudication in EC and National Law. Essays in Honour of Justice T F O'Higgins* (Dublin, Butterworths, 1992)

Mantu, S, 'European Union Citizenship Anno 2011: Zambrano, McCarthy and Dereci' (2012) 26 *Journal of Immigration, Asylum and Nationality Law* 40

Meduna, M, '"Scelestus Europeus Sum": What Protection against Expulsion EU Citizenship Offers to European Offenders?' in D Kochenov (ed), *Citizenship and Federalism in Europe* (Cambridge, Cambridge University Press, 2016, forthcoming)

Meij, AWH and Winter, JA, 'Measures Having an Effect Equivalent to Quantitative Restrictions' (1976) 13 *Common Market Law Review* 79

Middelaar, L, *The Passage to Europe: How a Continent Became a Union* (Yale, Yale University Press, 2013)

Minderhoud, P, 'Directive 2004/38 and Access to Social Assistance Benefits' in E Guild, C Gortázar Rotaeche and D Kostakopoulou (eds), *The Reconceptualization of European Union Citizenship* (Leiden; Boston, Brill Nijhoff, 2014)

Morris, R, 'European Citizenship and the Right to Move Freely: Internal Situations, Reverse Discrimination and Fundamental Rights' (2011) 18 *Maastricht Journal of European and Comparative Law* 179

Mortelmans, K, 'Article 30 of the EEC Treaty and Legislation Relating to Market Circumstances: Time to Consider a New Definition?' (1991) 28 *Common Market Law Review* 115

——, 'The Common Market, the Internal Market and the Single Market, What's in a Market?' (1998) 35 *Common Market Law Review* 101

Neuvonen, PJ, 'In Search of (Even) More Substance for the "Real Link" Test: Comment on *Prinz and Seeberger*' (2014) 39 *European Law Review* 125

Neuwahl, N, 'The Place of the Citizen in the European Construction' in P Lynch, N Neuwahl and W Rees (eds), *Reforming the European Union: from Maastricht to Amsterdam* (Harlow, Longman, 2000)

Newdick, C, 'Citizenship, Free Movement and Health Care: Cementing Individual Rights by Corroding Social Solidarity' (2006) 43 *Common Market Law Review* 1645

O'Brien, C, 'Annotation of *Hartmann, Geven* and *Hendrix*' (2008) 45 *Common Market Law Review* 499

——, 'Social Blind Spots and Monocular Policy Making: The ECJ's Migrant Worker Model' (2009) 46 *Common Market Law Review* 1107

——, 'I Trade, Therefore I Am: Legal Personhood in the European Union' (2013) 50 *Common Market Law Review* 1643

O'Keeffe, D, 'Equal Rights for Migrants: the Concept of Social Advantages in Article 7(2), Regulation 1612/68' (1985) 5 *Yearbook of European Law* 93

——, 'Judicial Interpretation of the Public Services Exception to the Free Movement of Workers' in D Curtin and D O'Keeffe (eds), *Constitutional Adjudication in European Community and National Law. Essays in Honour of Justice T F O'Higgins* (Dublin, Butterworths, 1992)

——, 'Trends in the Free Movement of Persons within the European Communities' in J O'Reilly (ed), *Human Rights and Constitutional Law: Essays in Honour of Brian Walsh* (Dublin, The Round Hall Press, 1992)

——, 'Union Citizenship' in D O'Keeffe and P Twomey (eds), *Legal Issues of the Maastricht Treaty* (London, Chancery Law Publishing, 1994)

250 Bibliography

—— and Bavasso, A, 'Four Freedoms, One Market and National Competence: In Search of a Dividing Line' in D O'Keeffe and A Bavasso (eds), *Liber Amicorum in Honour of Lord Slynn of Hadley: Judicial Review in European Union Law* (The Hague, Kluwer, 2000)
—— and Twomey, P (eds), *Legal Issues of the Maastricht Treaty* (London, Chancery Law Publishing, 1994)
O'Leary, S, *The Evolving Concept of Community Citizenship: From the Free Movement of Persons to Union Citizenship* (The Hague, Kluwer, 1996)
——, 'Putting Flesh on the Bones of European Union Citizenship' (1999) 24 *European Law Review* 68
——, 'The Free Movement of Persons and Services' in P Craig and G de Búrca (eds), *The Evolution of EU Law* (Oxford, Oxford University Press, 1999)
——, 'Developing an Ever Closer Union between the Peoples of Europe? A Reappraisal of the Case Law of the Court of Justice on the Free Movement of Persons and EU Citizenship' (2008) 27 *Yearbook of European Law* 167
——, 'Equal Treatment of and EU Citizens: A New Chapter on Cross-Border Educational Mobility and Access to Student Financial Assistance' (2009) 34 *European Law Review* 612
——, 'Free Movement of Persons and Services' in P Craig and G de Búrca, *The Evolution of EU Law* (Oxford, Oxford University Press, 2011)
——, 'The Past, Present and Future of the Purely Internal Rule in EU Law' in M Dougan, N Nic Shuibhne and E Spaventa (eds), *Empowerment and Disempowerment of the European Citizen* (Oxford, Hart Publishing, 2012)
—— and Fernández-Martín, JM, 'Judicially-Created Exceptions to the Free Provision of Services' in M Andenas and W-H Roth (eds), *Services and Free Movement in EU Law* (Oxford, Oxford University Press, 2002)
Oliver, P, 'Non-Community Nationals and the Treaty of Rome' (1985) 5 *Yearbook of European Law* 57
——, 'Some Further Reflections on the Scope of Articles 28–30 (Ex 30–36) EC' (1999) 36 *Common Market Law Review* 783
——, 'Of Trailers and Jet Skis: Is the Case Law on Article 34 TFEU Hurtling in a New Direction?' (2009–10) 33 *Fordham International Law Journal* 1423
—— and Enchelmaier, S, 'Free Movement of Goods: Recent Developments in the Case-Law' (2007) 44 *Common Market Law Review* 649
—— and Roth, W-H, 'The Internal Market and the Four Freedoms' (2004) 41 *Common Market Law Review* 407
——, Enchelmaier, S, Jarvis, M, Johnston, A, Norberg, S, Stothers, C and Weatherill, S, *Oliver on Free Movement of Goods in the European Union* (Oxford, Hart Publishing, 2010)
Peers, S, 'Free Movement, Immigration Control and Constitutional Conflict' (2009) 5 *European Constitutional Law Review* 173
——, 'Benefits for EU Citizens: A U-Turn by the Court of Justice?' (2015) 74 *Cambridge Law Journal* 195
——, and Berneri, C, 'Iida and O and S: Further Developments in the Immigration Status of Static EU Citizens' (2013) 27 *Journal of Immigration, Asylum and Nationality Law* 162
Pescatore, P, 'Some Critical Remarks on the Single European Act' (1987) 24 *Common Market Law Review* 9
Plender, R, 'An Incipient Form of European Citizenship' in FG Jacobs (ed), *European Law and the Individual* (Amsterdam, North Holland, 1976)
Prechal, S, 'Topic One: National Applications of the Proportionality Principle: Free Movement and Procedural Requirements: Proportionality Reconsidered' (2008) 35 *Legal Issues of Economic Integration* 201

Preuss, U, 'Constitutionalism—Meaning, Endangerment, Sustainability' in S Saberwal and H Sievers (eds), *Rules, Laws, Constitutions* (London, Sage Publications, 1998)

Reich, N, 'A European Constitution for Citizens: Reflections on the Rethinking of Union and Community Law' (1997) 3 *European Law Journal* 131

——, 'Union Citizenship—Metaphor or Source of Rights?' (2001) 7 *European Law Journal* 4

Reynolds, S, 'Exploring the "Intrinsic Connection" between Free Movement and the Genuine Enjoyment Test: Reflections on EU Citizenship after *Iida*' (2013) 38 *European Law Review* 376

Rieder, C, 'The EC Commission's New Adopted Baby: Health Care' (2007–08) 14 *Columbia Journal of European Law* 145

Ross, M, 'The Struggle for EU Citizenship: Why Solidarity Matters' in A Arnull, C Barnard, M Dougan and E Spaventa (eds), *A Constitutional Order of States? Essays in EU Law in Honour of Alan Dashwood* (Oxford, Hart Publishing, 2011)

Schmidt, S, 'Who Cares about Nationality? The Path-Dependent Case Law of the ECJ from Goods to Citizens' (2012) 19 *Journal of European Public Policy* 8

Schrauwen, A, 'Sink or Swim Together? Developments in European Citizenship' (1999–2000) 23 *Fordham International Law Journal* 778

——, 'European Union Citizenship in the Treaty of Lisbon: Any Change at All?' (2008) 15 *Maastricht Journal of European and Comparative Law* 55

Scott, J, 'Mandatory or Imperative Requirements in the EU and the WTO' in C Barnard and J Scott (eds) *The Law of the Single Market: Unpacking the Premises* (Oxford, Hart Publishing, 2002)

Shaw, J, *The Transformation of Citizenship in the European Union: Electoral Rights and the Restructuring of Political Space* (Cambridge, Cambridge University Press, 2007)

——, 'A View of the Citizenship Classics: *Martínez Sala* and Subsequent Cases on Citizenship of the Union' in M Poiares Maduro and L Azoulai (eds), *The Past and Future of EU Law: The Classics of EU Law Revisited on the 50th Anniversary of the Rome Treaty* (Oxford, Hart Publishing, 2010)

——, 'Citizenship: Contrasting Dynamics at the Interface of Integration and Constitutionalism' in P Craig and G de Búrca (eds), *The Evolution of EU Law* (Oxford, Oxford University Press, 2011)

Shuibhne, N Nic, 'The Outer Limits of EU Citizenship: Displacing Economic Free Movement Rights?' in C Barnard and O Odudu (eds), *The Outer Limits of European Union Law* (Oxford, Hart Publishing, 2009)

——, 'The Resilience of Market Citizenship' (2010) 47 *Common Market Law Review* 1597

——, 'EU Citizenship after Lisbon' in D Ashiagbor, N Countouris and I Lianos (eds), *The European Union after the Treaty of Lisbon* (Cambridge, Cambridge University Press, 2012)

——, *The Coherence of EU Free Movement Law: Constitutional Responsibility and the Court of Justice* (Oxford, Oxford University Press, 2013)

Skouris, V, 'Fundamental Rights and Fundamental Freedoms: The Challenge of Striking a Delicate Balance' (2006) *European Business Law Review* 225

Slot, PJ and Bulterman, M, 'Harmonization of Legislation on Migrating EU Citizens and Third Country Nationals: Towards a Uniform Evaluation Framework?' (2005–06) *Fordham International Law Journal* 747

Snell, J, *Goods and Services in EU Law: A Study of the Relationship between the Freedoms* (Oxford, Oxford University Press, 2002)

——, 'Who's Got the Power? Free Movement and Allocation of Competences in EC Law' (2003) 22 *Yearbook of European Law* 323A

——, 'And then there were Two: Products and Citizens in Community Law' in T Tridimas and P Nebbia (eds), *European Union Law for the Twenty-First Century: Volume II* (Oxford, Hart Publishing, 2004)
——, '"European Constitutional Settlement", an Ever Closer Union, and the Treaty of Lisbon: Democracy or Relevance?' (2008) 33 *European Law Review* 619
——, The Notion of Market Access: A Concept or a Slogan?' (2010) 47 *Common Market Law Review* 437
——, 'Free Movement of Capital: Evolution as A Non-Linear Process' in P Craig and G de Búrca (eds), *The Evolution of EU Law* (Oxford, Oxford University Press, 2011)
—— and Andenas, M, 'Exploring the Outer Limits—Restrictions on the Free Movement of Goods and Services' (1999) 10 *European Business Law Review* 252
Spaventa, E, 'From *Gebhard* to *Carpenter*: Towards a (Non-)Economic European Constitution' (2004) 41 *Common Market Law Review* 743
——, *Free Movement of Persons in the European Union: Barriers to Movement in their Constitutional Context* (The Hague, Kluwer, 2007)
——, 'Seeing the Wood Despite the Trees? On the Scope of Union Citizenship and its Constitutional Effects' (2008) 45 *Common Market Law Review* 13
——, 'Federalisation Versus Centralisation: Tensions in Fundamental Rights Discourse in the EU' in M Dougan and S Currie (eds), *50 Years of the European Treaties: Looking Back and Thinking Forward* (Oxford, Hart Publishing, 2009)
——, 'Leaving Keck Behind? The Free Movement of Goods after the Rulings in Commission v Italy and Mickelsson and Roos' (2009) 34 *European Law Review* 914
——, 'The Outer Limit of the Treaty Free Movement Provisions: Some Reflections on the Significance of *Keck*, Remoteness and *Deliège*' in C Barnard and O Odudu (eds), *The Outer Limits of European Union Law* (Oxford, Hart Publishing, 2009) 253
Starup, P and Elsmore, M, 'Taking a Logical or Giant Step Forward? Comment on *Ibrahim* and *Teixeira*' (2010) 35 *European Law Review* 571
Stein, E, 'Lawyers, Judges and the Making of a Transnational Constitution' (1981) 75 *American Journal of International Law* 1
Steiner, J, 'The Right to Welfare: Equality and Equity under Community law' (1985) 10 *European Law Review* 21
——, 'Drawing the Line: Uses and Abuses of Article 30 EEC' (1992) 29 *Common Market Law Review* 749
Sweeney, JA, 'A "Margin of Appreciation" in the Internal Market: Lessons from the European Court of Human Rights' (2007) 34 *Legal Issues of Economic Integration* 27
Syrpis, P and Novitz, T, 'Economic and Social Rights in Conflict: Political and Judicial Approaches to their Reconciliation' (2008) 33 *European Law Review* 411
Szpunar, M and López, MEB, 'Some Reflections on Member State Nationality: A Prerequisite of EU Citizenship and an Obstacle to its Enjoyment' in D Kochenov (ed), *Citizenship and Federalism in Europe* (Cambridge University Press, 2016, forthcoming)
Szydlo, M, 'Export Restrictions within the Structure of Free Movement of Goods. Reconsideration of an old Paradigm' (2010) 47 *Common Market Law Review* 753
Szyszczak, E, 'Building a Socioeconomic Constitution: A Fantastic Object?' (2012) 35 *Fordham International Law Journal* 1364
Tesauro, G, 'The Community's Internal Market in the Light of the Recent Case-Law of the Court of Justice' (1995) 15 *Yearbook of European Law* 1
Thym, D, 'When Union citizens turn into illegal migrants: the Dano case' (2015) 40 ELRev 249

Timmermans, C, 'Martínez Sala and Baumbast revisited' in M Poiares Maduro and L Azoulai (eds), *The Past and Future of EU Law: The Classics of EU Law Revisited on the 50th Anniversary of the Rome Treaty* (Oxford, Hart Publishing, 2010)

Tomuschat, C, Annotation of *Martínez Sala* (2000) 37 *Common Market Law Review* 449

Toner, H, 'Judicial Interpretation of European Union Citizenship—Transformation or Consolidation?' (2000) 7 *Maastricht Journal of European and Comparative Law* 158

——, 'Annotation of *Carpenter*' (2003) 5 *European Journal of Migration and Law* 163

Tridimas, T, 'The Court of Justice and Judicial Activism' (1996) 21 *European Law Review* 199

——, *The General Principles of EU Law* (Oxford, Oxford University Press, 2006)

—— and Nebbia, P, 'Introduction' in T Tridimas and P Nebbia (eds), *European Union Law for the Twenty-First Century* (Oxford, Hart Publishing, 2004)

Trstenjak, V and Beysen, E, 'The Growing Overlap of Fundamental Freedoms and Fundamental Rights in the Case-Law of the CJEU' (2013) 38 *European Law Review* 293

Tryfonidou, A, '*Mary Carpenter v Secretary of State for the Home Department*: The beginning of a new era in the European Union?' (2003) 14 *Kings College Law Journal* 81

——, '*Kunqian Catherine Zhu and Man Lavette Chen v. Secretary of State for the Home Department*: Further Cracks in the "Great Wall" of the European Union?' (2005) 11 *European Public Law* 527

——, 'Jia or Carpenter II: The Edge of Reason' (2007) 32 *European Law Review* 908

——, 'Was *Keck* a Half-Baked Solution After All?' (2007) 34 *Legal Issues of Economic Integration* 167

——, 'Family Reunification Rights of (Migrant) Union Citizens: Towards a Liberal Approach' (2009) 15 *European Law Journal* 634

——, 'In Search of the Aim of the EC Free Movement of Persons Provisions: Has the Court of Justice Missed the Point?' (2009) 46 *Common Market Law Review* 1591

——, *Reverse Discrimination in EC Law* (The Hague, Kluwer, 2009)

——, 'Further Steps on the Road to Convergence among the Market Freedoms' (2010) 35 *European Law Review* 36

——, 'Resolving the Reverse Discrimination Paradox in the area of Customs Duties: The Lancry Saga' (2011) 22 *European Business Law Review* 311

——, 'The Impact of EU Law on Nationality Laws and Migration Control in the EU's Member States' (2011) 25 *Journal of Immigration, Asylum and Nationality Law* 358

——, 'Redefining the Outer Boundaries of EU Law: The *Zambrano*, *McCarthy* and *Dereci* Trilogy' (2012) 18 *European Public Law* 493

——, '(Further) Signs of a Turn of the Tide in the CJEU's Citizenship Jurisprudence, Case C-40/11 *Iida*, Judgment of 8 November 2012, not yet Reported' (2013) 20 *Maastricht Journal of European and Comparative Law* 302

——, 'The Notions of "Restriction" and "Discrimination" in the Context of the Free Movement of Persons Provisions: From a Relationship of Interdependence to One of (Almost Complete) Independence' (2014) 33 *Yearbook of European Law* 385

——, 'The Federal Implications of the Transformation of the Market Freedoms into Sources of Fundamental Rights for the Union Citizen' in D Kochenov (ed), *Citizenship and Federalism in Europe* (Cambridge, Cambridge University Press, 2016, forthcoming)

Usai, A, 'The Freedom to Conduct a Business in the EU, Its Limitations and Its Role in the European Legal Order: A New Engine for Deeper and Stronger Economic, Social, and Political Integration' (2013) 14 *German Law Journal* 1868

Vandamme, TAJA, 'Annotation of Government of the French Community and Walloon Government v Flemish Government' (2009) 46 *Common Market Law Review* 287

254 Bibliography

Van den Brink, M, 'The Origins and the Potential Federalising Effects of the Substance of Rights Test' in D Kochenov (ed), Citizenship and Federalism in Europe (Cambridge, Cambridge University Press, 2016, forthcoming)

Van der Mei, AP, 'Cross-Border Access to Health Care within the European Union: Some Reflections on Geraets Smits and Peerbooms and Vanbraekel' (2002) 9 *Maastricht Journal of European and Comparative Law* 189

——, 'Union Citizenship and the Legality of Durational Residence Requirements for Entitlement to Student Financial Aid' (2009) 15 *Maastricht Journal of European and Comparative Law* 477

Van der Woude, M and Mead, P, 'Free Movement of the Tourist in Community Law' (1988) 25 *Common Market Law Review* 117

Van Elsuwege, P and Kochenov, D, 'On the Limits of Judicial Intervention: EU Citizenship and Family Reunification Rights' (2011) 13 *European Journal of Migration and Law* 443

Verschueren, H, 'Preventing "Benefit Tourism" in the EU: A Narrow or Broad Interpretation of the Possibilities Offered by the ECJ in Dano?' (2015) 52 *Common Market Law Review* 363

Weatherill, S, 'After Keck: Some Thoughts on how to Clarify the Clarification' (1996) 33 *Common Market Law Review* 885

——, 'Recent Case Law Concerning the Free Movement of Goods: Mapping the Frontiers of Market Deregulation' (1999) 36 *Common Market Law Review* 51

——, 'Consumer Policy' in P Craig and G de Búrca (eds), *The Evolution of EU Law* (Oxford, Oxford University Press, 1999)

——, 'Consumer Policy' in P Craig and G de Búrca (eds), *The Evolution of EU Law* 2nd edn (Oxford, Oxford University Press, 2011)

——, 'Free Movement of Goods' (2012) 61 *International and Comparative Law Quarterly* 541

——, 'From Economic Rights to Fundamental Rights' in S de Vries, U Bernitz and S Weatherill (eds), *The Protection of Fundamental Rights in the EU After Lisbon* (Oxford, Hart Publishing, 2013)

Weiler, JHH, 'The Transformation of Europe' (1991) 100 *Yale Law Journal* 2403

——, 'The Reformation of European Constitutionalism' (1997) 35 *Journal of Common Market Studies* 97

——, 'The Constitution of the Common Market Place: Text and Context in the Evolution of the Free Movement of Goods' in P Craig and G de Búrca (eds), *The Evolution of EU Law* (Oxford, Oxford University Press, 1999)

——, 'The Transformation of Europe' in JHH Weiler, *The Constitution of Europe* (Cambridge, Cambridge University Press, 2005)

Wenneras, P and Moen, KB, 'Selling Arrangements, Keeping Keck' (2010) 35 *European Law Review* 387

Wernicke, S, 'Au nom de qui? The European Court of Justice between Member States, Civil Society and Union Citizens' (2007) 13 *European Law Journal* 380

White, EL, 'In Search of Limits to Article 30 of the EEC Treaty' (1989) 26 *Common Market Law Review* 235

White, RCA, *Workers, Establishment, and Services in the European Union* (Oxford, Oxford University Press, 2004)

——, 'Citizenship of the Union, Governance, and Equality' (2006) 29 *Fordham International Law Journal* 790

——, 'Revising Free Movement of Workers' (2010) 33 *Fordham International Law Journal* 1563

Wiesbrock, A, 'Disentangling the "Union Citizenship Puzzle"? The McCarthy Case' (2011) 36 *European Law Review* 861

——, 'Granting Citizenship-Related Rights to Third-Country Nationals: An Alternative to the Full Extension of European Union Citizenship?' (2012) 14 *European Journal of Migration and Law* 63

Wilkinson, B, 'Towards European Citizenship? Nationality, Discrimination and Free Movement of Workers in the European Union' (1995) 1 *European Public Law* 417

Wils, WPJ, 'The Search for the Rule in Article 30 EEC: Much Ado about Nothing' (1993) 18 *European Law Review* 475

Wilsher, D, 'Does Keck Discrimination Make any Sense? An Assessment of the Non-Discrimination Principle within the European Single Market' (2008) 33 *European Law Review* 3

Wollenschläger, F, 'A New Fundamental Freedom beyond Market Integration: Union Citizenship and its Dynamics for Shifting the Economic Paradigm of European Integration' (2011) 17 *European Law Journal* 1

Index

Please note: authors are included in the index only where referred to in the main text but not in the footnotes.

Amsterdam Treaty   11
area of Freedom, Security and Justice   11
Armstrong, K   194
Ashiagbor, D   228
assessment of breach *see under* emerging questions on market freedoms

Becker, MA   215–16
benefit tourism   36–37
borders *see* cross-border specificity
breach of market freedoms *see* emerging questions on market freedoms, assessment of breach

capital, freedom to move   6
causation-based issues *see under* emerging questions on market freedoms
Cockfield, Lord   9
Completing the Internal Market (White Paper)   9
Constitutional Treaty   11
consumers' rights *see under* free movement of goods
Craig, P   4, 70
cross-border specificity
  dispensing with *see under* personal market freedoms
  terminology
    access to market approach/test   17–18
    discrimination-based approach   16–17

da Cruz Vilaça, JL   157, 173
Dashwood, A   66
Davies, G   125, 174, 203, 205
de Búrca, G   4, 70
de minimis test *see under* emerging questions on market freedoms
De Vries, S   115, 219, 223

economic self-sufficiency requirements   36, 39, 40–41
economically inactive persons   36–37, 41, 198
emerging questions on market freedoms
  assessment of breach   192–94
  building an internal market   163–64
  causation-based issues   180–81
    consumer protection   167

  cross-border context   164, 165, 166, 172
  cross-border neutrality   193
  current aims   162–73
  de minimis test   177–79
  dynamic/teleological interpretations   157
  expansion of scope
    invocation by Union citizens   176–77
    under literal interpretations   158–61
  filtering mechanisms   177
  invocation by Union citizens   173–92
    broad scope of application   174–75
    de minimis test   177–79
    expansion of scope   176–77
    filtering mechanisms   177
    national measures within scope   175–76
    purely internal rule *see* purely internal rule *below*
    remoteness test *see* remoteness test *below*
  judicial activism   156–57
  mutual recognition   193–94
  non-economic policy interests   167
  public health protection   167
  purely internal rule   182–92
    basis of rule   183–84
    definition   182
    EU/member state competence   183
    foreclosing effect on market   188–91
    neutral measures   185–86
    primary/non-primary rights, distinction   186–88
  remoteness test   179–82
    causation-based issues   180–81
    definition   180
    direct/indirect restrictions   181–82
  services, freedom to provide   160–61
  supranational legitimation/transnational integration   173
equal treatment principle   81
European Atomic Energy Community (Euratom)   4–5
European Coal and Steel Community (ECSC)
  aim   4
  individuals' role   66–67
  origin   3–4

family reunification rights *see under* personal market freedoms
Ferreira, N   52, 201–2
filtering mechanisms *see under* emerging questions on market freedoms
free movement of goods
　consumers' rights   135–39
　　choice, right to   135–36, 137–38
　　passive economic actors   135, 139
　　use restrictions   136
　economic due process clause   149
　MEQRs (measure having equivalent effect to quantitative restrictions)   119, 124–27, 135, 136, 144
　movement to another state to sell goods   135, 138–39, 140–43, 152
　non-discriminatory restrictions   144–46, 148–49
　passive economic actors   135, 139
　Sunday Trading Saga   127
　tariff/non-tariff barriers   118
　traditional interpretation   119–32
　　commercial/personal use, distinction   121–22
　　cross-border specificity   126, 127, 128, 130, 132
　　dual-burden regulation   126
　　equal burden rules   127–28
　　goods in transit   121
　　home state regulation   131–32
　　market circumstances rules/selling arrangements   127
　　MEQRs (measure having equivalent effect to quantitative restrictions)   119, 124–27, 135, 136, 144
　　nationality of parties   123–24
　　negative integration   130–31
　　production and sale of goods, separation   122–23
　　quantitative restrictions, definitions   124, 130–31
　　restrictions, justificatory grounds, exhaustive/non-exhaustive lists   119–20
　use restrictions   136
freedom to move capital   6, 218–19
fundamental human rights/fundamental economic rights, clash *see under* persisting conundrums in market freedoms
fundamental rights
　emerging questions on market freedoms   170, 171–72, 173, 196
　fundamental human rights/fundamental economic rights, clash *see under* persisting conundrums in market freedoms
　terminology   14–15

Gormley, LW   108
Goudappel, F   21

Hartley, TC   156
Horsley, T   166

imports/exports of goods, quantitative restrictions   6
individual rights/collective rights, clash *see under* persisting conundrums in market freedoms

judicial activism   156–57

Kochenov, D   53
Kostakopoulou, D   52, 201–2

Luxembourg accords   8–9

Maas, W   202–3, 214
Maastricht Treaty   10, 23, 25, 86, 201, 212
material scope (*ratione materiae*) *see under* personal market freedoms
MEQRs (measure having equivalent effect to quantitative restrictions)   119, 124–27, 135, 136, 144
more stationary personal market freedoms
　definition   13–14
　emerging questions on market freedoms   166–67, 171

nationals/non-nationals, differential treatment *see under* persisting conundrums in market freedoms
natural and legal persons, distinction *see under* persisting conundrums in market freedoms
negative harmonisation
　internal market policy   5, 7
Nice Treaty   11

O'Leary, S   42, 216

persisting conundrums in market freedoms
　free movement of persons, consolidation of provisions   204–7
　　argument for   204–5
　　fundamental rights issues   206
　　problematic aspects   205–7
　　role and aims, confusion possibility   205–6
　fundamental human rights/fundamental economic rights, clash   219–26, 240
　　double proportionality test   226
　　equal value starting point   224–25
　　margin of appreciation   222
　individual rights/collective rights, clash   226–30, 240
　　fundamental economic rights/collective interest in market regulation, conflict   227–28
　　individual economic rights/collective national solidarity, clash   229–30
　　soft proportionality test   227–28

nationals/non-nationals, differential
    treatment   197–204, 239
  economically inactive citizens   198
  individual bond with society   204
  length of residence   202, 204
  official authority exception   200–201
  public policy/public security/public health
    grounds   201
  public service exception   199–200
  special bond of allegiance   199
  and Union citizenship   202–3
natural and legal persons, distinction
    207–12, 239–40
  cross-border specificity   211
  freedom of establishment/freedom
    to provide services, entitlement
    dichotomy   207–9
  lack of clarity   211–12
  personal market freedoms, material
    scope   210
  solutions   212
  third-country nationals, and personal market
    freedoms   212–19, 240
  abuse incentives from exclusion   217–19
  economic problems with exclusion
    214–17
  free movement of capital   6, 218–19
  free movement of commodities   216–17
personal market freedoms   13–14
  background   61–62
  cross-border specificity, dispensing with
    87–88, 91–109, 112–15
    Community citizenship, emergence
      78–79
    direct restrictions   95–101
    discrimination-based approach   92–95
    disproportionate and unjustified
      regulation   100–101
    family reunification *see* family reunification
      rights *below*
    indirect restrictions   101–9
    movement-neutral rules   97–98
    non-discriminatory restrictions   95–97, 98
    raison d'être, post-Maastricht   112–13
  equal treatment principle   81
  family reunification rights   101–9
    prior lawful residence condition   103–4
    returnees case-law   104–9
  material scope (*ratione materiae*)
    beyond legislative competence   86–87
    cross-border specificity *see* cross-border
      specificity, dispensing with *above*
    fundamental human rights   87
    post-Maastricht   86–109
    pre-Maastricht   74–75, 76–79
    primary rights *see* primary law/rights, and
      more stationary freedoms *below*
more stationary personal market freedoms,
    definition   13–14

personal scope (*ratione personae*)
  cross-border healthcare   84–85, 230
  economic/non-economic activities,
    distinction   85–86
  former migrant worker, children of   85
  part-time workers   83
  post-Maastricht   82–86
  public policy/security/health limitations   63
Piçarra, N   157, 173
Preuss, U   66
primary/secondary rights, distinction
    21–22
purely internal rule *see under* emerging
  questions on market freedoms

Reich, N   135–36
remoteness test *see under* emerging questions on
  market freedoms
residence, right of, Union Citizenship
    36–41
reverse discrimination   12, 46–47

Schuman Declaration   5
secondary/primary rights, distinction
    21–22
Shuibhne, N   179–80, 209–10
Single European Act   10
Spaventa, E   97, 101, 168–69, 182, 192–93, 203
supranational legitimation/transnational
  integration   173
supremacy principle   66

third-country nationals, and personal market
  freedoms *see under* persisting conundrums in
  market freedoms
three-pillar structure   11
transnational integration/supranational
  integration   173
Tridimas, T   156–57, 228

Union Citizenship
  cross-border element, absence   56–57
  current legal regime   25–27
  free movement, right to   35–36
  fundamental rights   27, 38, 39, 41, 44, 58
  incipient citizenship case-law   31–35
  meaningful status   48–57
    1993–97 (infancy phase)   27–29
    1998–2005 (growth phase)   29–43
    2006–09 (early adolescence)   43–48
    2010–onwards   48–57
  non-discrimination on grounds of nationality,
    right to   30–35
  residence, right of   36–41

Weatherill, S   127, 135
White, E   129
White, RCA   30–31, 200–201, 208–9
Wiesbrock, A   215